T0238770

BigQuery for Data Warehousing

Managed Data Analysis in the Google Cloud

Mark Mucchetti

Apress®

BigQuery for Data Warehousing

Mark Mucchetti
Santa Monica, CA, USA

ISBN-13 (pbk): 978-1-4842-6185-9   ISBN-13 (electronic): 978-1-4842-6186-6
https://doi.org/10.1007/978-1-4842-6186-6

Copyright © 2020 by Mark Mucchetti

This work is subject to copyright. All rights are reserved by the Publisher, whether the whole or part of the material is concerned, specifically the rights of translation, reprinting, reuse of illustrations, recitation, broadcasting, reproduction on microfilms or in any other physical way, and transmission or information storage and retrieval, electronic adaptation, computer software, or by similar or dissimilar methodology now known or hereafter developed.

Trademarked names, logos, and images may appear in this book. Rather than use a trademark symbol with every occurrence of a trademarked name, logo, or image we use the names, logos, and images only in an editorial fashion and to the benefit of the trademark owner, with no intention of infringement of the trademark.

The use in this publication of trade names, trademarks, service marks, and similar terms, even if they are not identified as such, is not to be taken as an expression of opinion as to whether or not they are subject to proprietary rights.

While the advice and information in this book are believed to be true and accurate at the date of publication, neither the authors nor the editors nor the publisher can accept any legal responsibility for any errors or omissions that may be made. The publisher makes no warranty, express or implied, with respect to the material contained herein.

Managing Director, Apress Media LLC: Welmoed Spahr
Acquisitions Editor: Jonathan Gennick
Development Editor: Laura Berendson
Coordinating Editor: Jill Balzano

Cover image designed by Freepik (www.freepik.com)

Distributed to the book trade worldwide by Springer Science+Business Media New York, 233 Spring Street, 6th Floor, New York, NY 10013. Phone 1-800-SPRINGER, fax (201) 348-4505, e-mail orders-ny@springer-sbm.com, or visit www.springeronline.com. Apress Media, LLC is a California LLC and the sole member (owner) is Springer Science + Business Media Finance Inc (SSBM Finance Inc). SSBM Finance Inc is a **Delaware** corporation.

For information on translations, please e-mail booktranslations@springernature.com; for reprint, paperback, or audio rights, please e-mail bookpermissions@springernature.com.

Apress titles may be purchased in bulk for academic, corporate, or promotional use. eBook versions and licenses are also available for most titles. For more information, reference our Print and eBook Bulk Sales web page at http://www.apress.com/bulk-sales.

Any source code or other supplementary material referenced by the author in this book is available to readers on GitHub via the book's product page, located at www.apress.com/9781484261859. For more detailed information, please visit http://www.apress.com/source-code.

Printed on acid-free paper

To my parents, John and Dr. Roseanne, who have always been an inspiration, especially when they didn't know it.

Table of Contents

About the Author

 **Mark Mucchetti** is an industry technology leader in healthcare and ecommerce. He has been working with computers and writing software for over 30 years, starting with BASIC and Turbo C on an Intel 8088 and now using Node.js in the cloud. For much of that time, he has been building and growing engineering groups, combining his deep love of technical topics with his management skills to create world-class platforms. Mark has also worked in databases, release engineering, front- and back-end coding, and project management. He works as a technology executive in the Los Angeles area, coaching and empowering people to achieve their peak potential as individuals of bold, forward-momentum, and efficient technology teams.

About the Technical Reviewer

 **Björn Rost** is a customer engineer at Google Canada with a focus on data management and analytics. He has previously architected, implemented, and tuned many data warehouses and relational transaction systems as a consultant. His passion for sharing with and learning from others has led him to present on data, DevOps, and cloud at over 100 conferences and meetups around the world. He is an Oracle ACE Alumnus and a member of the OakTable Network.

Acknowledgments

Firstly, my thanks to the staff at Apress, who made the process so easy that all I had to do was write: Jonathan Gennick, Jill Balzano, and Laura Berendson.

Thanks to my technical reviewer, Björn Rost, for providing thoughtful direction under a deadline and whose suggestions consequently improved this book substantially.

Special thanks to my cadre of engineering stars, who reviewed excerpts, suggested use cases, and provided encouragement: Abby Cloft, Sasha Jordan, Clint Kumabe, Nick McKinnon, Andrew Melchor, and others whom I most certainly forgot. Equal thanks to the 606 crew (Derek Lieu, Abel Martin, and Geoff Stebbins), who have supported me since the previous millennium.

To Brit Tucker, who somehow remained a source of preternatural calmness and pragmatism, despite the unreasonableness that defines product management, thank you for the collaboration, insight, and triangle breathing.

Extra special thanks to Nick Campbell for his affable and insightful support across all topics. Undoubtedly he is the only engineer I know who would take my intentional omission of an Oxford comma as the personal affront I intended. Please reach him for advice on phenomena both Cloud-related and cloud-related. My friend, you are already both writer and technologist.

To Shari Laster, head of Open Stack Collections at Arizona State University, thank you for helping me interpret and visualize public data in a discipline-appropriate way and for exemplifying virtuous library science, and for everything else.

Thanks to my dear friend and adventitious counselor, Juan Ball, who taught me that physical strength and mental strength are mostly the same thing. Her unwavering confidence and faith have guided me through dark days.

To my sister Emily, who listened patiently and kept a very good secret.

To my children, John Luke and Amelia, who bring joy beyond measure. Finally, my deepest gratitude to my wife, Heather, who kept the children safe and the household humming while managing a demanding career of her own. I wouldn't have done it without you. Honey, if you're reading this, the book is done.

—Mark Mucchetti
Santa Monica, California

Introduction

The Organization of Data

The modern world is ruled by data. Even as I write this, dozens of my data points are being sent out over the Internet. Where I'm located, which websites I'm consulting for reference, my heart rate, and the lighting level in my office are all streaming continuously to servers worldwide. Even my keystrokes into this document are being streamed and recorded as I type, each generating its own event. Were I to look at the raw data collected on me alone in any given 24-hour period, I would likely be unable to make any sense of it without some in-depth review. Estimates suggest the world as a whole may be creating as much as 2.5 quintillion bytes of data every single day.[1] I'd take a large grain of salt with any such statistic—what does it even mean to "create data"?

As builders and architects, we can forget that data doesn't do anything on its own. Dealing with it in an abstract state, we are aware that it's something we have to get from source to destination without losing any and with a good idea of its provenance. We generally want to know that it's authentic too and comes from an authorized person. In its potential form, we move it around, extract, transform, and load it. However, it only becomes a tool for decision making when we synthesize it into information. Literally, to grow in understanding as a species, we must think both about how we collect and store data and how we turn it into information.

I don't think the emphasis on the word "data" in modern society is incidental; it's much easier for us to move boxes of books around from shelf to shelf than to open each book and read it. And there is certainly a time for that—we'll cover it in Part 2 as we build up the data warehouse. But this is all really about a journey. To continue with the book analogy, it's a process starting from the author to the commercial buyer, to the stocking and organization, to the reading and understanding, and finally to the librarians and archivists who work with the information. For the kinds of massive datasets we deal with now, it's too much for any single person to do. We use technology to fill the gaps and let us focus on the final step of information interpretation: knowledge.

---

[1]https://researcher.watson.ibm.com/researcher/view_group.php?id=4933

It's hardly a hop, skip, and a jump from raw data to knowledge. These problems have been fundamental to human society since the dawn of reading and writing. Technology adds a tremendous amount of power, but it also adds incomprehensible complexity. We've begun applying increasingly erudite labels to capture the technical work done by professionals in support of this: data engineer, architect, and, more recently, scientist. (I used to work with a person who styled herself a "data janitor", and in fact dressed as one for Halloween.)

We've reached a point where most business organizations understand the value of collecting as much data as possible. However, many don't excel at turning that data into information. There are undoubtedly large troves of raw data lying around in data centers and the cloud everywhere, with enormous potential but no plan. Some organizations are coalescing their data into information, but stakeholders don't know how to find it or use it. Sometimes stakeholders are adept at using it, but the feedback loop is too long and the data has been rendered obsolete by changing business conditions. Solely by optimizing that feedback loop in your organization, you can gain an edge over your competitors. But this advantage isn't going to last for long. One of the reasons for this is Google BigQuery and technologies like it.

BigQuery takes all the best parts of data warehouses—SQL compatibility, petabyte scale, and high availability—and puts them all in the same place. Even better, as a user, there is almost no difficulty in getting up and running. Whether you're migrating from an existing warehouse, a live operational store, or just a bunch of Google Sheets, we'll be able to extract key insights almost immediately. You can then get those insights to your non-technical stakeholders, decision makers, and senior leadership. Once you have everyone on board, you've created a culture of data, and the sky's the limit. I've seen it happen several times. I've never seen it happen as quickly as it does with BigQuery.

Google BigQuery

Data warehousing isn't a new concept, and in fact, its origins date back to the 1970s. The need for up-to-the-minute, global business data has been present for a long time. In the past, setting up the infrastructure to begin was a daunting and tedious undertaking. There would be multiple decision points around determining your scale and availability requirements, how to communicate system downtime to users, setting up disaster recovery plans… The list goes on. The nuts and bolts of this process could easily consume weeks and would be beyond the expertise of a business-focused analyst. Then, you could pretty easily consume two or more full-time roles solely with the responsibility of keeping the thing running and patched. You would have to do all of this before you could even dig into your business problems.

Gradually, as the concept of infrastructure-as-a-service emerged, we got increasing power for less work and limited maintenance. Virtualization in data centers gave way to managed SQL instances (Google Cloud Platform [GCP] SQL, Amazon RDS [Relational Database Service]) which in turn created cloud solutions for managing data. However, it is only with the advent of BigQuery that we have the best of both worlds: a fully SQL-compliant managed data warehouse.

If you're already a database administrator, this should all sound familiar. And in that case, good news for you: the next few chapters are going to be a breeze. You can use the extra time to reminisce about the bad old days. If you're just starting out, however, I strongly encourage you to focus on the concepts and strategies associated with building a data warehouse. They will serve you well far beyond the technologies we'll cover in this book.

This book is about BigQuery, yes; but this book is really about your data. Even if you don't know where your data is (or you're not even collecting it yet!), we'll cover all sorts of methods to work with data in BigQuery and take your practice up a couple of notches. As you prove the value to others in your organization, they will support you in taking it up a few more.

The best part about BigQuery is that you get to jump directly to solving your problems. Minimally, the benefit of managed infrastructure is that you don't need to retain resources in-house who can perform maintenance and upgrades. Beyond that, with a service such as BigQuery, you won't need to install any software on your computer or in a data center either. Your data will be fully available and equally accessible from everywhere, as you choose.

The most important thing this offers you is a lighter cognitive load to acquire your data and present it to others. You can spend your time working on improving your business and not remembering how to keep your machines running, build a maintenance schedule, and so forth. Furthermore, this means that delivering key, real-time insight to your business is now available to much smaller organizations. Even in a small business, you can harness BigQuery without needing to make a huge budget ask of your leadership.

Characteristics of BigQuery

Let's review some of the key characteristics of BigQuery. These may be more or less exciting for your specific use case, but you will most likely find one or two to convince you, your team, or your stakeholders.

Ease of Use

BigQuery runs in the cloud and is fully managed. You don't need to build an operating system or install a database. You don't even need to reserve a machine. BigQuery runs transparently without requiring you to understand anything about where or how it is deployed.

Availability and Reliability

As of this writing, BigQuery offers a ≥ 99.99% uptime service-level agreement (SLA). To save you the trouble of doing the math, this works out to only about 44 minutes a month. In practice, I have not seen any significant outages or performance impairment on a production workload.

Security

Configuring role-based permissions and user-level access can be a nightmare in traditional data warehouse applications. BigQuery configures basic permissions by default and allows you to get more granular as necessary. At all times, its permissions model is governed by Cloud IAM (formally, Google Cloud Identity and Access Management), meaning that you can keep permissions consistent among the rest of your Google Cloud Platform services, even out to G Suite.

Price

In the world of "Big Iron," fast, available database technology was traditionally the most expensive class of enterprise computing. Add in license costs for proprietary database software, and you are looking at an extremely expensive operation just to get under way. BigQuery does away with all of that: its default pricing model is pay-as-you-go, based on how much data your queries process. While it can be difficult to estimate costs sometimes, especially when comparing to a standard relational database, this approach means that when your users are dormant, the cost of your data warehouse is negligible. If you are running a global operation and consume a tremendous amount of data, Google also offers a flat rate based on the number of "slots" you consume. (We'll talk more about the concept of slots in Chapter 4.)

Speed

BigQuery performs very quickly and is consistent in response times. It also caches responses so that they are returned immediately after the first time (the query is also free). While it may not be the best choice for an edge-facing transactional database, you should find it more than sufficient for analytics workloads, or even the back end of a reporting system.

Business Value

It's hard to overemphasize this. Due to all of the other advantages mentioned earlier, you'll spend only a fraction of the time doing any of the routine tasks that may have previously consumed your day. Instead, you'll be able to focus on the overarching theme: turning your raw data into information and, ultimately, into knowledge.

The Structure of This Book

As with any journey, you may find yourself personally at various points along the path. The goal for you is to get your data into a managed state as quickly and easily as possible. This will probably tie to underlying goals for you as well. Your focus may be on proliferating information to more stakeholders, or it may be on visualizing it in a more compelling way. You may even just want to be able to sleep more soundly at night, not worrying about where all this data is and if it's being taken in properly. You should be able to find the right place along your journey for BigQuery to be helpful to you. I'll be starting with the basics and moving into more complex and innovative concepts as we go.

Part 1 will start from scratch. We'll discuss generally how to evaluate your data storage needs and ways of structuring it. Then we'll implement a few examples directly using BigQuery, again starting from the beginning, as if you aren't currently using any form of data warehouse or SQL. After that, assuming you do in fact have some form of existing data, I'll discuss strategies you might employ for it. Finally, we'll go over the economic efficiency equation, deciding how to make trade-offs between your budget and the availability you need for your data.

In Part 2, we'll go deep on getting data into your warehouse from existing sources in your production applications. We'll cover loading, streaming, and Dataflow. Loading and streaming can be handled directly by BigQuery. The chapter on Dataflow will cover more advanced techniques for building custom data pipelines to run at scale.

Part 3 is all about what you can do once your warehouse is up and running. In Chapter 8, we'll cover how to get your data program on solid footing after your initial launch. Chapter 9 will cover SQL and its implementation in BigQuery. After that, we'll cover scheduling recurring jobs using Cloud Scheduler, using Google Cloud Functions to perform data transformation, and setting up log sinks using Google Cloud Logging (formerly Stackdriver). You'll learn how BigQuery can provide a convenient resting place to perform analytics on all sorts of live data that might otherwise be lost in the ether.

By the time you reach Part 4, you'll have a smoothly running data warehouse humming along and delivering substantial value to your organization. But like any piece of business technology, it will start to drift without maintenance and careful planning of your ongoing strategy. In this part, we'll cover data governance strategies and discuss the value of a data program in your organization. Chapter 14 discusses how to handle large-scale change in your organization that will affect your warehouse.

Once you have the substance, Part 5 is all about the style. We'll talk about how to surface information to you and the organization, how to condense information into reports and real-time status dashboards, and how you can go deeper on analysis.

Finally, Part 6 is about pure innovation on what is possible in BigQuery. We'll look at the machine learning (ML) capabilities BigQuery provides and how they integrate with your existing data. We'll also look at the increasing prevalence of public datasets and how you can connect them with your data to go even further.

BigQuery is developing at an incredibly rapid pace. Pain points are getting smoothed over, and new features are appearing so quickly that it can be hard to keep track. Once you've been armed with the basics, you'll be equipped to understand and immediately utilize new improvements that Google makes. Best of all, due to BigQuery's managed nature, those features will become available in your instance without you having to do any work at all!

Let's get started.

Summary

Data and information are not the same thing. The technology of data warehouses is designed to intake huge amounts of raw data and assist the user in transforming that data into information which can be used by their organization. Google BigQuery provides a serverless, globally accessible, secure way of accessing data in a data warehouse. It doesn't require specific technical skills in database administration to set up or use. This book is about taking you through the journey from initial design and build, through data import and ongoing streaming, to maintenance, visualization, and innovation. You can start wherever you think you are along the path. You may find some topics more helpful than others with respect to your existing knowledge of databases, warehouses, and analytics. However you choose to proceed, this knowledge will help you beyond BigQuery and propel you toward the final step of the journey—where information becomes knowledge!

PART I

Building a Warehouse

CHAPTER 1

Settling into BigQuery

To get started, we're going to learn about Google's cloud offering as a whole, how to set up BigQuery, and how to interact with the service. Then we'll warm up with some basic queries to get comfortable with how everything works. After that, we'll begin designing our data warehouse.

If you're familiar with cloud providers and SQL syntax, you should feel free to skip ahead to the data warehousing section. If you prefer a tutorial or refresher on these topics, continue on.

Getting Started with GCP

Google Cloud Platform, or GCP for short, is a huge set of cloud services to accomplish pretty much any task you might have previously done on-premise or in a data center. Its offerings cover everything from virtual servers to all kinds of databases, software deployments, conversational AI, machine learning, content delivery... You name it. BigQuery is only one of hundreds of services available. One area in which Google has been continuously improving is connecting its services together to provide an all-in-one infrastructure on which to run your applications. Obviously, if you choose to host everything in your organization on GCP, you will get a lot of benefits like unified user authentication and direct access to your resources in other services. Throughout the course of this book, we will leverage other GCP services to show how your BigQuery implementation can work alongside other types of services to deliver your organization even greater power. And as with BigQuery itself, Google releases new features to each of its services on a regular basis, of which many start working automatically. Running your applications using a cloud provider can save you tremendous amounts of time along every step of the way. I hope that as we touch other GCP services and bring them into BigQuery, you'll see myriad opportunities in other areas of your organization.

© Mark Mucchetti 2020
M. Mucchetti, *BigQuery for Data Warehousing*, https://doi.org/10.1007/978-1-4842-6186-6_1

If you have worked with cloud computing before, you may want to understand how GCP differs from other major providers. Google maintains fairly comprehensive documentation from a marketing perspective. If you are familiar with Amazon Web Services (AWS) or Microsoft Azure, there is also plenty of documentation available on how to adapt the tools and technology into GCP. Apress has several other books and ebooks on other services in the GCP suite as well.

Beginning with GCP

If you have not already done so, make a Google account. This might be your Gmail address, or you may already be using GCP. Either way, log into that account and go to `https://console.cloud.google.com/`, which is the entry point for all Google Cloud Platform services.

You will be presented with a country selection and a checkbox for the terms of service. I encourage you to read the terms of service.[1] If you are unfamiliar with cloud providers, you may be concerned about what it means to store your data in the cloud. You may also have questions about the laws in your jurisdiction and how to ensure your data is compliant. Those questions are far beyond the scope of this book, but you should have a good idea of what your particular restrictions are and what your agreement with Google states. To ease your potentially largest concern, BigQuery data is encrypted at rest. Since mid-2019, you can also manage your own encryption keys for it. If you have geographical restrictions, you can also choose the region(s) in which to store and process your data.

It probably goes without saying, but there is cost involved as you begin to scale up your implementation. We'll cover this in detail in Chapter 4, but you'll want to pay attention to your budget constraints as you do more and more. A surprising amount of GCP is available for free to help you design and develop your solutions. This means the cost of entry is negligible—gone are the days of purchasing millions of dollars of hardware with a substantial investment to even discover if your idea will work.

After accepting the terms of service, the box will fade away, and you will be staring at the entire console in all of its glory. I want to draw your attention to a few things that will help throughout the course of using GCP.

---

[1]`https://cloud.google.com/terms`

Using Google Cloud Platform

You can work in basically any methodology you prefer when using Google Cloud Platform. Wherever possible, I'll be working in the web interface to make things as easy as possible. As we get deeper into the programming-heavy sections, we'll explore other methods. In reality, once you get the concepts, you can build it into anything you want. With the right configurations, you can use your data from anywhere in the world, with exactly as much granularity as you want. Googling any data technology and "BigQuery" typically yields a host of good (and bad) references for how to connect pretty much any two things you want to connect. The power and ease with which you can integrate any given data into your warehouse is phenomenally exciting.

The Cloud Console

The three horizontal lines on the left (or the hamburger menu, as we affectionately call it) open up the service list. As you might imagine, we'll be focused on the subheading labeled "Big Data," but you should take a few minutes to familiarize yourself with the other headings. We'll be using services under the Compute, Storage, Stackdriver, and AI headings later. You can also helpfully pin services to the top of your list; go ahead and pin BigQuery now, unless you enjoy scrolling.

Note that if you're familiar with older versions of BigQuery, there was a "classic" console available. This console was retired in June 2020, and all examples, code, screenshots, and so on will be from the new cloud console version. It's officially called the BigQuery Web UI, but suffice it to say that we won't use the classic console or SQL syntax anywhere in this book. You may still encounter references to the classic console or the classic SQL dialect in older documentation.

The Command-Line Interface

Google also offers a command-line interface (CLI) that you can use directly from the console. You may prefer to create your own virtual machine inside your project and use it through remote access tools you are more familiar with, but the CLI is a huge benefit to quickly execute commands and scripts on your project. Additionally, some new features in GCP will initially only be available through the command line.

You can activate it easily by clicking the icon in the upper right of your console with the tooltip "Activate Cloud Shell." The first time you click it, you will get a little introductory text about what it does. Just click "Continue" if necessary, and it will bring you to the command line.

Behind the scenes, this actually creates a virtual machine in your project with all of the GCP utilities installed by default. You'll also have access to a number of programming languages like Node.js, Python, and Go by default. It uses the bash shell by default, so if you're familiar with bash, then you can already use the console like a pro.

The primary CLI tool is gcloud. Type "gcloud" into the shell, and you will get a huge list of all of the things you can do. You may also try "gcloud help" to see all of the arguments you might pass to the tool itself. Or try "gcloud compute regions list" to see all the regions worldwide in which you can use GCP compute resources. (Documentation uses vim style here, so press space to page through and type q to quit.)

You can also take this opportunity to create a new project, if you like. (This is covered in detail in Appendix A.) Do that using the command

```
gcloud projects create YOUR-PROJECT-NAME
```

For BigQuery specifically, we'll be using the tool "bq". Again, try "bq" or "bq --help" to see all the options available. You could actually do many of the exercises in this book directly by the command line, but it shouldn't be necessary.

Programmatic Access

As with any good architecture, GCP also allows access to its services via APIs (Application Programming Interfaces). There are also SDKs (software development kits) that wrap around the APIs so you don't have to code a lot of boilerplate just to get information out of the services. As we get deeper into coding, we'll be using Python, but you can use whatever language you choose. GCP works with mostly anything you know already. However, Python has been widely adopted in the world of data science, is suitable for large-scale engineering, and has the latest machine learning libraries. Google also supports serverless functions coded in Python, so it will work in every context we'll need here.

If you're coming from academia or don't have a software engineering background, don't worry! Hadley Wickham and Jennifer Bryan have developed a package for R called bigrquery[2] which lets you query BigQuery directly from R. You can set everything up using the GUI and then access your data in R for advanced statistical modeling, visualization, or whatever you prefer.

BigQuery in the Cloud Console

To start using BigQuery in the cloud console, click the BigQuery item we pinned earlier. You'll get a brief introduction message with links to more information and the latest release notes. Click "Done" and...well, that's it. You're in. (If you want to get that introduction box back again, click "Features & Info" in the upper-left corner.)

If your morning cup of coffee is only half-empty and you are feeling as if you haven't accomplished anything yet, go out and build a server, install the OS, update all the packages, install your favorite database software, read all the patch notes, and start fiddling with the network so it can talk to your other servers. I can wait.

Querying

BigQuery uses SQL as its default language. It has been totally compliant with ANSI SQL since the introduction of the standard SQL dialect in 2016, and you can expect any standard statement to work properly. BigQuery supports any relational model without alteration. When you start loading hierarchical data like JSON directly into BigQuery, we may use parts of the SQL standard that are slightly less familiar, but this is also a significant area of advantage for BigQuery.

While the Classic Web UI has been deprecated, it is still possible to use the classic SQL dialect. You can do this either by opening a query window, clicking "More" ➤ "Query Settings," and scrolling down to the bottom to select "Legacy SQL." All further queries in that window will use the dialect you select. You can also use a decorator above the query, either #legacySQL or #standardSQL, to select the dialect. If you use the decorator, the option to switch dialects in the UI will be grayed out. As mentioned earlier, all examples in this book use the standard SQL dialect.

We'll cover this in more detail in Chapter 19, but another area of advantage for BigQuery is its ability to query public datasets directly. You can join your data directly to countless datasets in all sectors—healthcare, weather, genomics, politics, cryptography...

---

[2]https://bigrquery.r-dbi.org/

You name it. It's staggering to contemplate that even with this empty data warehouse we've just created, we already have access to exabytes of information.

Let's take a simple example. Say I wanted to know the most common species of healthy trees in New York City. In order to do this, I can use a BigQuery public dataset called new_york_tree_census_2015, which tracks the location of every single tree in New York City, including detailed accounts of their surrounding area and health.

You can run this SQL query directly in the browser without any loading or preparation:

```
SELECT spc_common AS species,
       COUNT(*) number_of_trees,
FROM `bigquery-public-data.new_york.tree_census_2015`
WHERE spc_common != '' AND health = 'Good'
GROUP BY spc_common, health
ORDER BY number_of_trees DESC
LIMIT 10
```

About half a second later, I know that the London plane tree, the honey locust, and the Callery pear trees (none of which I have ever heard of) are the most common healthy trees across the five boroughs. I have no insight as to why those are the most common trees, but that in itself is a pretty basic lesson in the perils of data science. You could stop reading here and spend the rest of the day connecting this information to all kinds of other data. You might discover that cherry trees are more likely to be on blocks with laundromats, but that probably wouldn't be the "information" we were looking to obtain with this data.

We'll be covering SQL with BigQuery frequently throughout this book. In fact, we'll be covering how to do a lot of new things like Dataflow and machine learning entirely within SQL. Here's a basic introduction to the concepts this query uses. If you're familiar with SQL already, go ahead and skip this section altogether.

Tables

The primary concept in relational databases is the table. Data is organized into columns and rows, where columns represent an attribute and rows represent a record of all attributes. In the preceding example, columns are attributes like the given name, the year, and the gender. Rows are specific records for those attributes, such as { 'London planetree,' '73311' }. At its heart, SQL is just a kind of set algebra, helping us to join and separate individual data values into the information we want.

BigQuery, incidentally, is described as a "columnar data store," meaning that under the hood it stores the individual values on a per-column basis. This grants a few advantages for large datasets. We'll get into this in the next section.

Aliasing

You can use the "AS" keyword to rename a column or other database object to something else. You will want to do this whenever bringing data together from two tables that have the same column name or when you are using an aggregate operator to return a new value (i.e., summing a value in all of the eligible rows). You may also want to do this when you would like a more descriptive name for your column—for instance, we might want to say "SELECT name AS given_first_name." Naming things is more of an art than a science anyway.

Since aliasing is so frequently used, conventionally the "AS" is omitted; you will therefore often see just "COUNT(*) number_of_trees" instead of "COUNT(*) AS number_of_trees."

Commenting

In order to comment your SQL, either to write notes about it or to temporarily exclude sections from running, you can use a double hyphen (--) at any point in a line to comment out the remainder of that line. Multiline comments are C-style, beginning with /* and ending with */, as such:

```
/* Here's a comment block to start a statement.
It will go until the closing characters
are reached, like most modern languages. */
SELECT 42 Answer --(to everything)
```

SELECT

SELECT specifies what data you are looking to retrieve FROM the dataset. You specify the columns you want to see in the results. You can also specify an asterisk (*) to indicate that you want every column in the table. In general, you don't want to use the asterisk in production queries, for a number of reasons that we'll discuss later. Additionally, you can specify a literal value, that is, "5," which will just display 5 no matter what row it is referencing.

FROM

FROM specifies what you want to use as a data source. While generally you will be accessing tables, you can also select from views, user-defined functions (UDFs), subqueries, machine learning models, and so forth. BigQuery makes no distinction in syntax between data in your own data warehouse, datasets shared with you, and datasets from federated sources outside of BigQuery.

WHERE

WHERE determines what rows to filter for. While WHERE is optional, you will generally want to use it for several reasons: queries will return less data; queries won't expand unpredictably if the table grows to accommodate new types of data; and most queries, at least in most implementations of SQL, will run faster. Because of BigQuery's distributed nature, you will sometimes end up accessing quite a lot of data to get a very small result. WHERE has its own expansive set of operators, allowing you to search with the usual =, !=, >, >=, <, and <=, but also IN, BETWEEN, STARTS_WITH, and others. You'll also typically need WHERE to make sure you find the correct subset when joining two tables together. Comparison in BigQuery is case-sensitive, unlike some other RDBMS systems; you can use UPPER() or LOWER() to make case-insensitive comparisons.

In the preceding query, we want to exclude trees with no specified species, and we want to restrict our query only to trees in good health. You can use AND, OR, NOT, and a variety of other keywords to combine restrictions.

GROUP BY

GROUP BY assists in aggregating data. When you would be returning the same row and value repeatedly, but you only want one copy, aggregated by some other value, you use GROUP BY to return the single value with its aggregation. This concept can be challenging for SQL beginners, but in our example, we want to know the most common trees. However, the same species name will appear many times in the table, but we only want one row for each. You can do this without any additional aggregation, but generally you will want to know some property of the aggregate as well.

ORDER BY

SQL result sets are non-deterministic. That means that there is no guarantee what order the results come back in. Often a given SQL engine will give the same results for the same query because of how it is built, but this behavior is not reliable. (Think of how in set theory {1, 2, 3} and {3, 2, 1} represent the same set.) To impose reliability, you can ORDER BY the set and obtain consistent results.

In this example, ordering gets us a further result: it's how we determine the order of the most common trees. The "COUNT(*)" is an aggregate statement as referenced earlier—it collects all of the rows with the species in the group and counts them. Then, it orders them based on how many it found for each species. Since there is one row in the table for each tree, counting trees by species is how we find the most prevalent examples. The DESC specifies we want to see the results starting with the highest count and working our way down.

The default ORDER BY type is ascending (ASC) and is implied when you don't write ASC or DESC. You can also ORDER BY computed columns by specifying the column number, that is, "ORDER BY 1." (In general, don't use this for any production query anyway. Column order is fragile. Referring to the results by index number will cause any further addition to the query to potentially slide the index you're looking at. This will typically break all the things relying upon the query.)

LIMIT

LIMIT simply specifies the upper bound on the number of rows you want to return. In this case, we only asked for the top ten tree species, so we see nothing beyond that.

LIMIT is a common-sense way to restrict the amount of data returned to the code (or person) executing the query.

Additional Things to Try

Shortcuts

Clicking "Shortcuts" in the upper left gives you a few platform-specific keystrokes to run queries. If you're like me and are used to hitting F5 over and over again, it might be worth glancing at them. As a personal note, I like to write lots of test queries in the same window and then execute them in pieces. To do this, select some text in the query box and press Cmd (or Alt)+E.

Statement Batches

You can also separate statements in the same window with a semicolon. If you run a batch separated by semicolons, BigQuery will summarize all returned queries, and you can open the result sets individually. This can be useful if you are doing live investigation on a dataset and are building up your sequence of queries to get the final result.

Query History

At any time, you can go back through all the queries you have performed in the query history. You can reload any version and rerun, and it will also show you in green or red whether the query succeeded or failed. Note that you can see the query history for yourself or for the entire project. If you have other collaborators, you can immediately load and run their queries. Of course, it can be a bit embarrassing if you have written a series of invalid queries and everyone else looks at them too.

Saving Queries and Views

At any time, you can also choose to save a query to either your personal list or to the project list. If you are collaborating with others, you may want to save your most useful queries to the project so they can be run directly by others. You can also save any result set as a view, meaning that it will create a new view into your data with those parameters. This feature allows you to build up a complex series of analyses by saving each query as a view and then joining them all together in another query. You may also want to preserve specific result sets for use in other applications which access BigQuery.

Scheduled Queries

You can also take queries you have written and schedule them in BigQuery to run repeatedly at certain times. If you have analysis functions that transform incoming data on a regular basis, this will allow you to easily automate that process without using other Google services.

Designing Your Warehouse

This may seem like an impossibly large topic, but every journey begins with a single step. You already have enough knowledge to think about how to store your data and what kind of information you hope to extract from it. You also know how to look at it and run queries on it to turn it into useful business intelligence. Now that that's out of the way and you know where your data will be living, how will it work?

Google BigQuery As a Data Store

I mentioned in the previous section that BigQuery uses a "columnar storage format." What exactly does this mean, and what implications does it have for your design?

Firstly, it's important to remember that data storage is ultimately one-dimensional. All the way down at the machine level, that series of ones and zeroes is linear. It's transmitted and stored linearly, one bit at a time. Consequently, no matter how fancy the data structures on top of it are, eventually it's going to be a stream of bits. The speed and performance of a database is related to how it stores the data at that level. Storage media like hard drives or RAM have their own characteristics, such as how long it takes to seek to a particular byte, how quickly it can perform a random access to any byte, and so on. This is a deep concept in both hardware and data engineering, and while not strictly pertinent at our level of discussion, it's worth knowing to understand what design decisions you can make to work appropriately with the underlying storage. In a SQL engine, this can often mean the difference between a cheap query that runs quickly and a query that would take years. For BigQuery, it may mean your data analysis budget itself.

Let's take a very basic table concept such as fruit. We'll creatively call the columns name, color, and shape. Here's our table (Table 1-1).

Table 1-1. The "fruit" table

name	color	shape
apple	red	round
orange	orange	round
banana	yellow	curved

Row-Oriented Approach

Traditional relational models use a row-oriented approach. Data is stored row by row, and new rows are added to the end. We'll ignore anything more complicated like indexes, metadata like the type of column, and so forth to get to the point. Imagine we were to store a database in a regular, sequentially accessed file. A table might appear on disk like this:

```
apple red round orange orange round banana yellow curved
```

This definitely has some advantages. When we want to add a new kind of fruit to the table, we can jump to the end of the file and append the next fruit. We don't need to know how many records are already in the table. Since the ordering is non-deterministic, we can even just insert the new record at the top of the file if we want. Or we can make a new file with new rows and then just concatenate them together, and everything will work fine.

But what if we want to know which fruits are round?

```
SELECT name FROM fruit WHERE shape = 'round'
```

In order to figure this out, the database engine needs to load up the whole table and go through it, stopping at each shape column, testing the value, and then backtracking or making a second pass through to stop at the name column and retrieve the results. If the table has hundreds of columns (is denormalized), this can be exceedingly costly.

Let's say we wanted to add a new column called size. To do this, we have to go through the entire table and insert a new value in the middle of the file for each row, all the way to the end. This would also be a very costly operation and in the real world can cause database performance issues and require reindexing or defragmentation.

Most performance enhancements implemented by these systems work around these limitations. Indexes allow the query engine to search a table without looking at every column. These systems are decades old, are well understood, and work extremely well for frequent retrieval and modification of data.

Column-Oriented Approach

We can invert this problem by using a columnar data store. In this model, the table we just saw would now be stored as

```
name: apple orange banana
color: red orange yellow
shape: round round curved
```

Now, for the same query, we can load the shape column, find all the instances of round, and then load the name column and match them up. We never have to look at the color column or the hundreds of other columns the table might have. If we add the size column, we don't have to go through anything else—we just make a new column store for "size" and populate it. Queries that don't know about size will never even know it exists.

There are also less obvious benefits to this. Since we know the data type of each column, it is much easier to compress a column store on disk. The same values also repeat over and over again, which means we can do some tricks so that we don't have to store them repeatedly. (One basic technique for this is run-length encoding, which just means you write the count of each value instead of repeating the value. { round round curved curved curved round round round round } would become { round 2 curved 3 round 4 }, taking up much less space.)

However, we have the opposite problem. In order to insert a new record into this table, we have to open every column and write a new value to the end of it. We also have to make sure that all our columns remain in sync and we have the right number of records for each value.

So, as with any engineering trade-off, there is no perfect solution. We need to pick the best tool for the job. Row-oriented stores are great for taking in new data quickly and fitting it to a schema. Column-oriented stores are better at doing analysis quickly and distributing queries in parallel. BigQuery uses the columnar storage format because it is designed for quick performance over large datasets. It's not designed to be used as an operational store for high volumes of inserts, deletes, and so on. In fact, you need never delete data at all. These considerations will have bearing on how we choose to structure our warehouse.

I've tremendously simplified these ideas—at a global scale, data engineers deal with the laws of physics and the theory of information itself. The point illustrates that even though BigQuery may feel like magic at times, it must make the same trade-offs as any database, and we can improve our results if we work to mesh with the model and not against it.

Google BigQuery As a Data Warehouse

Because BigQuery is SQL-compliant, if you have designed transactional databases in the past, you may be tempted to treat BigQuery as simply any other online transaction processing (OLTP) database. Don't! Google considers using OLTP with BigQuery to be an anti-pattern. Because it is a columnar data store, it is not designed for rapid sequences of INSERT and UPDATE statements done one row at a time. You can insert data much more quickly by using loading or streaming methods. BigQuery also does not have indexes that you might use in OLTP to do single-row lookups faster by key.

BigQuery is designed to be an analytics engine, and while it has many advantages over older data warehouse technologies, you will still need to apply your contextual understanding to increase performance and keep costs low.

Key Questions

When embarking on a data warehouse project, there are some questions that you should answer to figure out where to start. Think of these as requirements gathering. You may know the answers yourself, or you may need to go to business unit leaders and representatives to find out. You might also have been blessed with a product manager who can go and obtain these answers for you. Either way, you will want to know some things in order to establish your project charter.

I know, boring! We were already doing some work in BigQuery, and now it's back to paperwork. I promise it's worth taking these initial steps so you don't find yourself weeks into a project building something no one needs. As engineering itself gets easier and easier, we spend most of our time actually doing the work. And if the work's not suited to the purpose...well...we have a lot less technical scaffolding to hide behind. One of the reasons we set up the environment before design was to demonstrate that the several weeks you might have spent building and configuring while you deferred design no longer exists. All you need is a quiet morning and you're already there. Incidentally, if you took my facetious earlier advice to go build out a data center to feel productive, you can rejoin us now. You'd still have needed to do all this stuff.

Fundamentals

A key theme of this book is the establishment of a data charter and governance program. With massive, potentially multiyear endeavors like this, getting started is one of the most difficult parts. In the next chapter, I'll go into detail about how to form your charter and get business acceptance. Here are a few questions to form a basic idea of what direction that charter will take.

What Problem Am I Trying to Solve?

All projects, not just data warehouses, should have a simple, clear response to this question. The top-level answer is the theme of this book: to build a data warehouse which can provide insightful information to business users using an organization's data. Your answer should be one layer deeper. What kind of information is insightful for your organization? What business questions will you be able to answer that you could not answer easily or at all? Who will benefit from your work?

What Is the Scope of This Problem?

All projects need scope if they are ever going to be finished. As an agile practitioner, I believe strongly in iterative development and responding to change. Even so, projects need requirements, and everyone needs a clear idea of how to define success.

In order to answer this question, think about who your users are, what they will be able to do, and what they will gain from being able to do it. (Other agile-minded individuals may recognize this as a framework for creating user stories.) What actually **is** the data your organization collects? Is there data that isn't collected that needs to be? Whom can you find to help you answer these questions? You may discover projects that your warehouse depends on. In the end, you want to ensure that you can solve the problem you defined earlier with data that is actually in your warehouse.

Who Will Be the Primary Users of Your Warehouse?

You should have a good idea about this already from thinking about the scope of the problem. Of course, it depends a lot on the size and technical disposition of your organization. I've never seen any two organizations do it the same way, and even the same organization changes dramatically over time. You may have direct access to non-technical stakeholders who will be heavily invested in visualization. Or you may have stakeholders in the trenches who need up-to-date numbers to make critical business decisions. You may just want to do some heavy number-crunching and analysis on your own datasets. Your answer to this question will determine where you need to invest the most time and energy.

Are You Replacing Something That Exists Already?

If your organization already has a data warehouse, there are a whole host of other things to consider. You'll need to figure out how to migrate the existing data with minimal downtime, how to make sure nothing is lost, and how to train users on the new technology. You might be able to make the whole process seamless—but do you want to? If BigQuery will provide substantial improvements over your current solution, you may not want to hide them behind old paint.

If this is your scenario, we'll be covering it at length in Chapter 3. If the answer is no, well, you are the lucky owner of a greenfield project, you can just skip Chapter 3, and we're all jealous.

Thinking About Scale

Scale gets at how big your solution will be, how many users it will have, how available it needs to be, how much data it will store, and how that data will grow over time. Perhaps the most amazing thing about BigQuery is all the questions you **won't** have to answer. Most of the hardest problems of scale, such as how to keep the system performant over time and how to handle unexpected surges in user demand, are completely handled by Google.

Even though you won't have to think about hardware scaling, you will have to prepare for organizational growth. Perhaps unexpectedly, you will also have to prepare for popularity. As others become aware of what you're doing, they will want their own reports and analyses, and you'll be in the line of fire. This is a great thing at heart—a secondary objective of your project and this book is to create a "culture of data" in your organization—but if you value your free time, you will want to prepare for this.

How Much Data Do I Have Today?

No exact number is required here. You just want a sense of the order of magnitude. Are we talking gigabytes? Terabytes? Petabytes? A lot of our design will be predicated on how large the datasets are. But just as important:

How Quickly Will My Data Increase in Size?

All warehouses, including the one we just made, start at 0 byte. But depending on your data sources and who's creating them, the data may grow at tremendous speed. The baby name example earlier in the chapter will not: it's historical data and it's going to remain so. But if your organization is active and growing, more and more data will be pouring in. The good news is that you're not going to run out of hard drive space or crash the server; those days are over. You'll definitely need to budget for it though! Additionally, you'll want to make the best guess you can about it. Building for tremendous scale early can be inefficient and prevent you from finishing a project, but failing to account for it in time can be a disaster.

How Many Readers Am I Going to Have?

This depends on who will need access and the level of data they'll need to see. So far we've treated BigQuery like a tool that would be used internally to your organization. However, it's totally reasonable that you would open BigQuery analysis to the customers of your organization or to the public itself. I don't mean to say you'll give them all GCP accounts and let them log in, but you may want to expose some of this intelligence to the wider world. This raises both cost and security implications.

How Many Analysts Am I Going to Have?

Determining how many people will actually be working inside of BigQuery to write queries, load and transform data, and create new reports is also fundamentally important. It's important to make sure that information is on a need-to-know basis and that you configure permissions accordingly. As the central repository of data, it will likely contain personal information that must not be breached or at the very least trade secrets. Make sure you define granular access controls up front and don't leave it as an afterthought.

What Is My Budget?

One consideration that may be new to users of a traditional data warehouse is that cost is an ongoing concern. The initial outlay to start using BigQuery is zero: you can run all the examples in this book on a free trial or free tier and never spend a dime. However, as soon as you begin running at production scale, you will likely incur cost for both data storage and query processing.

This has two significant implications: One is how to specify and access your data in a way that respects your organization's budget. Two, individual users have the ability to run costly queries; this is another good reason to work out access controls before getting under way.

In Chapter 4, this will be covered in detail.

Do I Need to Account for Real-Time Data?

This question doesn't specifically affect BigQuery, but it does affect how your users perceive the availability of the system. If your reports and dashboards rely on up-to-the-minute information and something causes intake into BigQuery to fail, users will notice and complain. While BigQuery will be up and running, it will begin to fall out of date.

This may not be an issue for you if you only run reports on a daily (weekly, monthly) basis. But as I spoke to in the "Introduction," the way to gain an advantage over your competitors is to tighten this feedback loop as much as possible. You want data coming in and being processed as quickly as possible to be surfaced to your users. That level of availability comes at the cost of monitoring and safeguarding both BigQuery and all of the services that touch it. This will even extend to other applications in your ecosystem that may connect to BigQuery to provide charts and graphs, as we'll discuss later.

Data Normalization

The topic of normalization and denormalization is an early class session of any college-level database design course. Stated simply, normalization decreases duplication of data by storing attributes in a single place and joining them together on keys. Denormalization stores all the data in the same table, avoiding joins but taking up more storage space and possibly causing data integrity issues if the data is stored in multiple places and does not match.

Along this spectrum, there are all degrees. You may choose to normalize some tables and not others; you may create denormalized tables that load from a group of normalized tables underneath; and so forth. It is always worth considering the trade-off between your time and the system's performance. A great many datasets should perform adequately with minimal modification.

BigQuery also has another trick up its sleeve—nested and repeated data elements. Since you can represent a row in BigQuery in pure JSON, you can use a structure that more closely resembles a document store to hold information. This avoids the normal data warehouse strategy of storing a fact and all of its related dimensions into a flat structure. This is pretty close to the best of both worlds.

We'll talk a lot more about this as we get into the next chapter, in which we will actually create a data warehouse.

Summary

BigQuery is an analytics engine provided as a managed cloud offering from Google. It can be accessed via a web interface, command line, or software development kit (SDK). It's fully compatible with ANSI SQL, and you can use it as you would any other SQL system. However, it is not designed as a transactional database, and you should not use it in use cases with frequent updates and deletes. It's a columnar data store that offers some advantages over a classic data warehouse model. In order to use it most effectively, define your project and its scope and answer some questions about what you intend to use it for. You should also know how big it will be and estimate how it will grow over time. Lastly, we discussed data normalization practice and how it applies to BigQuery. In the next chapter, we will use BigQuery to create a data warehouse, reviewing data types, schemas, and table relationships.

## CHAPTER 2

Starting Your Warehouse Project

Building a data warehouse in a new organization can be challenging. While we tend to conceive of technology initiatives as mostly the hard technical decisions, anything involving data becomes far more investigative. You will want to use a lot of different skills aside from your ability to rationalize and normalize data structures. We'll talk extensively about how to frame that discovery and learn how to "right-size" your warehouse for the environment. You'll also want to figure out where you can make trade-offs and where you will want to invest your time to improve things in the future.

A major part of a successful warehouse project is business acceptance and understanding. Gartner estimated in 2005 that 50% of data warehouse projects failed.[1] Even with paradigm shifts provided by BigQuery, Amazon Redshift, Snowflake, and so on, the largest problem ahead of you is having a solid foundation to build upon. This chapter will help you to answer the key questions about your project, present a charter to stakeholders, and prepare you for the journey before you write even a single line of code.

Where to Start

In the previous chapter, we talked about the highest-level questions you should answer. These are things like overall scope, who your stakeholders are, the size of your organization and its data, and who the user group will be, at least initially. You should be able to do most of that groundwork yourself. In some cases, you will even get to define those parameters for yourself. That's a good deal—most engineers would be jealous of a greenfield project. Now let's go one level deeper and talk about the data itself.

---

[1]www.zdnet.com/article/50-of-data-warehouse-projects-to-fail-in-2005-2007/

© Mark Mucchetti 2020
M. Mucchetti, *BigQuery for Data Warehousing*, https://doi.org/10.1007/978-1-4842-6186-6_2

If you are new to this practice, you may want to open an empty document or grab a piece of paper and start taking notes on the answers. I'll also provide a worksheet { LINK: APPENDIX B } that you can print or download if you prefer to work that way. There's no right answer on how formal to be—it depends on your organization, the maturity of its project management, and your own particular work style.

Key Questions
What Are My Finite Resources?

In all projects, you will have constraints on time, money, and people. Figuring out what those bounds are will inform both how much you can build off the bat and how much margin of error you'll have as a result. You may not know these answers concretely, but at minimum, imagine a radar chart along these three axes. Do you have plenty of time but no money? Do you have a budget but no one to work with you? (Can you hire some people?) Do you have a team that can do this work, but they're stuck on other initiatives? Knowing what your limitations are will help you take a very technical problem and bring it into the real world.

You may recognize this as the project management iron triangle, and we'll be revisiting these concepts from a number of different angles throughout the book.

What Is My Business Domain?

Let's start with the easiest one. You probably know what your organization does. But let's pair it with the last chapter's key question—"What problem am I trying to solve?" I can't really think of an organization that, given the technical and logistical challenges had been solved, would not benefit from a data warehouse. Nonetheless, this question gets at a couple of important points. If you know your domain, you might know where you can go for help answering business questions. You can also avoid reinventing the wheel if there are off-the-shelf datasets that could save you time. For instance, if you run a pharmacy chain, there's no reason to collect your own information about drug names and dosages. You could find or buy a dataset for this purpose. We'll cover this in several other chapters (Chapters 5, 6, 19), but this is something you can file away for now.

What Differentiates My Business from Others in Its Domain?

This resembles a typical business question, namely, what do you do that your competitors don't. However, I would also challenge you to think about ways in which your business has a peculiar style of doing things which is not easily changed. You may or may not be interested in changing that part of your company's culture, but you must understand it in order to build an effective warehouse that people will use. Let's say you run a consignment shop. A customer brings items in and sells them to you—you record this, process them, and add them to your inventory. Later, another customer comes in and buys the same item, hopefully at a higher price. Simple. But let's say your employees don't record any information about the customer when they come in to sell. Is a "seller" entity important for your business? If it is, you'll face the obstacle of suggesting a business process change to collect it. These scenarios can be pitfalls if you design a completely standard model but find the business priorities are incompatible. Not unsolvable problems, of course, but a good callback to the finiteness of your resources.

Who Knows What Data I Need?

This question is somewhat like finding out who your stakeholders are, but it's taking the information that they would provide you and finding the person or people who know the actual attributes associated with it. For instance, you may have a stakeholder in your finance department who needs to know monthly revenue. Great! You note that you need revenue numbers. That's aggregate data though; you have to calculate that number from underlying data. Do you sell widgets? You'll need to know how many widgets you've sold and how much they cost. Do you provide consulting services? You might need to know the names of your consultants, their current engagements, and their blended rate. First, you have to figure out who knows the business domain well enough to tell you the formal definitions of this data.

Who Already Knows What Data They Need?

The difference between this question and the previous question is subtle but important. Stakeholders may not know how to generate their data, how to obtain it, or how to keep it up-to-date. However, some stakeholders will have very specific requests for reports or types of data. You'll want to know these requests in advance. You could certainly build something general-purpose and then build out these specific requests, and you may choose to do that. But answering this question gives you two specific insights. Firstly, it will tell you who is likely to be a power user of the system and which things you may want to invest in optimizing. Secondly, it will be an early hint about the layout of your data marts. As we discussed in the previous chapter, you may wish to align data marts to departments. Here you may learn that the data needs of each department overlap slightly or that different people in the same department have different interpretations of the data. It turns out that matching the organization of people to the organization of data isn't often clear. Asking this question and the previous question together can help you tease that apart before you get too far down the road to adapt.

What Are My Key Entities?

You will already know some of these and have encountered others. Using the answers you have already—what domain are you operating in and what data people are asking for—you can begin to conceptualize the important objects in your system. Don't worry too much about fields (columns) yet, although you will inevitably begin to do that. Do worry about how the entities are related to each other. Try composing some simple sentences about your business and note the nouns that emerge most frequently. Some basic examples are as follows:

- A customer purchases a product.
- An employee clocks in to begin a shift.
- A chef cooks three meals a day.
- A chatbot can answer several kinds of questions.
- Families can reserve cabins all summer long.

Again, you may recognize a user story structure emerging here (as an x, I want to y so that I can z). The similarity to functional requirements is obviously intentional. With a few of these, we can start taking these concepts into the real world.

What Are My Key Relationships?

Once you've established the most basic concepts for your warehouse, you can take it one step further and begin to determine relationships between data. In an operational store, you would design these using relational models that describe common functionality or are architected for performance. In a microservice architecture, the practice is to have a single data source for each service, which is too restrictive for our purposes. We are trying to make information from this data. You can think far more broadly in the data warehouse model about how things might be related. Once they understand the potential, your users will probably be even more creative combining data than you can be.

What Role Does Time Play in My Model?

This question has a couple of components. If your business cares about change over time (and most do), you'll want to know the range of relevant data and the interval that matters. For example, if your business operates on a monthly cycle, a lot of your reporting is going to look at a monthly range or a month-to-date value. If you're ingesting and storing logs, you may only care about the last seven days. You will have other use cases that might be major decision points for you. In the daily case, you can use BigQuery partitioned tables, which automatically structure the data on a daily basis.

What Role Does Cost Play in My Model?

A large mindset change to managed services is the idea of availability vs. cost. In the old days, if you miscalculated your resource needs, your system would fall over and stop responding to requests. In the world of Internet-scale cloud providers, if you don't set a limit, your system will respond to everything, and you will incur unwanted costs. BigQuery allows you to set custom quotas (we'll discuss this in Chapter 4) so you get the same effect, but you obviously don't want to design a system that's hitting its limits all the time either.

General Considerations

If you've designed or worked in a relational database before, you will be familiar with Data Definition Language, or DDL. If you've created tables and views, you will also know Data Manipulation Language, or DML. DDL and DML are both supported in BigQuery, but there are some things to keep in mind.

As a reminder, you should not be doing frequent UPDATEs or DELETEs on rows inside of BigQuery. As it is not designed as a transactional database, you should focus on loading data to it and then leaving it there. You can certainly do this work as part of maintenance, but your warehouse shouldn't rely on table modification to work properly.

Google considers using BigQuery as a transactional store (OLTP) to be an anti-pattern. In fact, in contrast to traditional data warehouses, Google sets no age limit on data. It is designed for indefinite scale, and you can keep inserting/streaming new data without hitting disk space or compute limits. Of course, you may care for cost or compliance reasons. While you don't have to consider it as a primary design consideration, you will want to keep data age in your mind moving forward.

One other note on time: Please do generally use Coordinated Universal Time (UTC). All of Google Cloud operates this way, and you should prefer storing datetimes in universal time and converting to a user's local time for display. Even if your business operates in a single timezone and all data collected is in that timezone, you should still use UTC. You can also store the user's UTC offset or the local time in another column for local analysis. For instance, if you want to know how often employees clock in late, it would be useful to look at all rows where their local time is later than the start of the shift, even though the UTC will vary by location and time of year.

Making the Case

Hopefully you see the value of having done the groundwork to answer the basic design questions ahead of time. If you have concerns about the next step—creating the model in your BigQuery project—try doing the worksheet exercise. If you feel you need additional help to understand the domain model itself, try searching for a glossary of terms for your industry and use it to form sentences about your business. It is often said that naming things is one of the hardest problems in computer science, and I am inclined to agree. With any luck, someone will have done this hard work for you already.

Even if you have an existing structure, you may still want to restructure your data to take maximum advantage of BigQuery's strengths at scaling to massive levels. This requires resources, obviously, and you may not have or want to spend them. So we'll talk primarily about the from-scratch implementation in this chapter and then revisit this question from the perspective of your existing data in the next chapter.

The focus on the project and the process for completing it is very intentional. A successful data warehouse requires broad support from the organization and an understanding of its politics. The theoretical knowledge and hard work to do the project is necessary, but it is only a prerequisite. If rallying troops and building consensus may not be your strong suit, now is the time to partner with an empowered project manager or a committed executive sponsor.

Interviewing Stakeholders

You should have an idea of who these people may be based on the questions in the previous section. Find out (or ask your partner) what the best way to get their attention is and get a meeting on their calendar. Busy people will undoubtedly deprioritize this exercise, since they may not understand its value until they are getting meaningful insight. If you have an idea what their data needs are, bring that outline to your meeting and use it to ask directed questions. If they receive existing dashboards or reports from you, those terms are probably front and center. You're liable to only get blank stares if you ask an open-ended question like "What data do you need?" Well, there will probably be a couple stakeholders who came from an organization with good data practices, and they'll just be thrilled you're asking at all.

Take detailed notes. Pay special attention if you hear a term you've heard in other contexts, but when you ask for a definition, it doesn't seem to agree. Start drilling down on what a given metric means, especially if it's custom to your business. How is something like "likelihood to repurchase" calculated? Does everyone agree?

You may realize that this exercise has never been undertaken before. It may have simply been unnecessary for two stakeholders to share the same context. Or, when they communicated with each other previously, they were careful to use more specific terms to disambiguate the scenario. Unfortunately for your blood pressure, one of our true needs as engineers is clarity—we can't build a system with inconsistent definitions or one that returns different answers to the same questions each time you ask. (Technically, BigQuery does support the RAND() function, but self-sabotage isn't really my style.)

Resolving Conflicts

By conflicts, I don't mean physical altercations. What I'm referring to is that different stakeholders will inevitably have different interpretations of the same piece of data. Your job here is to create a single, unified terminology, so that when people across the business use a term, it means the same thing to everyone. This may not be totally possible due to ingrained process, but you will at least be able to untangle domain-specific meanings of a word like "customer."

There are two straightforward ways to handle a terminology conflict like this. One is to apply the context to the term to differentiate them—for example, a "prospect" might become a "prospective customer" and a "prospective employee," since those two terms are not actually the same thing. The other is to unify the terms and apply the facets of both to the term. A marketing person and an operations person will both care about a "product," but the operations person would be concerned with its gross weight, size, shipping restrictions, and so on. The marketing person would care about the price, the marketing copy, the number of calories, and so forth. You'll pretty clearly need an entity with the name "product," but you can combine its attributes in the data warehouse, even if the source systems are totally disjunct.

If neither of these approaches applies, you probably have a "level" issue. What I mean by that is one person may be describing a thing that is a part of a whole that the other person is describing. To illustrate, the word "truck" may describe the physical object, with its attributes being size of gas tank, mileage on the odometer, radio frequency, and so on. But to a shipping person, it may refer to its contents—in reality, the truckload, not the truck. Those attributes would be internal size, number of packages contained, bill of lading, and so on. In this case, "truckload" could actually be an attribute of "truck" itself. To resolve, you can make a nested schema of truck which contains another business term, such as "manifest" or "pallet" or whatever it is that's actually being described. The data warehouse is then properly equipped to answer questions on either or both sets of attributes, for example, "How much gas did we use today?", "How many trucks (truckloads) reached their destinations today?", or "Are trucks on CB frequency 23 less likely to deliver on time?" It's always worth at least attempting to merge the sense of two terms, because there is almost certainly useful information to be found in the intersection. (Now as to how a particular CB frequency would affect truckers reaching their destinations, I'll leave to your imagination.)

Compiling Documentation

Once you've completed talking to your stakeholders and reconciling your terminology, you will want to produce three key artifacts. These will both help you prove the value of your case and serve as your template documentation for creating the warehouse in the next section. They'll also serve as guideposts if you lose track of (or others drift from) the original definition of a term over time.

Sources of Truth

You will need to understand all of the possible places your data can come from. This will obviously change over time, but you'll also get a sense of the level of effort that will be required to load up and maintain the data warehouse. Additionally, you'll get a sense of the kinds of attributes you need—once you get at this data, you'll know what's important or at least what's available.

You may see the same data point comes from multiple places, and that's okay. If it literally tracks the exact same data, then choose one and note it. If it tracks its own interpretation of the same data, you'll want to use nesting or aggregation to resolve and designate each piece of data as a source. Best example: Google Analytics, Facebook, and other marketing pixels are never going to match on exact number of impressions (for reasons beyond the scope of this book). It's fine to label "Google hit count," "Facebook hit count," and so on as separate metrics and deal with this in the transformation phase. They track the same thing in theory, but in practice they're never going to agree.

This will also bring to light another frequent and important problem—namely, that certain data points have no source of truth. It's common for finance to track to monthly or quarterly targets, but those targets may not exist anywhere outside of a spreadsheet or email, even though it is literally the most important metric. Forecasting, reforecasting, optimism, pessimism, random chance—all of these things can cause different people to have completely different numbers in mind. A stretch goal and what gets reported to Wall Street are totally misaligned. Take note of these and decide how much responsibility you can take for dealing with them. From a political standpoint, your warehouse function will suffer significant credibility loss if someone claims "the revenue target is wrong."

Data Dictionary

The data dictionary represents your clean, reconciled version of the terminology your business uses. This will become the bible for what any particular term actually represents. Remember that you can always change how data is visualized in an individual data mart, but the underlying warehouse definition must be pure. Don't compromise on this step. This is the nexus of your entire business intelligence operation, and without this to rely on, you will be lost.

If you have legacy BI solutions, they will stop agreeing with your solution in any place you have redefined a term. Make it clear to everyone that when the new system goes live, the legacy system will be deprecated. This will happen even if it's still receiving data and appears to be functional. Otherwise, stakeholders won't trust either set of data, and you will be constantly explaining that while they name the same metric, they are not measuring the same thing, and the data dictionary you published clearly states that this metric measures this, but in the legacy system it didn't account for this, and... Well, you get my point. It doesn't matter what the measurement did before; all that matters is that everyone will agree on the new measurement and that that measurement works properly.

The Charter

Now it's time to take the answer to the very first question—"What problem am I trying to solve?"—and formalize it in a charter. You can adapt this to your organization's particular work style and project management office requirements. It may just be a single-page document outlining the rough goals, or I hope not, but you could produce 200 pages of boilerplate to serve the same purpose. Ultimately the purpose of this part of the process is to give the business something to see and to sign off on.

Make sure all the key stakeholders sign off on this! Take it as high in the organization as you feel necessary. Even when all parties are acting with good intentions, standards can slip and internal sentiment can change. Once you get rolling, people will see the value in what you're doing, and acceptance will come more easily. Set a strong foundation now so that you have the chance to make that happen.

Understanding Business Acceptance

I can only approach this in a very general fashion, because it depends so highly on your particular culture. It also depends on you or your business partner's clout in the organization. A scenario where you would want to change the culture of the business in the process of gaining its acceptance would not be uncommon. Style yourself as a champion for data in your organization and see where it takes you.

I worked at an organization where there was very little process management and making decisions based on data was often a lost cause. Reports disagreed, no one trusted the information, and there was no sense of how to unify the definitions. The manager of the data team labored quietly for months constructing a real data analysis function. When it was ready, he began to tout it to the organization. Within a few months, he had earned the nickname "Data Steve," and his team received a large amount of positive recognition. Stakeholders hadn't even realized how many problems this function could solve. While your organization may have this structure in place, I have typically seen several phases of acceptance take place in the organization. I've written out the feel of an organization at each step. To gain business acceptance, you probably only need to talk about the benefits of going even one point higher. If you build a best-in-class warehouse using BigQuery, you can skip ahead, but you'll still need to build the culture at each point. See if you can score your own organization on this rubric (Figure 2-1).

0	Organization does not understand what data is. Major data points are not even being stored. Decisions are made without concrete input. Your title doesn't have "data" or "information" anywhere in the name and is probably something like "senior IT analyst." Stakeholders cannot answer even fundamental questions about the business without significant manual effort. Their desks are covered in papers. When you suggest building a "data warehouse," you are seen at best as harmless. Nothing could possibly improve the efficiency of this organization, so they might as well give you free rein. They're not sure what you do around here anyway.
1	Organization has "no data." While this statement isn't strictly true, you hear it a lot. Transactional data may be recorded, but it doesn't go to any central place. Individuals use different systems to look it up. Developers are querying live systems directly for lack of a better solution. Transactional systems have poorly defined schemas, leading to inaccurate or incomplete results. Business users mostly talk in terms of "reports." When you ask where to find these reports, they open their email. Reports needed on a regular basis often take days to arrive and sometimes have wild and inexplicable variance.
2	Organization has reporting, but it could "use some work." Business users can point you to some suite of reports, often in a customized and unattractive frame. It will be called something like "Phoenix." (Very clever.) Each report, even the most common, takes seconds or minutes to return. Developers talk about a "reporting system," but it is in reality just a replicated copy of the live transaction store. The reports run slowly because nothing is optimized. Also, they frequently break as developers remove or change database columns without considering the impact on the "warehouse." Most people at least know to go to this system to do their reporting, but there are still mysterious reports that come by email when the reporting system is insufficient.
3	Organization has a central business intelligence function. There is a team of analysts hidden in the IT department somewhere that can make new reports for you. The reports come out of a tool you can actually look up on Google. The data is accurate, although sometimes sluggish. Occasionally you will hear about "maintenance downtime," and the warehouse will be taken offline for the weekend starting at about 5 PM on Friday.
4	Organization has a data warehouse and data marts. Most of the work in the preceding sections was completed by your predecessor. Departments have data they can rely on, which is accurate. The most important reports perform well and are up-todate. You may also have real-time visibility on dashboards using a system like Looker, Tableau, or Qlik. Analysts in other business units are able to access and report on the data they need without much intervention from your IT team. Maintenance is rare or non-existent. By this point stakeholders have generally stopped complaining, and you can move into innovation.
5	Organization has tight, real-time feedback loops to business process. You couldn't even imagine making any significant decision without up-to-the-minute information at your fingertips. Anomaly detection flags any metrics that fall out of range. You have measurements tied to every aspect of your business. Analysts produce their own dashboards, which include metrics that you would never have thought of. When a truly oddball question emerges, your only role is to assist in the complicated query to obtain the information. You can visualize the information in charts or graphs almost immediately. Machine learning capabilities help you forecast accurately and prevent problems before they occur. New employees exclaim, "This is so much better than what we had at my last job!" Fresh flowers fill your cubicle each morning, and your beverage of choice sits on your desk when you arrive… Okay, well, maybe not that last part. If your organization scores a 5, you have my permission to close this book, put it on a shelf, and take the rest of the day off.

Figure 2-1. *Rubric for organizational data maturity*

Recording Decisions

You're all set now. You just need a way to ensure all the documentation and consensus you've produced can be recorded. You also want this as a safeguard for when things inevitably change. It's fine if they do and (agile hat on) probably desirable, but you'll want to keep a record of those changes.

You may opt to combine the data dictionary and the sources of truth at this point, but if you have a lot of hairy examples like the marketing tracker one I used earlier, you may not wish to do this. At the very least, define the sources of truth themselves and make sure you know who the owners are, should something change or you need additional clarification.

Regardless, I recommend keeping the three documents (charter, data dictionary, and sources of truth, if you haven't combined them) in an easily accessible location such as your intranet. You must be diligent about keeping them up-to-date as the organization evolves. In reality, these definitions shouldn't change too much if you have properly captured your business domain, but the sources of truth might.

The documents themselves should also have a version history, however you choose to track that. Here's that note again: all data models should be extensible, but they should not be modified. This includes the descriptions of those models. Changing the data dictionary to modify the definition of a certain term is a big deal, and all relevant parties should at least acknowledge the change. Failure to close the loop on this will get you more "my data is wrong" complaints.

By the way, this note applies as the "open-closed principle" across many areas of software engineering. We'll come back to it as we explore the evolution of schemas over time and how to handle what could be a design error.

You may also opt to keep tally of where you think your organization scores on the rubric. This could help you choose the correct pace of change and the level of formality your organization may require for success.

Choosing a Design

Google suggests that you can use nested and repeated fields to obviate the need for traditional OLAP data organization. Using partitioning can also eliminate some of the need for time-based dimension tables. However, if you have an existing model, you will probably also already have an OLTP database or an OLAP schema such as star or snowflake. You can revisit the question about your finite resources to decide how much work you can do when loading and transforming data into your database. We'll also discuss these considerations more in the next couple of chapters.

Transactional Store

If you have an existing transactional database using Microsoft SQL Server, MySQL, PostgresSQL, and so on , then your data is already structured. If you have dedicated database administrators, you may find this data is actually too normalized for use with BigQuery. We'll cover this use case in Chapter 5. If your dataset is small and does not frequently change, you can replicate it over to BigQuery directly, but in most applications this would only be a first step.

Star/Snowflake Schemas

In a star schema, you have a fact table in the center and dimension tables as the points of the star. It is so named because the arrangement looks like a star.

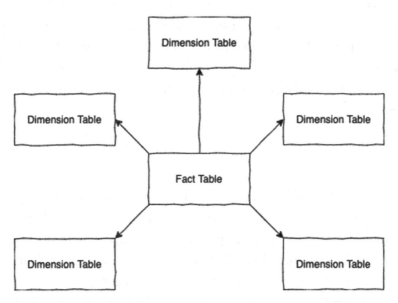

Figure 2-2. *A simplified star schema*

If you're migrating from an existing OLAP warehouse, this arrangement is perfectly viable in BigQuery. However, you may find[2] that BigQuery in a single denormalized table with nesting outperforms the star schema significantly. Two other advantages often cited are that analysts are more easily able to navigate this schema type and that it is optimal for disk space. In most cases, disk space will not be a consideration for you on BigQuery. As for navigation, this is a discussion you will need to have (see the "Making the Case" section). You may not be willing or able to restructure your existing schema.

A snowflake schema is essentially a star schema extended with normalized dimension tables. While with the preceding star schema there were no separate lookups for the dimension tables, the snowflake schema has additional tables to track lookups for dimensions. This makes changing dimensions a lot easier and the representation more compact, with a trade-off in performance.

NoSQL

This use case is increasingly common and covered in depth in Chapter 6. Essentially, the architecture is that you receive data live from your application and use a document-based storage system such as MongoDB or Google Cloud Datastore to store in a semi-structured format. Then, using an event-based architecture, you transform and load the data into a more structured format. BigQuery can serve as that structure, and you can even load your documents directly into it. However, unless you have a single NoSQL store and a single BigQuery dataset, and both are in the gigabyte range, you will still need to create a proper design.

BigQuery

Since the purpose of this book is to use BigQuery for your warehouse, I'm going to promote best practices for this wherever possible while also flagging alternatives or specific constraints. The pure BigQuery model encourages you to set aside these questions of normalization and other OLAP schemas. The message is clear: use nested and repeated data, and you can avoid these decisions altogether.

Obviously, your project won't have unlimited budget, and thus there will be some practical limitations to the amount of disk space you want to consume. But if you did

---

[2]https://fivetran.com/blog/obt-star-schema

have infinite storage and compute, how many of these trade-offs would go away? If your warehouse is likely to remain smaller than a petabyte throughout its lifetime, will you ever hit this theoretical limit? Again, if you're lucky enough to be starting from scratch, you can perhaps sidestep this entire part of the discussion. (You will probably still want to read Chapter 3 or 4 depending on where your live data sources currently are, though.)

Understanding the BigQuery Model

By now, if you have a reasonable sense of all of the preceding considerations, you're ready to get going. If you're itching to get started and you still aren't sure about everything, don't let that stop you. As much as I like to whiteboard all day, perfect is the enemy of the good when it comes down to these things. So do your best with the information you have available. You can always change it up when it becomes a runaway success.

I'll make this note many times: remember that, in general, all data models should be extensible, but they should not be modified. Changing the name of a dataset, table, column, or data type may have side effects that are extremely difficult to predict. You may have one or many brittle consumers of the data that are expecting a certain schema or response. Worse yet, they may be hiding in poorly written code (pesky developers) with no unit tests. This is not to say you can never modify anything—but as soon as your system is at a level of maturity where you cannot know all of its entry points, think carefully before you do.

Projects

In the last chapter, we created a Google Cloud Platform project to work with BigQuery. Google allows you to unify billing across projects, and you can also reach data stored in other projects if the owner allows it.

In principle, you probably only need a single project for your data warehouse. Unless you have a compelling reason to incur the overhead of maintaining multiple sets of services, you will have a much easier time if your permissions and other compute resources are all located in the same project.

If you are creating a warehouse that aggregates data over multiple tenants in a software-as-a-service environment, your clients may each have their own projects. However, your clients may also have their own clouds, on-premise installations, version issues, and so on. This consideration is best addressed as an abstraction over how you intake the data into the warehouse. From this perspective, it may be best to avoid reaching into client data sources directly and instead provide a unified interface for ingesting data.

If you have multiple GCP projects in your organization already, find out how they are administered and whether you will need direct access to them. For the remainder of this book, except when discussing public datasets and permissions, I will operate under the assumption that your warehouse lives inside a single project.

Datasets

The top level of organization in your project is a dataset. You can have multiple datasets inside the same project, and each of those datasets can contain tables, views, stored procedures, functions, and so on.

Hierarchical organization of data is a highly arbitrary subject. The two primary options are to use a single dataset in your project or to use many datasets. There are pros and cons to each approach. Storing everything in a single dataset makes it easy to query across any table without remembering which dataset it belongs to. However, you'll have to think more about permissioning, and if you are mixing sensitive and nonsensitive data, it may be easier to lose track. On the other hand, making many datasets for a small number of tables can be unnecessary overhead. Ultimately, you will want to refer to the answers to how big your data is now and how big it will become before making this decision.

Be wary of lining up your dataset definitions to data source. The place the data comes from may not be the most relevant structure for analysis. For example, you may take orders both in-store and online. Your in-store systems may be an antiquated point-of-sale using cash registers and Electronic Data Interchange (EDI) to send data to BigQuery. Meanwhile, the online systems send real-time order information directly to you. This doesn't necessarily mean they should go in two different datasets. The most relevant question your stakeholders might ask is how much money you've made in a particular day. If in-store outweighs online by a lot, and will continue to do so, put the data close together and unify the schema as best you can. Of course, this is only an example! I'm just trying to give some clarity around the kinds of questions you can ask yourself to help answer this question.

In case it matters to you, my personal preference is to make multiple datasets to contain logically distinct areas. For example, you might put your monitoring logs in a different dataset than your order information.[3] You might occasionally want to correlate logs to orders, perhaps to troubleshoot an issue, but BigQuery supports this, and you can take advantage of it when you need to.

Tables

The primary object in a dataset is the table. Your dataset will generally contain many tables, all of which you pull together in various ways for analysis. Tables also look a little different in BigQuery for a few different reasons. As mentioned earlier, Google considers OLTP to be an anti-pattern. So we'll be working primarily using OLAP concepts. That being said, there are still some BigQuery-specific patterns worth knowing.

Normalization/Denormalization

Favored by data engineer interviewers everywhere, this topic has decades of academic texts and research articles attached to it. If you're not familiar, the underlying question is this. Normalization is optimizing toward against redundancy of data and dividing the data into multiple tables which are then joined together. Denormalization goes the opposite direction, favoring performance and putting all of the data in as few tables as possible.

A classic example is a customer object. A normalized form of this might look something like the following.

---

[3]Cloud Logging (formerly Stackdriver) is the operational logging system for GCP, and we'll cover it in Chapter 12.

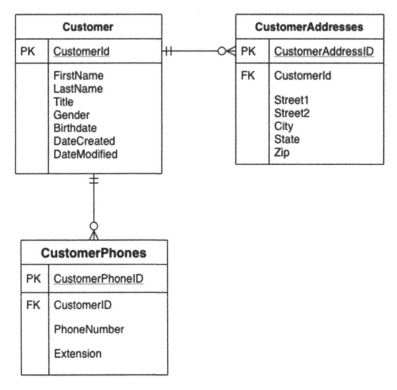

Figure 2-3. *A classic customer entity relationship diagram*

On the other hand, the denormalized form would put all of the customer data into a single table with a single identifier—no joins necessary. You just pull the columns you need.

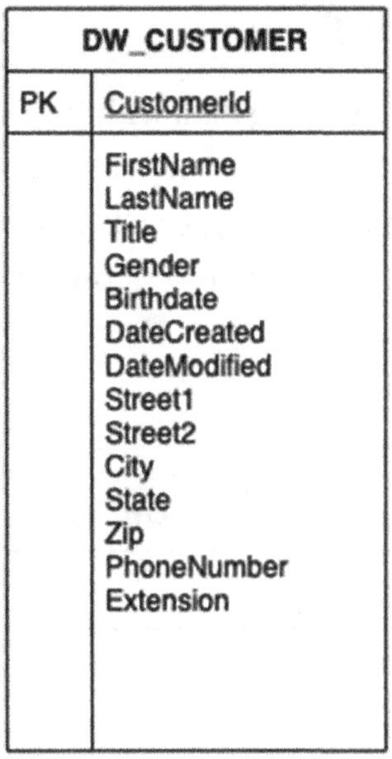

DW_CUSTOMER	
PK	CustomerId
	FirstName
	LastName
	Title
	Gender
	Birthdate
	DateCreated
	DateModified
	Street1
	Street2
	City
	State
	Zip
	PhoneNumber
	Extension

Figure 2-4. *The same data, denormalized*

This is a pretty succinct rule of thumb. You can override it based on the frequency and importance of UPDATE and DELETE operations. Remember, in general, you will want to primarily insert data into tables rather than overwriting or removing it. If you need to do this a lot, though, you may decide (and Google suggests) that it's better to have a normalized schema and take the performance penalty.

What if you don't have much data now, but you expect it to grow tremendously over time? Generally, you want to stick with standard procedure here and go ahead and denormalize the structure for future growth. The interesting implication is that if you know your datasets are going to stay relatively small, you could opt for minimal transformation on top of your existing transactional schemas. Generally, you would also care about data storage and costs due to the redundancy of denormalized data. In a managed environment, that's not going to pose any substantial risk. The other risk—loss of data consistency—is real. Data can lose synchronization among locations if it's stored in multiple places. Especially with rapidly changing data, you might deal with some inconsistency. This may or may not be a significant factor for your environment.

Hierarchical Data Structure

The other significant difference in storing data with BigQuery is using nested data. BigQuery can ingest native JSON and store each object as a row. This is the recommended method for schemas in BigQuery. BigQuery can also work with nested elements that repeat. This allows you to represent one-to-many relationships inside the row itself.

For example, consider the following.

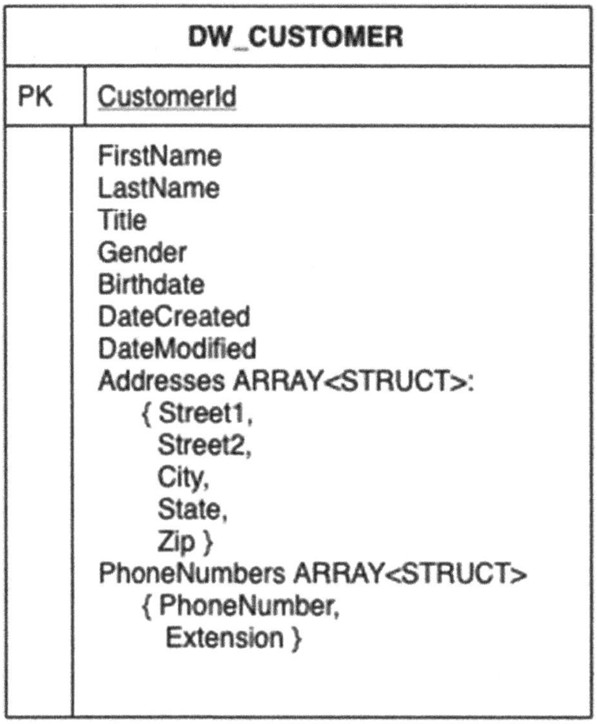

DW_CUSTOMER	
PK	CustomerId

	FirstName
	LastName
	Title
	Gender
	Birthdate
	DateCreated
	DateModified
	Addresses ARRAY<STRUCT>:
	    { Street1,
	     Street2,
	     City,
	     State,
	     Zip }
	PhoneNumbers ARRAY<STRUCT>
	    { PhoneNumber,
	     Extension }

Figure 2-5. *The same data, with a hierarchical model*

Modeling data this way allows you to get some of the advantages of normalization without actually having to do it. Of course, the disadvantages of denormalization also apply, namely, that this data isn't going to update as it would in a related table. This technique is fine whenever you are capturing point-in-time data, though.

Partitioning

Partitioning is a tool you can use when creating a table to automatically bucket rows by ingestion time, a timestamp, or an integer key. This is useful for two reasons: One, you get the range as a dimension without doing any extra work. This lets you more easily analyze data within or across those ranges. Two, you can set an expiration policy on partitioned tables. If you're storing ephemeral data and only need to keep it around for a certain amount of time, you can have BigQuery automatically remove older data. This technique could also be used in combination with a larger source table to create deeper analysis for a limited time.

Summary

To successfully start a data warehouse project, you need two major ingredients. The first is your technical skill and understanding of how to undertake a project like this. The second is business understanding and acceptance. Both are equally important. There are several key questions you can ask yourself or stakeholders to understand their needs. Once you understand the business domain and charter a project, you have the foundation to start building. This information will help you choose a design. BigQuery has some best practices for how to structure data and some decisions you can make yourself with your knowledge of the business. With this chapter, you should now be prepared to go full speed ahead. In the next chapter, we'll dive deep into construction to create a warehouse that handles all of your existing business cases and is prepared for new ones.

## CHAPTER 3

All My Data

One reason you're probably interested in this topic is that you agree with me that organizations run on data. Regardless of the maturity of the organization and any data collection practices you may already have in place, the purpose of a data warehouse is to centralize how users can access data accurately and reliably. Prior to the data lake concept, it was also to put all that data in a central place. With BigQuery, that last step is not always necessary. However, your job includes making that decision based on the nature of the data. The centrality in any warehouse model served the larger purpose of accurate and reliable data, and that consideration is unchanged regardless of this or any future model.

In this chapter, we'll discuss the nuts and bolts of building your datasets and other database objects. We'll also cover the other part of the process: satisfying your stakeholders and making sure that your execution satisfies the charter you've written. By the end of this chapter, you should have a shiny, new, and empty BigQuery project in which to begin loading or migrating your data.

If you don't have a charter, I strongly recommend you go back to Chapter 2 or Appendix B and sketch one out. Even if your organization is very small, projects have a tendency to "scope creep" and never quite get finished. A data warehouse is useless without users, and everyone's satisfaction level will be much higher if you can declare a start and an end to the project. Once your first phase is complete and the organization improves, I promise you will have more requests than you know how to deal with.

You may have the opposite problem, that is, you already have more requests than you know how to deal with. If this is the case, writing a charter should be even easier. However, finding the time to write one may be the challenge. As the venerable Admiral Jean-Luc Picard once admitted doing, don't make perfect the enemy of the good. Okay, lecture time over.

The Data Model

If you want to climb the ladder from data to information to insight, the first real rung is data modeling. Decisions made about the model are easy and malleable when you have

© Mark Mucchetti 2020
M. Mucchetti, *BigQuery for Data Warehousing*, https://doi.org/10.1007/978-1-4842-6186-6_3

nothing loaded, but once you're operating in the terabyte or higher range, it won't be as easy to make fundamental modifications. I'm hopeful that advances in technology will eventually eliminate that hurdle as well, but for now it's still a good practice to think about the model first.

In Chapter 2, we discussed these questions as relevant to project planning. As a result, you should have a pretty good idea what your key entities are, their relationships, and the relevant grain of time. Here, I'm going to revisit one additional concern: speed of event creation and value of historical data.

Intake Rates

When I talk about intake rate, I'm speaking generally about orders of magnitude. I typically use a brief rule of thumb to estimate based on how many people or things can generate the data. For example, if you need to insert a new row every time one of your salespeople signs a new client, that's a heavily manual process with a bounded maximum in the billions (conservatively, if you could sign up every human on the planet). If the event is a new order that any website user can input, that could move much faster. If it's an event per user click or keyboard stroke, you could see billions of records a day. And if it's something other machines are generating, like error or health logs, it could be trillions or more. Your model should take this into account.

Value of Historical Data

This principle tends to operate in inverse to the intake rate. Using the preceding examples, you are going to want to know about a client for the entire life of the organization. On the other hand, a server event log is rarely persisted for more than 30 days. Essentially this question informs your data model by helping you understand if the important property of a particular data point is recency, ease of analytics, or only in combination with other data.

Creating the Data Model

Armed with your charter and a rough idea of the entities and relationships that are important to you, it's time to get down to business. To start, we're going to make sure that you have a dataset to put all of your objects into. Throughout this book, we're going to stick to working mostly within a single dataset. At moderate scale, one dataset should be enough. However, if you need operations at the dataset level such as control of geographic location of the data or you want a permissions scheme that requires multiple datasets, there's no reason not to do that as well.

Making a Dataset

If you haven't already made a dataset throughout the previous chapters, let's do that now. The easiest way to do it is by clicking your project in the BigQuery UI and then clicking "Create dataset."

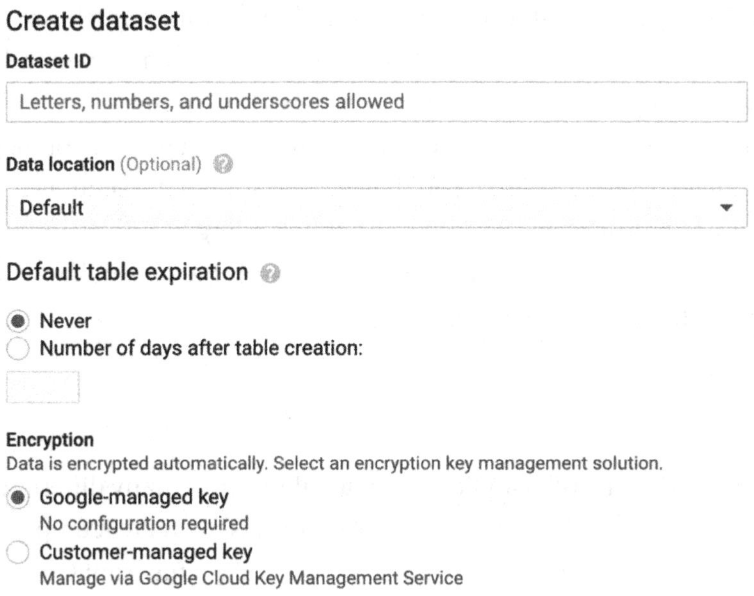

Create dataset

Dataset ID

Letters, numbers, and underscores allowed

Data location (Optional) ❓

Default ▼

Default table expiration ❓

● Never
○ Number of days after table creation:

Encryption
Data is encrypted automatically. Select an encryption key management solution.

● Google-managed key
   No configuration required
○ Customer-managed key
   Manage via Google Cloud Key Management Service

Figure 3-1. *Create Dataset View*

There isn't much configuration to do here. Enter a relevant dataset name (i.e., "companyname_data_warehouse" or "main" or whatever). For some reason, despite Google's typical convention being hyphenation, the only punctuation allowed in dataset names is underscores. That has deterred me somewhat from using overly complicated names, which is probably okay. You don't need to set a data location, but if you have legal or compliance reasons to do so, you can do that here too. You also likely do not want tables to expire in your data warehouse, so leave that set to "Never." Click Create, and you should immediately get a new entry in your project.

Another thing to consider when deciding how to create your datasets is you can copy a whole dataset from one project to another, but only one at a time. Similarly, if you want to make a dataset public, you can do that easily too. Google's order of magnitude for how many datasets you can have in a project is something like "thousands," so you don't need to worry about that limitation too much. Google also puts the maximum number of tables in a dataset at thousands too, so depending on how much you're going to store, this could be more or less important to you.

Creating Tables

Again, we'll start this through the UI to show all the available basic options. In this chapter, we're also focused on setting up your warehouse from scratch, so we'll stick to the basic methods of table creation. In later chapters, I'll go into greater detail about streaming from existing sources and setting up syncs from live data.

It's also worth noting that you don't even need to create a table if you're going to be loading data from an external source. You'll be able to supply the schema for that data (or in some cases, to auto-detect it) when you begin loading.

Open the dataset you just created and click "Create Table." A sidebar will slide open. Let's go over the options.

Source

One of BigQuery's strengths is its ability to create tables from many different sources and formats. The most basic way to make a table, of course, is to create it empty. The three following methods are variations on a theme: you can take a file from Google Cloud Storage (GCS), your local computer, or Google (G Suite) Drive and create a table from it.

Empty

Your table will be created with no data in it. If you are in fact starting from scratch, this is your only option!

Google Cloud Storage

Google Cloud Storage is the underlying file storage system for Google Cloud. If you're familiar with Amazon S3, this is an equivalent concept. You can load files of arbitrary size into buckets and then access them with a URI in the form gs://bucket-name/filename.

Upload

You can also upload a file from your local machine. Local uploads are limited to 10 MB. If you're uploading larger files, Google Cloud Storage is the best option.

Drive

Drive is Google Drive, the consumer G Suite product for storing and organizing files. You can load a file directly from its Drive URI. This includes things like Google Sheets, which actually create a live federated source against the Drive file.

Google Cloud Bigtable

The last method, Bigtable, is a little different. Bigtable is Google's NoSQL database solution, closely resembling Apache HBase (think Hadoop). When you link your BigQuery project to Bigtable, the data remains stored in Bigtable and uses its CPU cycles, but you can access and link it via BigQuery. This process is more involved than the others. If you have existing Bigtable implementations, it is worth considering.

Format

Let's cover the formats in which you can instantiate BigQuery tables.

CSV

Good old comma-separated value (CSV) files are probably the best way to intake your data if your current business intelligence tool of choice happens to be Excel (or Lotus 1-2-3, dBase, Notepad, etc.). It's suboptimal because CSV doesn't support nested or repeated fields. On the bright side, pretty much any tool can output it. If you're interfacing with older systems and need to load data periodically, it might be the only format that they can agree on.

When you choose CSV as an option, you will get several advanced options to do some basic data transformation on the file, such as setting the field delimiter, skipping header rows, and allowing jagged rows (i.e., rows that have empty data in trailing fields and don't use commas). You'll be familiar with all of these if you've ever used a standard SQL bulk import/export tool.

JSONL

JSONL, or JSON Lines, is a file where each line is a self-contained JSON object. This format has the advantage of allowing nested and repeated fields. You might ask why not place all the lines in a single JSON array to make it parsable by a regular JSON reader. The reason is that a parser would have to read the entire file to create one giant object before it could enumerate the individual array items. Using JSONL, the parser just reads one line at a time, parses it as standard JSON, loads it, and continues. This also enables parallelization and other desirable techniques for huge files.

```
 1 ▾ {
 2       "plays":
 3 ▾     [
 4 ▾       { "name": "Rosencrantz and Guildernstern Are Dead",
 5           "year": 1966
 6         },
 7 ▾       {
 8           "name": "Arcadia",          JSON
 9           "year": 1993
10         },
11 ▾       {
12           "name": "Rough Crossing",
13           "year": 1984
14         }
15   }
```

```
 1
 2   { "play": { "name": "Rosencrantz and Guildenstern Are Dead", "year": 1966 } }
 3   { "play": { "name": "Arcadia", "year": 1993 } }
 4   { "play": { "name": "Rough Crossing", "year": 1984 } }
 5
 6
 7                     JSONL
 8
 9
10
11
12
```

Figure 3-2. *JSONL vs. regular JSON*

Avro

Avro is an Apache data system used for serialization. It has some substantial advantages over plain JSON, namely, that it uses a compact binary format that takes up much less space than JSON. It also defines the schema for the data internally, which means you won't have to figure out what each column is supposed to be. It's supported by Kafka and other data streaming technologies, so if you're using one of those, you probably already have some Avro somewhere in your organization.

The format is not human-readable, so if you want to work with the data, loading it directly to BigQuery is probably even more convenient than converting it to JSON and trying to work with it that way.

Parquet/ORC

Parquet and ORC are similar Apache columnar storage formats used by Hadoop. If you're running a Hadoop cluster and want to pull data out of it for analysis in BigQuery, one of these two formats should work.

Destination

The project and dataset will be populated by default with the context you were in when you clicked Create Table. Ensure that's what you want and pick a name for the table. No hyphens!

A Little Aside on Naming Things

Computer scientists love to quote Martin Fowler quoting Phil Karlton that there are only two hard problems in computer science: cache invalidation and naming things. I am sure you have looked into a blank field countless times, stalling for far longer than necessary, trying to name something properly. It's torture.

Table name

Letters, numbers, and underscores allowed

Figure 3-3. *Table name with blinking cursor*

Not to add to the pressure, but your task here is even more daunting than your average programmer trying to name a loop variable. If you do this right, your entire organization will align on your names and definitions, and it will literally become the glossary for the business. Like I said, no pressure.

The reason the first two chapters of this book were so focused on understanding your business, building consensus, and getting ready is that by the time you reach this step, you shouldn't have that abyssal dread looking into the empty text box. You already know what your table names should be. They're things like "accounts" or "users" or "sales" or "clients" or whatever terms you've heard your stakeholders using. Where those terms overlap, you've teased out the difference between sales orders and invoices.

If everything is messy and people can't align on terms, you have an even bigger responsibility here, which is to disambiguate the names for them. If sales calls harvested email addresses "captures" and finance calls credit card charges "captures," you know they're not the same thing. You'll get it right.

Schema

Some of the source formats have schemas built in. If you use a format that does not, like CSV or JSON, you can have BigQuery attempt to auto-detect the schema. This works fairly well, so if you're in a hurry to get your data loaded, go ahead. For any critical (or basic warehousing) tables, I'd recommend manually specifying your schemas so you can be sure the data fits the schema and not the other way around.

Auto-detection works by randomly sampling entries from your source files and using them to extrapolate the likely type. In the case of CSVs, it can also auto-detect your delimiter and name columns according to header rows. If you attempt to load conflicting data into the same table, you will get unexpected and likely unwelcome results. In these cases, you could load raw JSON as a STRING type and use the EXTRACT_JSON() method to pull it out on-demand, but this is unconventional and you'll forfeit some of the performance and structural benefits of stronger typing.

If auto-detect is unchecked, you will see the view for adding columns manually. There are two ways to do this, using the UI or using text. The text mode is a JSON format for describing columns, and it's also what you would use for the command-line or API modes. You can switch freely between the two modes to see what the current JSON output for your column definition is.

Now's as good a time as any to go over the data types and their meanings. These will all be familiar to you if you have worked in SQL before, with the possible exception of RECORD, so skip over this if you've done it before. Google's own reference is far more exhaustive[1] so I won't reinvent the wheel here.

In addition to the value ranges specified here, all data types except ARRAY are nullable.

STRING

Strings are your garden-variety character data. Note that by default, these strings are all UTF-8 encoded. Unlike regular SQL, no size specification is necessary—any character-based data will get mapped to a UTF-8 string. There's no predefined maximum size; you'll just have the regular quotas on query length and record length to deal with. If you need a UUID, this would also be of STRING type. (Google supports UUID generation with the GENERATE_UUID() function.)

---

[1]https://cloud.google.com/bigquery/docs/reference/standard-sql/data-types

BYTES

Variable-length binary data. While the BYTES data type has most of the same functions as STRING, this is the raw byte array vs. the Unicode version stored by a string. This is good for things like password hashes, for example.

INTEGER

Your standard 8-byte integer storage.

FLOAT

8-byte, double-precision floating-point numbers. Conforms to the IEEE-754 standard and thus is not the preferred data type for encoding currency.

NUMERIC

16-byte, exact numerical values. This is the type to use for money and other financial calculations where you don't want to deal with IEEE-754 floating-point errors.

BOOLEAN

In this particular flavor, a two-value type represented by the keywords "TRUE" and "FALSE."

TIMESTAMP

Timestamps are your invariant, absolute point-in-time, microsecond precise types. Pretty much every row you store in BigQuery should have a timestamp on it somewhere. Additionally, it's the natural partition for any tables you are going to partition. When you view it in a table, it will show as a UTC date/time. Internally, it looks like a seconds offset from the UNIX epoch, that is, January 1, 1970, at midnight UTC. (As an aside, you can verify this with the simple command SELECT TIMESTAMP_SECONDS(0), to convert from epoch time to a timestamp.)

DATE

It gets a bit tricky here. Unlike the canonical TIMESTAMP, the DATE type describes a calendar date without a particular timezone. As such, it doesn't mark a specific period in time, but rather the date as a user would see it on a calendar. The canonical format here is simply YYYY-[M]M-[D]D.

TIME

This is the same thing: a time independent of a date. I may look at my clock and see it is 1:30 PM. This would be relevant for things like "Do customers purchase more frequently in the afternoon?" "Afternoon" is a subjective term based on where the user is located, so we would want to look at the civil time in all cases. On the other hand, what about looking at behaviors during a fixed event, such as a big football game in early February? In that case we'd want to look at the absolute TIMESTAMP in all timezones.

I'm going into detail here because this sort of nuance turns out to be really important in data warehouse construction. Granted, as long as you have the absolute point in time that an event occurred, you can reconstruct these other values, but non-technical users don't like being made to think in UTC, even if it is the most logical storage format. Just a thing to keep in mind as you continue building things out.

GEOGRAPHY

The GEOGRAPHY type is an extremely powerful addition to a dataset. Consider the days before GEOGRAPHY: designers had to encode latitude and longitude in separate floating-point values. Calculation of distance or a bounding box was an intensive trigonometric operation that was easy to get wrong. However, using the GEOGRAPHY data type, we eliminate all of that complexity. Now we can create deep insights against the specific location or area at which an event occurred. This helps us easily answer questions about the closest store to a customer or the density of spatial events. For now, it's best to remember that a single GEOGRAPHY value is not simply a latitude/longitude coordinate: it is in fact a collection of points, lines, and polygons describing topologies on the oblate spheroid better known as Earth.

ARRAY

An array is an ordered list of zero or more elements. Note that ARRAYs cannot contain ARRAYs—the Google documentation cheekily includes it as an invalid example since I suppose it's a common question. If you want to nest ARRAYs, you have to store an ARRAY of STRUCTs that themselves contain ARRAYs. Nothing like giving your data types a workout. But this is all critical to the discussion around using nested elements whenever possible; this is one way you are going to achieve that. ARRAYs can also not be NULL.

Another interesting property of BigQuery ARRAYs is they are neither zero- nor one-based. If you want to index into an array, you can use the OFFSET function for a zero-based offset and ORDINAL for a one-based offset.

STRUCT (RECORD)

You will see this referred to and used in standard SQL as a STRUCT, but BigQuery also calls it a RECORD. Creating and using STRUCTs, in general, creates anonymous types using the internal fields. This is how you will nest data inside rows. Remember that your internal fields should also be named if you want to use them in comparisons. You can't do much comparison on the STRUCT itself. Similarly, you can opt not to apply types to the fields of the STRUCT, but you will generally want to do this for any data with sufficient structure. Since this is such a crucial concept in BigQuery design, we'll come back to it again later in the chapter.

Mode

You will also have to specify the mode of each column. The options are nullable, required, and repeated. Nullable means the field doesn't need to be specified for every row, as with regular SQL. Required, predictably, means the field is required.

Specifying a column as repeated essentially means that you get an array for the column where you can have many values for the same field. You can use this instead of a standard outer join to get information about related data directly into the same table. We'll go deeper on this in the following section.

Once you've finished specifying your columns, switch back over to the text view so you can see the formal representation of your table schema. It's fairly easy to read, so you can also use this as a quick way to spot-check your design. (As a side note, the current quota for column count is 10,000. I can't personally think of a well-designed use case that would require more than 10,000 columns, but you never know.)

Partition and Cluster Settings

Next up are the partition and cluster settings. We'll cover these topics in more detail in the following. There are definitely trade-offs to using either, but in terms of cost savings and maintenance, they are each a huge benefit.

Advanced Options

The advanced options will change based on your other settings. Most notably, for the CSV format, you'll see the settings for delimiter and header row skipping, so configure those if necessary (and you're not using schema auto-detection).

There are also options here, as with most object creation, around key management. Don't worry too much about that; we'll cover key management in a later chapter as part of permissions and security.

Lastly, this is where you specify the behavior you want the import to take. The three options are Write if Empty, Append, and Overwrite. Write if Empty will only load data if the table is empty. Appending will add the data to the table at its end. Overwrite will wipe any data stored in the table. In this case, since we're making a new table, it's going to be empty, so you can leave the setting as is.

Partitioning

Partitioning is pretty basic to understand: imagine that if a BigQuery table were stored as a file (which sort of is), partitioning would split that file by date, creating many smaller files. This would be great if you tend to look over a small number of files (date ranges) at a time, but more intensive if you query across huge ranges. On the flip side, if you have a torrential amount of data going into this table, you can partition to prevent the table from growing arbitrarily large. Small tables won't benefit much from this optimization.

While you can continue to modify the underlying schema of the partitioned table, you can't rename the table or change the partitioning itself. The best way to handle this scenario when it arises is to create a new structure and copy the existing data to it.

BigQuery limits the number of partitions in a table to 4,000, which works out to a little under 11 years if you're partitioning by day. Luckily, you can also use other date grains to create partitions, such as months or years.

The value of this feature is in lowering query cost. If you have gigabytes of data coming in every day, using a partition will make sure that BigQuery only needs to scan some of the files to get you the data you need.

Let's say you have a log file storing data for the past year, and I want to see log entries from last Thursday. In a partitioned table, BigQuery is *only* going to search that single date's file to get me the data. In an unpartitioned table, it's going to search the entire year to find matching records, which is potentially 365 times more expensive. (Clustering might help; we'll get to that.)

A secondary benefit is that you can automatically set partitions to expire. In the case of storing logging or error messages, you might only need to keep a few days' worth of data. Setting the expiration date will cause BigQuery to automatically delete the data at the specified time, saving you money and query time across the full range of partitions.

Partitioning by Integer

The newest feature in this space is the ability to partition by integer. This opens up all kinds of other options to partition your tables by the right value. You could partition by other primary keys in your system, if the same pattern of thought applies. Translated into integers, it comes down to knowing the query pattern. Will you want to frequently access specific ranges of this integer? Is there enough data per integer range to make the effort of partitioning worthwhile?

To configure this, you will need a min, a max, and a range. For instance, if you specify min of 0, max of 100, and range of 10, you will end up with partitions on {0, 10, 20, 30, ... 90, 100}. If you can visualize your dataset being sliced in this way along some axis, then you have a good candidate for integer partitioning!

Another good use case for this is if you have an external system loading data that defines its own sequential identifiers and you can't change them. Even if you add your own ingestion time to make it compatible with traditional partitioning, users are probably going to want to use the external ID as a reference into the data. This way you can let them do that and still gain the benefits of not having one massive table.

Clustering

Clustering is a very powerful tool to control cost and to give BigQuery some hints about how to execute your query. I can't stress how important clustering is. Remember that BigQuery is column-oriented storage. Clustering tells BigQuery that you are likely to search tables by certain columns and applies some weak sorting so that it only needs to go look at those clusters when you run the query. Unlike partitioning, you don't have to be aware of it behind the scenes; BigQuery will use the hints automatically to optimize your query. Additionally, it's free, and it will recluster your data whenever you load more. Because of this automatic property, you don't need to do any maintenance on your table's clusters.

When you create your table, think about the columns users are likely to want to search by and specify them as clusters. For example, if you operate in the United States on a state-by-state basis, cluster on the state abbreviation to get additional efficiency when looking for rows that occurred in a specific state. If you're familiar with relational SQL design, this is a similar exercise to specifying clusters (or index hints) there. The limit for clustering columns is four, and you can't choose new cluster columns on a table after you create it, so this is a good time to go deep on design. To be fair, you will probably still get some benefits from clustering even if users mostly use other columns, but in the long run it will cost you more.

This also means you could in some cases use clustering as an alternative to partitioning. If you cluster by day, you get similar advantages to partitioning by day, but you don't have to query across partitions. Google recommends this when partitioning would create less than 1 GB of data in each partition or when partitioning would exceed the maximum limit allowed (4,000 at this writing, as mentioned earlier).

To most effectively use both partitioning and clustering together, first partition by date or integer, and then inside of that, specify more finely the columns to cluster.

I know this is a lot, but at the terabyte or petabyte scale, we're talking about a *lot* of data savings. Without any partitions or clusters, even a simple query to return the first row of your data is going to scan the entire table, adding up to a significant chunk of change over time. This is one thing worth getting right now as you design your models.

Reading from BigQuery

No doubt you will want to design methods by which your users will read data from BigQuery. In the later chapters, we will discuss all manner of methods for piping data in and out of the system, and ultimately in Chapter 16, we'll talk about the ways in which you will surface data to users. But what about the day to day, when you need data in the system for your own purposes? There are a few ways to go about doing this, largely mirroring the ways in which we access BigQuery for other purposes.

BigQuery UI

It goes without saying, since it is our primary interface, but you can always just access data using the web console. Using the web UI, you can download a limited amount to file or just view it in your browser. You can also use the BigQuery UI to directly pipe it to Google Data Studio, which is covered in Chapter 18.

bq Command Line

The command-line tool allows you to perform all of the operations you can perform in the UI and then some. It's also a way to retrieve data; you can run the query text directly, or you can refer to datasets and tables to retrieve them or send them to a file.

BigQuery API

The API is what the other two methods use to interact with BigQuery. You can also use it directly in your code to retrieve data. We'll interact with the BigQuery API to do data processing in other chapters, but it can be a simple retrieval mechanism as well.

BigQuery Storage API

The BigQuery Storage API is not the same as the BigQuery API. It doesn't provide a job construct, nor does it provide access to modify tables or datasets. What it does do is provide an extremely high-performance way of extracting data from BigQuery. It can export data in the Avro format or the Apache Arrow format, and you must write code to access it. There is a Storage API SDK for Python and other languages to facilitate access, but you can manage streams directly.

You can also initiate parallel streams over different ranges of data, allowing for efficient access to subsets of your tables for other purposes. One major use of the BigQuery Storage API is to allow fast connectors to third-party systems.

Summary

Understanding your data model is crucial to building a sustainable, extensible data warehouse. BigQuery has both familiar and unfamiliar patterns for those who have built a data warehouse in the past. Making good decisions about how to structure your data involves knowing its source, the relationships between your entities, and how to best store it following BigQuery practices. Use clustering and partitioning as much as possible to lower cost and optimize data loading. When it's time to pull data back out of the database, there are multiple ways to do so depending on your needs.

## CHAPTER 4

Managing BigQuery Costs

One of the most difficult questions to answer when building out a BigQuery implementation is how much it will cost. In a traditional model, you would answer questions about scale and storage before you began provisioning the system. With BigQuery, as we saw in Chapter 1, you can start loading and querying immediately without even understanding the cost model.

Managed, serverless models have different pricing models than regular cloud compute resources. Most prominently, you only pay for what you use. This means that your costs scale linearly with respect to your usage. You won't pay for idle cycles.

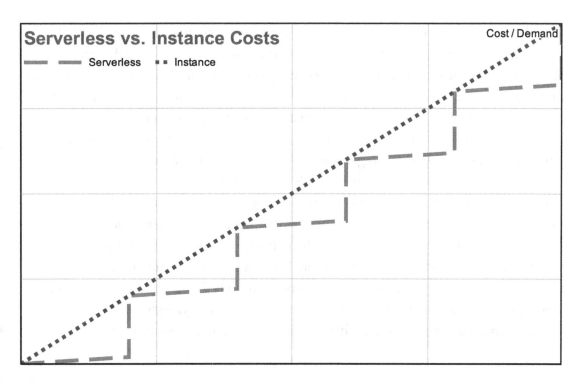

Figure 4-1. *Step function showing compute costs as you add more servers and a steadier line for serverless costs*

© Mark Mucchetti 2020
M. Mucchetti, *BigQuery for Data Warehousing*, https://doi.org/10.1007/978-1-4842-6186-6_4

This introduces the problem of high cost variability. No one is going to object to spending less money, but it's hard to budget if you don't know what to expect. In this chapter, we'll cover how costs work in BigQuery and how you can predict, optimize, and monitor your usage. We'll also cover reservation pricing, the newest BigQuery model specifically intended to add predictability to your spend.

The BigQuery Model

In order to understand what your costs are likely to be, it's important to understand how BigQuery is architected. Google generally prices a service in a way that matches how it consumes resources under the hood.

The key concept here is that BigQuery and other recent data storage systems separate storage from compute. This means that you pay one cost for the amount of data storage you're using and another cost for the compute resources you consume to query it. There are lots of other benefits to this scheme, but it can complicate your budgeting model.

Whenever you use compute power on GCP, you are essentially renting idle CPU cores—thousands and thousands of them—for the time you are running the query. Google chooses the most convenient place for the query to run. This means that running multi-region is actually cheaper; Google may route your query to any server in any data center it owns. BigQuery is also built so that a query can jump between places in a data center as it progresses through stages. In fact, it can jump to another data center, so even if the center your query is running in goes down, it can move to another.

A side effect of this system distribution is that BigQuery can also take advantage of idle cores to perform normal maintenance operations at no cost to you. Some normal maintenance operations don't exist in BigQuery at all. BigQuery doesn't have indexes, so there is no process to rebuild them. It also has no concept of "vacuuming," which is a sort of database defragmentation that moves blocks around to save space. (A Google employee shared with me that some customers thought their performance would degrade since they were never charged for vacuuming. Google had been doing automatic reclustering for quite a while, but hadn't thought to announce it.)

BigQuery Cost Models

Before you can figure out how much your BigQuery bill is going to be, you should understand the way in which Google charges for it. Throughout these sections, I will talk about the model, but I'll refrain from giving the actual pricing. Google has a habit of changing costs on a regular basis, although they change models less frequently.

For example, Google only published a flat-rate model with a minimum of 500 slots. Recently, they have begun offering lower flat-rate minimums, and I would expect this trend to continue. As a result, I suggest you consult the live BigQuery documentation for current pricing.

Storage Pricing

As mentioned earlier, storage and compute for queries are managed separately. As a result of this, you will also be billed for these things separately. In the case of storage, you will be billed directly for the amount of data you have. This data is billed at pennies per gigabyte, with a free monthly tier limit of 10 GB.

(It's worth noting that Google uses the binary form of gigabyte, often called "gibibyte." This represents 2^{30} bytes, not 10^9 bytes.)

Google also offers "long-term storage," which is charged at half price. (In Chapter 15, we'll go over the storage tiers; the Google Cloud Storage equivalent of this level is "nearline.") Any table that you do not modify for 90 days is placed into long-term storage. As soon as you touch the table in any material way, either by altering it, inserting data, or streaming data, it is moved back to regular storage and the regular price goes back into effect.

You may want to take advantage of long-term storage by loading all your lookup tables at the beginning and leaving them static, but in practice it may be difficult to account for this just to save a penny here or there. If you have large amounts of static data, that is, historical datasets, you will probably end up taking advantage of this discount without specifically preparing for it.

Loading data from Cloud Storage into BigQuery doesn't cost anything. As soon as it arrives in BigQuery, you will begin to pay the storage price for it. Similarly, copying a table is free, but you will then pay for the copy at the storage rate. Note: Streaming data is not free. One cost optimization we'll discuss later in the chapter is choosing carefully when to stream.

On-Demand Pricing

On-demand pricing is the default model used by BigQuery. In this model, you pay by "bytes processed." This number is not the same as bytes returned to you—it's whatever the query needs to access in order to return all the data.

On the bright side, cached queries don't cost anything. So once you run a query, you don't have to worry about being charged for it if it is run over and over again. This is useful in user analytics scenarios where the user may be refreshing or revisiting the report and would ordinarily get the same data. (It runs a lot faster too.)

You may have already noticed that when you write a query, BigQuery estimates how much data that query will return. You can translate this directly into how much that particular query will cost.

Google allows 1 monthly terabyte of query processing data for free. After that, you are charged per terabyte. Two caveats: One, the minimum query size is 10 MB. If you run a lot of tiny queries, you may use more data than you intend. Two, since you are charged for data processing, if you cancel a query or apply a row limit to it, you will still be charged.

Flat-Rate Pricing

Flat-rate pricing is offered primarily as a path to cost predictability. In this model, you purchase a certain number of "slots," which are used to execute your query. You are charged a flat monthly rate for the number of slots you make available.

While this has the advantage of being predictable, it creates another challenge, namely, knowing how many slots a particular query will consume. Roughly speaking, slots are a unit of computational power combining CPU, RAM, and memory, and BigQuery's query processor will determine the optimum number for maximum parallelization. Slots are requested by BigQuery based on the number of stages in the query.

When you run a query in the UI, you will see the number of stages the query is using to get the results. Each stage will then request the number of slots it deems necessary. If a query stage requests more slots than you have allocated, additional units will queue until slots become available.

This means that flat-rate pricing can also cause performance degradation under heavy load, as all slots become occupied by simultaneous queries in flight. This may be preferable over an unpredictably high cost under heavy volume.

BigQuery Reservations

BigQuery Reservations is the newest model for managing cost. In essence, it combines both the flat-rate model and the on-demand model, allowing for both predictable spend and unlimited capacity within the same organization.

Commitments

With the introduction of reservations, it became possible to use a GCP administration project to directly reserve slots with a monthly or annual commitment. You can make multiple commitments for different purposes or departments. This enables you to budget in an enterprise-scale environment and create different reservations for each use case. You can also take the same commitment and use it as you would have a regular flat-rate plan. However, there are additional benefits to commitments.

Reservations

Once you have created a commitment, you can split its slots up into separate pools called "reservations." When you first make a commitment, you will get a single reservation called default, with zero slot assigned. This means it will behave as a regular flat-rate plan. You can then add more reservations with specific departments or use cases in mind. For example, your finance team may need 200 slots for its daily usage, so you could create a reservation named "finance" and assign 200 slots.

Idle slots will automatically be shared across the full commitment. So if you've reserved 200 slots to "finance" out of a full capacity of 1000 and no one else is actively using the system, that reservation will be permitted to use the full commitment.

Assignments

Assignments are how you attach specific projects (or full organizations) to a reservation. BigQuery provides two types of job assignments to segregate load: QUERY and PIPELINE. QUERY is your standard slot processing as would have been used in a flat-rate plan. PIPELINE is for batch loading. Using these three concepts, you can ensure full predictability of your costs while constraining usage appropriately such that an individual department or process can't hog all of your resources.

Cost Optimization

You can see why cost is such an integral part of using BigQuery. If you are only running small workloads, you may be able to run exclusively in the free tier and never worry about this. Even if you are running in the sub-terabyte range, your costs will generally be fairly manageable. But petabyte workloads are not uncommon for BigQuery, and at that level you will want to be fairly aggressive about cost management. Reservations are a great tool to keep costs predictable, but there are also plenty of things you can do to optimize your costs.

Annualization

Both flat-rate and reservation-based pricing are discounted if you make an annual commitment, as opposed to a monthly one. If you are already seeking cost predictability, it probably makes sense to take the extra step to make it on an annual basis once you have begun moving your workloads to BigQuery.

Partitioned Tables

You will see the recommendation for partitioned tables appear in several places, as they perform better and allow for logical access to only the ranges that you need. They are less expensive for the same reason—you will be charged only for the range that the query accesses.

As an example, if you are typically accessing data on a daily basis, you can query the partition just for the current date. No data stored in the other partitions will be accessed at all. In the non-partitioned version of the query, it would hit every row in the entire table only to filter by the same date range.

Loading vs. Streaming

Loading data to BigQuery is free. Streaming, on the other hand, is billable. We'll talk more about the use cases for loading or streaming, but as a rule of thumb, prefer loading unless real-time availability is required.

In a scenario where you have a NoSQL data store that needs an analytics back end, you may be streaming data solely to query it. Or you may have a real-time logging solution that is immediately piped to BigQuery for analysis. In these cases, you will still want to stream; the cost is just something to be aware of in these cases.

Query Writing

This may seem obvious, but avoid SELECT * in all cases. Besides the fact that it is poor practice for consuming services, it is especially costly in a column-based store such as BigQuery.

When you request unnecessary columns either by using * or explicitly naming them, you immediately incur the additional cost of scanning those columns. This adds up quickly. As with any SQL-based systems, request only the data you need.

Google also recommends "SELECT * EXCEPT" to return columns using a negative filter, but I would also discourage this. This creates the same unpredictability in returns, and if another user adds a large column, those queries immediately become more expensive.

The row-based equivalent of this is the LIMIT operator, designed to only return a certain number of rows maximum. In relational systems, it's often used in combination with OFFSET for paging. In BigQuery, using LIMIT does nothing to affect the number of bytes processed, as it is applied after all rows in the table have been scanned. (Note that there are some exceptions to this rule when using clustered tables.)

Check Query Cost

The BigQuery UI will automatically estimate the amount of data that will be scanned by a given query. It recalculates every time you type or update a query. Use this as much as possible. You can even add and remove columns to and from your query and let it recalculate how much data it will use—this way you don't have to think about column data types and try to remember how many bytes each type uses. If you are writing a query that will be used on a frequent basis, you can save money simply by removing a column you know you won't use.

This query will process 42.6 MB when run.

Figure 4-2. *Picture of query data estimate*

Google Cloud Platform Budget Tools

Google Cloud Platform Pricing Calculator

The GCP Pricing Calculator can be found at `https://cloud.google.com/products/calculator/` and is handy for all manner of things. In addition to BigQuery, it has pricing models for pretty much every other service built in. Oddly, it also has a pricing tool for the pricing calculator itself—it's free. I guess every engineer likes a good recursion joke.

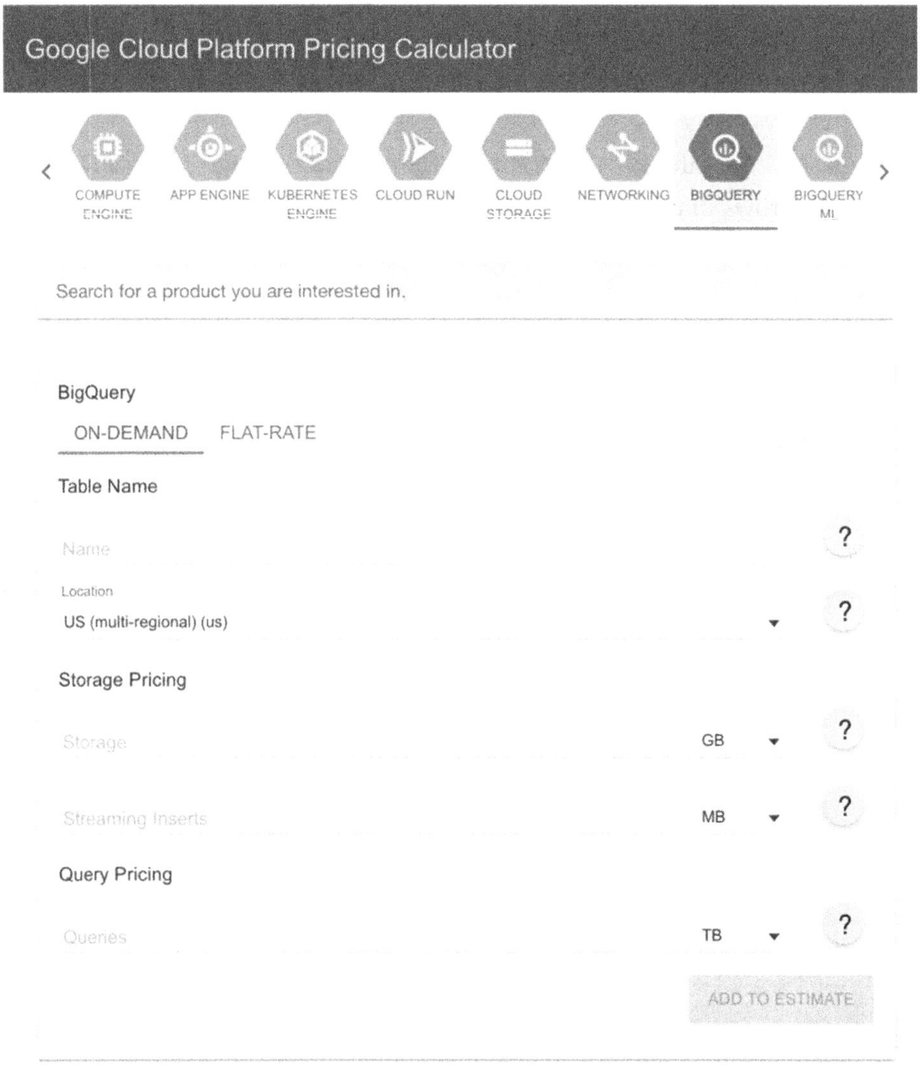

Figure 4-3. *Screenshot of the pricing calculator*

To use the calculator, plug in a descriptive name (for your reference only), the amount of storage it uses, and the amount of query processing data you think you will need. The calculator will use the prevailing rate and come back with an estimate.

For flat-rate pricing, you simply give it the number of slots you intend to reserve, and it will give you the rate. I would say that if you are really planning on spending a huge amount of money on this and you already know this, contact Google directly, get a sales representative, and negotiate some discounts. You may be able to obtain a lower rate than what the calculator returns.

Setting On-Demand Limits

The brute-force method of limiting your costs, even when using an on-demand model, is to set your own custom quotas. Effectively, you treat it as a traditional fixed-capacity system—when the allocation runs out, BigQuery no longer works until the next day starts in Pacific Time.

This is a good approach if your cost sensitivity outweighs your availability needs. It is also good if you know roughly how much processing your average workload should use, and you would want to restrict any unusual usage anyway. Neither of these models will be effective if you have any external users of your system or if stakeholders need potentially continuous access to the system.

You can also create a hybrid model, where you use one project with quotas set for some users and another project with shared access to the datasets and no quotas. In a scenario this complex, you should probably move to the reservations system unless your budget restrictions are so strict that you don't want to purchase even the smallest commitment.

Quotas are set in the same quota tool as for all other services, located at `https://console.cloud.google.com/iam-admin/quotas`. You can set two quotas relevant to query costs:

- Usage per day
- Usage per user per day

Once a user hits their quota, they can no longer run queries until the next day. As mentioned earlier, if the project quota itself is hit, BigQuery stops working altogether until midnight Pacific the following day.

If you use this as well as the pricing calculator, you can obtain pricing predictability without using flat-rate or reservation pricing. As a trade-off, availability may be too much of a sacrifice to make.

Setting a Reservations Quota

Reservations comes with a new type of quota, which is the total number of slots permitted by a reservation. If you intend to allow multiple users to reserve slots, you can use this quota to set that upper limit.

You are only billed for the commitments you actually make, but this will allow you to set a price ceiling based on your budget.

Loading Billing Information to BigQuery

When you need very fine-grained control of your billing information for BigQuery or other Google Cloud services, the best option is to export your bill into BigQuery itself and analyze it there. An example of this would be when you want to bill usage back to a client or another internal department.

To do this, go to Billing in the cloud console, and click "Billing export" on the left tab. This will open a window that allows you to edit your export settings. This will default to a BigQuery export page. Specify the project you want to export and choose a dataset in that project to receive the exports. Save this and you should see "Daily cost detail" showing that it is enabled with a green checkbox.

If you have multiple billing accounts and/or projects, you can go to each and enable the feature. From this point forward (no historical data is retrieved), a table in this dataset will begin to receive your billing data. Don't look right away; it takes some time for the results to appear.

The results will show up in a table of the form gcp_billing_export_v1_, followed by some hex values. You can immediately inspect your data usage. Of note are the service. description, cost, credits, and usage.units. Especially be sure to add the credits field (it will be a negative number) to show what you will actually be charged, if you are running against a free trial or other offset programs.

The Google documentation for this process is quite good, should you need further information.[1]

Summary

Measuring the cost of BigQuery can be challenging. Using an on-demand pricing model ensures you only pay for what you use, but cost variability can be high. Unpredictable spend can be difficult for enterprise organizations to understand and manage. You can increase cost predictability as a trade-off to efficiency or availability, but you should understand the equations at play before making a decision. Reservations allow you to get the best of both worlds. Regardless of how you structure your costs, some simple rules of thumb can help you to optimize your usage of BigQuery. Google provides tools to measure and limit spend; you may wish to use these to measure ongoing costs.

This concludes Part 1 of the book. In the first four chapters, you learned about the advantages of BigQuery over traditional data warehouses and how to design your BigQuery warehouse to optimally service your organization. You also learned how to prepare a migration or new data load into your newly built warehouse and how to understand the cost over time. In the next part, we will learn how to load, stream, and transform data from myriad sources into your new warehouse. We'll discuss how to set up pipelines for both relational and unstructured data and how to ensure your warehouse is populated with all the data your organization needs.

---

[1]https://cloud.google.com/billing/docs/how-to/export-data-bigquery

PART II

Filling the Warehouse

CHAPTER 5

Loading Data into the Warehouse

Now that you have a data warehouse up and running, the next step is to develop methods for populating it. In this and the following chapter, we'll go over the different methods you can use to set up paths for your data to load into BigQuery, depending on your needs and constraints. We'll start with the tried-and-true method, which is setting up loading and migration to populate the warehouse.

Another reason this set of strategies might work for you is if you already have a data infrastructure that uses traditional SQL models or even something like Microsoft Excel or flat files. You will need to lift them into a data warehouse framework to do analysis on them anyway, so the sophistication of the process to get them there is less relevant.

You should also consider the role that your data warehouse will serve when it houses all the data. Will it be a source of truth for transient data that lives in many different systems? Will it be an auxiliary system to an operational data source that is used for analysis of data? Are the sources bounded or unbounded (streams)? Will data ever leave BigQuery and go into another system? You could answer a lot of these questions in the project charter, but while that told you what to build, it didn't necessarily prescribe how to construct all the paths into and out of the system.

Long story short, you can use any of these tools and get your source data into BigQuery. The real test is how resilient and extensible those paths are. The more options you have, the easier it will be to choose the ones that work best for your organization. Also, with this information as a starting point, you can go off-road and build something entirely specific to your use case.

You've built a warehouse schema that is specifically designed for your business and the kinds of analytics and reports that it needs. That means if you're loading data from a

© Mark Mucchetti 2020
M. Mucchetti, *BigQuery for Data Warehousing*, https://doi.org/10.1007/978-1-4842-6186-6_5

relational database, you'll want to transform it into a model appropriate for you. If you're loading data from some other source, you may need to build appropriate schemas for it yourself or to impose data types on it.

In this part, we'll start with pure loading and then move to additional considerations for streaming and finally into Dataflow. These three classes of techniques will give you a wide breadth of possibilities, but there are a panoply of others to address your specific use cases.

Loading and Migration

Migration makes sense if you are already storing data in a database or warehouse and you plan to bring it over to BigQuery and decommission the existing system. It also makes sense if you have data that isn't being stored in any live system and you want to operationalize it. In either case, the primary use case for migration is when you want to bring your data into BigQuery once or twice and not on a regular basis.

A secondary case is to use migration techniques, but at a recurring interval. Your existing databases might be updated less frequently, and you want to establish synchronization on a daily or hourly basis. You might also want to sync slower data sources using these techniques and use streaming for your high-velocity data.

Another plus to these methods is that loading data into BigQuery is free. It's obviously in Google's best interest to capture and store your data, but if you're planning to use BigQuery anyway, just use straight loading wherever you can.

If you need high-velocity, immediate access to your data, the next chapter is about streaming data, which will likely be more appropriate.

From a File

The most basic method of doing a one-time synchronization is to use a file import. Most systems will have some method of exporting their data to a file. This is also a process that most business users will understand as well. If your current database system is Microsoft Excel (or paper!), then this is a good place to start. You can also use this to pull information out of any existing BI tools you might be using.

Many organizations also do a great deal of information sharing through FTP/SFTP using flat files. If you receive regular data dumps in this fashion, this method will be the simplest. If you're interested in how to automate and repeat this process, one great way is to use a serverless technology like Google Cloud Functions. We'll talk at length in Chapter 11 about how you can build pipelines using Cloud Functions to manage these tasks.

This is also helpful if you have a data source that doesn't change often, but you need the metadata as a dimension in the warehouse. For example, your HR department may maintain codes for things such as full-time, part-time, hourly employees, and so on. They'll probably be most comfortable providing you with a file of codes that you can load into the warehouse and use indefinitely. These also are not likely to change much, so it's most efficient to load them and leave them.

I personally use this method for smaller datasets where I want to use the power of BigQuery analysis without setting up a pipeline at all. Even a spreadsheet program (like Microsoft Excel) can export into CSV, which you can then load into BigQuery to do offline analysis on an ad hoc basis. I used to use Microsoft SQL Server or MySQL for that purpose, but being able to hook the data up to all the data that BigQuery already has is pretty compelling. For example, if I'm working on a dataset involving retail purchase history, I can seamlessly join in the historical weather data. Or I can join it directly to an organizational product catalog and immediately link in all of the details. Don't underestimate the utility of BigQuery to easily set up an environment for exploratory data analysis.

If your organization is still building out its data strategy, you may find yourself doing this a lot just as a function of the kind of requests you get from stakeholders. There's nothing wrong with this, but you can also come to see it as a reason to increase automation. If someone is emailing you a file, why not have them drop it in a Google Storage bucket? You can even share a Google Drive folder and automatically load it from there.

Here's an example. I once worked for a company that would frequently receive files from clients to be loaded into our database. Clients would email these files to their account managers, who would forward those emails to me. I would then run the file through a script to validate it for formatting errors before sending it to the import tool for processing. I tried in vain to get clients to FTP the files directly to the server or even to email me directly instead. I couldn't change the process. Finally, I made a new email account with the handle "filevalidator" and asked account managers to send their files to that inbox instead. A cron job read the emails, looked for attachments, processed the files, and then replied to the emails with the results. Pleased with myself, I moved onto the next task and forgot all about the pain of the manual process. A few weeks later,

I hadn't heard a single comment on my automation prowess. I opened the filevalidator email box to see what was going on. All the account managers were using it—and they were also replying to it! Many of the validation results emails had replies saying thank you or commending me for the speed with which I'd processed the file. They never knew they'd been transferred to an automation task. My point is that creating a data culture in your organization may require some creativity too. Build pipelines which make sense, even if they start with a lot of manual flat file loading. You got the structure correct already in Part 1—you can always upgrade the methods as your culture matures.

Preparing Files for Upload

The BigQuery UI only allows for files up to 10 MB to be loaded. In the most basic cases, you may have to load files in this fashion, manually defining schemas and checking data as you go. However, that will be extremely time-intensive. Let's go over an example where we need to load many data files of average quality. In this case, we'll tackle the scenario where we have daily historical transaction records from a system that is offline or otherwise inaccessible.

Source

With respect to flat files, there are really only two options: local and Google Cloud Storage. Given the 10 MB limit and the vagaries of network connections from your local machine to the Google Cloud perimeter, you will generally want to stage your files in Cloud Storage first. Note that this incurs the extra cost of Cloud Storage holding your file.[1]

While you can create buckets and load files from the Google Cloud Storage UI, in this case, a better approach is to become familiar with the command-line syntax for copying files to a bucket. This is straightforward:

```
gsutil -m cp {source} gs://{bucket}/{location}
```

The -m switch is optional and allows the copy to run in parallel. If you have a reasonably good connection outbound to Google Cloud, this should increase performance. A couple of caveats: Slow connections will show worse performance because they will saturate, unable to take advantage of extra bandwidth. A parallel

---

[1]Assuming you exceed the current 5 GB free tier.

process will also need to be restarted from the beginning if it fails. (See Appendix A for information on installing the command-line tool.) Take note that BigQuery can accept wildcard loads, so you can stage all files with the same format simultaneously.

Format

If you have a choice about input file format, there are several things to weigh. The primary consideration here is size, which determines ideal format and whether or not you can or should compress the data. The secondary consideration is obviously what your source system can support. A tertiary consideration is how human-readable the raw files need to be.

CSV and line-delimited JSON (JSONL) are the easiest to obtain from other systems that may not be designed for large datasets. However, they are less expressive and may require preprocessing. BigQuery can accept gzip-compressed files and load them directly. However, for CSV and JSON, gzipped files cannot be loaded in parallel, which means slower load times. You'll have to make a trade-off between file size and processing time. In most cases, BigQuery can process compressed files faster than you can upload huge files, and compression is a better option.

Remember also that JSONL is not regular JSON; each line of the file needs to be an independent JSON object. This is to prevent the parser from having to traverse the entire file to parse a structure, which would nullify any benefit to reading from a stream. Python has a library to convert JSON objects to JSONL,[2] if that's something you need. There are libraries in other languages as well.[3]

BigQuery's preferred format is Avro. Avro benefits from being compressed natively, allowing for BigQuery to process compressed data and also use parallelization. Two drawbacks: First, most non–big data-fluent systems won't be able to output in Avro. Second, this format is not human-readable, so the intermediate files won't be useful. Parquet and ORC are Apache Hadoop columnar data formats; if you have these file types available, you can choose them along a similar decision path, based on available formats from your source.

One other substantial benefit to these files besides speed is their built-in schema, ensuring a higher quality of data right off the bat.

---

[2]https://jsonlines.readthedocs.io/en/latest/

[3]Yes, in some cases you can just strip the [and] from a JSON array and add commas after each object. But JSON and CSV both share the property that they look like trivial formats, but they have quirks that can easily foil hacky solutions.

Schema

Defining and using data schemas will typically constitute the bulk of your preprocessing data wrangling. If you're using a compressed serialization format like Avro, Parquet, or ORC, you're covered: these files will import with their schemas intact. BigQuery has a mapping that it uses to automatically convert the underlying types in these formats into its own native formats.

With CSV and JSONL, you will have to get a schema into the relevant BigQuery table somehow. There are two primary options: auto-detection and schema import.

Auto-detection

By checking the box or specifying the --autodetect flag to the bq load command, you can instruct BigQuery to attempt schema derivation on its own. There are a few cases where this is appropriate:

- You don't know the quality of the data and would prefer to process it into a more appropriate schema using SQL, after you've looked at it.

- You do know the quality of the data, it's high, and columns are well populated with appropriate values. BigQuery takes a sample from the file to detect types, so if a column has many or most rows empty, its chance of success is low.

- You're in a hurry, want to do data analysis, and are comfortable using the SAFE_CAST function to coerce the data if necessary. If you're lucky, it'll be good enough.

By no means is BigQuery's auto-detection poor. It can detect multiple types of delimiters, header rows, and timestamps. However, if you need specific data formatting for numbers or dates or you have a spare dataset, you'll want to define a schema.

Schema Definition

The BigQuery schema format is a JSON file containing an array specifying row names, descriptions, and types, for example:

```
[
    {
      "mode": "NULLABLE",
      "name": "Author",
      "type": "STRING"
    },
    {
      "mode": "NULLABLE",
      "name": "Title",
      "type": "STRING"
    },
    {
      "mode": "NULLABLE",
      "name": "LexicalDiversity",
      "type": "FLOAT"
    }
]
```

For a better example, you can print the schema for any BigQuery table you have access to with this command line:

```
bq show --format=prettyjson {dataset.table}
```

Look for the schema.fields property.

You can generate the schema file manually, by using the preceding command to retrieve it from an existing table or by adding the fields in the UI, which will generate the schema file as it goes. There is also a Python package which generates an improved schema by using all of the file records, not just the first hundred.[4] It also does a neat thing where it determines whether columns are NULLABLE or REQUIRED based on the presence of data in every row of the file, something the BigQuery schema detector can't do.

---

[4]https://pypi.org/project/bigquery-schema-generator/

In any event, you will want to store the schema in a file for reuse. If you use the Python package or the bq show command, pipe it to a file (like schema.json), which we'll use in the loading section.

Preprocessing Files

If your files are of unknown or poor quality, you will need to do some preprocessing on them so they can be loaded to BigQuery. You can do this using the local files, if they're human-readable, accessible, and small enough to operate on. In other cases, you will want to load them into a staging table in BigQuery first and then process them into another table. Let's say you have a table of the following format:

```
Frank,Megan,3,2005-01-03
Wu,Derek,4,2009-09-04
Stebbins,Jeff,,2008-07-12
Myerson,Kate,2,2013-09-03
```

This data is notably obtuse. There's no header row, and thus it's unclear what any of these fields mean. The date format is ambiguous and may be YYYY-MM-DD, but could just as easily be YYYY-DD-MM. There's no way we'll know what we're looking at without clarification. So let's provide some context clarification. This is a list of names, GPAs, and enrollment dates.

Let's see what BigQuery makes of this file by running the load and showing the generated schema:

```
bq load --project_id='{YOUR_PROJECT}' --autodetect 'dataset.gpa_table'
./gpa.csv
bq show --format=prettyjson {dataset.table}
  "schema": {
    "fields": [
      {
        "mode": "NULLABLE",
        "name": "string_field_0",
        "type": "STRING"
      },
      {
        "mode": "NULLABLE",
        "name": "string_field_1",
```

```
      "type": "STRING"
    },
    {
      "mode": "NULLABLE",
      "name": "int64_field_2",
      "type": "INTEGER"
    },
    {
      "mode": "NULLABLE",
      "name": "date_field_3",
      "type": "DATE"
    }
  ]
}
```

Well, not too bad. It got the date. The default is YYYY-MM-DD, so no changes there. None of these fields are nullable besides the GPA, though, and the GPA is supposed to be a NUMERIC. We have two options here: We could take the output from the command and save it to a file (add "> schema.json" to the end of the command) and then reload the data with the new schema and a header row. Or we could just create the new table in the BigQuery UI with the column names and schema and then run this same command again.

However, if we've loaded thousands or millions of rows into BigQuery and we want to work with what we've got, then we can repair this within BigQuery. There's no way to modify columns in BigQuery once the data is already in there, so we'll have to project into a new table and then delete the old one. Let's write a query that adds column names and fixes the data types. We could also take this opportunity to add any additional calculated columns or things we will need later. We could also write filters or aggregations if we needed to additionally manipulate the data. We can also do this entirely in SQL using a Data Definition Language (DDL) statement instead of the command line:

```
CREATE TABLE dataset.gpa_table_temp
 (LastName STRING NOT NULL,
  FirstName STRING NOT NULL,
  GPA NUMERIC,
```

```
  EnrollmentDate DATE NOT NULL,
  ExpectedGraduationYear INT64 NOT NULL)
AS
SELECT
string_field_0,
string_field_1,
SAFE_CAST(int64_field_2 AS NUMERIC),
date_field_3,
EXTRACT(YEAR FROM date_field_3) + 4
FROM dataset.gpa_table
```

Here, we create a new table with the schema we want, using SQL instead of the JSON schema format (just to show it can be done). We then cast our numeric GPAs into FLOAT64s, using SAFE_CAST to ignore the null values. Finally, we calculate an expected graduation date by getting the year out of the date field and adding 4.

Also, you don't need to specify the column names in both the select and the create, but it's probably a good idea if you have more than a few, to avoid getting confused. Once we run this statement, we have the table we want.

	Schema	Details	Preview		
Field name		Type	Mode		P
LastName		STRING	REQUIRED		
FirstName		STRING	REQUIRED		
GPA		FLOAT	NULLABLE		
EnrollmentDate		DATE	REQUIRED		
ExpectedGraduationYear		NUMERIC	REQUIRED		

The last step in this exercise is to delete the old table and copy the temporary table back to it. This is easily done on the command line:

```
bq rm my-project:dataset.gpa_table
bq cp --project_id='my-project' dataset.gpa_table_temp dataset.gpa_table
bq rm my-project:dataset.gpa_table_temp
```

Of course, you can also do this through the BigQuery UI if you prefer. This isn't totally straightforward, but in practice, that's okay: changing the schemas of tables people are using is not a good business practice. (We'll talk about this more throughout the course of the book.)

Loading Files

Now that you've decided what format you're going to use, it's ready to go, and you've got a schema for it, it's time to load the data in. This can be done using the command-line tool bq load. The command takes a huge variety of flags which vary based on type, but the basic structure will look like this. This loads a CSV file with a schema we generated in the previous step:

```
bq load --source_format=CSV dataset.table gs://data-bucket/file.csv
./schema.json
```

Loading from a local file is similar; just replace the Google Cloud URI with your local filename. You can also specify a schema inline with a limited format, which defaults all columns to nullable and doesn't support the RECORD type.

```
Author:STRING,Title:STRING,LexicalDiversity:FLOAT
```

is equivalent to the inline version of the preceding sample schema.

For Avro/Parquet/ORC, no schema is necessary, as it will be auto-detected. There are a couple twists you can put on this command to handle other common scenarios.

Wildcards

Thankfully, BigQuery accepts loading of files from a wildcard—you can even specify one in the UI. This can be done with local files or from Google Cloud Storage. Do this like so:

```
bq load --source_format=CSV dataset.table gs://data-bucket/file*.csv
./schema.json
```

This will load all found files into the table in question. Obviously they should all share a schema and belong to the same table. You can supply a comma-separated list of files to pull in all matching files from multiple directories (or Storage URIs).

When working on the command line, you can take advantage of scripting to process the command line before feeding it to BigQuery. The lore of UNIX scripting is decades deep, but here's one tantalizing example for bash, which should be cross-compatible with MacOS and Linux:[5]

```
ls  **/*.csv | sed 's/.*/"&"/' | tr '\n' ','
```

This example finds all CSV files in all subdirectories below your current working directory, quotes them, and concatenates them into a single line.[6] You can use this directly as an argument to load files to BigQuery.

In this example, we still dealt with the basic scenario where we're migrating or loading to BigQuery on a one-time basis. What about routine processing? Good news! Staging your files in Google Cloud Storage opens up other methods that we'll cover throughout this book. You can automate file loads from Google Cloud Storage using a number of methods:

- Dataflow, covered in Chapter 7

- Google Cloud Scheduler, Cloud Composer, or BigQuery Transfer Service, all covered in Chapter 10

- Google Cloud Functions, covered in Chapter 11

You can, of course, roll your own using the SDK. You'll see other Python examples, or you can look at the googleapi documentation for a massive list of usage snippets.[7] In general, though, here's a stripped-down version of annotated steps for your reference:

---

[5]If using Windows 10, look into the Windows Subsystem for Linux (WSL). It removes a lot of the friction associated with trying to translate bash or Python to PowerShell, and it also makes following installation instructions a lot easier.

[6]There are dozens of other ways to do this using purely sed or ls options or other commands entirely. It's fun to find them and play code golf to optimize, but that would take us too far afield.

[7]https://github.com/googleapis/python-bigquery/blob/dc389498391798235383fbec20 e48a23128ddc6a/docs/snippets.py

```python
# Load BigQuery from the Python GCP Library
from google.cloud import bigquery

# Load a performance timer (optional or comment out)
from timeit import default_timer as timer

# Specify your fully-qualified table name as you would in the UI
import_table = 'YOUR-DATASET.bortdata.bookdata'

# Choose the GCS bucket and file, or override it with a full gs:// URI
gcs_bucket = 'YOUR-BUCKET'
gcs_file = 'book-data.csv'

# gs://mybucket/book-data.csv OR local file ./book-data.csv
location = ''
# location = 'gs://YOUR-BUCKET/book-data.csv'
# location = './book-data.csv'

# Load the references to the table for import
[project_name, dataset_name, table_name] = import_table.split('.')
client = bigquery.Client(project_name)
dataset = client.dataset(dataset_name)
table = dataset.table(table_name)

# Create the configuration and specify the schema
config = bigquery.LoadJobConfig()
config.schema = [
    bigquery.SchemaField("Author", "STRING"),
    bigquery.SchemaField("Title", "STRING"),
    bigquery.SchemaField("LexicalDiversity", "FLOAT")
]

# If you have a header row
config.skip_leading_rows = 1

# Uncomment to change import file type
# config.source_format = bigquery.SourceFormat.CSV

# Uncomment and remove config.schema to autodetect schema
# config.autodetect = True
```

```python
# Default to GCS
local = False
gcs_uri = ''

# Format the GCS URI or use the pre-supplied one above
if (len(location) == 0):
    gcs_uri = "gs://{}/{}".format(gcs_bucket, gcs_file)
elif not (location.startswith('gs://')):
    local = True
else:
    gcs_uri = location

# Create the job definition
if (local):
    with open(location, "rb") as file:
        job = client.load_table_from_file(file, table, job_config=config)
else:
    job = client.load_table_from_uri(gcs_uri, table, job_config=config)

print ("Loading {} file {} into dataset {} as table {}...".format \
      (("local" if local else "GCS"),(location if local else gcs_uri),
      dataset_name, table_name))

# See if we have a timer
try:
    timer
    use_timer = True
except NameError:
    use_timer = False

if (use_timer):
    start = timer()

# Performs the load and waits for result
job.result()

if (use_timer):
    end = timer()
    result_time = " in {0:.4f}s".format(end-start)
```

```
else:
    result_time = ""

# Prints results
print("{} rows were loaded{}.".format(job.output_rows, result_time))
```

You can run this script to compare timings for loading the same file from GCS or from local, testing schema auto-detection, or loading different formats. The load job will automatically create or append to the table without deletion, so you can run this script multiple times in succession to compare results. Running this script is free, but you will be charged for the cost of the data storage once it's in the table.[8]

From a Live Database

Organizations often start their journey toward data management by cloning their productionalized relational database into an offline version at regular intervals and performing analytics there. While this plan may not hold up over time for a variety of reasons including having more than one such source, performance, schema, integration, and so on, at the very early stages, it may save a lot of time. There are several options to do this.

Of course, if you are already familiar with exporting your database to a file, you could set up a cron job for that to run it at regular intervals and drop back to the file-based method. The fastest way to see results is to integrate whatever your pipeline already supports.

In any event, you still don't want to do expensive queries on any live database under load, so you may need a replica purely to execute some of the simpler methods.

Cloud SQL (MySQL/PostgreSQL)

I'd be remiss if I didn't mention Cloud SQL, Google's managed offering for database hosting. It supports managed MySQL, PostgreSQL, and Microsoft SQL Server. While in many ways it functions similarly to Amazon's Relational Database Service (RDS), it has one significant advantage with respect to BigQuery. This is that you can establish a connection directly to Cloud SQL from BigQuery to access its data.

---

[8]If you go over the free-tier allotment of 10 GB.

This in turn creates another potential way to load your data—use Cloud SQL as an intermediary replica of your OLTP solution. This allows for minimal disruption to existing ELT (extract, load, transform) processes that run to a MySQL or PostgreSQL instance. Use this solution to reach the processed data in the Cloud SQL copy, and you can run workflows between your transactional system and BigQuery transparently. You

In order to access data in Cloud SQL, you can use what's known as BigQuery Cloud SQL Federation (what a mouthful). To do this, first enable the BigQuery connection API. BigQuery will ask you to do this automatically when you try to add a connection to a federated data source. It will also let you know that it takes a minute to provision your project to do so.

After this happens, you can create the external connection to the Cloud SQL database by clicking "+ Add Data" next to Resources and then "Add Connection." This will open a sidebar that gives you the configuration to set up the connection.

Connection Type

As mentioned earlier, you can currently establish connections to MySQL or PostgreSQL. You'll be using the SQL dialect native to these engines, as opposed to BigQuery, so there's no operational difference from the BigQuery side as to which you connect to.

Connection ID

Give your connection a descriptive name that makes it clear what kind of connection you are planning to establish and, if it's relevant, the purpose of this connection. Connections go to a specific database, so you might conceivably have names like "production-users," "production-orders," and so on.

Connection Location

Specify where you want the connection itself to be stored. This can't be changed later. You probably don't need to modify this from the default unless you have compliance-specific regulations to adhere to such as the European General Data Protection Regulation (GDPR) or similar.

Friendly Name/Description

An optional friendly name and description to help identify this connection as separate from its formal identification.

Cloud SQL Instance ID

This represents the GCP instance designation for your particular Cloud SQL database. Atypical for GCP, no helpful dropdown allows you to auto-select the right one. You can get it by clicking the instance in the Cloud SQL console and copying it out of the "Instance connection name" box. It should be in the format project:regionid:server-id.

Database/Username/Password

To create a connection string, you will also have to supply the name of the database, username, and password to connect to the instance. This also means that you can specify the permissions you want the connection to have from the database side.

Once you've populated all of this data, create the connection. The connection is not actually validated or tested at this time, so if you've mistyped something, you won't know it yet. To test the connection, find it under "External connections" in the Resources hierarchy and click it to open a query window. Click "Query Connection," and a statement will appear in the window.

```
SELECT * FROM EXTERNAL_QUERY("projectID.US.connectionID", "SELECT * FROM INFORMATION_SCHEMA.TABLES;");
```

Figure 5-1. *An external query statement*

Running this statement will validate that your connection works properly. If it doesn't, log into your MySQL/PostgreSQL database and ensure that the database exists and that the username/password you're using has the required access.

If this works, you're off to the races. The secret sauce here is the keyword EXTERNAL_QUERY, which is actually a table-valued function that runs the query and returns its results to you. Migrating an individual table, or even materializing a view into a data warehouse table, is now as simple as INSERT INTO (SELECT * FROM EXTERNAL_ QUERY (...)).

If you rarely need data from the operational database, but it needs to be up-to-date, you can continue to use the federated query as a permanent solution. However, I would recommend against that in most cases, for a couple of reasons. One, you don't control the schema on the Cloud SQL side, and there's no way to easily validate it. Since you can query the information schema, you could write an elaborate function that verifies your source table looks the way you want before accessing it, but that creates even more moving parts for error. Two, federated queries can be slower than native BigQuery calls. They also create one of the problems you were trying to avoid by building a data warehouse in the first place—the source database needs to be available to service the query, and your query will compete with real production user load. Three, your external SQL query is now essentially operational code living in a string in a non-verifiable way. It could be hidden, hardcoded, and forgotten, until someone turns off the database...

However, if you just need a quick way to migrate or access data out of your operational store, this is a really simple way to do it.

Data Types

One other thing to be aware of with the federated query method is that even if you specify a schema for the load, data types do not totally correspond between database systems. BigQuery will fail an EXTERNAL_QUERY immediately upon encountering an unsupported data type.

Microsoft SQL Server

As I mentioned earlier, you cannot add a connection to a Microsoft SQL Server, even if it is hosted in Cloud SQL. There are several companies that have stepped in to fill this void and others in data migration pipelines. Typically they support real-time replication and streaming as well. Notably, Alooma, which was acquired by Google in early 2019, has a product to load/stream Microsoft SQL Server into BigQuery. Several other companies such as Striim have products as well. If you're not keen on bringing another provider into the mix, you may be able to run a convoluted path of your own via Microsoft's Java Database Connectivity (JDBC) drivers—see more of this in the following.

MySQL (Non-Cloud SQL)

If your MySQL instance is not hosted in Cloud SQL, but is instead a standalone instance in Google Compute Engine (GCE), Amazon Web Services Relational Database Service (RDS), or a data center, then you can't use the connection technique. You might also prefer to migrate the entire database into BigQuery and work from there, especially if you are doing a nonrecurring load.

The easiest way to do this is to use the mysqldump command that comes with MySQL to generate static files from the database, load them to Google Cloud Storage, and then process them from there (how to use GCS to load to BigQuery is in the following). This method has a couple of caveats.

First, it is really only for a one-time load if you're migrating an existing structure. MySQL dumps can take hours. The original purpose of the mysqldump command was to create and maintain backups; even restoring to another MySQL instance could take a long time. (You could also combine this with a Cloud SQL migration, using this process to transfer from a VM into Cloud SQL and then setting up the external connection.)

Second, mysqldump doesn't actually produce a CSV file that is compatible with BigQuery. You need to do some additional work on the files to make BigQuery accept them. One good starting point is a script by James Mishra that converts MySQL dumps into CSV.[9] It's unmaintained, however, so you may have to make additional modifications depending on your MySQL installation.

Third, BigQuery expects all data to be encoded as UTF-8. You either need to use UTF-8 or override BigQuery's default encoding to match the format of your data.

Lastly, if you wanted to make it a repeatable process of your infrastructure, you would likely need to write a series of scripts and cron scheduler jobs to keep it updated. As with any direct connection between an operational database and your data warehouse, changes in schema or table structures can cause imports to fail. Your custom scripts are less likely to have the robustness, error-checking, and logging that a more formal solution would have. It's still a totally valid solution: it's just worth thinking about the trade-off between tool cost and development cost.

Another way to get data out with mysqldump is to generate a tab-separated value (TSV) file and import it into BigQuery that way. That could work better if you are having issues with the CSV approach.

If you want to take this approach, a couple steps will remain the same. I'll summarize all of these suggestions below each step, and you can choose your own adventure. (GitHub is littered with scripts in every conceivable language to do this sort of thing. Tread lightly!)

---

[9]https://github.com/jamesmishra/mysqldump-to-csv

Export from MySQL

Do one of the following.

- Write a mysqldump command to export one table or an entire database in CSV, TSV, or MySQL's almost-CSV format.

- Write a MySQL query using SELECT ... INTO OUTFILE to do the same thing.

Clean the Data

- If you chose to export in MySQL almost-CSV, run a script such as the one James Mishra wrote to convert it into a CSV format that BigQuery will accept.

- Alternatively, take the database dump and load it into a Cloud SQL instance, stop following this set of steps, and use the EXTERNAL_ DATA method detailed earlier.

Load the Data to Google Cloud Storage

- You can do this in any of the usual ways. The easiest is to use the command line and execute a command like "gsutil cp table.csv gs:// bucket-name/path." To copy an entire folder, use "gsutil cp -r folder-name gs://bucket-name/path."

- You can also do this from the GCS web console by creating a bucket and uploading either a file or folder to this place.

- Make sure your bucket is not publicly accessible!

Load the Data into BigQuery

- Taking note of what format you left your files in, use the bq command-line tool to load them into the database.

- To repeat this process for multiple tables, write a script to enumerate all the files in the bucket and load them in one at a time. This could be done with shell scripting or the language of your choice.

- Details for loading a file from Google Cloud Storage into BigQuery are in the following.

The last piece of this is how you intend to specify the schemas. Data types between MySQL and BigQuery don't completely match, which means you might run into additional problems with loading the data because of incompatibility. As we'll cover in the following, you can auto-detect the schema, but that may give undesirable results. Another solution for this is to stage the data into BigQuery without typing it (i.e., make everything a STRING) and then do your transformation on the BigQuery side.

Things like column lengths, primary and foreign keys, and indexes won't matter, as BigQuery doesn't have those concepts. The important part is to get the right data types out of your source system so that they can map cleanly to BigQuery. If you're going to introduce nested or repeated fields, you can do that once the data is available in a format which matches closely to your OLTP source.

The ANSI SQL standard supports INFORMATION_SCHEMA views, which allow you to programmatically investigate the metadata of your SQL objects. BigQuery supports these too, but in this case we're more interested in extracting schemas from our external OLTP sources. This bit of SQL trickery will extract the BigQuery JSON schema from a MySQL table. Note that this is a MySQL query (the only one in the book!). It won't work on BigQuery. It also doesn't handle advanced data type conversions like GEOGRAPHY or anything, but if you find yourself using this method, you can extend it:[10]

```
SELECT CONCAT('[', GROUP_CONCAT(field SEPARATOR ', '), ']') FROM
(SELECT JSON_UNQUOTE(JSON_OBJECT('name', COLUMN_NAME,
                          'mode', CASE IS_NULLABLE WHEN 'YES' THEN
                          'NULLABLE' ELSE 'REQUIRED' END,
                          'type', CASE DATA_TYPE
                                WHEN 'TINYINT' THEN 'INT64'
                                WHEN 'SMALLINT' THEN 'INT64'
                                WHEN 'MEDIUMINT' THEN 'INT64'
                                WHEN 'LARGEINT' THEN 'INT64'
                                WHEN 'BIGINT' THEN 'INT64'
                                WHEN 'DECIMAL' THEN 'NUMERIC'
```

---

[10]The exact command will depend on your type and version of SQL; this worked on MySQL 5.7, which is about as low as I wanted to go. I also intentionally eschewed JSON_ARRAYAGG here so it would work with Cloud SQL (gcloud sql connect).

```
                                        WHEN 'FLOAT' THEN 'FLOAT64'
                                        WHEN 'DOUBLE' THEN 'FLOAT64'
                                        WHEN 'CHAR' THEN 'STRING'
                                        WHEN 'VARCHAR' THEN 'STRING'
                                        WHEN 'TINYTEXT' THEN 'STRING'
                                        WHEN 'TEXT' THEN 'STRING'
                                        WHEN 'MEDIUMTEXT' THEN 'STRING'
                                        WHEN 'LONGTEXT' THEN 'STRING'
                                        WHEN 'BINARY' THEN 'BYTES'
                                        WHEN 'VARBINARY' THEN 'BYTES'
                                        WHEN 'DATE' THEN 'DATE'
                                        WHEN 'TIME' THEN 'TIME'
                                        WHEN 'DATETIME' THEN 'DATETIME'
                                        WHEN 'TIMESTAMP' THEN 'TIMESTAMP'
                                        ELSE '!!UNKNOWN!!'
                                        END )) field

FROM INFORMATION_SCHEMA.COLUMNS
WHERE TABLE_NAME='gpa'
ORDER BY ORDINAL_POSITION) R;
```

A couple of limitations: While you should map the datetime types to their equivalent in BigQuery, the underlying string format is not the same. You will have to adjust the field as part of your loading process.

Additionally, some of the tables online suggest that a BIT type should go to a BigQuery boolean. Unfortunately, BIT in MySQL is not the same as BIT in Microsoft SQL Server; it is actually a bitfield. I omitted it from this conversion because you'd have to decide if you wanted to parse the bitfield out into separate BOOLEAN columns or do something else. For BLOB fields, you can also store them as BYTES, but you might want to output them as Google Cloud Storage files and replace the columns with URI strings.

You can pipe this directly to a JSON file and use it as input for a BigQuery load.

This whole process is definitely suboptimal. As we proceed through the following chapters into streaming and Dataflow, you will see more sustainable methods for continually bringing data into your BigQuery instance. Sometimes you just need a quick and cheap method for getting data into your warehouse once or twice. And of course, as we discussed earlier for file loads, there are ways to automate regular loading if you can get your data into Google Cloud Storage in any fashion. We'll cover a nightly load process in Chapter 11.

From Google Cloud Storage

Many of the sources listed earlier can export to Google Cloud Storage (GCS). In fact, as long as you can get a file from somewhere, you can push it to GCS and have BigQuery look for it from there. GCS is also a supported destination for Dataflow, so you can use it as an intermediary location if you need files for some reason. Using objects from GCS to power other Google Cloud services is a common pattern, so you will see it again.

We've mostly used the console up until now, but we'll do this one from the command line, where it's easier to see the options and a path to repeating this process for other things. You can do this directly from your cloud shell. Here's that example again with a few more of the flags we saw from the SDK version.

```
bq --location=US load --source_format=CSV {dataset.table} gs://{bucket}/{datafile.csv} [schema.json]
```

Figure 5-2. *Loading data into BigQuery from Google Cloud Storage*

This is pretty self-explanatory, but to break it down, bq is the command-line tool for BigQuery. You specify the source format, which dataset and table to put the file in, and where to find the file on Cloud Storage. You can also specify a schema for the table.

Some variations:

- --autodetect will attempt to auto-detect the schema. The success will depend on your input file.

- --replace will overwrite a table, if it exists.

- --noreplace will append to the table, if it exists.

- --field_delimiter=tab will cause BigQuery to treat the incoming file as a TSV (yes, leave the source format as CSV).

- --skip_leading_rows=1 will skip a header row, if the file has one.

- --encoding can be either ISO-8859-1 or UTF-8. UTF-8 is default.

Data Types

As with the federated query approach, BigQuery will fail the load if data does not match the schema. You can avoid this by auto-detecting the schema, but that will cause unsupported types to show up in an unpredictable form. If you have many tables using fundamentally incompatible types (at this point, geometry-based fields are a problem, along with some datetimes), this may be an excuse to use a slightly higher-grade solution or a third-party connector.

Third-Party Transfers

Google also recommends (but does not guarantee) all kinds of external providers of connectors. Companies such as Fivetran and Supermetrics publish a host of different integrations to other systems. If you are doing a migration from an existing MySQL or PostgreSQL instance, you might save time by using a third-party connector.

Additionally, some connectors exist for solutions which use relational databases as an underlying structure, but have additional abstraction on top. If you have a lot of data bound up in an ecommerce platform such as Magento, this is probably an easier approach than trying to understand the underlying schemas the platform uses or trying to figure out data synchronization using an API. You will incur additional cost with these methods, however, and it can be significant depending on your volume.

Something that you may see as either an advantage or a liability is that you are also at the mercy of the provider to fix any issues that arise with the connector. If you're doing a pure migration, that's not really a concern; you use the connector and then you're done. If you're doing a near–real-time approach, you will want to vet the provider and ensure that issues are fixed quickly and without substantial interruption to your services. These sorts of compatibility issues will arise even if you are maintaining your own integrations too, so it's quite possible that a third-party provider will have an even better service-level agreement (SLA) than you'd be able to obtain with your own internal resources.

One other thing to note is that since many of these connectors rely on a third-party platform, they can do some interesting things with source data. While GCP has been improving its cross-cloud support by allowing imports from Amazon Web Services S3, you can also use connectors that sync data from AWS Relational Database Service (RDS) or Aurora to automatically pull your data across clouds. If your infrastructure is hosted primarily on Amazon, but you want to use GCP purely for BigQuery and/or machine learning, this is a low-hassle way to do it.

Java Database Connectivity (JDBC)

There's one other way to roll your own migration, but it involves a little bit of black magic. Using Dataflow, which we will cover extensively in Chapter 7, you can create data pipelines to do processing of large amounts of data in a massively parallelized way. In general, this is useful for streaming data on a continuous basis from unbounded datasets. However, there is an interesting little trick that makes it potentially suitable for one-time load, when you've exhausted some of these other options.

Google supplies a series of Dataflow templates that save you the trouble of coding your own pipeline. One of those templates is Java Database Connectivity (JDBC) to BigQuery. Using this template, you could use any JDBC driver to load data into BigQuery. Microsoft publishes official JDBC drivers for SQL Server. There are also companies that produce custom JDBC drivers for decidedly non-relational systems. For example, Simba Technologies maintains JDBC drivers for things like Excel, Salesforce, Amazon DynamoDB, and even PayPal. Since the templates Google uses are open source, you could even code up your own custom connector that modifies how the rows come in.

If you're interested in giving this a try, you can go to the Google Dataflow console and click "+ CREATE JOB FROM TEMPLATE." Choose a job name and region, and select the template "Jdbc to BigQuery." This will expose a number of required parameters you need in order to execute the job. Most of these are explained in more detail in Chapter 7, but I will call out the ones unique to this template.

JDBC Connection URL String

This is a JDBC formatted connection URL. For Microsoft SQL Server, it'll look something like this:

```
jdbc:microsoft:sqlserver://HOSTNAME:1433;DatabaseName=DATABASE
```

JDBC Driver Class Name

The Java class name required to operate the connector. For Microsoft SQL Server, it's

```
com.microsoft.jdbc.sqlserver.SQLServerDriver
```

JDBC Source SQL Query

This is the query you want to run on the target database. Use the SQL dialect of the remote database, since this will be run directly on that server.

BigQuery Output Table

The BigQuery project, dataset, and table name you want the results to go to. Note that you need to match the schema of the source table to the destination. If you're using one of the more exotic JDBC drivers, you're probably going to need to look up the schemas in its documentation to figure out how to construct the destination table.

GCS Paths for JDBC Drivers

This is the fun one. You also have to supply the JAR (Java ARchive) files from a location somewhere on Google Cloud Storage accessible to the given Dataflow service account. This means the JARs also have to be from a Java version compatible with Dataflow. At this writing, that appears to be Java 8.

Other

The remainder of the fields are described in more detail in Chapter 7. At this point, you should be able to create the job, and it will execute the remote query and pipe it into your desired BigQuery table. As I said, this is somewhat convoluted. But unless or until BigQuery adds native support for external connections of other types, this might work for you.

Document-Based Storage/NoSQL

Now that we've covered all the many ways that you can get a CSV file, stick it in the format that BigQuery is looking for, and use bq load or the UI console to get it loaded, you might imagine that most of the loading-based methods are going to look similar. This is pretty much the case. The major functional difference is that NoSQL systems generally operate in or can export JSON. The other is that many of them do not have a strongly typed system for data. This means you will have to impose your own schema on the data as it arrives in BigQuery.

To load JSON to BigQuery, it will need to be in line-delimited JSON format. This is because in order to support streaming and very large datasets, each line of the file needs to be its own JSON object. If the entire file were one object, the parser wouldn't be able to work on it until it had loaded the whole file. Obviously this isn't optimal for large files. So you'll have to make sure that each element in your file can stand on its own as a JSON object.

The switch for bq load is

```
--source_format=NEWLINE_DELIMITED_JSON
```

Many NoSQL systems like MongoDB will have a similar export command to get JSON out of their tables. (Mongo's, e.g., is mongoexport.) There are far too many to try to cover all of them, but if you combine the techniques we've already gone over, there will likely be a viable path. If not, on to streaming.

Google Firestore

Google Firestore is a serverless NoSQL database. Originally a product of Firebase, a subsidiary of Google, it is the successor product to the Firebase Realtime Database and has been folded into GCP at large. It is capable of producing exports in the DATASTORE_ BACKUP format, which can be read directly by BigQuery. (Firestore and Cloud Datastore share this backup format.)

Firestore is very good at scale and extremely easy to develop with, but querying it directly is nigh on impossible, and getting any analytics out of it without putting the data in some other form is also very difficult. The best way to deal with large amounts of data in Firestore is to either load or stream it into BigQuery.

To load it, use the bq load switch:

```
--source_format=DATASTORE_BACKUP
```

External Data Sources

Finally, there's another way to access your data from inside BigQuery, which is in fact not to load it at all. As we talked about earlier, federated data sources are slower than native BigQuery tables. You can also create a table from an external source and then save it directly to BigQuery so it is no longer pulled from the outside. We talked about use cases for this in Chapter 3: the trade-off here is speed vs. accuracy. If you prefer to have the data up-to-date and potentially slower, leave it in the external source. If you want the data natively in BigQuery and will develop a process to refresh it periodically, bring it over. There are three systems aside from Cloud SQL that you can set up as external data sources. They are Google Cloud Storage, Google Bigtable, and Google Drive.

There are a couple of limitations. In addition to the slower speed, BigQuery (by definition) cannot guarantee consistency of data from the external source. There's no way for it to impose a transaction-level scope on a document that can be edited directly by end users. This could lead to some unpredictable results if the data source is being modified while BigQuery is trying to access it.

Google Cloud Storage

As opposed to the "bq load" method we already discussed, this method leaves the data in Cloud Storage. After you establish the table in BigQuery, you could still copy it into an internal table instead of using "bq load."

One other thing this method would grant you over loading directly from GCS into BigQuery is that you could use the external table as a staged data source, doing the remainder of the transform inside a BigQuery. (This would constitute an ELT pipeline—you already loaded the data and are now transforming it inside the destination.)

Google Bigtable

Google Bigtable is Google's highly available NoSQL database. It's actually the system Google invented to maintain its search indexes. Datastore and Spanner, two of Google's other database technologies, are in some ways overlays on Bigtable. (Spanner is how Google runs search now.) It is also designed not as an OLTP system, but as a big data, real-time analytics system. However, it doesn't support SQL, and so BigQuery is still your best bet for a SQL data warehouse. If you already have Bigtable workloads, though, you can get the best of both worlds by using it as a BigQuery external data source. (The amount of ink that could be spent just comparing and contrasting Google database technologies against each other is not inconsiderable.)

Google Drive

You can also establish a table from a source located in Google Drive. This method supports CSV, JSON (newline delimited as with other sources), Avro, or, intriguingly, Google Sheets. It also works on shared documents available to BigQuery's account's permissions.

This opens up some interesting processing ideas. If your organization uses G Suite and you have employees doing manual data entry into Sheets, you could get at that data through an external data source and incorporate it. You would want to use a similar ELT method so that you can adequately cleanse and filter the data before combining it with any of your system-generated BigQuery data.

Summary

After you have designed and built the data warehouse, you need to construct paths to get your organization's accumulated data into it. The most straightforward way to do this is to do a one-time load of data into BigQuery, which is a free operation. There is a vast array of methods, scripts, connectors, and BigQuery features to do this. Choosing the right ones is a delicate balance among cost, speed, reliability, and future-proofing. Weighing all of these considerations, you can combine these methods to create a data warehouse that has all of your organization's historical data and some good processes to keep that data current.

In the next chapter, we'll move into streaming, which will allow your data warehouse to accept updates in near real time, allowing for rapid analytics and storage of live user activity as it happens.

CHAPTER 6

Streaming Data into the Warehouse

In the last chapter, we covered myriad ways to take your data and load it into your BigQuery data warehouse. Another significant way of getting your data into BigQuery is to stream it. In this chapter, we will cover the pros and cons of streaming data, when you might want to use it, and how to do it.

Streaming bears little resemblance to loading. Most notably, there's no way to activate it using the UI in the BigQuery console. Consequently, we'll be using Python for our examples. In practice, you could run this code inside a Google Compute Engine (GCE) or Google Cloud Function. You might also run this code at the end of a processing pipeline you already have in your current architecture. Or you might add BigQuery as a streaming destination for data in addition to other sinks.

Also, the streaming methodology we're discussing here is not Google Dataflow. Dataflow is another Google service that integrates closely with BigQuery, as well as external systems, Pub/Sub, Cloud Functions, and so on. Dataflow is capable of both streaming and batching incoming data. However, it has a different origin and requires a completely separate set of concepts and services. It definitely warrants a treatment of its own, which we'll get to in the next chapter.

Another important note: BigQuery streaming is not available on the free tier of Google Cloud Platform. Most services have a threshold under which Google will not charge you, and in fact if you stay on the free tier, you may never even provide billing information. BigQuery streaming has no such threshold. To enable it, you must provide your billing information. The cost for the test data we're messing with will not be high (at this writing, streaming costs a nickel per gigabyte), but it's something to be aware of.

With all that out of the way, let's dive in.

© Mark Mucchetti 2020
M. Mucchetti, *BigQuery for Data Warehousing*, https://doi.org/10.1007/978-1-4842-6186-6_6

Benefits and Drawbacks

With loading, you have to wait until the job completes for your data to be accessible. You gain access to streamed data very quickly. This makes it ideal for scenarios where you want to query the data as soon as possible. These are things like click streams, user event tracking, logging, or telemetry. This is the signature and primary benefit of streaming. Data becomes available to query within a few seconds of the stream beginning to insert. You can begin to aggregate it, transform it, or pass it to your machine learning models for analysis. In high-traffic scenarios, this can give you rapid insight into what is happening with your business and application.

For example, let's say you run an application with a fleet of mobile users. Each event a user performs on the application is streamed to BigQuery, and your analysis runs on the aggregate across users. Suddenly, after a code deploy, the rate for one of your events drops precipitously. This would give you a clue that there might be an undetected error occurring that is preventing users from reaching that page.

There are also great use cases for adaptive learning algorithms. For an ecommerce site, you might log an event every time a customer looks at a product, adds it to a cart, and so on. If you are streaming all of those events as they happen, you can monitor changes in sales trends as they occur. If you also store the referring URL for a given product view, you would know within minutes if a high-traffic site linked to yours and could adapt to present that new audience with other product opportunities. This could even all happen automatically at 3 AM while you were sleeping. (Of course, if these views were resulting in sales, you might want an alert to wake you up in this situation...)

I'm focusing on aggregations, trends, and speed because the trade-offs you make to get these benefits are not insignificant. Streaming is most appropriate for those situations because of the deficiencies.

Many of these scenarios would also be applicable for a Dataflow pipeline. Dataflow also requires a fair amount of code and tends to be more expensive than streaming. Once you have a solid grasp on loading, streaming, and Dataflow, you'll be able to decide which of your use cases fit best with each technology. In reality, your business will have many use cases: the double-edged sword of being the data architect is that you get to (have to) understand all of them.

There are a few additional considerations around streaming.

Data Consistency

There is no guarantee with streaming that your event will arrive or that it will arrive only once. Errors in your application or in BigQuery itself can cause inserts to fail to arrive or to arrive several times.

Google's approach to this is to request a field called insertId for each row. This field is used to identify duplicate rows if you attempt to insert the same data (or an insert is replayed) twice. The specifications say that BigQuery will hold onto a given insertId for "at least" one minute. If a stream errors and the state of your inserts is unknown, you can run the inserts again with the same insertIds, and BigQuery will attempt to automatically remove the duplicates. Unfortunately, the amount of time BigQuery actually remembers the insertId is undefined. If you implement an exponential backoff strategy for retrying after error, cap it under 60 seconds to be safe.

Even insertId comes with a trade-off though: the processing quotas are much lower if you are supplying insertId. Without insertId, BigQuery allows a million rows a second to be inserted. With insertId, that number drops to 100,000 per second. Still, 100,000 rows a second is nothing to scoff at. Even with thousands of concurrent users generating several events a second, you'd still be within quota. (The non-insertId, 1,000,000 rows/second quota is currently available only in beta.)

In scenarios where you are looking at data aggregation and identifying patterns, a few lost or extra events are no big deal. In a scenario that requires transactional guarantees, streaming is not an appropriate choice. Google provides guidance for querying and deduplicating rows after your stream has finished, so if you just need the guarantee *later*, that might be sufficient.

For the record, I have not often seen streaming either drop events or duplicate them, but that's not a guarantee on which I'd want to base the integrity of my business's data. (Side note: Google Dataflow implements insertId automatically and thus can guarantee "exactly-once" processing.)

Data Availability

As mentioned previously, data streamed to BigQuery becomes available in a few seconds. However, the data does not become available for copy or export until up to 90 minutes. You can't implement your own aggregation windows by running a process every minute to grab all the new streamed data, dedupe it, and push it elsewhere.

There will be a column in your streamed table called _PARTITIONTIME which will be NULL when the data is not available for export/copy. You can use this to set up behaviors that do aggregate and additionally transform the data, but those pipelines may take a while to run.

Google does not specify what determines the delay for data insert or availability, but it is likely a factor of adjacent traffic, latency between GCP data centers, and the amount of free I/O available to the data center(s) your stream is executing on. They do say that "Data can flow through machines outside the dataset's location while BigQuery processes..." and that you will incur additional latency if you're loading to a dataset from a different location.

When to Stream

So when should you prefer streaming over loading data? When your data conforms to these characteristics:

- Very high volume (thousands of events per second).

- No need for transactionality.

- Data is more useful in aggregate than by individual row.

- You need to query it in near real time.

- You can live with occasional duplicated or missing data.

- Cost sensitivity is not a major issue.

You may be thinking that these are a lot of constraints for the benefit of immediate analytics. That's true. Dealing effectively with data at such high velocity comes with trade-offs. With infinite budget and resources, a careful decision wouldn't be required. Ultimately this decision will be based on whether the benefits outweigh the costs, both in money and in time.

Writing a Streaming Insert

In order to write an insert, we'll have to put our code somewhere. You can run this code from your local machine or on the cloud shell. You can run it from there as well, or you can deploy it to Google App Engine.

Google App Engine

Google App Engine (GAE) is a great place to easily write code and deploy it with minimal configuration and no server management. Google has more ways to host and run your code than I can even properly describe, but if you want something easily comprehensible that handles most everyday workloads, Google App Engine is it.

One of the fun things about GAE is the number of runtimes it supports out of the box. I give a Google Cloud Platform Introduction talk for people who are just getting started out with cloud or GCP, and one of the exercises I sometimes do is to show a deployment to Google App Engine on every supported language. Java, Ruby, Python, Node.js, Go, C#, PHP—I do them all. Once your application is up and running, it looks the same from the outside no matter how you built it.

GAE is slowly getting supplanted by other technologies such as Google Kubernetes Engine (GKE), Cloud Run, Cloud Functions, and others, but I still use GAE for examples because it's so easy to get rolling.

(If you want to follow along using GAE, note that this also requires you to enable billing. If you're already doing that to check out streaming, then this will work too. I'd also recommend you do this in the same separate project, so when you're finished, you can delete this BigQuery instance, GAE, and so on and not incur any charges inadvertently.)

Check out Appendix A for instructions on setting up the Cloud SDK and creating projects via the command-line interface, if you haven't done that already. Once that's done, create a new App Engine app with the following command:

```
gcloud app create --project=[YOUR_PROJECT_ID]
```

You'll be asked to choose a region. For simplicity's sake, choose the region that your target BigQuery dataset is in.

Now, install the Python App Engine components. You only need to do this if you are running on your local machine; the cloud shell already has App Engine support. You may also need to prefix "sudo" to obtain elevated privileges:

```
gcloud components install app-engine-python
```

Now you're ready to code the sample. You might also want to update python3 and pip3 package manager to the latest version. You'll need one more thing in order to use your application with Google App Engine, and that's an app.yaml file. This file tells Google what to do with your package when you deploy it. For the moment, it only needs a single line:

```
runtime: python37
```

GAE will use that to deploy the application on a Python 3.7 runtime. You'll additionally need two dependencies for this sample to work: the Google BigQuery SDK and Flask, the web server we'll use so that you can see the application working. You can do that with

```
pip3 install google-big query
pip3 install flask
```

If you're running on the cloud shell, you may also need to append the "--user" flag to install with your permissions level.

Now make a file called main.py and we'll code up the sample. You can manually enter the sample from Figure 6-1, or you can download it from the source code associated with this book.

Make sure Cloud Build and BigQuery APIs are enabled

/static/index.html

```
<html>
<body>
    <p>Enter your string for streaming here</p>
    <form action="/stream" method="post">
      <label for="str">String</label>
      <input type="text" id="s" name="s"/>
      <button type="submit">Go</button>
    </form>
</body>
</html>
```

app.yaml

```
runtime: python37
handlers:
  - url: /static
    static_dir: static
```

```
requirements.txt
Flask==1.1.2
google-api-core==1.17.0
google-api-python-client==1.9.1
google-bigquery==0.14
google-cloud==0.34.0
google-cloud-bigquery==1.24.0
```

Figure 6-1. *Source code for main.py*

```
main.py
from flask import Flask
from flask import request
from google.cloud import bigquery

app = Flask(__name__)

# define your project.dataset.table here

table_id = 'bort-qaliwo.wbq.stream'

# define number of repetitions you want
count = 1000

# you can modify the schema if you wish
schema = [
    bigquery.SchemaField("streamed_data", "STRING", mode="REQUIRED")
]

# define the root page
@app.route("/form")
def index():
    return app.send_static_file('index.html')

# define the behavior for loading the stream
@app.route("/stream", methods = ['POST'])
def stream():
```

Figure 6-1. (*continued*)

```
    if "s" in request.form:
        s = request.form.get('s')
    else:
        return "No string passed!"

    client = bigquery.Client()

    table = bigquery.Table(table_id, schema=schema)

    # the true ensures you will not get errors on subsequent runs of
the script
    # when the table already exists
    table = client.create_table(table, True)

  rows_to_insert = [{"streamed_data" : s+str(i)} for i in
range(count)]

    errors = client.insert_rows(table, rows_to_insert)
    if errors == []:

        return "Successfully streamed! Check your table."
    else:
        return errors

if __name__ == "__main__":
    app.run(debug=True)
```

Figure 6-1. (*continued*)

Lastly, make sure your requirements.txt has the necessary dependency versions listed for Flask and BigQuery. Yours will be different than mine, so just use whatever the latest is.

Now all you need to do is sit back and deploy to Google App Engine. You do that as follows:

```
gcloud app deploy
```

App Engine will confirm your target project, sources, and URL. If you're satisfied with the defaults, press Enter, and the service will begin deploying. This will take a minute or two. You should see something similar to Figure 6-2.

```
Beginning deployment of service [default]...

  Uploading 1 file to Google Cloud Storage

File upload done.
Updating service [default]...done.
Setting traffic split for service [default]...done.
Deployed service [default] to [https://b          .appspot.com]

You can stream logs from the command line by running:
  $ gcloud app logs tail -s default

To view your application in the web browser run:
  $ gcloud app browse
```

Figure 6-2. *Screenshot of successful deploy*

Once it's done, fire up the sample either with the recommended "gcloud app browse" or by going to the browser. You should see a simple text box and a form submit. Put any string into the text box and click "Submit."

Enter your string for streaming here

String [   ] Go

Figure 6-3. *The UI for the sample*

Once you do this, the sample will multiply the data and stream it into BigQuery to the dataset and table you specified in your source. Open up a BigQuery console window and select from that table. You'll see the rows made from the submission you made to the website.

And that's it! You've successfully streamed data!

Common Problems

Of course, it's not always going to be wine and rows when you're streaming data to BigQuery. Occasionally, you will run into the messy result of one of the trade-offs you made to support streaming. There are compensation scenarios for all of them, but you have to manage them yourself. Here are a few issues you may run into and some suggestions for compensating for and resolving them.

Insertion Errors

In all cases, when you successfully complete a job, you must inspect the "insertErrors" property to see if any rows failed.

The insertErrors property will typically contain an empty list, indicating everything went fine. If there are rows in there, then you'll need to programmatically check to see what went wrong in order to repair it.

If some rows indicate a schema mismatch, no rows will have been inserted, and you can jump down to the following "Schema Issues" section. In this case, *all* the rows you tried to stream will be in the insertErrors list.

If only some rows are in the insertErrors list, you will have to check for the specific failure message to see whether you can simply retry them or if you have to do something to repair them first.

Copying Unavailable Data

If you attempt a copy or export operation before data in your streamed table has become available, the data will be silently dropped from the operation. This could be a major issue if you copy out of a table that has both extant data and incoming stream data without checking.

As mentioned earlier, before you do a copy or export operation, check the _ PARTITIONTIME column of all rows in the table to make sure that none of the rows are still in the streaming buffer.

If you are running a scheduled, periodic process on the table, the data will be picked up in a later run. If you have built your process with some tolerance for late-arriving data, this should be sufficient. Combine this with any deduplication strategy to make sure you don't copy or export the same row twice.

Duplicate Data

In most cases, if you're using the insertId field, BigQuery will be able to detect any scenarios in which you have to retry the data and automatically deal with the duplication.

In some cases, this may be insufficient. For example, if you used insertId, but waited too long before retrying, BigQuery may have lost track of those particular insertIds and will allow duplication. Google also notes that "in the rare instance of a Google data center losing connectivity," deduplication may fail altogether. Google just wants to helpfully remind you that BigQuery streaming is not transactional.

So, if you want to be sure your data was not duplicated, you can wait until you have finished the stream and then search for duplicate ID_COLUMNs to clear out the extras. This feels especially inelegant, so I would tend to recommend not even bothering with streaming if you need to go to this end to validate your data. (Dataflow would be a better choice.)

Schema Issues

What happens if you modify the schema of the insert table as you are running a stream? In short, nothing good. If you have changed the schema or deleted the table before you start the job with the old schema, it will fail outright. If you manage to change the schema *while* the job is in progress, BigQuery should still reject all of the rows and give you information about which rows that conflicted. The rest of the rows, while not inserted, were acceptable and can be retried.

In short, don't change the schema of tables you are streaming to until you have finished a job and the streaming buffer has cleared. Don't change a drill bit while the drill is in motion either.

Error Codes

Sometimes the stream will just fail. Most often, this will be due to a network error somewhere between the machine initiating the stream and the BigQuery API. If this occurs, your job will be in an unknown state.

As we discussed earlier, you have two choices here: One, do nothing and accept the uncertainty; or, two, supply the insertId with all of your streaming batches so that BigQuery (or, failing that, you) can attempt deduplication. The first approach is obviously unacceptable for many workloads, so unless you are planning to exceed the 100,000 rows per second quota, use insertId.

If the stream fails right off the bat because it couldn't connect, you have invalid authentication, or you're already over quota, the job won't start and you can safely assume that no rows were inserted at all.

Quotas

If you are running into issues with quotas, the call (or any other call on GCP) will return HTTP code 429: "Too Many Requests." GCP is generally very good at enforcing quotas right at the published levels, so you can push close to the limit without much risk.

A common pattern for dealing with 429s is to implement an exponential backoff strategy. Often, when implementing such a strategy, you don't know either the exact rate limit or how many calls you have left to make. In that case, you want to implement a strategy with "jitter," that is, a random interval tacked onto the backoff interval. Jitter is a good idea whenever a quota is shared by multiple disconnected jobs on the same system. BigQuery streaming quotas are set across your entire project, which means that even if you are only streaming one row per second, if another job is currently monopolizing the quota, your job will still receive 429s. Jitter helps to prevent those disconnected jobs from syncing up with each other and all retrying simultaneously at the same exponential spike.

The most typical way to implement backoff in this way is to start with one second and double each time. This works well for streaming, since the quota resolution is also one second. So, assuming that you add jitter of between zero and one second, one sample pattern would be the following.

Exponential Backoff

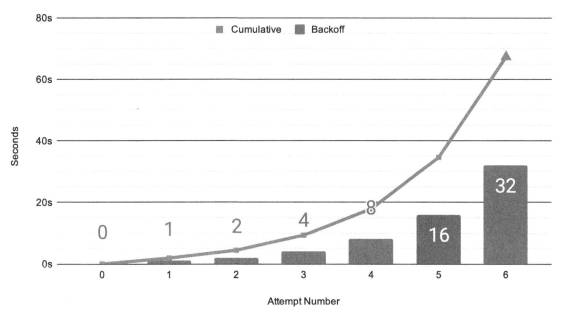

Figure 6-4. *Exponential backoff with jitter calculations*

Remember that the intervals should be cumulative, that is, don't hit it 1, 2, 4 seconds after failure; wait the next interval after each try. Obviously, if the call succeeds, stop retrying.

This strategy will help you balance multiple streaming jobs against each other. What I mean by "syncing" is that if all of your jobs receive 429s simultaneously, without the jitter, they will all retry again at 1 second and likely get the same error.

Lastly, if you are using insertId, cap your exponential backoff rate at 32 or 64 seconds. Since BigQuery is only guaranteed to remember the ID for a minute, going beyond this interval risks additional duplication of your data.

If you're hitting quotas and you know for a fact that you shouldn't be, find the other data analyst on your team and tell them to knock it off. If they swear up and down it's not them, then open a ticket with Google. (I'm serious. While you can look through logs and figure out the source of quota violators, it is usually either you or the person sitting next to you. Save yourself the trouble of doing the forensics and just ask!)

Advanced Streaming Capabilities

There are a few more things you can do with BigQuery streams to prioritize the performance of insertion. You can divide inserts either by date or by a suffix of your choosing. Either will help you maximize accessibility to the data you want to analyze.

Partitioning by Timestamp

Partitioning by date, as covered in Part 1, is also available for streaming applications. This is great if you're not planning to do additional transformation on the data, but you want it to be available on a partitioned basis for later querying. Since this is done automatically by the streaming job, all you need to do is ensure that you have a DATE or TIMESTAMP column in your insert (and in your destination table), and the streaming buffer will automatically partition the data into the correct tables.

The limits for auto-partitioning are as follows:

- Eighteen-month window: This window (in UTC) starts 12 months before the current datetime and ends 6 months after and is the maximum partitioned range for streaming. If you attempt to partition data outside of this window, the insert will fail.

- Ten-day window: This window (in UTC) starts 7 days before the current datetime and ends 3 days after. It is the maximum range for direct partitioning. Data in this range will go directly from the streaming buffer into the correct partition. Data outside this range (but inside the 18-month range) will first go into the unpartitioned table and will then be swept out into the appropriate table as it accumulates.

This emphasizes the use case around temporal data for streaming. While I've already broken down the use case around the idea that this should be data that you need available for immediate analysis, this reinforces that that data should be *temporally* relevant as well.

Here's a relevant Internet of Things (IoT) example. Let's say you have a fleet of sensor devices that stream current data to BigQuery. You collect this data on a daily basis into partitioned tables and use it to calculate daily trends. At some point, some of the sensors go offline and stop reporting their data. Several weeks pass as the rest of the sensors continue to report data continuously. Once the sensors are fixed, they begin transmitting the samples that were queued while they were offline. These samples contain new information, but also contain the stale information from the previous couple of weeks. BigQuery will correctly prioritize the relevant, recent information. It will still collect the stale rows, but they'll accumulate for a while before being partitioned.

Partitioning by Ingestion

The default partition scheme is to insert data into date-based partitions based on current UTC. This assumes either that you have low latency between the event sources and your insertion or that you care more about when the data was received at BigQuery than the event occurrence time.

The preceding sensor example wouldn't be appropriate for ingestion partitioning, because the event timestamp itself is more important and suddenly reporting stale data as current would presumably cause issues for your metrics collection. However, it's good for most sampling use cases, like user activity on a live website, logging, or system monitoring.

In fact, when you set up an event sink from something like Cloud Logging (formerly Stackdriver), it also will automatically partition tables by ingestion. For decent performance on large-scale querying of ephemeral data, this is definitely the way to go.

Template Tables

If you want to partition your tables by something other than date, BigQuery streaming supports the concept of template tables to accomplish this. This particular methodology only appears here. BigQuery supported this methodology before it supported date partitioning for streaming, so users would fake out date partitioning using template tables. Now, it is still useful for other partitioning schemes.

To use this methodology, create your destination table to accept stream jobs as you normally would, specifying a schema that will be shared across all implementations of the template. Then, decide what you want to partition by.

In the preceding IoT sensor example, we might choose to partition our inserts by sensor ID instead of date. Or we might want to do two streaming jobs and partition our inserts by date in one table and by sensor ID using template tables. We could also use one or the other method for whatever requires real-time analysis and then copy the data into the other format later on.

Generally, you would want to choose whatever field is the primary key of your data. If you were tracking all movements on an order, you could partition by that order ID. Or you could partition by an account or session ID.

Once you have decided, add your identifier to the call as a templateSuffix. When BigQuery detects that you have supplied both a table name and a suffix, it will consult the table for the schema, but it will automatically create and load into a table in the form tableName+templateSuffix.

To go back to the sensor example, if you used the sensor ID as the suffix, each sensor would supply its insertAll command with its own sensor ID, and BigQuery would take care of the rest, creating tables like SensorData000, SensorData001, and so on.

Summary

Streaming is a technique for inserting data at extremely high velocities into BigQuery with minimal latencies. This speed comes with significant trade-offs, however; data consistency and availability may both be degraded in order to enable inserted rows for analysis as quickly as possible. This method is different from both data loading and Dataflow pipelines and is most appropriate for datasets where you care more about aggregates and trends than about the individual rows themselves. Even when streaming, there are compensatory strategies you can take to minimize the impact of trade-offs. You can also divide inserts by date or a field of your choosing to create a greater number of smaller tables that are easier to query.

We've covered two of the methods you can use to get your data loaded into BigQuery. In the next chapter, we'll cover a technique you can use for loading, migration, streaming, and ongoing data processing, using another Google Cloud Platform service called Dataflow.

## CHAPTER 7

Dataflow

Once you have your data warehouse built, its schemas defined, and all of your external and internal data migrated into BigQuery, it's time to start thinking about your data pipeline architecture and how you can enable your organization to accept stream or batch processing into the warehouse.

Your organization may already have a well-established system of relational or NoSQL databases collecting and distributing data to end users. The trick is to get that data into BigQuery as efficiently as possible so you can begin analysis. If your organization has or requires big data pipelines, at some point you are going to hit a limit that might be bounded either by scale or by the amount of time you have to devote to the problem.

When you reach this point, there are still plenty of options—you could employ a custom architecture using functions as a service (FaaS), or you could use any of the available transfer mechanisms through the native features of your SQL or NoSQL platforms. You might even rely on some of the basic methods we discussed in earlier chapters, like maintaining read-only replicas or streaming data directly from sources.

However, at massive scale, it becomes difficult to keep track of your data configurations. With manifold data sources and disparate transforms, an organization can become quickly overwhelmed with preprocessing raw data to do analysis. Dumping your data rapidly into lenient BigQuery schemas and crunching it later can become the equivalent of shoving all your dirty laundry into a closet. While efficiently dealing with a problem at the beginning, you pay for it later in the amount of time required to retrieve and organize the data (or socks). This is not an ideal system of prioritization for data at scale.

Enter Google Dataflow. Dataflow is Google's managed service for processing and transformation. Like most of the other Google Cloud Platform (GCP) products in this book, it uses a serverless model and is designed to abstract the challenging management of concurrency and parallelization so you can focus purely on what you want to do with the data.

© Mark Mucchetti 2020
M. Mucchetti, *BigQuery for Data Warehousing*, https://doi.org/10.1007/978-1-4842-6186-6_7

Google Dataflow was originally developed at Google ("Dataflow Model") and intended as a successor to technologies like Apache Hadoop MapReduce and Apache Spark. In 2016, Google joined a group of other developers with a proposal to open source the Dataflow Java SDK as an Apache Software Foundation incubator project. When the SDK was open sourced, it took the name Beam, a portmanteau of "batch" and "stream." Google's Java Dataflow SDK retained compatibility with Beam. In 2016, Google added Python support and, very recently and most excitingly, Dataflow SQL. The Dataflow SDK is also being deprecated and will use the open source Beam SDK. All this to say, you will see both Dataflow and Beam, and while they are not equivalent, they are closely related.

The development of Dataflow SQL and its underlying Apache Beam work is fascinating because it seems like an obvious choice, and yet Java and Python (and Go) appeared on the scene first. However, at the dawn of big data, when Hadoop and other map-reduce technologies were becoming popular, that was all that was out there. This has some pretty deep historical precedent. Björn Rost, the technical consultant on this book, surmises that this could be partially because SQL was designed originally for fixed storage, as opposed to streaming datasets. Streaming was also something organizations tended to do in a few isolated use cases. And yes, if you think about the world of RDBMS and how query engines were constructed, it made sense at that time to do certain data processing in procedural languages, outside the database. This was also convenient for software engineers, who were often nervous about SQL and considered query optimization to be a black art. (Those who embraced SQL also found welcome parallels in functional programming techniques and happily adopted relational algebra all over the place.) The merging of these two streams (no pun intended) is fairly recent, starting around when Kafka released KSQL (now ksqlDB). Both ksqlDB and Dataflow have had to contend that SQL is not built for streaming operations and have introduced extensions to compensate.

In the last several years, technologies like Google BigQuery, Amazon Redshift, and Azure Synapse Analytics have allowed SQL to regain its throne as a language at the terabyte and petabyte scale. As a long-time practitioner and admirer of SQL, I couldn't be happier. Colonizing the entire data ecosystem with SQL feels like it was the natural choice from the start. And finally, the technology is catching up.

(Side note: Engineer-adjacent professionals like product managers and sales architects often ask me if they should learn to code. Whatever my specific answer is, I seem to always find myself veering into the recommendation to learn SQL. I really do believe that it changes your perception of how the world's information is organized. Of course, you already know this.)

Key Concepts

Since Dataflow emerges from a map-reduce school of thought, its model resembles more of a phased workflow. Understanding the model and execution phases will help you design pipelines that best suit your needs.

Driver Program

The driver program, or just driver, is the execution unit that constructs the pipeline. In Java and Python, it is the actual executing program that instantiates the pipeline, supplies all the necessary steps, and then executes on an Apache Beam runner, in this case, Google Dataflow. In Dataflow SQL, this actually gets all abstracted away, but we'll get to that later. Essentially, just be aware that if you are working with a procedural SDK like Java or Python, you'll actually be writing the program to contain the job. (There are plenty of templates to assist with all kinds of common tasks.)

Pipeline

The primary object in Dataflow is the pipeline. The pipeline runs from start to finish and governs all the aspects of your task. Your ultimate deployment unit to manage Dataflow jobs is this pipeline. Beam drivers must implement a pipeline in order to do anything. The pipeline will in turn be responsible for creating the datasets (PCollections) that will be loaded and transformed throughout the life of the job.

The job is intended to represent a single workflow and to be repeatable. Thus, it can both be parallelized and run continuously inside a Beam-compatible framework like Google Dataflow. Under the hood, a Beam pipeline looks a lot like something you would see in Apache Spark or really any other workflow tool: a directed-acyclic graph (DAG).

Directed-Acyclic Graphs

If you're at all familiar with graph theory, skip this section.

Directed-acyclic graphs, or DAGs, come up theoretically as great interview questions in a wide variety of mathematics and computer science subdomains. They tend to pop up anywhere you want to understand or generate a static graph of an execution flow, in compilers, and so on. If they're not interesting to you in this context, they'll probably surface somewhere else.

"Pipeline" is an evocative term that summons large industry to mind. It also implies a straight line from input to output, and in some ways it doesn't really touch on the importance of data transformation in the process. The reality of a workflow-based structure is slightly more complex. As far as your business owners are concerned, expressing data processing as a series of tubes is a perfectly fine approximation, but as you come to work with the technology, it's useful to go one level deeper.

When we speak of graphs in this context, it is in the mathematical sense, not the common sense of bar or line graphs. A graph is a formation of vertices and edges, which creates paths along which you can traverse. Many of the greatest-of-all-time graph theory problems involve using graphs as a representation of physical space, that is, the Traveling Salesman Problem, in which you attempt to compute the most efficient route among cities, with the distance between the cities represented by the weight of the edges. Dijkstra's Shortest Path algorithm determines the shortest number of hops required to get from a given vertex to another.

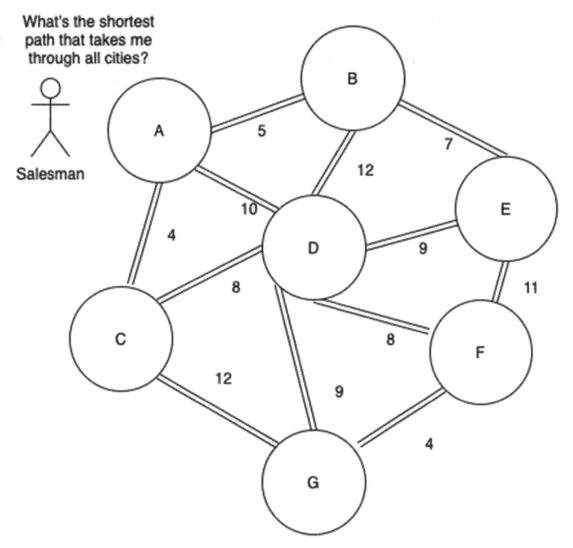

Figure 7-1. *a graph as might be seen in the Traveling Salesman Problem*

DAGs impose two additional constraints upon a graph, which, as you may have guessed, are "directed" and "acyclic." Informally, they're defined as follows:

- Directed: This means that the edges between nodes have a direction, typically represented with an arrow. You may only proceed along edges in a valid direction.

127

- Acyclic: This means that there are no "cycles" in the graph, meaning that you can never start at one node and, following the arrows, end up back at that same node. This should be a familiar programming concept—a cycle connotes an infinite loop. Infinite loops in tasks that are supposed to complete are bad!

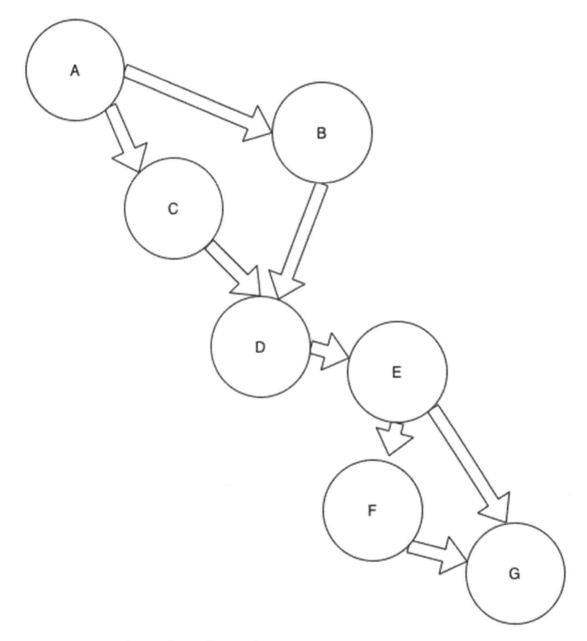

Figure 7-2. *a directed acyclic graph*

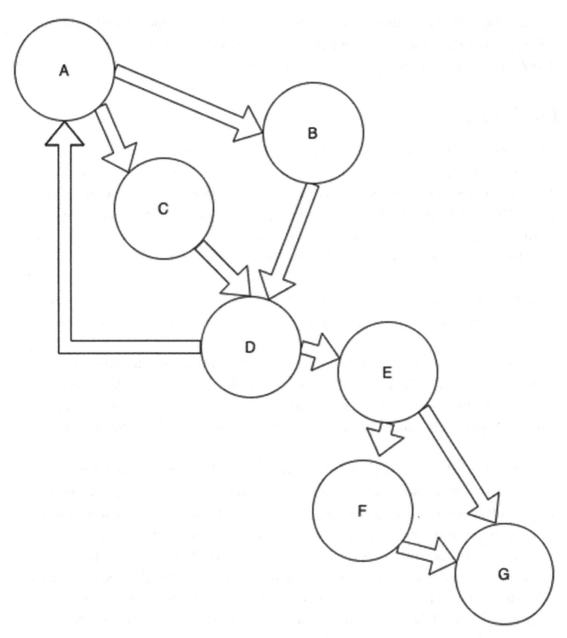

Figure 7-3. *a graph with directed cycles*

There's usually one additional restriction for workflows that operate using a DAG, while not part of the formal definition. Usually disconnected nodes aren't permitted— that is, every step in the workflow has to be reachable. It doesn't really make sense to write steps that can't be executed.

129

With the difference between the admittedly friendlier term pipeline and a directed-acyclic graph, thinking about this in terms of graph theory may assist you in quickly distinguishing between valid and invalid workflows.

PCollection

A PCollection is the input and output object for the pipeline's steps (graph vertices). The whole pipeline will start by initializing a PCollection. That PCollection will represent the dataset, which comes from a bounded (like a file) or an unbounded (like a stream) data source. This also helps establish the basis for a job that will run on finite input files or for one that will run continuously hooked up to a queue. This data source is generally also provided from a location external to the pipeline's starting point.

Technically, you can initialize a starting PCollection with values internal to your driver program as well. This could be a handy use case if the primary concept you need to transform is a fixed list of data, and you're going to be collecting auxiliary data to join from the external source.

In general, however, I would encourage you to think of the pipeline as being controlled by the input data. Thinking about the pipeline in terms of widest to narrowest will create the highest degree of parallelization and avoid the bottlenecking that might be caused by running a small dataset over and over again and trying to join it up to larger sets.

(A job that *only* looks at internal data may be fast and repeatable, but it won't accomplish anything useful. If that's what you are hoping to do, you can probably get the same result by running a BigQuery query by itself. Techniques in earlier chapters would probably suffice without the cost and effort of following the data flow path.)

Each PCollection's elements get assigned a timestamp from the source. (Bounded collections all get the same timestamp, since they aren't continuously streaming.) This will be important as it drives the concept of windowing, which is how Dataflow is able to join datasets when it doesn't definitively have all of the data for any of them, except again in the case of bounded sets.

Another important note: PCollections are immutable. One of the key properties of the Beam model is that you must not modify the elements of a PCollection that you are processing. This is a familiar concept in functional programming models, but the underlying reason is because parallelization doesn't work if objects can change unpredictably. A given PCollection may undergo multiple transforms in a non-deterministic order of execution. If any of the relevant transforms modify the object, all the others will get a different copy, which will yield different results.

This could happen easily with branched transforms, where you send the same PCollection to multiple PTransforms for different purposes. For instance, say you have a bounded dataset with the numbers 1...100. Transform F should filter all the numbers divisible by 3, and Transform B should filter all the numbers divisible by 5. Let's say that one of those transforms removes the number 15 from the PCollection, which is applicable to both filters. This means that the order of execution will now determine how one of the transforms operates. One transform will see the number 15, and the other will not. The results will become only more unpredictable and distorted as future PTransforms try to operate on disjoint datasets. The Java SDK will detect and reject transforms that modify PCollections, but if you find yourself running into this issue, remember that parallelization is dependent on consistent data.

PTransform

A PTransform is the actual step in the pipeline, which takes one or more PCollections as input and returns zero or one PCollection as output.

Thinking about it from a graph perspective, this means that instances of the PTransform object each do the work from beginning to end, by passing PCollections around. A PTransform object might take multiple PCollections as input because it needs to join or filter them. However, it can only produce one PCollection as output because it should only have a single responsibility, to do something with the data and output a dataset (PCollection) that's slightly closer to the final form you are looking for.

When a PTransform outputs zero PCollection, that's the end of that particular journey. Note that you could have several destinations in your pipeline that output zero PCollection if you are writing to different places or writing different kinds of data. (Directed-acyclic graphs don't mandate that there only be a single termination point to the graph.)

Applying a Transform

To apply a transform, you perform the "apply" operation on a PCollection using a PTransform. In Java, the method name is "apply." In Python, you use the pipe operator "|".

```
p = beam.Pipeline()

# apply a series of transforms for the pipeline
(p
    | 'LoadFile' >> beam.io.ReadFromText(input)
    | 'DoSomething' >> beam.FlatMap(lambda line: doSomething(line) )
    | 'WriteFile' >> beam.io.WriteToText(output)
)

p.run().wait_until_finish()
```

Figure 7-4. *code example to show application of transformation*

Basic Transforms

Beam supplies a number of general-purpose transforms, which are available to Google Dataflow. We'll cover some of them here as an aid to conceptually understand how the pipeline works. I've used the same ordering as the official Apache Beam documentation, in case you want to cross-consult it:

- ParDo: From "parallel do," this is the generic parallelization method. To use it, you create a subclass of DoFn and pass it to the ParDo.

- GroupByKey: This transform operates on key-value pairs. Much like SQL GROUP BY, it takes a list of elements where the key is repeated and collapses them into a PCollection where each key appears only once.

- CoGroupByKey: This transformation operates on two or more sets of key-value pairs, returning a list of elements where each key in any of the datasets appears only once. This is somewhat like doing a UNION of the same primary key on multiple tables and then using a LEFT OUTER JOIN on all of them to retrieve the distinct data for each key. A key only needs to appear in a single input dataset to appear in the output.

- Combine: This is actually a set of transforms. You can take action to combine all elements in PCollections, or you can take action which combines across each key in a set of PCollections with key-value pairs. You can also create a subclass of CombineFn and pass it to Combine to perform more advanced operations.

- Flatten: This is much like a SQL UNION ALL operation in that it takes multiple PCollections and returns a single PCollection of all of the elements in the input collections. You're most likely to see this approaching the end of a pipeline, when eligible data has been through several separate branches of transformation and is getting prepped for writing.

- Partition: This transform takes one PCollection and, using a subclass of PartitionFn that you define, splits it up into multiple PCollections stored in the form of a PCollectionList<>. This partitioning cannot be dynamic, which I'll cover in the following.

Learning about these transforms may have raised a couple of questions with respect to how Dataflow will actually work. Before we get into the actual nuts and bolts of building a pipeline, let's address a couple of them.

Firstly, some of these operations appear to work like joins or aggregations. But how can those operations work if the full content of a dataset is unknown, as it definitionally is for streams? The answer is windowing: Dataflow needs to either be able to estimate when the dataset has been delivered, or it needs to break the datasets up into time-based windows. Remember from earlier when I said that PCollection elements all get a timestamp? That's what this is for. Advanced windowing is quite complicated. We'll discuss it in Dataflow SQL, but for now remember that we're not operating with fully materialized datasets here. Each dataset must be divided in some way. Furthermore, if you try to perform a combine operation on two datasets that don't have compatible windows, you won't be able to build the pipeline. This is critically important in both the Java/Python and the SQL flavors of Dataflow.

Secondly, as to why partitioning cannot be dynamic, the workflow graph must be constructable at runtime. You can't do anything once the workflow is running to change the number or order of steps. This is often cited as a weakness of the Apache Beam model, and there are certainly data processing scenarios where it could pose a problem for you. It is definitely something to keep in mind as a limitation of the system as you proceed.

Building a Pipeline

So now you have a good idea of all of the basic elements of the pipeline and what kinds of operations are possible. Everything up until this point is common to Apache Beam, but from this point, we'll jump into Google Dataflow and use practical examples.

Let's summarize. A pipeline consists of a series of steps where one or more PCollections pass through a PTransform either to emit another PCollection or to end the pipeline.

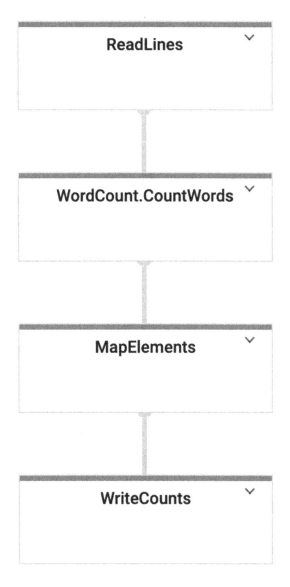

Figure 7-5. *a simple Pipeline*

I suppose if you follow a simple graph where each step takes one PCollection and yields one PCollection, then it really does feel more or less like a pipeline. However, as I hinted earlier with branching transforms and streaming PCollections, you can do a great deal more as you move beyond this.

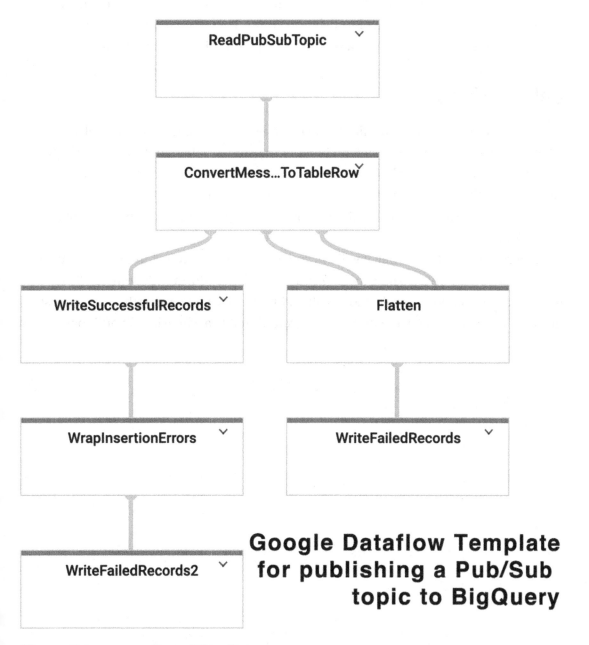

Figure 7-6. *a complicated Pipeline*

Once you have succeeded in conceptualizing your data in a way that is compatible with this paradigm, the sky's the limit. You can easily run hundreds of thousands of elements a second through your Dataflow jobs. Many enterprise clients already do.

The Dataflow pipeline corresponds to an ELT (extract, load, transform) process. The extraction is done via the input PCollection; transform is the PTransform; and the load would typically be done with the PCollection output. There's no requirement that you load the results, but it wouldn't be a very useful pipeline if it didn't output anything.

Getting Started

Head to the Dataflow page and click "Try Dataflow." I've found this to be useful to get all of the necessary services turned on in order to use it. A helpful note: If you're doing this as a test, for something like Dataflow, you may want to make a completely new GCP project. That way, when you're finished with your testing, you can just delete the whole thing. You won't incur charges later on because you forgot to turn off one of the dependent services that Dataflow uses.

When you start the tutorial, it will ask you to choose an SDK. I chose Python, but you can choose Java as well. (I know that SQL button looks so alluring; it's coming.) Then it will ask you to choose a project to install in. Choose one you have or the one you just made for testing. The step after that will ask you to enable a whole bunch of Google Cloud services that Dataflow relies on.

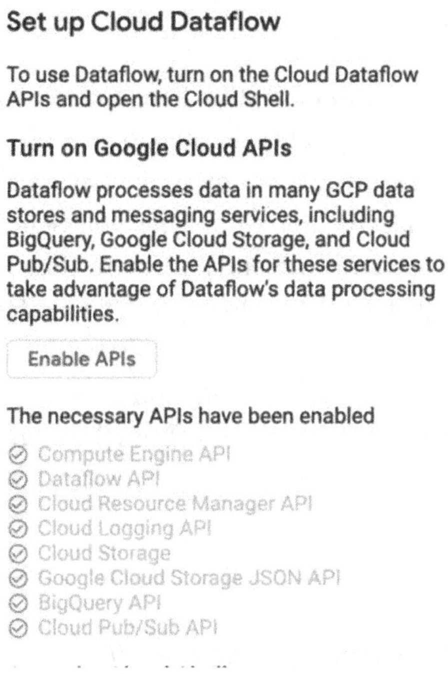

Set up Cloud Dataflow

To use Dataflow, turn on the Cloud Dataflow
APIs and open the Cloud Shell.

Turn on Google Cloud APIs

Dataflow processes data in many GCP data
stores and messaging services, including
BigQuery, Google Cloud Storage, and Cloud
Pub/Sub. Enable the APIs for these services to
take advantage of Dataflow's data processing
capabilities.

> Enable APIs

The necessary APIs have been enabled

- ⊘ Compute Engine API
- ⊘ Dataflow API
- ⊘ Cloud Resource Manager API
- ⊘ Cloud Logging API
- ⊘ Cloud Storage
- ⊘ Google Cloud Storage JSON API
- ⊘ BigQuery API
- ⊘ Cloud Pub/Sub API

Figure 7-7.

You may have some or all of these turned on already, but clicking "Enable APIs" does
the hard work for you and sets them all up.

The tutorial also recommends that you use the cloud shell to deploy a sample job. I
concur with this: if you happen to have a Python 3.x environment on your local machine,
you can do it there, but the cloud shell already has Python and pip (the Python package
manager) installed—and is pre-authenticated! It's also disposable, so make sure you
familiarize yourself with the expiration rules (see Appendix A) before storing scripts on it
that you don't want to lose.

If you are more comfortable with Java, there is thankfully a host of documentation
available. The official Apache Beam documentation is equally fluent in Java and Python,
but leaves out Go. The Google documentation also has samples in Go. Historically, the
Java SDK has been superior to Python; while the gap has closed, I only choose Python
here to keep the book's primary language choice consistent.

Tutorial Annotation

I'm also not going to replicate the tutorial steps here and reinvent the wheel (a little Python humor there), but I will annotate each step to provide context for the demo against what we've covered already. GCP tutorials are amazing and easy to run. In fact, they are sometimes so easy that you aren't sure what you've just done or its significance. This is not a criticism! No one wants to spend hours wrestling with operating systems and package dependencies just to see "Hello World." It does, however, provide a great opportunity to apply the theory.

After you've created the Python 3 virtual environment, you'll need to install the Apache Beam SDK for Python. This can be done from the command line with --quiet apache-beam[gcp].

```
pip3 install --quiet apache-beam[gcp]
```

Figure 7-8. *pip3 install --quiet apache-beam[gcp]*

The tutorial uses sample files that are downloaded by the SDK from Cloud Storage. This way you can stage a job with all of the necessary dependencies built in. Now it's getting kind of confusing. Where is everything going to run? Here is a quick diagram to show you where all the pieces are and where they'll run.

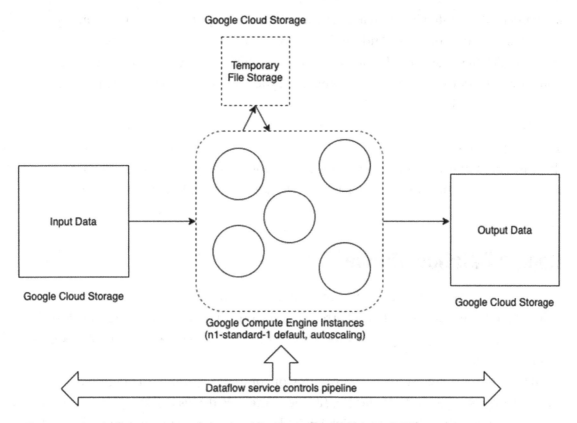

Figure 7-9. *infrastructure for running Dataflow jobs in GCP*

The missing piece to get going is that the GCP runner will need some place to store files that it can get to, both for input and output and also for temporary storage. Conveniently that location is Google Cloud Storage. You'll need a location to store things no matter what runner you're using. The tutorial has you create such a bucket—it uses the shell for this too, but you could also hop over to the Cloud Storage UI and make a bucket yourself.

Now that you have the pipeline, the sample files, and a place to put them, you can deploy the pipeline to the Cloud Dataflow service. To do that, you're running python with the -m flag, which indicates you want to run a module as a script. That module is an Apache Beam sample that specifies that you want to run a job with a specific, unique name in GCP using the DataflowRunner, which is the name for Dataflow in Beam. You also specify the scratch location and a location for the output and the GCP project you want this all to take place in. And...that's it. Once you run that command, you'll start seeing INFO messages from Python appear in the shell telling you interesting things about the job's current status. After some time, you'll see that the job has finished and produced result files.

My favorite part about this whole tutorial is that it doesn't actually tell you what you are doing. As it turns out, it takes the text of Shakespeare's "King Lear" and counts the number of times each word appears. Before you go and look at the helpful UI representation of the pipeline, see if you can figure out which PTransforms it needed to do this.

Google Dataflow Runner

One really nice convenience about using Google Dataflow is that it gives you such a helpful graphical view into what is currently going on. I have a deep and abiding love for console logs, but being able to see what's happening—and share with your coworkers—is very valuable.

If you click a Dataflow job that is running or complete, you'll see a tab called Job Graph. Hey, it's a directed-acyclic graph! One of the nice things Google Dataflow does for us is visualize the job's steps, which it will do regardless of what language you used to stage the job. You can also click each step and see how many elements it processed, the throughput, and the total timing for each phase.

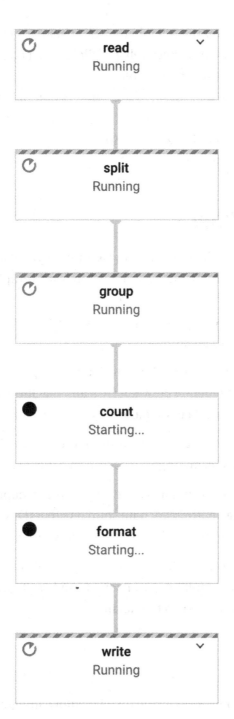

Figure 7-10. *graph view of Dataflow*

You can see the metrics for the full job, which is useful for troubleshooting steps that might be slow or jobs that are not effectively parallelizing. It can also help you make sure that the cost of your jobs remains reasonable.

Finally, you can view the logs for all of the workers that processed the job, which you can use to troubleshoot jobs that aren't working the way you expect. Both these logs and the metrics are logged to Cloud Logging and Monitoring (formerly Stackdriver), which we'll cover in depth in Chapter 12.

Dataflow Templates

For many tasks, there are predefined Dataflow templates you can use rather than building one yourself. Clicking "Create Dataflow Job from Template" in the top bar of the Dataflow console will open the page to do so.

The templates currently available support a number of useful pipelines. Some examples involving BigQuery are as follows:

- Google Cloud Storage to BigQuery with data loss prevention: Uses Cloud DLP in the pipeline between GCS and BigQuery to automatically obfuscate sensitive data in uploaded files before loading it

- Kafka to BigQuery: Takes a Kafka topic and Bootstrap Server list and pipes the streams on an ongoing basis into a BigQuery table

- JDBC to BigQuery: Automates the exercise from Chapter 5 where we discussed hitting an arbitrary data source with a JDBC-compliant driver and loading the results into a BigQuery table

Most of the templates come with an associated tutorial you can use to replicate the underlying pipeline. These templates are all Java-based, as far as I could see, but you don't need to get into the code to run the defaults.

Dataflow SQL

Now that you've seen the power of setting up a Dataflow, imagine doing it purely in SQL, using the same concepts we have used for querying and joining in BigQuery. Dataflow SQL became generally available in May 2020, and it's already heralded a new world for constructing data processing pipelines. (Credit where credit is due, of course. Google Cloud Dataflow is only possible because of the joint development of Apache Beam SQL.)

Beam SQL sits on top of Beam Java to allow SQL queries to become PTransforms for the Java runner. When using Apache Beam Java directly, you can use both SQL PTransforms and regular PTransforms interchangeably. This also means that you might be able to upgrade some of your existing pipelines with SQL where appropriate.

Key Concept Extensions

Beam SQL uses two dialects of SQL. One, Calcite SQL is a variant of the Apache Calcite dialect. While it's the default Beam SQL dialect, we won't be using it here since our primary focus is BigQuery. The other dialect, ZetaSQL, is a language that was created at Google and open source in 2019. We'll use it here since it is in fact the same SQL dialect used by BigQuery.

If you used BigQuery at its inception, you may recall that there was a second dialect of SQL there too, now called Legacy SQL. We don't use BigQuery Legacy SQL anywhere in this book since it is no longer recommended by Google. I call this out to indicate that ZetaSQL may not be the predominant language extension even a few years after this book goes to print. This area of data processing is changing rapidly, and many people are contributing to repos to explore and standardize this. Hopefully this makes clear why I try to focus on the underlying concepts and their practical application to business. The concepts don't change: Euler invented graph theory in the 18th century, and it's just as applicable today. Edgar F. Codd codified relational algebra in 1970, but the underpinnings go back much further. Don't sweat it—if you need to learn EtaSQL or ThetaSQL, so be it. That being said, Google has a decent track record at keeping their standards supported,[1] and the goal of ZetaSQL—to unify the SQL dialect used across Google Cloud—is a good point in favor of its longevity.

The following are some additional terms you need to understand Beam SQL.

SqlTransform

The SqlTransform extends the PTransform class and defines transforms that are generated from SQL queries. (Beam allows you to initialize the runner with either Calcite SQL or ZetaSQL by default; as in the preceding text, we'll use ZetaSQL.)

---

[1] I said their standards, not their products.

Row

A row is an object representing a SQL-specific element, namely, the row of a table. Rather than using the table nomenclature, the Java implementation appropriately uses the collection PCollection<Row> to represent a database table.

Dataflow SQL Extensions

In order for Dataflow SQL to have the expressiveness required to handle external data sources and processing pipelines, a few extensions to standard SQL are required. This is where the ZetaSQL dialect comes in. Its analyzer and parser have the extra keywords required to define SQL statements that can be converted into Apache Beam's PTransforms.

Inputs and Outputs

Currently, Dataflow SQL can accept inputs from three GCP services: BigQuery itself, Cloud Storage, and Pub/Sub. It can supply outputs to two of those: BigQuery and Pub/Sub. You do accept a reduction in customization from working in Dataflow SQL. However, since Pub/Sub is so widely used as an asynchronous mechanism outside of data processing and Google Cloud Storage is an easy destination to integrate with file-based systems, you can shift the burden of data collation to outside of the pipeline itself. (In Chapter 11, we'll talk about doing data transformation using Google Cloud Functions. You could just as easily have a Cloud Function pipe its results to a Pub/Sub queue, which would then attach to a Dataflow job.)

Formatting

Constructing pipelines in Dataflow SQL entails some specific formatting restrictions. At this time, messages arriving from Pub/Sub queues must be JSON-formatted. Avro support should be available by the time you read this. They must also be configured as a data source in BigQuery, and they must have schemas that are compatible with BigQuery. These restrictions make sense—even if you were writing your own pipeline in Java or Python, you have to match a BigQuery schema to insert data anyway.

Windowing

Recall that Dataflow is designed to work as easily with bounded data sources as with streaming (unbounded) sources. If you are using an unbounded data source like a Pub/Sub queue, you can't simply use a key—the key may keep recurring in the incoming dataset, and you will never have a completely materialized "table" to work with. The solution to this is windowing. Windowing uses the timestamp of the incoming data as a key to logically divide the data into different durations. The elements in these data windows comprise the aggregation that is used as the input PCollection to the pipeline. This mechanism continues for the lifetime of the job.

There are two other methods of dividing unbounded datasets, known as watermarks and triggers. Neither is currently supported in Dataflow SQL. For more information, you can learn more about streaming pipelines at `https://cloud.google.com/dataflow/docs/concepts/streaming-pipelines`.

Types of Windows

What are tumble, hop, and session? There is no relationship to rabbits; I am instead referring to the various names for the window types used by Google Dataflow. (If you look these up in Beam, they will be referred to as fixed, sliding, and session windows.) You may want to be familiar with these so you can control the aggregation behavior of your SQL-based pipelines.

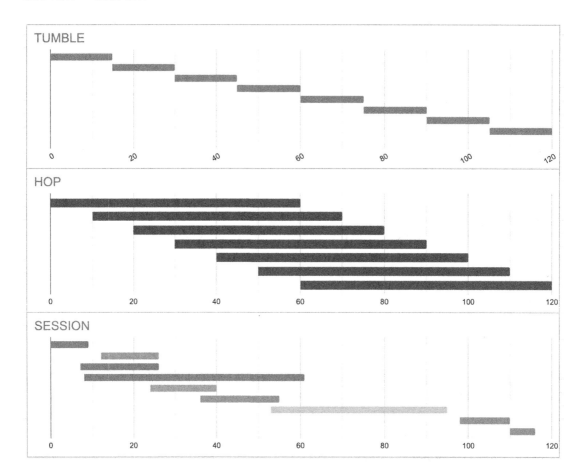

Figure 7-11. *windowing types*

Tumble

A tumble is a fixed interval that does not overlap with other windows. If you specify a tumble of 15 seconds, this means data will be aggregated every 15 seconds, in 15-second increments.

Pick an interval that gives you the best compromise between latency and cost. If users are only looking at the data on an hourly basis, there's no need to run it with second-level frequency. On the other hand, if you're receiving data constantly and need to immediately process and forward it, set a small interval.

Hop

Hop defines a fixed interval, but it may overlap with other windows. For example, you may want to see a minute worth of data, but you want it to roll a new minute window every ten seconds (i.e., 0:00–1:00, 0:10–1:10, 0:20–1:20, etc.).

This is useful for times when you want to be able to generate rolling averages over time. You may need a minute's worth of data to do the processing, but you want to see an update every ten seconds.

Session

A session will collect data until a certain amount of time elapses with no data. Unlike tumble and hop, a session will also assign a new window to each data key.

The best use case for sessions is—unsurprisingly—user session data. If you are capturing user activity on a real-time basis, you want to continue to aggregate over that key (the session or user ID) until the user stops the activity. Then you can take the entire activity's data and process it as one window. All you need to do is define the amount of time a key's activity is idle before it is released.

Remember, if you are joining tables, you *must* ensure their windows are compatible. Data must be aggregated from all of the streaming data sources with the same frequency and timing.

Creating a Dataflow SQL Pipeline

And now, the fun part. Let's see where you do this. The most interesting part of all of this is that you will literally not need to write a single line of code. You can make a SQL pipeline without knowing anything about PTransforms or DoFns or any such thing.

In fact, to create a Dataflow SQL pipeline, you don't even need to go into the Dataflow console itself. The Dataflow mode is set up through the BigQuery UI. Once you create a job, you'll be able to watch its deployment and progress through the Dataflow UI.

Accordingly, go back to our old friend, the BigQuery console. From there, open a new query, and click "More" ➤ "Query Settings." You'll see an option to select the query engine.

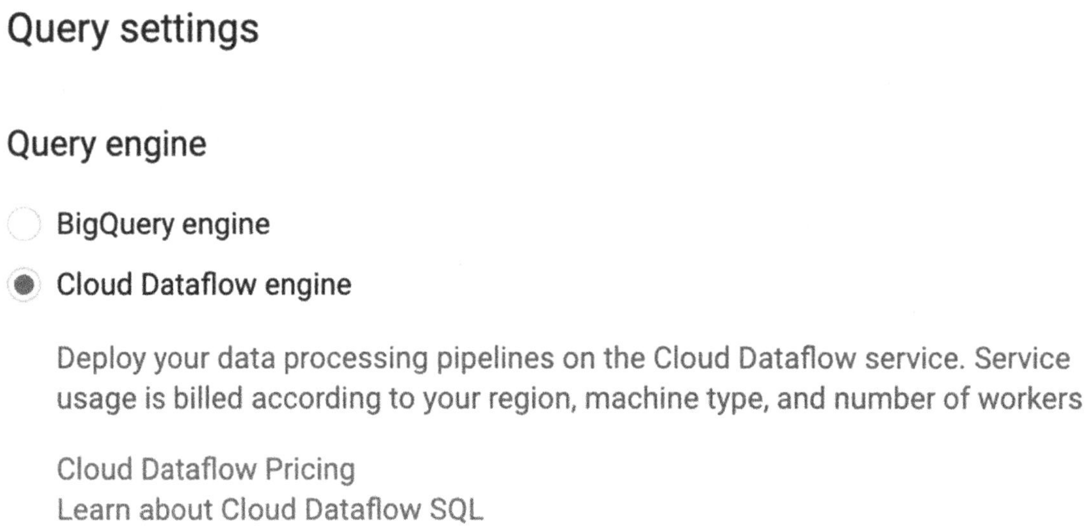

Query settings

Query engine

○ **BigQuery engine**

● **Cloud Dataflow engine**

Deploy your data processing pipelines on the Cloud Dataflow service. Service usage is billed according to your region, machine type, and number of workers

Cloud Dataflow Pricing
Learn about Cloud Dataflow SQL

Figure 7-12.

Select Cloud Dataflow engine and click Save. Now, instead of running on BigQuery, you will see that the tag "Cloud Dataflow engine" has appeared and query execution has been replaced with "Create Cloud Dataflow job."

In order to add sources from Dataflow, click "+ Add Data" next to Resources and click "Cloud Dataflow Sources." This will bring up a window from which you can automatically search your project for valid Pub/Sub or Cloud Storage sources. (You can actually configure a Dataflow job from the Pub/Sub console as well with "Create Subscription." This will allow you to choose a template from a list of supported Google Cloud operations.)

Once you select the source you want, a "Cloud Dataflow resources" section will appear in the Resources hierarchy with your topic below. The last thing to do is to configure the schema for incoming messages. Only JSON is supported right now, and the JSON must contain an "event_timestamp" field of type TIMESTAMP. (The UI actually lets you delete this required field. Don't do that.)

Supply the schema in which you expect messages to arrive from the topic. This schema definition is the same as for BigQuery tables, so you can also "edit as text" and paste in the schema from one of your existing tables.

Now that that's done, you're free to use this streaming data source as if it were a regular table in BigQuery, plus the addition of a windowing aggregate if you want one. That's it! No Java, no Python, and no PCollections or PTransforms, just (almost) plain old SQL.

Having finished setting up the new data source, you can now write queries against it, using both the streaming Pub/Sub and the existing BigQuery table. Doing this, you might end up with a query like

```
SELECT TUMBLE_START('INTERVAL 1 MINUTE') interval,
  t.Name, SUM(Price) TotalSales
FROM bigquery.table.`{PROJECT}`.{DATASET}.Products t
INNER JOIN pubsub.topic.`{PROJECT}`.`NewSales` d
USING(SKU)
GROUP BY
  TUMBLE(d.event_timestamp, 'INTERVAL 1 MINUTE'), Name
```

This query, when converted to a Dataflow job, will collect the live sales from a Pub/Sub and then join to an existing BigQuery table to get the name and total sales of that item automatically. You can then pipe the result anywhere else you like.

Note the additional prefix of "bigquery.table." required to reach the table from Dataflow. Even though you're in the BigQuery UI, you're using the Dataflow SQL engine, and the syntax is a little different. (None of the "tumble" stuff would work in BigQuery SQL either.)

Deploying Your Dataflow SQL Job

Now that you have written your query, it's time to convert it into a Dataflow pipeline. This means GCP will be handling the underlying Java runner, creating a SqlTransform object from your query, generating the pipeline, and deploying it to the Cloud Dataflow runner. You don't have to do any of this manually, but aren't you glad you know how much work that would have been?

When you click "Create Cloud Dataflow job," you will have to go through a bit more ceremony than your average five-line SQL query requires. Let's walk through the options available to us, since we no longer have access to the underlying code in which to write them ourselves. (These parameters are available in Java/Python jobs as configurations too.)

Name and Region

Choose a descriptive name that is unique among your running jobs. This is the job name you'll see in the Dataflow console, so pick something you'll be able to recognize.

Dataflow pipelines run by default in the us-central1 region. You can modify the zone in which your underlying worker instances will run. You may need to control this for compliance reasons but otherwise can leave it alone.

Max Workers

This is the number of Google Compute Engines the pipeline will use. You can prioritize cost over time or leave allocation for other, higher-priority jobs by changing this number.

Worker Region/Zone

As mentioned earlier, you can actually specify that the Google Compute Engine VMs use a different region than the job is using. You can further specify the zone they will operate in within that region. Google recommends not setting the zone, as they can more efficiently optimize the job by choosing the zone themselves.

Service Account Email

The service account is the security principal used for the execution of the job. (It's like a username for robots.) GCP will generally create a new service account when one is needed, but if you have one with permissions or security that you need, you can specify it directly.

Machine Type

Since Dataflow jobs are building and tearing down virtual machines on the fly, you can specify what kind of virtual machine you want to be used as a worker.

Network Configurations

With these configurations, you can assign the network and subnetwork you want the virtual machines assigned to. If you have protected resources in a certain network needed for the job to run, you will want the VMs to run in that network as well. You can also specify whether the virtual machines will have public or internal IPs. Note that some runners (like Python) actually need Internet access in order to reach their package repositories upon spin-up, so you might not want to touch this. If you want the machines to have both internal IPs and limited Internet access, you will have to perform all the NATing yourself—contact an experienced cloud engineer!

Destination

This section is how you specify where you would like the results of the job to go. As referenced earlier, the two options are Pub/Sub and BigQuery. Selecting either of these will open up the required options to select/create either a Pub/Sub topic or a BigQuery dataset table.

Note also that you can check the box marked "Additional Output" and specify a second output for the job. This gives you the ability to store your results in a BigQuery table and also to send the results to a Pub/Sub, which you could then connect to another pipeline or a Cloud Function or anything else!

Creating the Job

After you click "Create," GCP will get to work. It can take a couple minutes for it to prepare everything, but you'll be able to see it in the BigQuery UI, the Dataflow UI, and the Pub/Sub UI (if applicable). Dataflow will follow the same steps that you did when you deployed the Python pipeline. Once it has done this, the workflow graph will appear in the UI, and you will be able to track metrics and CPU utilization. This job will run until you manually stop it.

And there you have it! You now have everything you need to do real-time processing on massive, unbounded datasets without needing to do any manual administration whatsoever. Now go out there and get the rest of your organization's data into BigQuery.

One final note: This is where things can start getting expensive. Running a continuous streaming job from Pub/Sub to BigQuery involves having Google Compute Engine VMs running constantly, plus the cost of BigQuery, Pub/Sub, and Dataflow themselves. Batch jobs can be relatively cheap, but streaming will incur charge for as long as you have the pipeline up and running. Don't let this deter you, but if you are running intensive processing on large amounts of data, keep an eye on your bill.

Summary

Google Dataflow is a powerful data processing technology built on Apache Beam, an open source project originally incubated at Google. Dataflow allows you to write massively parallelized load and transformation jobs easily and deploy them scalably to Google Cloud. Although originally Dataflow and Beam supported only procedural languages like Java, Python, and Go, they recently introduced Dataflow SQL, which allows you to write your transformations in pure SQL. Regardless of the method you choose, building your own Dataflow jobs can allow you to quickly and reliably process huge amounts of data into BigQuery.

PART III

Using the Warehouse

## CHAPTER 8

Care and Feeding of Your Warehouse

We've come a long way. In Part 1, we covered all the logistics of preparing both your organization and data for the transformation necessary to increase your data maturity. In Part 2, we've discussed a staggeringly wide range of options to migrate, load, or stream your data into your provisioned data warehouse. In Part 3, we'll discuss all of the ways in which you can use your data warehouse to grow your organizational data maturity.

The success of your warehouse project depends very much on understanding the cost, speed, and resiliency of your solutions. While BigQuery and other modern technologies allow you to get off the ground relatively quickly, they don't do the work of building either your data culture or consensus among your stakeholders. In fact, a secret silver lining of longer projects is that they give more calendar time for other activities to occur. In the weeks or months required to requisition hardware from your IT department and get it racked and stacked, secured, approved by compliance, and so on, you would have time to draft a comprehensive charter and conduct as many conversations as you needed. Executives, seeing the eye-popping price tag, would at least vaguely understand the priority of the project. These aren't actually advantages, but the lengthy timeline could obfuscate all kinds of issues caused by poor planning. Projects like that fail because after a certain amount of time and money have been spent (usually way, way too much) with no results, someone pulls the plug.

Another double-edged sword is that with BigQuery, you can get away without ever "launching" officially. You can just begin to accumulate and analyze data in small pieces, gradually building power but never making a splash. This will create a sort of data "gray" market, where information about your project spreads unevenly across the organization and yields inconsistent or incomplete insight. You're effectively letting other people tell your story. People who understand the value of what you've done will flock to you. Those who don't get it will dismiss your efforts as "yet another attempt to fix reporting."

© Mark Mucchetti 2020
M. Mucchetti, *BigQuery for Data Warehousing*, https://doi.org/10.1007/978-1-4842-6186-6_8

To avoid that, continue to follow discrete phases in your plan and communicate frequently about what you officially support and what datasets are currently available. This also means guarding the perimeter if someone asks for data that you haven't formally ingested yet. The effects of incorrectly onboarding data and reporting on it can be catastrophic: one major issue with accuracy caused by misinterpretation or misreporting of data will be difficult to recover from when the project is in its infancy. We are all fans of iterative development and continually proving ever-increasing value. Do that. But also, package the highlights up and get feedback from stakeholders on a regular cadence.

Google BigQuery can do nothing to mitigate poor planning. If anything, it accelerates problems because you will be forced to confront them so quickly. You can no more embark on a project of this magnitude without careful preparation than you could before. The good news is following a charter, getting the necessary buy-in, and making the warehouse useful are the hardest steps in the process. Once momentum has been established, your data warehouse will seem like a natural destination for all data. Engineers will appreciate that they don't have to think about custom logging and storage requirements for every project they do. Once stakeholders trust the data, they won't even bother going to engineering to get "the real answer" either. And as you repeatedly prove out the power and insight that a functioning warehouse is generating, the organization will begin responding to insights. Better decisions will be made. People will have less arguments because they can point at the real information. Departments will want to hire data scientists—and data scientists will want to work for your organization, because they have the tools they need to do their jobs.

Looking Back and Looking Forward

First, let's review some success criteria for the initial launch of your data warehouse:

- Project charter created and signed off

- Meetings with key stakeholders concluded and core data models constructed

- Historical data pre-populated where applicable

- Ongoing data flows redirected or created to load to BigQuery

- Line of sight to creation and automation of currently manual business processes

- Formal launch and release to stakeholders

If you've completed all of these steps, then your data warehouse build project was a success. If that's all there was—an initial launch—the book could end right here. (And certainly, any consultants who helped you generate and build the data model could probably roll off the project here too.) However, as a data custodian, you now have the challenge of making the project continually useful to its users, understanding their needs, and mitigating their frustrations.

The key here is retaining momentum. The temptation will always be to categorize this as "just a project" that is now complete. Rather, think of the data warehouse as a continually evolving program that needs your support and the support of others in your organization to keep it healthy and relevant. This program goes beyond BigQuery too; eventually, a new technology will come along to fill this same niche. If you have been steadily improving the program over time, that leap won't seem quite as daunting.

You can now shift your focus to the day to day, which is actually a clue for constructing the near future. When you get reporting, data, or other requests, ask yourself the following questions:

- Is this a request that needed me to handle it, or could it have been self-serviced?

- If it could not have been self-serviced, was the reason a knowledge gap or a technical gap?

  - If it was a technical gap, is it something I might reasonably have anticipated when designing the warehouse?

  - If it was a knowledge gap, was the requestor open to receiving that knowledge?

- Is this request likely to come only once, or will I get it again?

- If I get it again, will it be completely identical or just similar?

- How many different ways have I received a request like this one? How many different ways have I received a request like this from the same person or group of people?

- How will the requestor know I have fulfilled this request?

- How will the requestor receive the results of this request?

It's easy to get wrapped up in the day-to-day routine and not take the extra few minutes to determine if there is a way to systematize the patterns you're seeing. These questions can help triage whether your warehouse has any fundamental issues, as well as how your users are acclimating to having a data warehouse.

If you already had a warehouse and have launched the new-and-improved version, here are a few additional questions:

- Am I getting the same requests now as I got before?

- For requests which I got before, what can I do now that I couldn't do then? (Speed of turnaround, age of data, method of presentation, etc.)

- For new requests, are people specifying that they want them from the new system? Are they specifying that they want them from the old system?

- Am I hearing comparative statements about the two systems? What kinds of statements? ("Well, before I could...", "I couldn't do this last week!", "This was so much easier!", "This didn't seem to have changed things at all.")

In these questions, you are looking for a qualitative signal of adoption rate and whether users understand and want to use the new system. If they don't, that doesn't necessarily mean something is wrong with it. It just gives you a clue that you may need to conduct some training or recommunicate the aims of the project.

The Retrospective

While you should be in contact with your primary business stakeholders as you are building out the data warehouse and following a project plan, you should also conduct a formal retrospective at the conclusion of the project. This has several well-known side effects, but primarily it indicates to the cross-functional team that this phase (construction and loading) is over. It reopens the conversation about what kinds of resources and time need to be allocated to go forward, and it allows for some time to breathe and take stock of the current situation.

Organizations often forgo retrospectives when they are intent on moving into the next phase, when projects never have a stated completion date, or based on a sense that looking back is bad business. *Dwelling* in the past, or accepting its limitations, is bad business. Learning from the past and using its lessons to improve the next iteration is a worthy expenditure of time.

You should conduct a retrospective no more than two weeks after you have declared the launch of the warehouse. Broaden the circle somewhat; include anyone who gave you feedback on designs that informed your schemas, as well as any business stakeholder who helped explain a process that the warehouse has automated. Also, include people even if you think they may say primarily negative things (be they warranted or not). Those people may surprise you, but even if not, your other stakeholders will see your commitment to improvement.

If you're unfamiliar with the format of a retrospective, there are many methods and many schools of thought. As an agile practitioner, I tend to conduct them with the three simple questions:

- What went well?

- What didn't go well?

- What can we improve next time?

This will give you a pretty good idea of common areas of feedback, as multiple stakeholders will align and say similar things. You can solicit feedback anonymously as well, but unless your group is especially contentious or reserved, that's probably not necessary.

Remember way back in Chapter 2 when I suggested that you might partner with a project manager or committed executive sponsor? Did you forget about them while you were heads down building models and imports? Now's a great time to reengage and ask for feedback on how you might best conduct this process.

Also, those stakeholders you interviewed back then are now your first users. They were critical to getting your project funded, and now they will be critical to its ongoing success. More on that...

A Story About Productionalization

Here's a story about my own experience with production launches. Since you have reached this point in your project, you may find it helpful.

The first platform I launched at scale was as a software engineer in the data center days. My team spent weeks agonizing over how many servers we would need to run the workload. We calculated mean scale, peak scale, growth over time, and whether we could afford it. We optimized code tirelessly to ensure the servers wouldn't buckle under high load. We managed the load on our single, monolithic SQL database. And in the end, we were successful. We all had a solid grasp on the performance characteristics of the application and knew what it would take to support it.

In contrast, a few years ago, I had the privilege and rare opportunity to build a high-traffic, high-revenue platform from scratch. I had a group of extremely talented engineers; however, many of them were early in their careers, and this was their first platform at scale. We had been experimenting with serverless technology on both Amazon Web Services and Google Cloud Platform and made the decision to build the back end entirely serverless.

Most of the benefits I've described in this book came to fruition. We didn't worry about how we'd scale or how many servers we'd need. We didn't have to think about queues running out of memory or figuring out how to fail over critical infrastructure. The build pipeline was almost too easy. It was hard work, but it seemed like a vision of the future. Then, the users arrived.

When we launched the platform, every quality issue was magnified by scale. For every issue we observed, we had hundreds of user reports. If we experienced a database issue for a few minutes, then thousands of rows were affected. We couldn't triage problems manually because while the platform scaled, *nothing else could*. It's not an option to horizontally scale engineers and QA analysts to look at bug reports (at least, not on this timescale). You can't read 100× more emails or tickets, even if they're all variations on a theme. If you apply a change to fix an issue and it makes it worse, you can't go case by case and resolve. The software scaled up to handle demand without a hitch. But the people didn't.

In my fascination with the utter ease of serverless architecture, I neglected to notice that all of the steps I'd done pre-cloud had served a purpose. In those days, calculating software scale meant understanding all of the other moving parts that were not software. Even if a product could somehow be bug-free, users would need training and to ask questions. Discovering answers to those questions also informs you about the support structures you'll need around the software.

I knew all of these things, but my teams hadn't needed to go through the exercise. When we abruptly stopped being architects and designers and became maintainers and operators, we weren't prepared for the transition. An application in production has very different characteristics than one in development, and serverless technology allowed us to forget about that, rather than to encounter it as a by-product of the design.

I relate this as a richer explanation of what I mean when I say that "your stakeholders have become users." In constructing the data warehouse, you could easily sidestep concerns about how many users you'll have, what they need, and how quickly they need it. They wouldn't come up in your design as a technical decision to be made: the warehouse will be fine no matter what you throw at it. Conversely, if no one ever uses it, it won't burn money. There's negligible risk on either side of the calculation. Nevertheless, the success of your project will still be based on scale. It will be dependent on how well you meet your users' needs.

The Roadmap

The retrospective should have given you a good sense of the general perception of the project. This information is helpful twice, at face value and directionally. At face value, you receive concrete feedback on things that might have gone better and your next area of focus. Directionally, you get a sense of where you can improve communication and things you may have done that didn't land as expected.

In order to keep the program going, you will have to both operate and improve the data warehouse. Many books have been written about backlog prioritization and conducting programs over time, so I'm not going to focus on the nuts and bolts. Instead, let's go over the types of things to plan for.

Most of what drives the long-term change in your data management strategy will be driven by business goals and objectives. Part 5 is all about long-term change, keeping your strategy relevant to the business, and how feedback loops will resonate so that your data management helps to inform the strategy (more on that later). On the first day your warehouse is open for business, you probably won't have that insight. Coupled with the natural evolution of business markets and your own organization's rate of change, focus your roadmap initiatives on the areas that make sense.

If all goes well, you can expect to see new insights from the warehouse change organizational thinking around potentially long-held beliefs. A statistic someone once generated by hand several years prior may be what everyone has been carrying around in their heads since then. Suddenly having access to real-time updates will be jarring at first.

Production Defects

Hopefully, you caught any major issues with the warehouse—especially issues affecting data integrity—before you launched. But if not, your prioritization will have to carry some capacity for issue remediation. These aren't roadmap initiatives; they're just part of daily operation. However, you can ask yourself the same questions about defects as for new requests. Repeated defects in the same area or defects that hint at underlying design issues may actually be a sign that additional systemization is needed. Defect reporting in a certain pattern could indicate hidden technical debt or a need for additional system work.

The most important question here is to ask yourself (honestly) if the defect represented something you could have reasonably prevented during construction. If so, the issue may not be failure to systematize; it may be an actual quality control issue somewhere in the process. That happens too, but the approach to resolution would differ.

Regardless of whether it is a quality issue or a series of unforeseen circumstances, strive to correct severe defects as quickly as possible. At this stage of development, everything is under test. Your response will determine users' reactions to you, your team, the project, and even the underlying technology. I can't tell you how many times I've gone into a design meeting without context and said that it seems like [Product] would be an easy solve to the problem. At that point, someone scoffs and says [Product] is terrible. My reply: "Is [Product] terrible, or did someone do a bad implementation of it?" It's always a red flag to lambast a common technology, even if you don't like it. It would be hard to defend a blanket argument that BigQuery is just a "bad" technology, no matter how you personally feel. Unfortunately, non-technical users are apt to just do word association, and failure to correct defects could result in a lot of additional friction that isn't truly warranted.

Technical/Architectural Debt

Most projects incur technical debt. Usually this debt is incurred at an increasing rate as the project approaches its deadline. Technical debt is a value-neutral term. Intentionally taking on debt to launch a minimum viable product on time is not inherently a bad thing. However, you must be careful to log it and leave room on your post-launch timeline to mitigate or resolve it. Take on technical debt strategically in areas that aren't critical for a first launch. If it took four hours to run your previous reporting suite every night and it now takes 30 minutes, don't sacrifice other important launch criteria to get it down to 20, even though you know it could be 20. You can't merge onto the highway if the car never makes it out of the driveway. Make sure the car can start before you try to increase its top speed.

Why are production defects separate from technical debt? This is a bit nitpicky and not everyone agrees, but I believe that technical debt is the result of a choice. In order to launch the project on time and/or on budget, you accept some inefficiency in one or more non-functional characteristics. So to be more precise, bugs are only technical debt if you knew about them and left them there on purpose. And why would you do that? I might leave a bug and classify it as debt if it were unreachable. Let's say I cut scope and decided not to log a certain type of event. If there were a bug in that logging code, I'd classify that bug as part of the debt. That's the difference: you can plan which debt remediation you want in your roadmap, but not bugs. You can leave capacity for bugs, but by definition, you don't know what specific bugs those would be.

This distinction is relevant specifically because it allows you to go back and clean things up without losing efficiency to the amorphous black hole of "fixing bugs."

Maintenance

This bucket used to be a lot bigger when server drive space and memory was an issue. There were OS and database patches to perform and indexes to defragment. While some of the work associated with periodic maintenance is now handled automatically by Google, there is still plenty of change to account for.

External integrations update their API frameworks. Some integrations are deprecated. The business may replace one accounting vendor with another. You may have to change how certain tables are partitioned to account for a sudden rise in volume. Not everything in this bucket will rise to the level of roadmap consideration, but plan for those that do.

Scope That Was Cut

In addition to the non-functional pieces you incurred as debt, there are probably a few functional pieces that didn't make it either. These likely represented use cases that stakeholders weren't especially concerned about or features that blocked on other teams or issues. Maybe you wanted users to switch to using Google Sheets for data and they wouldn't or couldn't, so you deprioritized that flow. Or a particular department was pushing really hard for a certain dataset, but their priority changed midstream and now they no longer need it.

Whatever the reason was, it's a good time to go back and look at scope that was shed to hit the first release. Don't automatically drop it back on the roadmap; evaluate if it is still necessary. If it is, you may have already learned a better way to do it. Take the opportunity to rescope it if you need to.

This also gets back to the earlier point about having a defined launch date and marking the phase completed. As you approach launch date, stakeholders will begin to throw words around like "phase 2" and "fast follow." These have the effect of endangering the launch or engendering a sentiment that even though it launched, the project was not done. Of course the project is not done—it's a program that you will be operating in perpetuity. The purpose of creating the charter and getting broad consensus is so that everyone can agree on what the project comprises. Phase 2 should not be a wish list of things that weren't valuable enough for phase 1. The same prioritization system should apply, so that you can continue to target your effort where most needed.

Systemization

It is said that the mark of a good architect is that they see a better way to build a system as soon as it's finished. Alas, there is no Totally Average Tower of Pisa. You don't often get the resources to do it a second time. One advantage that you have over architects of buildings is that you can restructure major pieces of a system while in operation. This is where asking those questions about incoming requests comes in handy. You will see patterns in the requests that tell you what would benefit from greater systemization.

These may be phrased as complaints ("Why does this report take so long to run?") or as hopeful requests ("This is so much better than before, but I'd love if..."). Your most valuable users will see the pattern themselves and preemptively inform you ("I've requested variants on this three times in the last two weeks. Maybe we could..."). No matter how it arrives, this feedback will help you lower your operational workload. That gain in efficiency will leave you free time to plan the final type of things for your road map, which is...

Optimistic Extensibility

I use a term of my own coinage, "optimistic extensibility," to refer to the process of reasonably predicting likely enhancements and creating empty shells for them. One of the best things you can do to set yourself up for enduring success is to create new extensibility points to anticipate things which do not yet exist. This is the class of work that allows the leap to the next plateau of complexity. When the successor to BigQuery comes out and you find compelling value in piloting it, this is the work that will show you the path there.

Some of this is abstraction work. If you are building a data pipeline to a destination and it seems likely that the same data will need a second destination in the future, take the time to add the layer of abstraction so that you can target multiple destinations. When that destination inevitably comes along, you won't have to write an entirely new pipeline to target two destinations (and then three destinations and so on). I'm not saying to add complexity for the sake of non-existent use cases: just watch out for unnecessary coupling and smooth the path to the obvious next steps.

Incidentally, this work also makes great candidates for "cut scope," so if you were already thinking along these lines in phase 1, you may have trimmed some of these extensibility points. You made the right call—they weren't necessary yet.

This work could also be R&D. If BigQuery has a feature in alpha that you'd like to use, you can do the work to prepare it and wait until it becomes generally available to launch it. The details of the feature may change, but if the concept was good, then you'll be able to use it as soon as you deem ready.

As I described, this doesn't mean necessarily building a feature. To go back to the analogy in physical architecture, suppose you've just built a house. The land adjacent to the house becomes available for sale, and you have the money, so you buy it. You might go so far as to commission some blueprints to make sure that a pool would fit on the lot. It does not mean building the pool. The land is your extensibility point, and you are optimistic that you will build on it in the future. You've made a good decision to keep that option open for when you're ready.

As Donald Knuth said, premature optimization may be the root of all evil, but preparation is not optimization. Try to find a balance between looking to the future and doing work that you'll never be able to use.

Prioritization

This is all up to you. It may take a few weeks or months of warehouse operation to collect items from all of these areas, but when you do, you'll have plenty of options for where to go next. Prioritization is not an easy exercise, but it's impossible without the prerequisite of having things to prioritize.

As your business grows and changes around you, your roadmap will come to be dominated by business-driven initiatives. That's good. Those who are tasked with developing the business will be able to suggest things that add more value than you are able to do alone. You can still perform systemization on those initiatives to understand whether there is a deeper need. You can also use this information to develop the next tranche of optimistic extensibility. Finally, you can use these relationships to develop a feedback loop: your data improves the strategy as much as the strategy drives the data collection.

Push-Pull Strategy

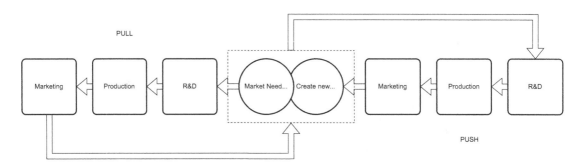

Figure 8-1. *Technology push vs. market pull. See Creative Commons (https://commons.wikimedia.org/wiki/File:Technology-Push_Market-Pull.png) for reference, CC BY-SA 3.0*

The push-pull strategy originated in supply chain management as a way to plan production against demand. Based on the type of good you sell, you can use push, pull, or a combination of the two to satisfy the market need for your good. In brief

- **Push-based supply chains** use forecasting to approximate the demand for the good and then produce and push that product to market. This works with goods with relatively static demand variance, like toothbrushes or (usually) toilet paper, and high economy of scale. People are going to buy about the same amount all the time, and it's not cost-effective to make toothbrushes to order.

- **Pull-based supply chains** wait for an input from a consumer before making or delivering the product. This works with goods with variable demand variance and reasonable tolerance for latency, such as jewelry.

- **Push-pull supply chains** use a combination of the two techniques. This works when a good is made upon request, but the raw materials or component parts can be pushed ahead of time. Think of a full-service restaurant: your salad isn't made until you order it, but the lettuce is already on hand.

It also appears in marketing in a similar fashion, but the product in this case is advertising. Push advertising is direct mail campaigns, email blasts, and so on, where you reach out directly to a potential consumer. Pull advertising could be a partnership with a related brand, where interested customers hear about your product and go to your website to buy it.

Software engineers deal with these strategies as part of agile development processes. The Kanban methodology, which also originated in supply chain logistics, is an example of a pull process because engineers pull from the stack of available tickets and there is a limit to work in progress.

I'm not aware of anyone consciously using this methodology on a data warehouse, but I have applied it to all manner of core product development processes, and I think it's equally applicable here.

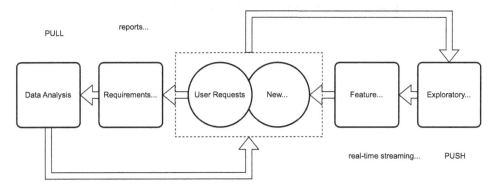

Figure 8-2. *Proposal to apply this strategy to data warehouse planning, more built out than this model. Warehouse users ➤ Data warehouse ➤ Data analysts*

As laid out in Figure 8-2, the reasoning goes like this. Your users have data and reporting needs, which they pull from the warehouse and which you are able to "make to order." A traditional reporting suite fills this role. In contrast, you push newer and better ways of accessing data to your users—dashboards, real-time analysis, machine learning, and other things that your users haven't asked for yet. Each side of the model complements the other, and a feedback loop of ever-improving insight is formed.

I have no doubt that a similar model is in use in many organizations already, even if this isn't the terminology they use. The advantage of carrying over this model is that it informs the formalization of roles and responsibilities. It frees the owners of the data function to contribute as much to the shared ownership of the product as the users requesting results and features.

In summary, as you receive incoming requests and systematize them into patterns, you then push these improved systems back to your consumers, who then derive even better patterns.

Data Customers

My stress on the non-technical aspects of the data warehouse underlines its core importance to the organization. Even if it sits off in the corner of the chief architect's systems diagram, it will play a central role to the business. This centrality means that the data warehouse is truly a product of your organization, and products need marketing. You're not going to put up a billboard advertising your company's data warehouse, as Figure 8-3 facetiously suggests, but the insights that it will produce will really be that important.

Figure 8-3. *A billboard advertising a data warehouse. This just illustrates a joke*

You very well **may** see a tech company's billboard that cites a statistic about how many users use their platform or how much money they've saved or something that illustrates a key performance indicator (KPI) of that particular business. Where do you think the information for the billboard came from?

Another common technique in product management is the development and study of "personas." A persona represents the profile of an average customer of your product. You can break your target market down into several personas, each of which represents the characteristics and motivations of a segment of potential customers.

There's no compelling reason to do this as a formal exercise for your data warehouse (unless you want to), but framing potential data "customers" in this way can be another useful way to build relationships and understand how to truly add value.

There's a meta-layer on this, which is that by prioritizing data projects that produce insights that drive larger amounts of revenue, you can affect the targeting of your organization's *actual* users. That is to say that if some of your users are generating more revenue based on the data you can provide, they are more valuable customers to you too.

Every business will be different, and in a small one you might as well name your personas "Ana," "Brit," and "Nick" after your users, because there are literally only three of them. My point is that the symbiosis between product builders and users is critical to its success. This tenet is easy to overlook for something abstract like a data warehouse.

Personas often have cutesy names like "Ana the Analyst" and seemingly irrelevant details like "loves pizza." I'll leave it to you to decide how much you want to try that marketer hat on. Instead, here are a couple common users of an organizational data function. How might they react to the shiny new BigQuery warehouse you just launched?

Data Analysts

Data analysts are looking for the insights they need to do their jobs effectively. They have access to advanced tools and statistics and need ways to get at the data and then to get it into their preferred method for doing analysis. BigQuery has the advantage of operating in native SQL. In addition to that, you want to make it as easy as possible for them to push their own datasets into BigQuery and to retrieve them via API, SDK, or file for use in their own analytics packages.

For data analysts who prefer R, you can use BigQuery from R using Jupyter notebooks. There is also a CRAN package called bigrquery. RStudio can also integrate directly with BigQuery, and you can even run RStudio on a Google Compute Engine instance.

In short, enable self-service as much as possible.

Engineers

Engineers will want to know how they can use BigQuery data in their applications without performance loss or substantial extra work. They will also be happy if you can solve thorny problems like where to put logs and how to retain them or how to report events needed for analytics.

The easier it is for engineers to adopt a methodology that they can easily insert into their code, the more data telemetry you will get from the running application. As we'll discuss in Chapter 12, you can also use BigQuery to assist in application performance monitoring and root cause analysis. Ideally, you will find that engineers want to log their own data to BigQuery too—just as they did at Google.

Leadership

I hesitate to paint this with a broad brush, but there are a few commonalities. Time management is a priority for executives, and they need access to their important reports and data without interruption and at any time. You may begin to see an easier or different way to do things, but be wary of changing a methodology without a lot of preparation.

Senior leadership is perfectly capable of adapting and learning new methods (how do you think they got there?), but the cognitive load of learning a new way to do an important thing must be calculated carefully. If they're used to seeing a revenue number in the upper-left corner of their daily report, don't just change it. Don't push value to them expecting that they'll be happy about it, even if they recognize that value. This isn't a skill set thing; it's all about time management.

Many decisions executives make based on data are extremely time-sensitive, and they only have one window in which to look at all the data, evaluate, and make a decision. Most leaders in that circumstance will make the best decision they can with the data at hand, and if it is poor quality or seems wrong, they will make their best judgment. But they will not be happy about having to do that!

Most leaders prize and welcome innovation and will see the raw value in your efforts. If you've built consensus with your leaders as part of the project charter, this will come more easily. But in any event, don't underestimate your leaders, but don't bottleneck them either.

Salespeople

Salespeople have a similar mentality, but they are laser-focused on their prospects and customers. The more data you can provide in that process, the better—they will want both self-service and their standard reporting suite.

Even better, one of your goals for a data culture should be for that data to be ambiently available wherever they need it. Sales is all about relationship management, and having data about how to do that close at hand will both help target the need and impress customers.

Salespeople are also why you should never even ask to take the system down for maintenance during business hours. All joking aside, isn't it great you don't really have to worry about that with BigQuery?

Summary

Launching your data warehouse is a major accomplishment. Now, the work is just beginning. Documenting progress to this point should be done in a retrospective process. Following that, you can construct a roadmap containing a series of priorities to continue work. Prioritization is extremely specific to your organization, but the items will come in several common types that you can mix and match appropriately. Due to the data warehouse's unique and central position in an organization's business strategy, a shared product ownership scheme can deliver the greatest amount of value to your users. The types of users your system will have will also be extremely specific to the organization, but several roles are common and can help you construct relevant user personas.

In the next chapter, it's back to SQL! We'll talk about common query patterns and how to use BigQuery SQL in a variety of ways to get value out of the warehouse you've built.

CHAPTER 9

Querying the Warehouse

You've built the whole warehouse, loaded and streamed the data, set up your workflows, and defined your warehouse's roadmap for the next several months. You probably feel pretty accomplished, and you know now what you have to do to make your data program a success. You also have a massive amount of data pouring into your system—and I'm sure you're anxious to do something with it.

In this part, we'll touch on several other Google services that will be useful to you in dealing with your data, making it accessible to your users, and defining automated tasks to limit the amount of manual work you have to do. We'll discuss scheduling, functions as a service, logging, and monitoring. Combining these additional tools with the ones you have already will free you to focus on the actual work of analyzing your data. After that, we'll go into the analytic functions.

But before we get there, let's turn our attention to all of the power you now have available in BigQuery itself. Remember the goal of your data program is ultimately to take all of this raw data, turn it into information, and productively use that information to generate insights. The hard part was getting all the data into one place to begin making "information" out of it.

In order to work effectively with BigQuery, you will need a working understanding of SQL. This means working with SQL both in the ANSI-compliant sense and the BigQuery-specific concepts that make it so powerful. In this chapter, we'll run the gamut from basic SQL concepts through querying nested columns, partitions, and many different underlying data types. Buckle up. There's a lot to talk about!

A navigation note: If you're already familiar with SQL, you can skim this chapter. For BigQuery specifically, nested data and partitions may be of interest. I've reserved advanced discussion around analytic functions for later in this text, so you can skip this chapter entirely if you are looking for that.

© Mark Mucchetti 2020
M. Mucchetti, *BigQuery for Data Warehousing*, https://doi.org/10.1007/978-1-4842-6186-6_9

BigQuery SQL

In Chapter 1, we looked at a sample SQL query and analyzed its constituent parts. For reference, that query was

```
SELECT spc_common AS species,
COUNT(*) number_of_trees,
FROM `bigquery-public-data.new_york.tree_census_2015`
WHERE spc_common != '' AND health = 'Good'
GROUP BY spc_common, health
ORDER BY number_of_trees DESC
LIMIT 10
```

Yep, still works. The big difference between Chapter 1 and now is that now you also have your own datasets to run queries against, and they're likely to be more useful to your particular business domain than tree species (unless you work for the New York City Parks and Recreation Department, in which case maybe these are also your datasets).

This query demonstrates most of the basic principles of how SQL works, but it's really only scratching the surface of the kinds of queries you're likely to write. And it doesn't even begin to touch all of the other database objects you can use to compose your queries into complicated functional units. And even then, it doesn't cover some of the tips and tricks you might use to operate on extremely large datasets. BigQuery is designed to operate up into the petabyte range. As your data gets larger and larger, you will have to start to understand what's happening behind the scenes in order to optimize and understand your query performance.

Querying Basics

As we covered in Chapter 1, a query that retrieves information from a database always has the same anatomy. You SELECT data FROM a table WHERE certain conditions are true. Everything else modifies that basic concept.

Let's revisit the other concepts from the sample query, with more information about their options. For grouping, which is far more complex and has other associated keywords, we'll cover the basics here and then go deeper in the "Aggregation" section later.

Limits

Using LIMIT and OFFSET to restrict the number of rows returned or to page through the data is a critical BigQuery concept. When your tables have billions of rows, failing to specify a limit for the data returned could result in gigabytes of results. This isn't cheap or fast. In general, always use a limit on your data unless you are returning a static value set that you know to be small.

Limits and offsets both have to be positive numbers. And unless you specify an order, the rows that will be returned are non-deterministic; it's simply the first qualifying n rows the query processor encounters.

Ordering

Applying an ORDER BY specifies the sort order in which you want to see the results. In combination with a LIMIT, the ordering is applied first, and then the results are restricted to the top n rows.

You can sort either ascending (the default) or descending, and you can sort by multiple columns using both ascending and descending.

Some examples are in Figure 9-1, to give you a sense of the options here.

Figure 9-1. *ORDER BY examples*

Note that in the last example, instead of using column names, we used numbers. This lets you sort by columns where 1 represents the first result column, 2 the second, and so on. Prefer named sorts over numbered columns, solely because if you change the number or order of the columns in the SELECT statement, the sort behavior will change too, usually unintentionally. (But for scratch queries, it does save you the trouble of retyping the column names, especially when they have been aliased or joined or you're doing a star SELECT and you don't remember the name of the column.)

BigQuery also supports choosing whether you want NULL values to appear before or after the non-NULL values. You can configure this with the parameter "NULLS FIRST" or "NULLS LAST." The default behavior is nulls come first for ASC ordering and nulls come last for DESC ordering.

Note that in BigQuery, certain data types are "unorderable." These types are STRUCT, ARRAY, and GEOGRAPHY. You'll get an error if you attempt to include columns of these types in your ORDER BY clause. This is because for the first two types, there's no top-level value to sort by; they are multivalued. For GEOGRAPHY, it is because there is no canonical ordering for spatial data types. The operation for ordering New York, Chicago, and Los Angeles by location is undefined. (You can, of course, order by distance from or to a given point, and we'll be looking at that later.)

Grouping

You will also want to group matching data together in order to perform aggregate functions on it. In the sample query, we used grouping to ensure that we only got one result per name. In the raw table, each name appears for each year. In order to find the most popular names, we needed to know, when you looked at each name, which one had the highest number across the datasets.

Typically, you use GROUP BY in conjunction with other aggregate functions in order to give you a single row calculated from multiple matches. This pattern is nearly ubiquitous in warehouse queries. You generally want to know how many or the most or the least or the average over millions of candidate rows. For example, the average response time of your website per page might look like this:

```
SELECT PageName, AVG(ResponseTime)
FROM PageLoads
GROUP BY PageName
```

This query will look at every page load and response time in the table, grouping on the key PageName and then taking all rows that match and averaging the value of the ResponseTime column. From there, you can easily apply

```
ORDER BY AVG(ResponseTime) DESC
```

to immediately show you the slowest pages on your site. Aggregate analysis is the bread and butter of reducing giant datasets into usable information.

BigQuery supports a whole load of aggregate functions, so many that we'll review them in a following separate section. For the sake of completion, there are a few straightforward ones that you'll see commonly used in most SQL implementations:

- MAX: Return the maximum value in the group.

- MIN: Return the minimum value in the group.

- SUM: Return the sum of all values in the group.

- AVG: Return the average of all values in the group.

- COUNT: Return the number of values in the group.

With a little bit of creativity, you can actually write your own aggregate functions by piggybacking on the ARRAY_AGG aggregate function. BigQuery doesn't have official support for this, but we'll talk about this sort of thing in Chapter 13.

Additional Options

There are additional clauses you can supply to SELECT that we haven't yet covered.

Star Queries

This has come up a few times, but I'll iterate it for completeness. Using the * character in a SELECT indicates that you want all of the columns from a result set.

If you use it in a single table query, that is, SELECT * FROM Table, you'll get all of the columns in Table. Using it in a query that has joins or subqueries will get you *all* columns in the combined set, that is, SELECT * FROM Table JOIN Table2... JOIN Table3... JOIN TableN will get you all columns from all the tables.

In a multi-table scenario, you can qualify the star with a table name to get all the columns for that one table:

```
SELECT A.*, B.Name FROM A JOIN B USING (Key)
```

will get you all the columns in table A, but just the Name column from table B.

As we've covered before, selecting all the columns is generally not best practice for production queries. Column restrictions are the primary way to avoid accessing (and paying for) unnecessary data. Additionally, it's quite brittle, since any change in column ordering or column renaming will break the query. It's good for exploratory data analysis when you don't remember the names of all of the columns and you want to get a sense of the data.

To get a sense of this in BigQuery, try writing the same query against a large table using a few column names and then by using *. You will see the data estimate skyrocket. For example, running the preceding trees query estimates 12.5 MB of processing; the same query with * is 223.1 MB.[1]

EXCEPT

The EXCEPT modifier allows you to use the SELECT *, but exclude specific columns from the result set. At least in BigQuery, this is useful for seeing query results in a more compact way by excluding nested columns that can make it hard to read.

REPLACE

The REPLACE keyword allows you to do a sort of batch aliasing of column names. This is an interesting concept for * queries because you can rename certain columns without remembering to name them in the SELECT statement itself.

Especially in a highly denormalized table as BigQuery is likely to have, it's a nice feature to be able to rename a few out of a hundred of column names without having to specify all hundred names first.

DISTINCT

The default behavior of a SELECT query is SELECT ALL, which means return every row in the set, including duplicates. The purpose of DISTINCT is to filter duplicate rows from the result set and give only one copy of each.

Specific to BigQuery: DISTINCT cannot do comparisons on STRUCTs or ARRAYs, and thus you cannot run one of these queries if you are returning one of those data types.

---

[1]And this is still small potatoes. The public Wikipedia datasets on BigQuery range from 1 to 2+ TB.

WITH

WITH is a prefix you can place before SELECT to create a temporary named query result you can use in the following statements. It can be easier to read than a subquery, especially when you need an intermediate result with aggregation to perform additional processing on.

In standard SQL, you can also use WITH to join the table to itself, creating a recursion. BigQuery does not support this, and I honestly shudder to think about recursively self-joining a petabyte-size table.

WITH must be immediately followed by its SELECT statement; it cannot stand alone. The following query counts the number of "Kinds" in a table and uses it to select the row with the highest count. This could also be written as a subquery:

```
WITH Result
AS
(SELECT Kind, COUNT(*) C FROM T GROUP BY Kind)
SELECT MAX(C)
FROM TableQuery
```

Querying the Past

There's also one additional feature that FROM has, which is that you can use it to look at older versions of the table. This is SQL standards-compliant too; Microsoft SQL Server has supported it since 2016, and several other database systems support this sort of temporal querying.

This feature doesn't give you unbridled access to all previous versions of the table ("Where we're going, Marty, we don't **need** rows!"), but it can be eminently helpful in doing a before/after when you are making table changes, if you want to do some comparison to ensure something about the table has changed in the way you expect. You can retrieve the state of the table as it looked up to one week ago from the current time.

The syntax for this type of query is

```
FROM Table FOR SYSTEM_TIME AS OF [Timestamp]
```

where [Timestamp] represents some sort of BigQuery timestamp expression. The following restrictions are in effect:

- The timestamp must be a constant (no ARRAY flattening, UNNESTing, WITH clauses, subqueries, user-defined functions, etc.).

- The timestamp must not be in the future or more than 7 days in the past.

- You cannot mix multiple timestamps anywhere in the query. You can't join a table from an hour ago with a table from yesterday, nor can you join the current table with the table from an hour ago.

You can use this feature to track changes in both data and schema. Let's say you have a scheduled job that runs at 9:30 AM to delete all the rows in a table. At 9:45 AM, you can check to make sure the table is empty. This alone doesn't tell you that the table *wasn't* empty earlier. Using this feature, you can also check the table as it was at 9:29 AM to see that it had rows that were then deleted.

You could also use this to recover from everyone's favorite SQL mistake, deleting or overwriting rows without specifying a WHERE clause. As long as you catch the issue within a week, just pull the table state as it existed before you made the error, and overwrite the current table with it. (If it's a live table, also stash the rows inserted in the meantime somewhere else while you do this. Recall that you can't join the current version to the previous version to do it automatically.)

(My favorite flag in MySQL is undoubtedly the --i-am-a-dummy flag, which is an alias for a flag called --safe-updates. This switch prevents you from running any UPDATE or DELETE commands that don't have a WHERE clause. Every database should have this, and it should be turned on by default. I don't know a single data engineer who hasn't accidentally done this at some point in their career. Most people are lucky enough not to be on production when it happens.)

Unions and Intersections

A union has basically the same meaning in SQL as it does in set theory. There are three types of set operations that BigQuery supports. Note that databases don't really adhere to set theory, since in pure set theory elements cannot be duplicated within a set.

An element, for purposes of these operators, is the value of all returned columns. That means that to perform any of these operations, the subsets all must have the same number of columns. For the examples in this section, we'll use a single integer column for simplification.

UNION ALL/DISTINCT

The union of two sets is defined as the set that contains all the elements from either. The use of the ALL or DISTINCT keyword determines whether you want duplicates in the union or not. You use DISTINCT when you care about the presence of a given element; you use ALL when you care about the number of times that element appears.

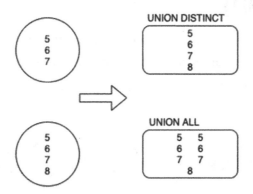

Figure 9-2. *UNION ALL vs. DISTINCT*

INTERSECT (DISTINCT)

The INTERSECT operator only supports the DISTINCT mode. This will give you the elements that appear in both sets, that is, the set intersection.

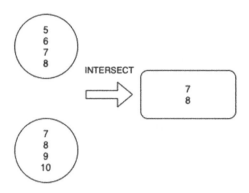

Figure 9-3. *INTERSECTION*

EXCEPT (DISTINCT)

The EXCEPT operator is a non-commutative operation that excludes elements found in the second set from the first set. Because it is non-commutative, the order in which you specify the sets matters.

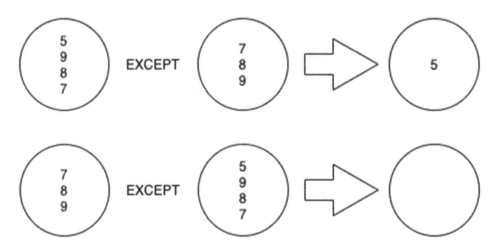

Figure 9-4. *EXCEPT*

Joining

Joining is the process of connecting two tables together by use of a common value. In data warehousing strategy, denormalization means that you limit the number of joins required to do a given operation. With BigQuery, the use of nested columns can limit the number of joins you must do to extract the desired data, even within the denormalized table structure.

In general and also for BigQuery, JOINs are not as performant as denormalized table structures. If you are finding that you are joining across large datasets as a matter of course and performance is degrading, this is an indication that your design needs adjustment.

(We won't address if and how you should use joins in this section, only what they are and how they work.)

There are three basic types of joins: CROSS, INNER, and OUTER.

CROSS JOIN

Cross joins are much maligned because they simply calculate the Cartesian product of two tables and return everything. This can be a massively expensive operation, and should you do it without a WHERE clause, you will probably be visited by people in expensive black suits asking for "a word." (Side project: What's the *most* expensive single BigQuery call you could make that actually returns? It almost certainly involves cross joins.)

The cross join is so basic that it is implied if you select from multiple tables separated with a comma. There's not even a need for a common key. In other words, if you have table A, table B, and table C and they each have 100 rows, the query

```
SELECT *
FROM A, B, C
```

will return 100*100*100: a million rows. You can also, and maybe should, considering the implications of the operation, explicitly declare the CROSS JOIN:

```
SELECT A CROSS JOIN B CROSS JOIN C
```

At least then, someone might catch it in code review and ask you what you are even doing there.

That being said, there are some valid use cases for the cross join. The best example is if you need to return data for every combination of certain variables. For instance, if you had ten data entry workers and you wanted to see how many records they had input in each one-hour period, you could cross join a list of the workers to a table containing the numbers (0..23), which would give you all workers and all hourly periods, to which you could then OUTER JOIN the data you need. This example is a stretch, since there's a better way to do it in BigQuery using UNNESTing.

(That way is SELECT * FROM UNNEST(GENERATE_TIMESTAMP_ARRAY(...)).)

INNER JOIN

An INNER JOIN combines two tables on a common value. (It's the same as A CROSS JOIN B WHERE A.column = B.column, if that helps.) You use this join type when you only want rows where the key appears in both tables.

Incidentally, you always need a join condition unless you're doing a cross join (or an UNNEST). Otherwise, there's no method the parser can use to determine which rows you want.

A basic example of a question you can answer with an inner join is "For all users in my system, return their pets' names." In a normalized structure, you would definitely never store a list of pets for a user in the same table as the user is defined. (In BigQuery, you very well may avoid this join by having Pets as a nested column inside your denormalized Users table.) This query would look something like

```
SELECT UserID, UserName, PetName
FROM Users
INNER JOIN UserPets
ON Users.UserID = UserPets.OwnerID
```

The ON clause specifies the join condition and is required. This join will look at both tables and find rows in UserPets that have an OwnerID matching a UserID in a Users row. Assuming that users appear only once in the Users table, the result will look like the following.

UserID	(Users.)**UserName**	(UserPets.)**PetName**
1	matteom	Pepper
2	nicom	Sparky
3	chrisd	Sir Bunnsington Parsley

Figure 9-5. *Inner join results diagram*

We'll revisit this in querying with nested columns in the following.

OUTER JOIN

OUTER JOINs often trip people up when they first encounter them. Think of an outer join as the following—no matter which option you choose, at least one of your tables will remain intact. Then, the other table will come along and attempt to match on the join condition. If it succeeds, the data will appear in those columns. If it fails, the row will remain, but its columns will be NULL.

For a LEFT OUTER JOIN, your first table remains intact. For a RIGHT OUTER JOIN, your second table remains intact. For a FULL OUTER JOIN, both tables remain intact.

(Using this model, an INNER JOIN is like mutually assured destruction. Two tables collide, and if they can't find a match, they destroy the row.)

LEFT OUTER JOIN

In the LEFT OUTER JOIN, rows from the first table will always be retained, even if no data was found in the second table matching the join condition.

RIGHT OUTER JOIN

Amazingly, this is the opposite, where rows from the second table will always be retained, even if no data was found in the first table matching the join condition.

FULL OUTER JOIN

A full outer join is essentially doing a LEFT and a RIGHT outer join at the same time. All rows from both tables will be preserved, even if none of the rows matched the join condition.

This is not the same as a CROSS JOIN—a CROSS JOIN does a direct Cartesian product, which means that if one of the tables in a CROSS JOIN has zero row, you will get zero row. A FULL OUTER JOIN will instead return the schemas of both tables, but all the data on the side which was empty will be NULL.

USING

USING is helpful readability syntax that you use when the column in both joined tables has the same name. In the UserPets query from the INNER JOIN example, we could replace

```
ON UsersID.UserID = UserPets.UserID
```

with

```
USING(UserID)
```

In this example, they would be equivalent. However, in SELECT * queries, USING behaves a little differently than INNER/ON. Consider this query:

```
SELECT *
FROM A
INNER JOIN B
ON A.x = B.x
```

In the INNER JOIN form, the result set will return both A.x and B.x as columns. Since it's an inner join, the columns will always have the same value. This often happens when you're building an INNER JOIN query for the first time—you'd try to SELECT x, and it would give you an ambiguity error and require you specify whether you want A.x or B.x, even though you know they're equivalent by query definition.

However, you can do

```
SELECT x
FROM A
INNER JOIN B
USING (x)
```

with no trouble at all. This is a nice bit of syntactic sugar that improves readability and avoids those ambiguous column errors.

Self-Joins

You can also join a table to itself. You would generally do this when you need to traverse some sort of hierarchy. Typically it means that there is a relationship modeled within the same table, as in an organization chart or a category tree. You want to get both the original record and its related record back in the same row.

There's nothing inherently wrong with this, but in the same way that you want to model relationships with nested and repeated columns, you would want to do that here too. Yes, that means duplicating information in some columns in rows of the nested column. That is also a form of denormalization, and it's worth considering here.

Subqueries

Subqueries comprise the intermediate results of a more complicated query. They're useful when you need to do multiple steps of aggregation or transformation within the same query. In places where you only get a single statement context, like Dataflow SQL or a scheduled query, they allow you to do more.

However, once you begin using subqueries, your statements can start getting pretty complicated, so this is where you will want to begin focusing on readability. The easiest way to do this is to give your subqueries alias table names to indicate the intermediate step.

Declaring a subquery is easy; you just place a query in parentheses. Once you've done this, you can treat the subquery as a table to perform additional operations. For example, take the subquery from a users/pets example:

```
(SELECT UserID, COUNT(*)
FROM UserPets
GROUP BY UserID)
```

As a primary query, this returns each user and the number of pets they have. However, if you use it as an aliased subquery and JOIN it, you get the following:

```
SELECT Username, PhoneNumber, NumberOfPets
FROM Users
JOIN (SELECT UserID, COUNT(*) NumberOfPets
FROM UserPets
GROUP BY UserID) PetCount
USING (UserID)
```

In this query, you use the subquery to make a table value called PetCount. Then, you can join that as if it were an actual table to the Users table and return all the users, their phone numbers, and the number of pets they have.

While extremely powerful, you can see how nesting several levels of subqueries could be very difficult to read. If you mix that in with BigQuery nesting and array syntax, you are creating a potential nightmare for others or future you.

WITH Clauses

One way you can head this off at the pass is by declaring your subqueries as WITH clauses. The primary purpose of WITH is in fact readability—BigQuery will not execute the subquery on its own. If we rewrite the preceding query to use WITH, it will now look like

```
WITH PetCount AS (SELECT UserID, COUNT(*) NumberOfPets
FROM UserPets
GROUP BY UserID)
SELECT Username, PhoneNumber, NumberOfPets
FROM Users
JOIN PetCount USING (UserID)
```

This is slightly more readable, but as the number of subqueries grows, you will see increased benefit to this technique.

If you find yourself writing the same WITH clause over and over again at the top of each of your queries, it may be a good candidate for a denormalized table or a view.

Nested Data

So far we've stuck to concepts that are equally applicable to online transaction processing (OLTP) databases. And, as we've discussed, if you're operating on small amounts of data, you may opt to retain some of the normalization and join syntax that you would use in the operational store. (As a reminder, BigQuery's recommended threshold is that you can leave any dimension smaller than 10 GB normalized if you wish.)

At scale, your queries should definitely be minimizing joins and subqueries to achieve maximum performance. Google's recommendation for BigQuery suggested nested and repeating columns wherever possible. Possible has a broad definition here; you don't need to optimize anything until you start to see performance issues. As covered in previous chapters, many datasets won't require any transformation at all to perform acceptably on BigQuery.

UNNEST

The UNNEST operator takes an ARRAY type from a column and turns it into a table. Were you to denormalize the structure of pets and owners into a single BigQuery table, you could have UserID, PhoneNumber, and all of the pet data stored as an ARRAY. Now you can run the preceding same query without any joins at all:

```
SELECT UserID, PhoneNumber,
(SELECT COUNT(*) FROM UNNEST(UserPets)) PetCount
FROM DW_Users
```

(I used the prefix DW, for "Data Warehouse," to differentiate it from the earlier, normalized version of the table.)

You can also replicate the original query, returning users and all of their pets' names, still using the JOIN syntax but without the need to access a second table:

```
SELECT UserID, P.PetName
FROM DW_Users
JOIN UNNEST(DW_Users.UserPets) P
```

This query will run faster and use substantially less data, since it doesn't need to scan a second table at all. Note that there is no join condition here, since the nested column is already "joined" to the table.

If you query a table with nested columns in the console, those columns will generate subtables inside the table view, as seen in Figure 9-6.

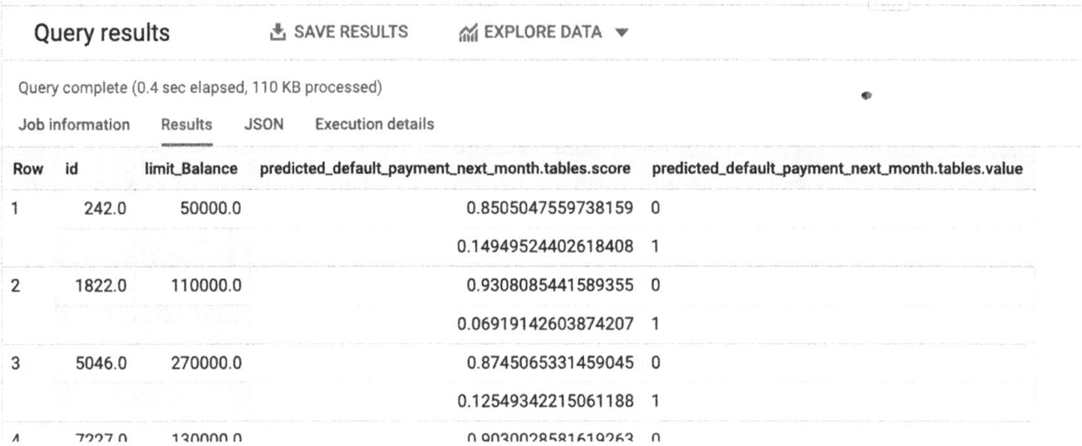

Query results		± SAVE RESULTS		⟪ EXPLORE DATA ▼	

Query complete (0.4 sec elapsed, 110 KB processed)

Job information   Results   JSON   Execution details

Row	id	limit_Balance	predicted_default_payment_next_month.tables.score	predicted_default_payment_next_month.tables.value
1	242.0	50000.0	0.8505047559738159	0
			0.14949524402618408	1
2	1822.0	110000.0	0.9308085441589355	0
			0.06919142603874207	1
3	5046.0	270000.0	0.8745065331459045	0
			0.12549342215061188	1
4	7227.0	130000.0	0.9030028581619263	0

Figure 9-6. *Console screenshot of nested table*

This can get quite difficult to read and seems to be the biggest barrier for visual learners to jump in. You can explore these tables with UNNEST or with EXCEPT to exclude the record columns while you're looking to understand the schema.

Another common early error with BigQuery nesting is that when you see a column with a repeated type, it seems somewhat intuitive that you might go and query it directly, as in

```
-- This query is invalid
SELECT UserPets.PetName
FROM DW_Users
```

The reason this doesn't work should make sense now; you can't access a repeated field inside a table without flattening or aggregating it in some way.

If you're still having trouble grasping this concept, I encourage you to get into the console and explore the syntax. Working fluidly with nested columns is a critical part of using BigQuery successfully.

Working with Partitions

Most of the loading and streaming options recommend or automatically generate partitioned tables. The primary purpose of partitioning is to reduce the number of partitions a given query needs to look at; this is known as partitioning pruning. When querying partitioned tables with BigQuery, your objective is, whenever possible, to look at the fewest number of partitions to retrieve your results.

As you may recall from earlier chapters, there are three different types of partitioned tables:

- Ingestion-time partitions
- Date/timestamp partitions
- Integer range partitions

Each of the three has slightly different ways of expressing queries.

Ingestion-Time Partitioned Tables

For these tables, which you created when you streamed data into the warehouse in Chapter 6, you don't actually specify the partition column. It's inferred and created automatically when the data is inserted into the table.

This is done by the creation of two "pseudocolumns" called _PARTITIONDATE and _PARTITIONTIME, which are reserved by BigQuery. In order to effectively prune partitions, you need to use these columns to filter the query to look at only the qualifying partitions.

You do this with a query like

```
SELECT *
FROM IngestionTimePartitionedTable
WHERE _PARTITIONDATE = '2020-01-01'
```

This will throw out every partition except the one for that date. Be careful to avoid subqueries or functions that will make it impossible for the BigQuery parser to prune partitions.

Date/Timestamp Partitioned Tables

For tables that are configured to partition by TIMESTAMP or DATE, you specified the partition key when you created the table. That means that pruning partitions is as simple as using that column in the WHERE clause. For example, a TIMESTAMP partitioned table might be accessed like this:

```
SELECT * FROM
`bigquery-public-data.ethereum_blockchain.blocks`
WHERE timestamp BETWEEN '2018-07-07T07:00:00Z' AND '2018-07-07T08:00:00Z'
```

One way to know that you're hitting the partition is that BigQuery can detect partitions as part of its estimate. There was a time when it did not do this, and it was scary for everyone, but now you can be sure before you start. In this case, the preceding query accesses only 6.1 MB. Without a partition filter, it would access a whopping 9.5 GB. So it makes a huge difference.

However, be sure to avoid subqueries or complex WHERE conditions when seeking to filter. BigQuery can only prune partitions if the query doesn't need to look outside of your requested partitions in order to satisfy the WHERE clause. In the preceding example, no math or extra calculation is done on the TIMESTAMP. You may want to experiment a bit, since BigQuery's partition optimization ability seems to be steadily improving.

You can also set a rule on a table you created this way that queries must specify a partition filter to execute. This rule is called "Require partition filter," and it can save you a lot of money if you have analysts who have a tendency to use a lot of *s.

If you only need to access a single partition, and you know which one it is, you can use the $ syntax to reach it. For example, SELECTing from a date-partitioned table called DatePartitionedTable$20200101 would go directly to the underlying partition for that date.

Integer Partitioned Tables

Integer partitioned tables behave basically the same way as date-partitioned tables, except that the query in question is a number. As long as you perform a WHERE clause on the partition key and don't perform any calculations or subqueries using it, the partitions will automatically be used.

Also as with the date-partitioned tables, you can go directly to an underlying partition by using the $ syntax, that is, IntegerPartitionedTable$100.

Date, Time, and Timestamp Functions

Data usually has a strong connection to temporal data. Learning to slice and dice time and intervals and convert between types is another critical step on the road to BigQuery success. There are four time-related data types:

- DATE

- DATETIME

- TIME

- TIMESTAMP

Of the four, only TIMESTAMP represents an absolute point in time. The other three represent what I've been calling "local time" and Google calls "civil time," namely, a timezone-independent representation of a logical date and/or time.

This can be pretty hard to grasp when you're dealing with events. I find it easiest to think of it in terms of which context is relevant: the record's or the absolute time. Let's look at an easy example: January 1, 2001, at midnight, otherwise known as the beginning of the current millennium.

Since I haven't told you anything about where this takes place, your mental image is probably of "local" midnight—champagne bottles popping, couples kissing, and so on. But as a an absolute UTC timestamp, it is

```
2001-01-01T00:00:00Z
```

Cities who shared a timezone with UTC, like London, were indeed singing "Auld Lang Syne". But in Chicago, the clock said 6 PM on December 31st. So which time matters? The answer is the same as the answer for whether you are thinking about a TIMESTAMP or a DATE/DATETIME/TIME. A TIMESTAMP occurs at the same microsecond everywhere. (No letters about relativity, please.) A DATE represents an arbitrary period where the calendar had that value on any particular date.

Coordinated Universal Time (UTC)

Use UTC whenever possible in storage. This allows you to do date math without trying to account for timezones, and it also allows for the very common pattern where a user in a certain timezone would like to see the results as local to them. For example, if someone logged in at 5:36 PM Pacific Standard Time and I'm looking at an event log while in Eastern Standard Time, I'd like to see that the event occurred at 8:36 PM "my" time. Storing the event at the absolute UTC timestamp would allow you to perform that conversion without manual error.

I'm not going to sugarcoat it; managing time data is one of those things that seems like it should be really easy until you actually start to get into globally distributed systems. Basic assumptions don't hold true—you can't *actually* calculate the distance between the current time and a UTC timestamp in the future, because leap seconds may occur. And ultimately because time is a human construct and we're modeling a physical process, that is, the rotation and orbit of the Earth, there will always be discontinuities. Luckily, as long as you stick with UTC, pretty much all of them will be at a higher level of precision than we care about.

Common Use Cases

Let's briefly cover each of the data types and their precisions. After that, we'll look at some of the functions and their common uses. The majority of functions have a suffix for each data type. For example, CURRENT_TIMESTAMP, CURRENT_DATE, CURRENT_TIME, and CURRENT_DATETIME are all valid. For further reference, the BigQuery documentation on these functions is quite good.[2]

DATE

DATE takes the form YYYY-[M]M-[D]D and as such has a maximum precision of one day. The valid range is from 0000-01-01 to 9999-12-31, so if you want to represent the ancient Egyptians or the Morlocks, you're out of luck.

---

[2]https://cloud.google.com/bigquery/docs/reference/standard-sql/datetime_functions

TIME

TIME has microsecond precision and a form of [H]H:[M]M:[S]S[.DDDDDD]. You can go from 00:00:00.000000 to 23:59:59.999999, which means no Martian time here.

DATETIME

As a logical combination of the preceding two types, the DATETIME object ranges from 0000-01-01 00:00:00.000000 to 9999-12-31 23:59.999999. This gives you the full range of precision from year to microsecond. The canonical form is a DATE plus a TIME, with either a "T" or a space between them.

TIMESTAMP

As mentioned earlier, the TIMESTAMP is the only data type of the four that represents a fixed, absolute point in time. This adds one more value, which is the timezone. The default is UTC, but you can also represent absolute timestamps in other timezones. This means that the same canonical form of DATETIME can be accepted for a TIMESTAMP, but you can also append the timezone code at the end.

Note that BigQuery doesn't actually store the timezone—it doesn't need to. Each timezone has its own representation of the UTC fixed time. You use timezones when searching or inserting and to format the value for display; the internal value doesn't change.

You can represent a timezone either with a "Z" (Zulu) to explicitly indicate UTC or by specifying the name or offset.[3]

Date Parts

When working with these data types, you will frequently need to operate at an arbitrary level of precision. Across all of the date and time types, BigQuery recognizes the following date parts:

- MICROSECOND
- MILLISECOND
- SECOND

---

[3]Please see https://data.iana.org/time-zones/tz-link.html if you have any interest in this topic and about three weeks to kill.

- MINUTE

- HOUR

- DAY

- WEEK

- WEEK([SUNDAY, MONDAY, TUESDAY... SATURDAY])

- MONTH

- QUARTER

- YEAR

MONTH and YEAR also have ISO variants using weeks as defined by ISO 8601.

Intervals

In order to work with lengths of time, you need to declare an interval. An interval consists of an integer combined with a date_part, like (INTERVAL 5 MINUTES) or (INTERVAL 13 DAY). The construct has no use by itself; you must use it in combination with one of the date functions. Note that the numeric part must be an integer. You can't add 1.5 YEAR or 0.25 HOUR.

CURRENT

CURRENT_(TIMESTAMP/TIME/DATE/DATETIME) will return the current date and/or time.

_ADD, _SUB, _DIFF

These three functions exist across all four data types (i.e., DATE_ADD, TIMESTAMP_DIFF, TIME_SUB, etc.).

You use them to add or subtract an interval to and from a datetime or to find the distance between two datetimes using a given date part.

_TRUNC

DATE_TRUNC, TIME_TRUNC, DATETIME_TRUNC, and TIMESTAMP_TRUNC allow you to quantize an object to a lower level of precision. For example, you can use DATE_TRUNC(DATE '2001-01-13', MONTH) to truncate to month-level precision, 2001-01-01.

EXTRACT

Using a date_part, you can extract just that piece from a date/time value, for example:

```
SELECT EXTRACT(YEAR FROM CURRENT_DATETIME())
```

Again, if you specify a date_part that isn't part of that data type's precision, it will fail with an error message like "EXTRACT from TIME does not support the YEAR date part."

Formatting and Parsing

A number of the other date functions convert between string-based values and date/time objects or vice versa. When dealing with data from external data sources, you will frequently need some conversion to deal with another system's data formats. You can use ISO date specifications as a common format. Watch out for timezones!

UNIX Epoch Operations

When dealing with UNIX-based external systems or older timestamp systems, you will often encounter the concept of the epoch. This is the amount of time that has passed since UNIX's arbitrary second 0 on 1970-01-01T00:00:00Z. You can use UNIX_SECONDS, UNIX_MILLIS, or UNIX_MICROS to get the current epoch date for a given timestamp. To go the other direction, you can use TIMESTAMP_SECONDS, TIMESTAMP_MILLIS, or TIMESTAMP_MICROS.

The epoch format has three levels of precision, which depend on your use case. The original UNIX version used only second-level precision. Javascript's underlying support uses millisecond-level precision. Systems analysis, performance counters, and the global positioning system (GPS) itself have microsecond resolution.

Grouping Operations

Earlier in the chapter, we explored basic grouping. There are more things we can do with grouping, and it is important for dealing with large datasets to return data in the buckets that we need.

Much like ordering, there are also data types that do not support grouping, and they're the same data types: ARRAY, STRUCT, and GEOGRAPHY. You can also use integers positionally in GROUP BY clauses as with ordering (i.e., GROUP BY 1), but I also discourage their use for similar reasons (in a word, brittleness.)

ROLLUP

Using the rollup keyword allows you to use grouping "sets," instead of grouping by only the one grouping set defined in the initial GROUP BY. To do this, it multiplies the GROUP BY set into its constituent subsets and then unions them together.

Effectively, this gives you multiple levels of GROUP BY without having to specify the grouping sets directly. For rows representing a "rollup," the grouping key will be null.

This concept can be a little weird to understand at first; I usually use the concept of budgeting to explain it. Suppose your organization has three departments: accounting, HR, and executive. (This company obviously doesn't do anything.) Each of those departments has individual expenditures, and you want to see the amount of money they have each spent.

Using just the GROUP BY, you can see one level of grouping by department:

```
SELECT Department, SUM(Cost) TotalCost
FROM Expenses
GROUP BY Department
ORDER BY TotalCost DESC
```

This will return a list of each department's total expenses, ordered by decreasing cost.

Row	Department	TotalCost
1	Execution	500.0
2	Executive	400.0
3	HR	125.0
4	Accounting	120.0

Figure 9-7. *Result table*

With ROLLUP, you can get an additional level of grouping that "rolls up" the departments together for a company-wide sum:

```
GROUP BY ROLLUP(Department)
```

This query gives the same result, with an additional row at the bottom.

Row	Department	TotalCost
1	*null*	1145.0
2	Execution	500.0
3	Executive	400.0
4	HR	125.0
5	Accounting	120.0

Figure 9-8. *Result table with null row*

That NULL row represents the SUM applied to the individual buckets' sums.

HAVING

The HAVING keyword is much like WHERE, except that it follows GROUP BY in the order of operations. This keyword lets you filter the results of a GROUP BY for additional conditions.

Using HAVING requires that you are employing aggregation somewhere in the query; otherwise, HAVING has no group selection to operate from. In the preceding example, we can easily add a HAVING clause to show departments that spent more than $1,000:

```
SELECT Department, SUM(Cost) TotalCost
FROM Expenses
GROUP BY Department
HAVING SUM(Cost) > 1000
```

After the GROUP BY is applied, the HAVING clause filters its rows to just those that qualify. Note that aggregation is present both in the SELECT and the HAVING, but you could also filter by rows HAVING AVG(Cost) > 50, for example, to only return departments whose average expenditure exceeded $50.

Aggregation

As a related item to grouping, we also looked at some common aggregate functions earlier in the chapter. In addition to those (MAX, MIN, SUM, AVG, and COUNT), let's look at the others. You can find dizzyingly comprehensive documentation for every type of function in the BigQuery documentation. (For reference, I'm repeating the preceding five as well.)

ANY_VALUE

Sometimes, you just need a representative value from the bucket, and it doesn't matter which one. In that case, there's ANY_VALUE, which non-deterministically pulls one qualifying value for the group and returns it to you.

You can also use MIN or MAX in any of these cases, but ANY_VALUE is faster, since it doesn't have to do a sort.

ARRAY_AGG

ARRAY_AGG takes any value (except an ARRAY) and converts it into an array. It can handle values with multiple columns too, which means you can use it as a sort of opposite to UNNEST.

Even better, in combination with user-defined functions, which we'll get to later, you can actually define your own aggregate functions that use ARRAY_AGG to filter elements in a way that you choose.

ARRAY_CONCAT_AGG

This aggregation only takes ARRAYs and creates the concatenated array containing all of the subelements. For example, if you had three rows, { [1, 2, 3], [4, 5], [6] }, running ARRAY_CONCAT_AGG on these values would generate a single array, [1, 2, 3, 4, 5, 6]. You can also specify an ORDER BY on the array concatenation, and you can LIMIT the number of arrays you will allow to be concatenated to a constant integer.

AVG

Returns the average value across all the rows in the group. This only works on numeric types, so don't expect to average some strings together. (Yes, yes, I know you think the average of {"A", "B", and "C"} should be "B". I just told you you can use ARRAY_AGG to write your own aggregate functions, so go ahead and implement it yourself.)

COUNT

Returns the number of rows in the group.

COUNTIF

Returns the number of rows in the group that match the boolean expression you specify. This is a good way to avoid the need for subqueries or additional WHERE constraints by simply specifying the query in the aggregation. For example:

```
SELECT Department, COUNTIF(Cost > 25)
FROM Expenses
GROUP BY Department
```

will give me the number of expenses by department, but only where the expense was greater than $25. (WHERE HasReceipt = 0 would give me a list of offenders who didn't submit expense reports that were over the $25 limit!)

MAX/MIN

As discussed before, returns the maximum or minimum value for that group.

STRING_AGG

STRING_AGG takes a series of values and concatenates them together into a single STRING (or BYTES) value. This handles the very common case that you have finished operating on the individual values and need to return or display them in a readable format.

SUM

This gives me the cumulative SUM across all rows per group. There is no corresponding SUMIF, as in Microsoft Excel and other database systems, but it's quite easy to approximate:

```
SELECT Department, SUM(IF(Cost > 150, Cost, 0))
```

The IF function evaluates the expression in the first argument and produces the second expression if true and the third if false. (Programmers recognize this as equivalent to ternary operator expressions like (sum > 150 ? cost : 0)). If the cost is greater than $150, the cost is supplied to the sum; if not, 0 is supplied, effectively skipping the row.

Bitwise Aggregation

Using the INT64 type, you can use BIT_AND, BIT_OR, and BIT_XOR to perform bitwise operations across values. (To specify hexadecimal values in BigQuery, use the form 0x0000.) LOGICAL_AND and LOGICAL_OR are similar, but operate on boolean values.

In databases where space was a constraint, data engineers would use packed fields to fit multiple values into a single column. For example, using an INT64, you could store 64 individual bits of data, that is, 64 boolean columns. To retrieve individual values, you'd first need to know which bit held the flag you wanted, and you would then apply a bit mask to get the value out.

These operators are still useful for manipulating columns that have been stored in this way, especially if you are transforming them into proper columns or arrays upon load.

BigQuery GIS

Geospatial calculations are a fundamental part of most data warehouses. Most businesses have the need to track what location things are in, whether it be consumer goods, vehicles, store locations, and so on. Being able to pinpoint something in time and space is a basic feature of much data analysis.

The BigQuery feature supporting geospatial data is called BigQuery GIS, or just GIS. Like most SQL geography packages, it has a series of common functions and operators designed to make it easy for you to do work with spatial coordinates and bounding boxes—no trigonometry required.

For the purposes of this book, BigQuery, and anyone outside of a space agency, we are using the WGS84 coordinate reference system, which takes the Earth to be an oblate spheroid 6378.1... No, sorry, geodesists. For everyone else, we're using the longitude/latitude system to establish locations on the face of the planet.

If you weren't paying attention in geography class, crash course. Latitude can go from +90 degrees (90°N, the North Pole) to -90 degrees (90°S, the South Pole). Longitude goes from -180 longitude (180°W) to +180 longitude (180°E). -180 and +180 degrees of longitude represent the same meridian, the farthest away from 0° longitude, which is *almost* at the site of the Royal Observatory Greenwich in London, United Kingdom, but not quite. Using this system, you can specify any location on Earth to an arbitrary degree of precision. The history of coordinates is incredibly fascinating and almost entirely irrelevant to BigQuery, other than at this one intersection point.

The breadth of this issue is enormous, and a full treatment would deserve a book of its own. But you will almost certainly encounter use cases requiring it, and there's no need to subject yourself to the pain of trying to manage a separate latitude and longitude column in all of your tables. If working with the GEOGRAPHY type seems natural to you, you will be able to do all kinds of fascinating analysis.

There's only one data type in play here: GEOGRAPHY. But the GEOGRAPHY type is pretty complex, so we'll break it down.

GEOGRAPHY Concepts

Point

The simplest unit of location is a point. A point can be constructed with just the latitude and longitude, which uses the ST_GEOGPOINT function to yield a GEOGRAPHY type.

Line

A line is the shortest distance between two points. Using ST_MAKELINE, you can take two or more points (or lines) and join them together to make a single, one-dimensional path called a linestring.

Polygon

A polygon is a geography consisting of multiple linestrings. To form a polygon, you must have at least three linestrings where the first point of the first linestring and the last point of the last linestring are exactly the same point. That is, to form a valid polygon, you have to end where you started. Then, you use the ST_MAKEPOLYGON function to generate the GEOGRAPHY which contains the surface area.

Because the Earth is round (seriously, no letters) and thus the coordinate system is contiguous, any given polygon specifies two surface areas—what's inside it and what's outside it. Think about it—if I draw a square on a globe, am I enclosing the space inside it or outside it? By convention and common sense, the ST_MAKEPOLYGON function defines the space to be the smaller of the two options; so, if you draw a polygon around the state of Wyoming, MAKEPOLYGON will create the geography of the inside of the state, as opposed to the geography of everything *outside* the state. You can change this behavior with the ST_MAKEPOLYGONORIENTED function.

GIS Functions

Whew. Let's skip ahead and say you've just inherited some GEOGRAPHY data. Honestly, this is probably exactly what will happen. You don't generally need to define your own GEOGRAPHYs; they usually come prepackaged from other data libraries. For example, if you go to www.arcgis.com, you can download datasets that represent the boundaries of common geographical objects like states, rivers, streams, and so on. Luckily, the work of centuries of surveying has given us extremely accurate representations of the world we live in. (Well, reasonably accurate. The state of Colorado, despite its appearance on a map, is a polygon containing hundreds of sides. And did I mention US zip codes have no canonical polygonal representation at all? But...when you use a store locator... Not now.)

Assuming you have some GEOGRAPHY objects lying around now (Chapter 20 has some too), let's look at a sampling of the functions we can use on them. Note that since a GEOGRAPHY may contain one or more polygons, lines, or points, functions are not always applicable to a given value of the data type.

ST_DIMENSION

I include this one so you can get a sense of your bearing when first looking at GEOGRAPHY objects. ST_DIMENSION(geography) will return 0, 1, or 2, indicating whether the highest-order element in the input is a point, line, or polygon, respectively. (Empty geographies return -1.)

ST_AREA

This function works on one or more polygons to tell you the total surface area covered in square meters. The area of a line or point is 0.

ST_CENTROID

This function will return the centroid of all of the elements in the geography, using the function for the highest dimension available. A centroid, in basic terms, is the "center" of a group of points, lines, or polygons. The math can get fairly complicated in higher dimensions, but in practical terms, this tells you where you might center your map to visualize all the values inside. (You can also then apply ST_MAXDISTANCE to figure out the zoom level for that map.)

ST_DISTANCE

ST_DISTANCE gives you the shortest possible distance between two GEOGRAPHY objects in meters.

ST_LENGTH

ST_LENGTH operates on lines to return the total length of all lines in the GEOGRAPHY in meters. If the GEOGRAPHY contains only points or polygons, the result is 0.

ST_X/ST_Y

ST_X and ST_Y are how you take a single point and break it back out into its longitude (ST_X) and its latitude (ST_Y). You will have to do this for any external system to plot points on a map; for example, if you pull ST_X and ST_Y for any GEOGRAPHY point, you can pop them into Google Maps with (`www.google.com/maps/place/`) [ST_X],[ST_Y] and see that point on the map.

Other Functions

The other geographic functions allow you to do things like see if GEOGRAPHY objects cover each other's area, if they intersect at all, or if they touch, perimeters, boundaries, and a whole set of conversion functions from other common geography data representations.

Joins

You can use some of these functions as join predicates too. For example, you could write a query to join a list of service areas with a list of state areas on whether their geographies intersect: this would tell you which states had any service areas. You could then use a GROUP BY to SUM the ST_AREAs of each of the service areas to figure out what portion of the state's area was covered by your service areas.

This query uses geographic intersection to find all of the zip codes in a US metropolitan area and then orders them by decreasing land area. The ratio column tells you what percentage of a given metro that particular zip code covers:

```
SELECT
  zip_code,
  zipcodes.area_land_meters zip_area,
  urban_area_code,
  name,
  cities.area_land_meters metro_area,
  (zipcodes.area_land_meters / cities.area_land_meters) ratio
FROM
  `bigquery-public-data.geo_us_boundaries.zip_codes` AS zipcodes
  inner join `bigquery-public-data.utility_us.us_cities_area` cities
  ON ST_INTERSECTS(zipcodes.zip_code_geom, cities.city_geom)
WHERE urban_area_code = '51445'
ORDER BY 6 DESC
```

With a little extension, you could easily discover which metropolitan areas are covered by the fewest zip codes. By simply removing the WHERE clause, you can learn that the zip code 99752 is actually 4,000 times larger than its designated metro area of Kotzebue, Alaska.[4]

Visualization

Dealing with arbitrary locations in numerical form can be aggravating. Sometimes you just want to see what you're dealing with on a map.

There are several options available, including Google Earth Engine, but we'll focus on the simplest in order to help you understand and work better with your geographic data. That's BigQuery Geo Viz, located at `https://bigquerygeoviz.appspot.com/`. I found this tool to be invaluable when learning about geographic data types.

---

[4]Actually, zip codes don't describe areas at all... Enter the ZCTA and some very interesting analysis. Read more at `www.georeference.org/doc/zip_codes_are_not_areas.htm`

Authorize the site to access your BigQuery instance, and your project IDs will populate in step 1. Select the project you're using, and type in a query which returns a GEOGRAPHY result in a column. The map will automatically visualize all of the points for you. You can click each point to see the rest of the row for that location.

This tool is not really intended for production use. You can't share or download maps. But it gives you an easy, valuable visualization directly out of BigQuery. I hope that they incorporate it directly into the query results at a future date.

Other Functions

Frankly, the SQL standard is massive; and even with a broad survey, we haven't even scratched the surface. There are hundreds of other functions for string manipulation, math, networking, and encryption. Google's documentation is excellent on these points, and you can read it here (`https://cloud.google.com/bigquery/docs/reference/standard-sql/functions-and-operators`).

Suffice it to say, if you need to do data transformation using only SQL statements, you're still well-covered.

Summary

SQL is a huge language, and thousands of books have been written just about writing effective queries. BigQuery is SQL-compliant, so all of that power is available to you in your data warehouse too. Retrieving data from a database always follows the SELECT/FROM/WHERE pattern at heart. You can also join tables together, or you can use nested and repeated columns to avoid them. SQL offers a variety of functions for date math, aggregation, field manipulation of all kinds, and geospatial support. Even that barely begins to tell the story; there are hundreds of other functions available.

Before returning to SQL, we're going to diverge in the next few chapters to explore some other GCP services that work well in tandem with BigQuery to solve common problems. First up is how to schedule queries and jobs so that you can run operations inside BigQuery on a prescheduled or recurring basis.

CHAPTER 10

Scheduling Jobs

Configuring tasks to run at a scheduled time or on a recurring basis is a conceptually simple idea. Ken Thompson wrote the original cron at Bell Labs sometime in the mid-1970s, and we use it mostly the same way today. It's only recently that cloud technology has taken upon itself the improvement of this most venerable of basic task schedulers. Google's foray into the area came startlingly late, only reaching general availability in March 2019. (Microsoft Azure had scheduling as early as 2015; Amazon Web Services has had it in Lambda nearly since inception, and the Batch service has been available since 2016.)

The use cases for scheduling are varied and endless. Interfacing with older systems may require you to poll periodically to sweep any new data available into BigQuery. Routine maintenance and compliance backups can occur nightly. You may just want to pre-stage reports into views every once in a while.

In Chapter 1, I mentioned that BigQuery has the concept of scheduled queries. It's true; it does. Unfortunately, the BigQuery native feature has some limitations which might be deal breakers for you. It's also limited to BigQuery, so if you wanted to chain scheduled queries with some other functionality or run them as part of a larger scheduled job, it wouldn't suffice.

Cloud Scheduler fills an important gap because it is a serverless complement to all of the other infrastructure we've been building and using. As you succeed in lowering or eliminating your self-managed virtual machines, you will come to regard the ones you have left as a burden. Once the majority of your applications are running without the need for manual tuning, you look for ways to eliminate the remainder as soon as possible.

© Mark Mucchetti 2020
M. Mucchetti, *BigQuery for Data Warehousing*, https://doi.org/10.1007/978-1-4842-6186-6_10

I'll take the opportunity here to razz some of my support engineers at Google. A few years ago, when I first came across a use case that required scheduling in GCP, I went to the docs to see what my options were. Seeing as I could think of three or four ways to do it in Amazon Web Services without even looking at docs, I was puzzled when I couldn't find an obvious solution. I contacted my partners at Google and told them what I was looking for. They told me to make a Google App Engine instance and run cron on it—this was the recommended pattern at the time. I am pretty sure I replied with "You want me to muck up my fancy pure serverless infrastructure where the only server runs cron?!" or words to that effect. Now Google Cloud Platform has Cloud Scheduler, everything is serverless again, and all is forgiven. (I very nearly ran schedulers on Amazon Web Services with triggers across to Google Cloud to solve this problem.)

In this chapter, we'll go over both the native BigQuery scheduling feature and Cloud Scheduler. We'll also touch on Cloud Tasks' scheduling capabilities. Using one or more of these tools will help you automate activity on your BigQuery instance that you must do on a regular interval or at a specific time.

BigQuery Scheduled Queries

First, let's cover the scheduling capabilities built into BigQuery directly. If your needs are limited to operating within BigQuery and its connected services, there may be no reason to incur the overhead of a totally separate service.

BigQuery scheduled queries operate using the BigQuery Data Transfer service. In order to use them, you will first have to enable that service. The first time you go to the Scheduled Queries sidebar, it will first have you do this and then direct you to the main UI screen. If you have no scheduled queries, the main screen will direct you back to the regular console to enter and schedule a query.

Scheduling Queries

To schedule a query, type it into the console window as you would any other interactive query. Run it once to ensure that it returns the data you want. Also, ensure that this data will be changing over time to justify running it on a scheduled basis. You may want to apply a date filter in the WHERE clause to give you only new rows in the last given interval, or you may just want to select all rows that have not been processed by the query yet. A column named ProcessedTime that holds the timestamp of when the query ingested this row could do the trick; then you only need to select all rows where ProcessedTime is NULL. You don't need to format the query as an INSERT—doing a simple SELECT will still insert the results of that query into the table when you schedule it.

Once you're satisfied with the query, click "Schedule Query" and "Create New Scheduled Query." A sidebar appears on the right to allow you to configure the parameters.

Name

Name the query. If you are going to be making a lot of jobs, you can develop a rational naming scheme to keep them straight. For scheduled jobs, I try to use a format like source-destination-action. I don't put the schedule in the name of the job, because this should be flexible and you may want to change it over time. So, for example, I might name a job "bigquery-email-reporting-sales" to indicate that I'm going to take some sales information from BigQuery and report it over email. Trust me a year from now when someone asks you to stop sending that nightly report, you'll appreciate that you can distinguish between all of the different jobs you made.

I've mentioned it in other contexts, but it's really important to name things properly. While in an ideal scenario you'd have supplementary documentation for everything you do, in practice things will slip through the cracks. Even if you're the only person who configures your project, things you did more than a few months in the past may as well have been done by someone else. If many people are working on your project, it is more valuable to standardize and agree on naming conventions for each application than to try to keep up with the rapidly changing names themselves. I have had to excavate many half-finished cloud configurations where it takes me a day to set up the new structure and six weeks to figure out which one of the "sched-job-old-nightly" processes is actually delivering the emails.

Schedule Options

You'll see common options in the dropdown, where you can just configure hourly, daily, weekly, or monthly. You can also select custom or on-demand.

Custom

Custom schedule uses its own string-based specification to say when you want the query to run. Frustratingly, there's no validation for the custom scheduling string. So while it looks like you might be able to get pretty fancy, as shown in Figure 10-1:

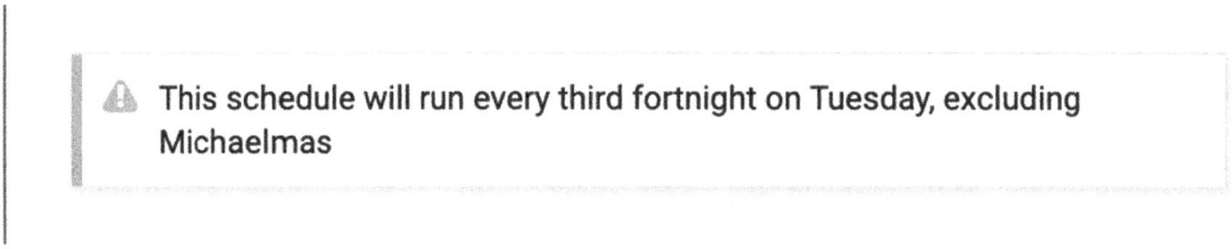

 This schedule will run every third fortnight on Tuesday, excluding Michaelmas

Figure 10-1. *This isn't going to work*

When you actually go to schedule the query, it will be rejected. This makes it fairly difficult to determine what formats are actually valid using this sidebar, and it caused me quite a lot of confusion. If you save a custom schedule string and then edit the query, it will appear in the dropdown format, which at least will let you confirm that you did what you expected.

Anyway, the minimum interval is 15 minutes (longer than the 1-minute resolution of Cloud Scheduler), and the maximum interval is 1 year, which you can get with a custom string like "1 of January 00:00".

To save you the trouble of trial and error, here are some common use cases and their associated strings. Note that the parser will take variants (like "jan" or "Jan" for "January"), so some modification will be tolerated. I found other parts of the syntax to be strangely restrictive, though, so your mileage may vary.

every day 09:00
every monday at 04:30
every thu, wednesday at 09:00
every 8 hours
every 2 hours from 08:00 to 18:00
1st tuesday of month 10:00
1,4,7,10,15,20,24,28 of jul at 09:45

Figure 10-2. *An actual list of schedule strings that work with BigQuery scheduled queries*

On-Demand

You can set a query for scheduling and never actually schedule it. If you do this, the only options available for running the query will be via API or by manually running it from the details page. You might use this if you want to save some queries for scheduling but haven't decided on a schedule yet.

You could also do this to have a safe place to store the queries outside the code and then use an external scheduling solution to invoke the API. That way all of the BigQuery-specific code stays there.

Start Time/End Time

You can also specify when you want this schedule to be active by specifying a start and end time for the recurrence. You could, for example, run your query on every Tuesday at 9 AM, but not start this schedule until a future date and end the schedule some time after that.

Another odd thing that could trip you up is timezones. The schedule options default to your local timezone *unless* you use a custom time string, in which case they default to UTC. However, for the start and end times, you must specify a timezone, which defaults to your local timezone, but can be changed. Furthermore, you can accidentally set the start time and the end time in *different* timezones, raising the possibility that your scheduled query actually uses three timezones in its specification—UTC, start timezone, and end timezone.

Even beyond that, once you start using custom schedule strings and timezones, the timezone specifications will lose options, sometimes showing GMT offsets and other times not even allowing the selection of GMT.

Lastly, the scheduler will actually let you specify a recurrence end time which is *before* the recurrence start time. This should cause the job to never run. Worse yet, it silently removes the end time and creates a sequence that starts on your chosen start date and never ends.

The reason for all of these validation issues is undoubtedly that this sidebar is just an adapter into the transfer service API, which means it has separate logic to construct the API call. Often, when Google does this, there is some way to see what your selections are doing to the generated API call, but I couldn't find such an option here.

Given all of these inconsistent behaviors and poor timezone handling, I strongly recommend that you review the generated schedule after you save your query and ensure that it does what you expect it to do. (At this writing, this feature is still in beta, so hopefully this will all be resolved by the time it reaches GA.)

Destination for Query Results

This specifies where you want the results of the query to go. At the specified times, the query will be run and the results placed into this table. The table will be created on the first scheduled run. After that, you can choose append or overwrite; append will add the new rows to the bottom of the table, and overwrite will wipe the table and replace it with new data.

Advanced Options

There are two notification options to help you track status of jobs.

Send Email Notifications

If this box is checked, all failed jobs will send an email to the address associated with the query owner. The owner is whatever account you're logged in as to create the scheduled query—probably your personal email address. This doesn't give you a lot of options for notifying a distribution group, but for lower-priority work, it's a good thing to have.

Cloud Pub/Sub Topic

You can also publish job results to a Pub/Sub. Note that while the email only sends failures, the Pub/Sub will receive results for any job run. Since Cloud Scheduler has a similar mechanism, you might write a single function that collates status on all of your scheduled jobs and takes action if something goes wrong. One significant advantage both the BigQuery scheduler and Cloud Scheduler have is that they can tell you when jobs fail. (Traditional cron would just never fire, and so if your job was never invoked, you'd never know it had failed until angry users began calling you.)

Reviewing Queries

After you save your query, you can go to the Scheduled Queries sidebar again, and it will show you a list of your scheduled items. You can also delete or disable them from this window.

Clicking an individual job will let you see its run history and the current configuration. As I mentioned earlier, verify the configuration of your job, specifically the schedule string, start date, and end date, to ensure it matches your expectations. Thankfully, all times are in UTC here, so you should be able to do a straight comparison.

While less robust than the Cloud Scheduler, which we'll cover next, the BigQuery scheduler works well for operations isolated to BigQuery. These include all kinds of routine maintenance and data preparation. There's no reason you can't use more than one solution to fit your needs either, so you may find yourself deploying both scheduled queries and Cloud Scheduler after you've learned both.

Cloud Scheduler

To go to the scheduler console, open the hamburger menu and scroll down to tools. "Scheduler" is listed in the tools menu. When you go to the console for the first time, your only option will be to create a new job, or you will see scheduled jobs if you have already made them. Click "CREATE A JOB" to open the scheduling options.

Name

Choose a name for your job, as usual, that is descriptive and doesn't duplicate other jobs in your project. If you need help, follow the instructions in the preceding "BigQuery Scheduled Queries" section.

There is a nice filter option on the console that supports name, as well as target and the last time the job was run, so worst-case scenario, you can probably still find that needle in the haystack.

Frequency

You can skip this section if you're familiar with cron. Google Cloud Scheduler uses default cron syntax to describe job frequency. If you are new to cron or need a refresher, read on.

Cron (and, by extension, Cloud Scheduler) uses a shorthand that has been well established for decades. It is relatively flexible and easy to specify and works with pretty much any Unix or Linux scheduler tool. Unfortunately, I have yet to find an appointment scheduling system that lets me schedule my recurring meetings in cron syntax, but one can dream.

Point of note: You will hear both "cron" and "crontab" used to indicate this syntax. Cron is the daemon, or background-running process, that actually executes the scheduled tasks at the desired time. Crontab is the program that allows you to view and edit the syntax of the crontab file, which is the input that cron uses to run its jobs.

Formatting

As shown in Figure 10-3, the cron format is a space-separated list of five values, indicating the expression for recurrence:

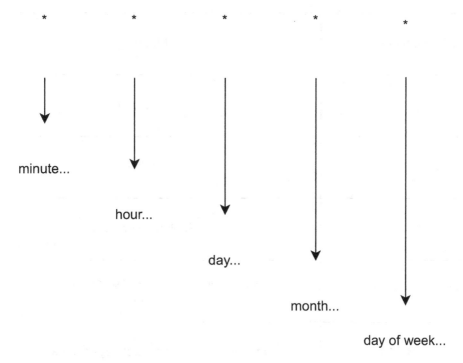

Figure 10-3. *** * * * (min, hour, day of month, month, day of week)*

The values thankfully predate JavaScript and are zero- or one-based as appropriate for the unit. So minutes are 0–59, hours 0–23, day of month 1–31, month of year 1–12, and day of week 0–7, where 0 is Sunday and 6 is Saturday. (7 is Sunday again, interchangeable with 0 in an attempt to support both Sunday and Monday as the start of the week.[1])

Cron implementations vary in how they handle illegal specifications. Cloud Scheduler is pretty good at catching invalid dates (like February 30th), but best practice is not to specify schedules that might be interpreted ambiguously, that is, every month on the 29th. Most systems will only run February 29th's job on every leap year.

Accordingly, here are some examples of common cron expressions.

---

[1]Thanks, Björn!

Expression	Meaning
* * * * *	Once a minute
*/30 * * * *	Every half an hour
0 9 * * *	At 9am every day
0 */1 1 1,4,7,10 *	Every hour on the first day of each quarter (Jan 1, Apr 1, Jul 1, and Oct 1)
*/15 9-18 * * 1-5	Every fifteen minutes on weekdays from 9am to 6pm

Figure 10-4. *Garden-variety cron expressions: once a minute, every Thursday, every other Saturday at 3 AM, once an hour from midnight to noon, that kind of thing*

If you want to use the cron format and have some odd use cases (undoubtedly specified by that one stakeholder you couldn't talk out of it...), you can start your job by doing some additional checking to see if the case is fully met. For example, if you want to run on the first of the month unless it's a full moon, you can set a cron expression to run on the first of the month and then check at the top of the code in the job if it's currently a full moon.

I really don't recommend this if you can avoid it, because you'll be coupling the schedule of the job to the job itself, which both makes the job less portable and imposes some additional restrictions that are difficult to document. Chances are in the future that some user will reschedule the job and then wonder why it's not firing. If you do have to do this, make liberal use of both code commenting and logging so that it doesn't create a tricky situation for someone else trying to reuse the job.

BigQuery Scheduling Format

It's inconsistently documented, but you can use the "English-like schedule" format from BigQuery scheduling here too. This could give you a little more flexibility when a single cron expression doesn't capture your schedule. I would still recommend using the cron format if you can, since it will be more widely recognized and understood.

I also found some references in the Google documentation calling it "App Engine cron format," which makes sense, since Cloud Scheduler was originally a cron service for App Engine only.

Tools

Considering the venerable age of the cron format, there are countless tools for helping you specify, test, and convert cron parameters for usability. One tool I have found especially useful is crontab.guru (`http://crontab.guru`), which you can use to generate expressions or to parse them into something you can read. It's also great if you're just trying to get a feel for the capabilities—you can click "random," and it will generate and parse a random cron expression. It does use non-standard syntax like @yearly and @daily, which Cloud Scheduler does not support. (Another quick tip: If you don't like this particular tool, I guarantee there are others for your desired stack or operating system.)

Timezone

Specify the timezone in which you want the job to run. This is actually a nice touch for jobs that need to run in local time to a particular user, but in general as with most time-based applications, you want to use Coordinated Universal Time (UTC).

The primary reason for this is that local time may observe Daylight Savings Time (DST). As we'll get to in the following, this may cause undesirable results unless you are specifically looking to follow local time.

Target

Cloud Scheduler allows three targets, from which you can trigger anything else you need to. Note that BigQuery itself is not a target, so you will be scheduling jobs in concert with other techniques to hit BigQuery directly. For example, you could use this in tandem with the App Engine stream we set up in Chapter 6 in order to stream data into BigQuery at a given time. That process works for any other code you would want to put into that function as well.

HTTP

HTTP is the most generic of the options. You can hit either an HTTP or an HTTPS endpoint with any method and a request body if required.

One major problem with the UI console is you cannot specify custom headers. Often, if you are hitting an arbitrary URL on a scheduled basis, you will need to identify yourself in some way using the HTTP headers, and that's not possible in the UI. It is, however, possible in the command line call, and we'll cover it there.

Scheduler supports all the HTTP methods, including PATCH and OPTIONS. I enjoy the idea that you'd want to make an OPTIONS call to an HTTP endpoint on a recurring basis with no ability to do anything with the output. I can think of only one minimally valuable case for doing this, which is if you wanted to ensure that a given endpoint was currently supporting some form of Cross-Origin Sharing Request (CORS). Either way, you aren't going to need OPTIONS for BigQuery!

If you specify POST, PUT, or PATCH, you will have the option to supply a request body. This may be useful if you are triggering calls to your APIs on a scheduled basis and need to distinguish between multiple behaviors.

Auth Header

If you have endpoints running on the public Internet (or, really, even if they aren't), it is a best practice to secure all of your endpoints. The last thing you need is unauthorized users learning about your scheduled endpoints and conducting denial-of-service attacks on them by hitting them repeatedly. Worse yet, the responses to those jobs may have sensitive information about your application's architecture that may render it vulnerable to other attacks.

Google Scheduler supports two basic methods of authorizing to HTTPS endpoints, OAuth and OIDC (OpenId Connect). Both require additional configuration and have some limitations.

The first is that you can only use the HTTPS scheme. This is a limitation of all authorization schemes, Google or otherwise; the HTTP headers must be transmitted securely so that they cannot be intercepted and used by malicious entities.

The second is that you will need to have a service account with the correct permissions to authorize at the destination. If you are using an OAuth token, that also means that you can only use endpoints on the googleapis.com domain. That service account must also have the proper permissions. At minimum, this is the Cloud

Scheduler Service Agent role. The default Cloud Scheduler principal already has this permission. Additionally, the account must have permissions to run whatever the destination service is.

Pub/Sub

This method lets you publish messages to any Pub/Sub endpoint in your project. To use it, you need only specify two things.

Target is the name of the topic in your project. The payload is the string you want to send to that topic. The payload should be specified in whatever format the subscriber to that queue is looking for. Note that some payload is required, even if you don't need parameters for whatever reason.

This method is best when you need to trigger an external workflow on a schedule. Since services like Dataflow support Pub/Sub as a trigger, you can initiate a Dataflow pipeline on a defined schedule by using this method. Set Cloud Scheduler to trigger a Pub/Sub on your schedule, and have Dataflow subscribe to that Pub/Sub as the job trigger. That pipeline could then handle multiple actions on your data, including insertion to both BigQuery and other destinations, custom logging, and so forth.

One thing to be aware of is that using a Pub/Sub pattern disconnects your scheduled job from the thing that will execute on it. It is fully asynchronous, which means that Cloud Scheduler will consider the job to be successful when it has pushed your message to the queue. If nothing is on the other side to receive it, the job will continue running successfully, but nothing will happen. A job configured to run on a minute-by-minute basis with no target will stack over a thousand messages in the queue, all of which will sit unread.

If you are using Pub/Sub, design defensively around this pattern so that the job behaves in a failure condition.

App Engine HTTP

The presence of this item hints at Cloud Scheduler's origins. Before Cloud Scheduler existed, App Engine had a built-in cron service—the very same service as was recommended to me in this chapter's introductory story. That scheduler worked with some substantial limitations. (For example, it only supported the GET method. Maybe that's why they overcompensated and now you can schedule OPTIONS?) Now, with Cloud Scheduler, you can recreate all of your legacy App Engine crons as scheduler jobs.

This form is also very simple to use: specify the URL and the service. The URL must start with a slash, as it represents an App Engine URL available to your project. The service represents the API on that App Engine application that you want to call.

You specify the usual HTTP method here (minus PATCH and OPTIONS) that you want the endpoint to receive. And as with the HTTP target, if you specify POST or PUT, you will also need to supply a body.

App Engine gives you two additional features here, both of which remedy limitations with the earlier App Engine Scheduler. You can target specific instances or versions of your App Engine applications, whereas before, the App Engine Scheduler was locked to a specific instance and the version that instance was using. Probably also not super useful features for integration with BigQuery, but I note them for the sake of completeness.

As for authorization, with App Engine, Google will automatically be able to authorize the call inside the same project using its built-in security model. This is one area in which GCP has been steadily improving, allowing security parameters to be handled directly by the Identity and Access Management (IAM) system.

Target Use Cases

There is some substantial overlap between targets, and many use cases can be supported by all three. Here's a quick overview to help you decide:

- HTTP/HTTPS: Use this option for synchronous calls to endpoints either inside or outside of GCP, excepting App Engine:

  - With OAuth for services inside of GCP

  - With OIDC for services outside of GCP

- Pub/Sub: Use this option for asynchronous calls to workflows within GCP, where you know that the message will be received in a timely fashion or with which you can tolerate stacking or delay.

- App Engine HTTP: Use for any endpoint inside App Engine.

Once you've specified all of your options, you can save the job. If this was the first job you've scheduled, you will now see the regular console, showing all of your jobs.

Status

A couple of nice columns appear here which help you to see the progress and results of your jobs. You can see the last time the job ran (or if it has never run), the result of the job (failure or success), and the logs. You can also trigger a one-time run for testing or to compensate for a missing job.

Two notes on this: First, remember when I said earlier that you shouldn't couple scheduling logic into the job itself? If your job checks to see if it's currently a full moon, running an off-schedule job won't do anything if the conditions internal to the job aren't met. Keep in mind that you'll be giving up this flexibility as well as some intelligence about why this particular job didn't run—although you can compensate for that with the next note.

Scheduled jobs produce events which are recorded in Cloud Logging, which we'll be covering in greater detail in Chapter 12. You'll be able to store the logs from the Cloud Scheduler in BigQuery and produce detailed reports of how often jobs succeed and fail, how often they run, and so forth.

You can also, with some loss of precision, use the logging to determine whether a job was run by the scheduler or manually from the console. The first event the scheduler logs is an "AttemptStarted" in this event. This log contains both the received timestamp and the scheduled time for the job. When you run a job manually, the scheduled time remains the next scheduled time the job was to run, whereas the timestamp will be the current time. Assuming you didn't click the "Run Now" button precisely when the job was supposed to run, you can probably tell what triggered it and use that to inform a different behavior in your job. If you reach this level of complexity for scheduling, you should probably solve the problem with documentation, that is, write a detailed description for the job that includes all of the non-standard things it is doing.

However, I encourage you to take a look at the logs for Cloud Scheduler anyway, since they are relatively simple compared to other services and will help you understand the process of creating event sinks and acting on logging when we get there in Chapter 12.

Command-Line Scheduling

Another way to schedule jobs is to use the Google Cloud command-line tool (gcloud). Since schedulers evolved on the command line, it seems completely natural to continue the trend. Also, Google tends to release new features to the command-line tool that are not available, or not yet available, in the UI. Since Cloud Scheduler is a relatively new service, some of the useful features are not exposed in the UI.

The command to interact with Cloud Scheduler is

```
gcloud scheduler jobs list
```

The default behavior is to show you all of your scheduled jobs. The full documentation on the command at https://cloud.google.com/sdk/gcloud/reference/scheduler/jobs is comprehensive and will show you how you could convert the job specification from what we just reviewed on the Cloud UI to the command-line version. However, here are some flags that will configure the behaviors not exposed to the UI.

--attempt-deadline

The --attempt-deadline flag will allow you to set a timeout for initial response from the endpoint. If your request doesn't respond within this deadline, the job fails.

--headers

The --headers flag will let you specify HTTP headers to send with the job. This works with the HTTP and App Engine targets. (Pub/Sub has no HTTP interface.) If your destination endpoint requires certain headers to operate, this is the only way to specify them.

Yes, you could also use this to allow the scheduler to hit endpoints with Basic Authorization enabled. Please avoid this if at all possible; your credentials will be stored with the job for anyone with the scheduler read permission to see, and this is not in any way secure.

--message-body-from-file

You can create a job's POST/PUT/PATCH body from a file, rather than in the UI console. This is useful for interoperating with a tool that you may already be using to construct POST bodies, like Insomnia or Postman.

Retries and Backoffs

The other major feature set supported by the CLI but unavailable to the UI is control of the retries and backoff system. Cloud Scheduler will automatically retry the job on a schedule you specify, if you want it to. This lets you get some of the advantages of the asynchronous Pub/Sub method without having to write any code to deal with failures or stacking.

Configuring these uses a combination of five flags, as follows:

- --max-backoff: The longest amount of time between retries along the exponential backoff path

- --max-doublings: The number of times to double the wait between retries, that is, how many iterations of exponential backoff

- --max-retry-attempts: How many times to retry

- --max-retry-duration: How long to retry, in total, from the first attempt

- --min-backoff: How long to wait before the first retry

For a deeper explanation of how exponential backoff works, see Chapter 6, where I explained it in the context of request quotas for BigQuery streaming.

Good Scheduling Practices

When creating jobs and managing their environment, there are a number of practices that are worth following to ensure that jobs run the way they are supposed to, have no intended side effects, and are easy to understand and maintain.

Rescheduling

The behavior for how jobs behave if you disable/enable them varies by system. In Cloud Scheduler's case, if a job was scheduled to run while disabled, that job will run immediately as soon as you reenable it, rather than waiting for the next scheduled time.

This is an important note if you disabled the job because it became unsafe to run or had a potentially negative effect. If the job clears all of your commission values on the fifth of the month and you disable it on the fourth to prevent that, turning it on the sixth will do it anyway, rather than waiting for the next fifth of the month. This has potentially catastrophic consequences.

Idempotency

Idempotency refers to a condition where a function has the same results no matter how many times it is invoked. It's important in functional programming as a related principle to immutability. The easiest way to comply with idempotency is to have the first call take the action and subsequent calls recognize that the action has already been taken and do nothing.

Cloud Scheduler operates on an "at least once" delivery model. This means that your job is guaranteed to run. However, in some cases it may run more than once. This seems like a silly thing to note, since by definition a recurring job is going to hit an endpoint more than once. However, if your job is doing something that relies on the external environment, make sure you protect it from this situation.

In the full moon example, say that you schedule your job to run daily, but the job does nothing unless it is also a full moon. The job's responsibility is to toggle the werewolf state for all werewolves in a given GCP region. Correspondingly, it may assume that since only one job in the month will qualify for the full moon state, it can just toggle the state regardless. This means that if Cloud Scheduler sent the message twice and it were a full moon, the job would first turn everyone into werewolves, but then turn them back again! In cases like these, protection for idempotency is critical. (The solution in this case would be, in addition to checking if it is a full moon, to check if the werewolves have already been activated and do nothing if so.)

Timezones

In any event, if you are not using UTC, be sure to choose the correct timezone, even though multiple timezone specifications will have the same UTC offset at any given time. For example, even though in the summertime Pacific Daylight Time and Mountain Standard Time (i.e., Arizona) are both UTC-7, this will not hold true once DST ends in October and the west coast returns to one hour earlier.

This also ties into idempotency in that local time may repeat or skip hours. Daylight Savings Time is implemented in the United States such that when clocks move forward in the springtime, they go from 1:59:59 AM local time directly to 3:00:00 AM. If you have a job scheduled to run every night at 2 AM, this job will not run in US local time that night. In UTC, it will be a fixed time, which means it will run one hour later in local time, but will not be skipped.

If your business operates in a single timezone and you are doing business-related activity that is meant to occur at a given local time, the behavior to run one absolute hour later during part of the year could be correct. I agree that if you are scheduling the start and end of a sale, it's unusual to have the sale start at midnight in the winter and 1 AM in the summer. In those cases, you'll have to decide which time is more relevant. But for all these reasons, and many more, prefer UTC everywhere unless you have a compelling reason to do something else.

Testing

When you first create a job, test it both by clicking "Run Now" and by scheduling an invocation to occur several minutes in the future. You might do this when you first buy an alarm clock, to make sure that it works one minute from now, reasoning that it will then also wake you up in the morning. While in most cases running the job manually should replicate all of the test conditions, I also prefer the peace of mind that Cloud Scheduler is running as intended.

Also, be sure to check the logs for the first couple invocations of your job, to make sure it is stable. As I mentioned before, you can run the scheduler logs into a BigQuery sink if you need more detailed information available there.

Resolution

The maximum resolution of Cloud Scheduler (and most standard cron implementations) is one minute. The mechanics of running a serverless and globally distributed timing system make it difficult to guarantee timing to a shorter interval. Additionally, while the task will run inside the minute you specify, it's not guaranteed to start precisely at the zeroth second of that minute, though it usually gets pretty close. Anyway, you shouldn't use Cloud Scheduler for tasks that you need to schedule more precisely.

Overlap

Cloud Scheduler will not allow two simultaneous executions of the same job. If your job is still running when the next invocation fires, the second invocation will be delayed.

There are a few ways to handle this. If your job takes too long, set the schedule farther apart; by definition you'll be running continuously anyway. If your job only takes too long under heavy volume, you could use the Pub/Sub architecture to stack executions asynchronously. When traffic is heavy, the stacked calls will cause the process to run continuously. After traffic falls again, the job will "catch up" and begin running on the regular process again.

Cost/Maintenance

At this time, the free tier for Scheduler allows for three jobs. Additional jobs cost 0.10 USD per month. This is unlikely to break the bank, but if you aren't using a job, pause or remove it anyway.

Additionally, if the job remains running and is still consuming destination resources, you'll continue to get billed for those too. A rogue Dataflow pipeline operating on a frequent schedule can become quite expensive. (BigQuery can save the day again, though! You can export Cloud Billing reports to BigQuery too, where you can do analysis on where your costs are leaking.)

If you're only using Cloud Scheduler for light-duty work, you can almost certainly remain on the free tier. The Pub/Sub free tier allows 10 GB of free data a month. Say you run a job every minute using your free-tier schedule allowance. You could send 3-kilobyte payloads per message and still not pay a penny.

Other Scheduling Methods

Besides Cloud Scheduler, there are several other options for scheduling BigQuery activity. Here are a few additional possibilities.

Cloud Tasks

Cloud Tasks is a service on GCP designed to allow for asynchronous workflows. Essentially, it is a distributed execution queue. The primary use with respect to BigQuery is that you could use Cloud Tasks as an intermediate layer between a user and a long-running database update.

For example, let's say that you surface data from BigQuery to users on a custom report portal. When the user clicks the button to request a report, BigQuery initiates a process that could take minutes or hours to complete. The user's synchronous call from the application could create a task in a Cloud Tasks queue and then immediately return to the user to let them know that their report will be ready later. The application flow can continue uninterrupted while the report is queued and executed.

In the context of scheduling, Cloud Tasks also supports running a task at a future time. However, it is not for recurring tasks; a single task is queued and executed once, even if the execution is not until a later point.

Cloud Tasks has no UI for creating and managing tasks, and since it's not a recurring scheduler, we won't go into greater depth here. This topic is more of note to applications engineers, who can build it into workflows which have downstream calls to BigQuery.

Nonetheless, it is a powerful tool for separating the user interface of a custom application from long-running processes like complicated BigQuery analysis workflows. If, after your warehouse is up and running, you hear users complaining that "reports take forever" or "when I try to download a report, I have to wait for minutes," suggest that your engineering team look into Cloud Tasks as a way to let the user know that the process will take some time and they can come back later to retrieve the results.

Cloud Composer

Cloud Composer is the Google Cloud implementation of Apache Airflow, a general-purpose workflow scheduler. On the surface, it looks somewhat similar to Apache Beam (see Chapter 7); but despite its utilization of a DAG (directed-acyclic graph) to execute nodes in a sequence, it is not a data processing solution. You can certainly use Airflow to trigger Beam pipelines—well, let me rephrase. You can certainly use Composer to trigger Dataflow—but the concept of "streaming" really doesn't make sense in the Airflow paradigm anyway.

GCP will handle the server provisioning for you when you create an environment. You specify the characteristics of the underlying Google Kubernetes Engine (GKE) cluster, and it spins it up for you as an Airflow environment. This takes a while, but then you can begin to build your DAG. Airflow is Python-native, but it can speak other languages as well. Using "operators," you can connect to other systems and invoke tasks as part of your workflow. There is, of course, a BigQuery operator,[2] among many others.

Ah, but back to the main point: Airflow DAGs can be scheduled using cron syntax. Specifying a start date, an end date, and a cron schedule will automatically create an instance of the workflow at the specified times.

If you're comfortable in Python and want to build more complex workflows, Composer is a good choice. By centralizing the workflows in an open source tool, you also gain some portability, as well as better self-documentation of what your workflows are doing and how they are performing.

---

[2]https://airflow.apache.org/docs/stable/_api/airflow/contrib/operators/bigquery_
operator/index.html

BigQuery Transfer Service

The BigQuery Transfer Service is an option if you need a single operation, namely, transferring data inside of BigQuery or from other services such as Amazon S3. To use this service, click "Transfers" on the left side of the BigQuery UI. For a simple dataset operation, choose "Dataset Copy" as the source. You can transfer datasets within the same region or to other regions.

Note that this appears to be a different UI than the Google Cloud Platform "Transfer" service, which can load data into Google Cloud Storage on a recurring basis. Of course, you could combine that with Cloud Scheduler to get regular data imports from Amazon S3 or Azure Storage.

Summary

Google Cloud has several methods you can use to schedule BigQuery processes at a later or recurring schedule. BigQuery has a scheduler built in, which is based on the BigQuery Data Transfer service. The BigQuery scheduler is useful for controlling processes that run entirely inside BigQuery and which can be represented in a BigQuery SQL command. For more complex processes, Google Cloud Scheduler can trigger any arbitrary HTTP, App Engine, or Pub/Sub endpoint, which you can then use to initiate BigQuery tasks. The command-line application for Cloud Scheduler exposes a few additional features that the UI does not. Google Cloud has several other scheduling systems that you may be able to use if you have a specific use case.

In the next chapter, we'll look at Cloud Functions, GCP's solution for functions as a service and which will allow you to make your data processing pipelines even more powerful while still remaining completely serverless.

CHAPTER 11

Serverless Functions with GCP

If you've been building on the cloud, you have likely encountered the functions-as-a-service (FaaS) paradigm already. Amazon has offered the Lambda service since 2014, and Google's equivalent, Cloud Functions, has been generally available since 2016. Other public cloud providers have this capability as well, and increasingly we are seeing it even in specialized platforms. For example, Twilio, the popular communications management platform, has its own flavor called "Twilio Functions." Twilio Functions is actually AWS Lambda under the hood, but augmented with tool-specific logic and shortcuts.

This term is frequently used along with "serverless technology." Serverless doesn't specify a compute boundary specifically to be a function, but the premise is related in that you don't manage (or know about) the underlying servers. Serverless is also somewhat of a marketing misnomer, since there are still servers involved. This technology is distinct from paradigms like peer-to-peer, which do not actually have a "server" designation.

Google Cloud Functions is a great tool to have in your arsenal. Let's dig into how they work, how they work with BigQuery, and when you can use them to your advantage.

Benefits

Before we get into the construction of functions that augment the power of BigQuery, let's talk a little bit about what function as a service offers that differs from other solutions. This solution may or may not be appropriate for your use case. There are a few key benefits that make cloud functions worth considering for your workload.

231

© Mark Mucchetti 2020
M. Mucchetti, *BigQuery for Data Warehousing*, https://doi.org/10.1007/978-1-4842-6186-6_11

Management

You're already enjoying one of the major benefits of serverless, which is that BigQuery itself is a serverless technology. It's not a function as a service, since it has underlying persistent data storage and divides its queries into compute units on its own.

BigQuery and Google Cloud Functions have this benefit in common. Just as you don't have to provision and configure a data warehouse to use BigQuery, you don't need to configure a server, set up a runtime, and scale an application in order to use functions.

Scalability

Functions scale automatically based on usage. To the previous item, since you aren't managing the server, the cloud provider is free to distribute the queries however it needs to in order to service your requests. This is generally accomplished by setting some hard limits on what you can do inside a cloud function, which we'll go over in "Drawbacks."

Cost

As we have discussed in earlier chapters for BigQuery, Cloud Functions are also extremely low cost due to the small resource demand they exert per call. Just as with database servers, the cost of running your own application is stepwise and doesn't decrease with demand. If you're paying a dollar per hour per server, you're going to incur 168 dollars in cost a week no matter what you are doing. As soon as you have too much traffic for one server to support, you go to two servers and pay 336 dollars a week, even if you only need that second server to make a few extra calls.

With serverless, you're paying only for what you use, per function call. If no one uses your application for a week, you maintain availability without paying anything. This technique, where applicable, can generate huge cost savings over more traditional provisioning.

Reliability

One of the largest problems with maintaining your own servers is making sure they are available at all times to service requests. One misbehaving API call might interfere and crash the entire service layer. Tying up resources on the server for one user might impact the experience for all other users. Wearing my platform architect hat, I can guarantee that no client wants to be told their service is degraded because of another client.

Running functions as a service allows you to be confident that your calls will be available to users when they are needed, without any need for effort on your part.

Drawbacks
Latency

If you've heard anything from functions-as-a-service detractors, it's about the dreaded "cold start." Cold start refers to the latency from when you initiate a function call until a server is ready to handle that call. In the early days of serverless, this was often considered to be a deal breaker for running a back end. Cloud providers have worked to minimize the frequency and duration of cold starts, but deploying a function in a user-facing capacity may cause frustration when a user has to wait several seconds for the application to start responding.

While it's not something to ignore, there are ways to mitigate this drawback. In my opinion, the best way is not to use serverless in these use cases, but if you're set on it, you can use a runtime that spins up more quickly or have a scheduled call that pings your functions periodically to "keep them warm."

Resource Limits

Generally, cloud providers impose limits on how much memory, compute power, or time an individual cloud function can use. This means that serverless is inherently inappropriate for long-running processes.

However, using a more event-driven model, you can parallelize work so that time traditionally spent waiting for the next step in a workflow is spent idling. For example, you can set the trigger for a function to be on an item entering a queue. The function does its work and then submits a message to another queue for the next step in the process.

Portability

You may be familiar with Docker or the concept of containers. Containers aim to bring portability to computing by allowing you to create a package that has all of the dependencies and code necessary to run your application. FaaS is one step more granular and, as such, doesn't come with any of the same guarantees. Different cloud providers will have different deployment mechanisms, different supported runtimes, and different ways to interface with file systems and databases.

If it's important to you to have your code easily deployable across clouds and your own data centers, this may be of concern to you. In the scope of this book, you're already using BigQuery in the Google Cloud Platform so using the companion services is not as much of a hurdle.

It's also worth noting that there are several solutions intended to address this drawback. NodeJS has a package called "serverless," which abstracts serverless compute across multiple clouds and allows you to write code that can run in multiple places. While not especially applicable to BigQuery, this may be a consideration for you if you are already running the majority of your workload in another cloud and still need to pipe data around. There are also ways to use the Node serverless package to package and deploy functions you've written in other cross-cloud–compatible runtimes such as Python, but that one I'll leave as an exercise to the reader.

This area is evolving rapidly. Cloud Run—based on knative—reached general availability in late 2019. This allows you to run containers in a serverless environment without dealing with container management. The collection of technologies that comprise Google Anthos are beginning to enable cross-cloud and on-premise deployment in a managed and transparent fashion.[1]

Organization

In my opinion, this drawback of serverless systems is under-considered. To manage code and databases, we have reliable source control systems and documentation structures rooted in the best practice of several decades ago. When using managed cloud systems, it is a lot harder to understand what you've built and how it is working and, to the uninitiated or newly introduced, can appear like magic. Public cloud providers have hundreds of services and, as we've repeatedly seen, countless valid implementations across services and clouds. Once you have an arbitrarily large number of cloud functions, it can become difficult to organize and track them.

---

[1]This only scratches the surface of what breaks down into the current iteration of the monolith vs. microservice conversation. It hasn't sent a shockwave through the data analysis community—yet.

There are plenty of companies whose technologies solely serve to automate the creation and reconstruction of cloud infrastructure. If this sort of tool is not applicable at your scale, at least be sure to document what you have done for the benefit of others who need to understand and work on it. Unfortunately, on several occasions I've only been able to figure out what portions of a cloud infrastructure are actually active and relevant by looking at the monthly bill.

I'm aware this shades fairly far out of data warehouse management and into DevOps, but I think it's an important skill to develop as you venture outside of the BigQuery walls to build functions and pipelines that interact with other services. Even in the managed services world, these things are often not intuitive.

Cloud Functions and BigQuery

Some interactive workloads are not appropriate for serverless functions, specifically those that will take a long time to return to a user who is waiting for results. Most of the processes we discuss in this book are batch jobs run without a waiting user, that is, scheduled jobs, ETL, or analytics post-processing. These cases are perfect candidates for Cloud Functions, which is why it's worth the effort to become familiar with them and how they can give you capabilities beyond what is available strictly in BigQuery.

Generally you will be accessing BigQuery from a cloud function, not the other way around. BigQuery can't execute cloud functions directly, although there are some convoluted ways around this, which we will cover in Chapter 12 with Cloud Logging (formerly known as Stackdriver.)

Creating a Cloud Function

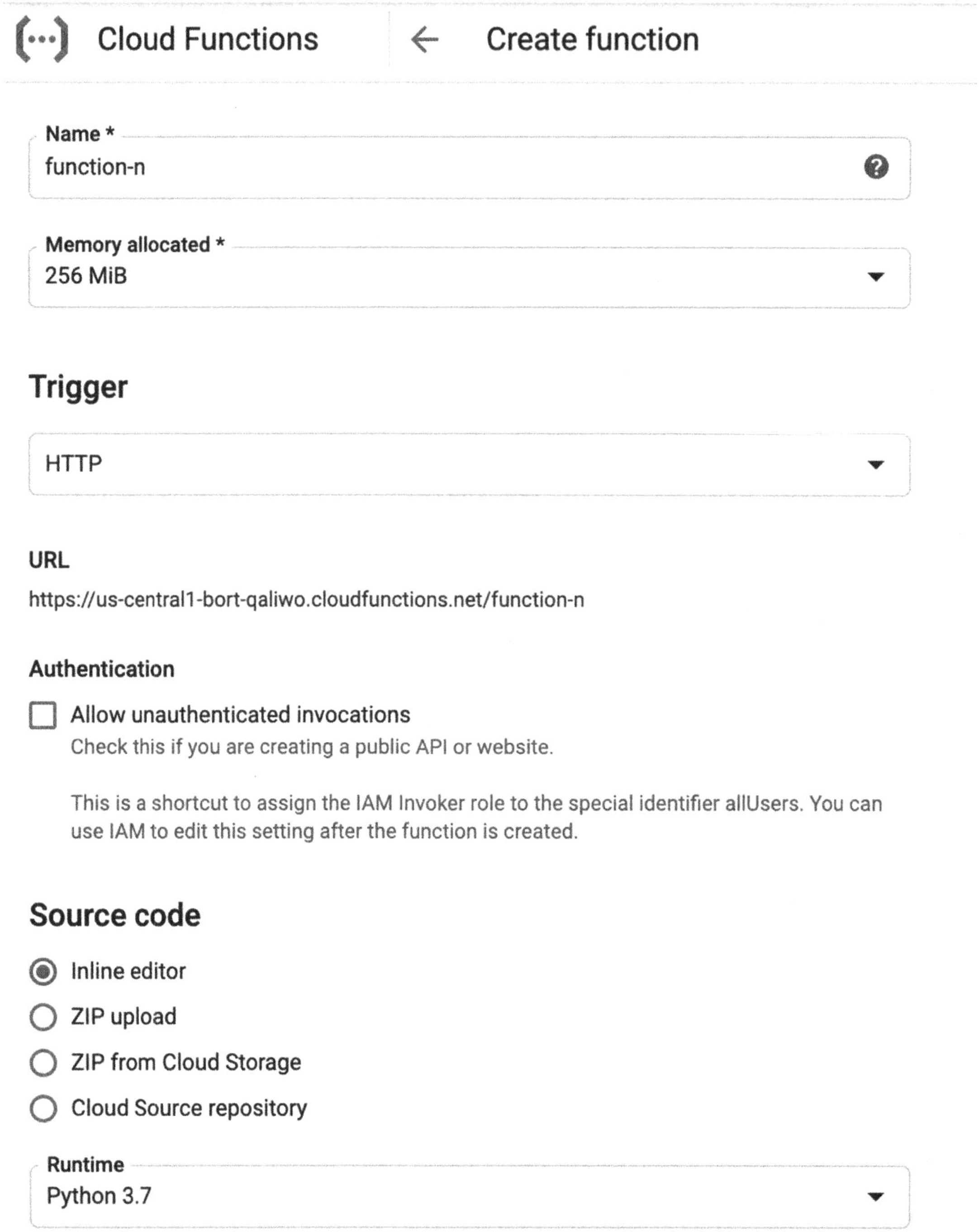

[⋯] Cloud Functions   ←   Create function

Name *
function-n   ❓

Memory allocated *
256 MiB   ▼

Trigger

HTTP   ▼

URL

https://us-central1-bort-qaliwo.cloudfunctions.net/function-n

Authentication

☐ Allow unauthenticated invocations
Check this if you are creating a public API or website.

This is a shortcut to assign the IAM Invoker role to the special identifier allUsers. You can
use IAM to edit this setting after the function is created.

Source code

◉ Inline editor
○ ZIP upload
○ ZIP from Cloud Storage
○ Cloud Source repository

Runtime
Python 3.7   ▼

Figure 11-1. *Cloud Function creation screen*

Creating a cloud function is pretty straightforward. If you've used AWS Lambda before, then these steps will be familiar to you, and you should have no trouble getting under way.

Go to the hamburger menu on the cloud console and find "Cloud Functions" under the Compute heading. You may have to enable it for your project, after which you can click "Create Function." This will open a configuration window for you to specify the parameters.

Name

Your cloud function's name will determine the URL on which you access it. Choose a name carefully, proceeding from general to specific, that is, application-feature-function-activity. (For example, ramen-bq-ingest-performance-load might take a performance file and load it into the BigQuery instance for the "ramen" application.) There is only one namespace for functions inside each GCP project, so you want to make sure you can distinguish among a lot of things that load data. Using load-1, load-2, load-3, and so on is a good way to cause problems quickly: don't be that person.

Memory Allocated

You can allocate up to 2 gibibytes of RAM for your function. This directly affects the cost of your function, so choose a reasonable number for the workload your function is performing.

Less commonly known is that this also controls the approximate CPU clock your function will run at. If you need faster invocation, raise the amount of RAM. If you're serious about this, you would probably also want to time your functions to ensure you actually need the increased processing time. To be clear though, cloud functions cost something along the order of magnitude of a penny an hour, so you might not want to spend too much time tuning this.

Trigger

How your function will be called. This is covered in detail in the next section, but note that as you change the options in the dropdown, the accompanying code sample also changes. This is because the function will expect a different message format depending on where it originated.

Authentication

This is a checkbox indicating whether you want to allow unauthenticated invocations. Essentially, checking this box makes your cloud function public. Only check this box if you want to do that! For ETL, data transformation, and so on, your functions will likely not be public. Using Google Cloud Identity and Access Management (IAM), you can ensure that your internal functions have access to BigQuery and your other services without making anything public.

Source Code

Here, you get to choose where the source for your function comes from.

Inline Editor

If you're writing an incredibly simple function, you can get away with using the inline editor. You wouldn't really want to do this at any substantial scale because your source control of that function won't be very good—Google Cloud will keep track of versions as you update the source, but every time you save a change, it will be automatically deploying the function, which is not great if it's in production and you break it.

More importantly, you can only upload one code file and one definition file (i.e., requirements.txt) in this mode, which will be pretty severely constraining if you need lots of external packages or any substantive amount of logic.

ZIP Upload

In this mode, you can upload a ZIP file containing all of your code and dependency files. This would at least let you use a code editor, from which you could then zip the file and upload it here. In some ways, this is even more unwieldy than inline, because you have no access to the code, but it's also not part of any formalized build process.

ZIP from Cloud Storage

This method is the same as the previous, except that the file comes from Cloud Storage instead of your local machine.

Cloud Source Repository

Unknown to nearly everyone, Google has its own GitHub competitor called Cloud Source, and you can use git-like syntax to manage code and builds inside of it. You can load cloud functions directly from Cloud Source branches, enabling a pretty seamless build process from end to end.

While out of scope for this book, Cloud Source also supports mirroring repos to GitHub, and Cloud Build supports automatic triggers to deploy cloud functions, so you can tie auto-deploy, environments, and your full continuous integration solution to cloud functions as well.

Runtime

Google Cloud Functions supports three major flavors of runtime: Golang, NodeJS, and Python. A note if you do use Python: With Python 2.x's official discontinuation on January 1, 2020, GCP is gradually deprecating support for it. At this writing, Cloud Functions only support Python at version 3.7.

Google Cloud SDKs function equally well in any of these runtimes, so choose the language you are most familiar with or that your organization uses elsewhere. Another major difference between GCP Cloud Functions and other offerings like AWS Lambda and Azure Functions is that runtime support is more limited. GCP does support languages like C#, Java, and Ruby on Google App Engine and Cloud Run, but not here.

There are a few undocumented and unsupported ways to make Cloud Functions use other libraries using dynamic compilation, but I would not recommend them due to lack of official support, increased cold start times, and the relatively easy alternatives.

Function to Execute

The function needs to know its entry point, that is, which method it's going to start in when the function is invoked. This specification varies by language, but this method will also need a signature that can accept the appropriate payload you asked for earlier, like an HTTP request or Pub/Sub payload.

Region

You can choose the region in which to load your function. Choose the location closest to the majority of your users. Note that some locations are more expensive than others, so consult tier pricing if this is important to you.

Timeout

This specifies how many seconds you want the function to run before aborting unsuccessfully. The default is 60 and the global maximum is 540 (9 minutes). Set this value to the maximum amount of time you expect your function to ever take: if the function churns away uselessly for nine minutes, you'll be charged for time you didn't really need to take.

Maximum Function Instances

This specifies how many instances you want to coexist. The default is 0, which means you'll get as many as you need. You might want to limit this if you are concerned about public denial-of-service attacks or if a huge number of concurrent requests would indicate a bug in the system and you don't want to pay for that. (I once had a developer rack up a several-hundred-dollar bill in the span of a few minutes because an infinite loop set off thousands of concurrent function requests.)

Service Account

Any activity in GCP needs a principal identity to execute against. Nonuser interactions use service accounts as principals to do this. Following the principle of least privilege, best practice would mean using a service account for this function which has the minimum permissions required to do its job. For instance, if the function is reading a file from Google Cloud Storage and writing it to BigQuery, it needs only Cloud Functions permissions, Cloud Storage reader, and BigQuery writer.[2] This prevents someone from being able to upload code that takes other, unwanted actions.

Ingress Settings

This is an additional setting you can use to make sure your cloud function can be accessed only by appropriate parties. By default, it allows all traffic. You can further

---

[2]roles/storage.objectView, bigquery.dataEditor, and bigquery.jobUser, respectively.

restrict its accessibility to a single cloud project or a single Virtual Private Cloud (VPC) perimeter.

Egress Settings

This is another security setting you can use to prevent your cloud function from accessing things it shouldn't. By default, cloud functions will have access to the Internet. Using this feature, you can set them to access only resources within a single Virtual Private Cloud.

The same least privilege principle applies here: if your cloud function doesn't need access to the Internet to do its job, don't give it Internet access.

Environment Variables

The purpose of environment variables in any context is to supply settings to code without modifying that code. You can use them similarly here—any variables outside of execution that your function can use to execute can be provided to the environment. This also lets you maintain the same code across multiple environments merely by altering the associated settings.

Your data pipelines may not have multiple environments, but you still might want to store variable values in here like the names of BigQuery datasets or Cloud Storage buckets.

Deploying the Cloud Function

Once you've completed the settings, click Create. If all the settings have been filled out, you'll go to the main Cloud Functions view, which will show a spinner indicating that your new function is being deployed.

		Name ↑	Region	Trigger	Runtime
☐	⬤				
☐	↻	function-n	us-central1	HTTP	Python 3.7

Figure 11-2. *Function deployment*

After a short amount of time, you should see a green checkbox showing that the function has been deployed successfully. Clicking the function will show you top-level information about the performance of the function. There shouldn't be any data here since no one has used the function yet.

You'll also see all the settings you just selected. If you click Edit, you'll be brought back into the previous window where you can modify those settings however you like. There's also a built-in tester you can use to try out your function with the permissions properly set.

Lastly, if you click Trigger, you'll see how the function is invoked, which we're just about to cover in the next section. If it's an HTTP request, you can actually click the link directly and see the function's URL.

Assuming that you configured it not to be accessible to the Internet, you'll get a 403 error. That's good—your function is secure.

Invoking Cloud Functions

There are quite a few ways to execute your cloud function now that you've built it. Setting up your execution pipeline will require some operational architecture know-how to serve your particular use case(s). Let's cover each invocation method with an eye to how it might be useful in your data processing workflows.

HTTP Trigger

This is the lowest common denominator for invoking a function and generally presumes there are other systems out there managing their own infrastructure. You would use this for receiving webhook calls or event data from external systems or even if you just wanted to accept a payload directly from an application for processing into BigQuery.

(If you want to process files, you can use Cloud Storage triggers directly and skip the API call.)

Cloud Pub/Sub Triggers

Cloud Pub/Sub is Google Cloud Platform's native service for queue management. This is your best bet for gluing services together and making asynchronous workflows for processing. A simple example would be that you want to insert a row into BigQuery to log a certain event. Rather than pausing the event for the BigQuery insert to occur, you can have the event drop a message into a Pub/Sub queue. A cloud function would then pick it up, read the payload, and insert the results into BigQuery. In this case, you have effectively disconnected the BigQuery performance load from the event load itself.

Queue-driven programming is a very common paradigm, so it is good to be familiar with it as you will see it frequently. With BigQuery in the mix, it gives you two benefits: One, as we discussed earlier, is disconnecting the two steps in the process. The other is that you can isolate them logically as well—you can connect whatever you want to the other side of the queue, making more and more complicated responses to the event's log, without ever changing the code of the event itself.

Cloud Storage Triggers

This may be the most interesting of the bunch for its relevance to BigQuery, and in fact we have talked about this in earlier chapters as useful for all kinds of ETL.

In the bad old days, developers used to spend months writing "importer" applications, which often didn't even do the ETL, later handled by the database layer. Importers only had one job—to monitor for the presence of files in a folder, parse them in some format, and stage them for the database to do something with. I can't even enumerate all the problems you encounter when building such an importer from scratch: memory overflow, importers failing to notice a file being created, validating records... It's a wonder these things worked at all.

Using a Cloud Storage pipeline, you can build a serverless importer in an irresponsibly short amount of time. Cloud Storage triggers use Pub/Sub under the hood, but automatically fire events when objects are created or deleted. I'll detail a working example in the following section.

Cloud Firestore

As we discussed in Chapter 7, Cloud Firestore is Google's NoSQL managed database technology. It's great for dumping in data directly for end users, but it's not designed for (and frankly is terrible at) querying or analyzing the data. The best way to use this with BigQuery is to write a function that listens to changes in your Firestore instance and loads some portion of the data into BigQuery. For straightforward applications with less complex ETL, this can save you the trouble of spinning up a heavy-duty Dataflow pipeline or messing with custom mappers.

That being said, you really do want to watch out for schemas if you go this route. Firestore uses JSON documents, and you will need some way of translating them into a columnar format for BigQuery. If your documents have a lot of nesting and repeating fields and you want to represent those in BigQuery, you may need a more robust approach.

You can also opt just to dump the JSON into BigQuery directly and deal with it later, but that may cause you to have lower performance and higher costs from dealing with the unstructured data directly.

Direct Triggers

I include this for the sake of completeness; direct triggers are only for debugging and not to be used in production workloads. They let you trigger cloud functions directly from the command line for testing. You can use this to simulate the other methods too, that is, by supplying a mock payload for a Pub/Sub message as if it had been triggered directly from the queue.

There's no direct application to BigQuery for this one, other than that you will want some method of being able to test your cloud functions.

Firebase Triggers

There are some other Firebase triggers that you can use to trigger Cloud Functions. These could be useful to you if you run your mobile back end entirely on Firebase and want to collect data about that application's performance in BigQuery. In practice, you would use these the same way as the other triggers, having a function collect this information and trigger an insert into BigQuery.

Cloud Scheduler

We covered Cloud Scheduler in the previous chapter, but in this particular area, it can deliver massive benefits to asynchronous workflows. Before Cloud Scheduler debuted, you could set up an amazingly complicated matrix of functions and triggers and quietly humming infrastructure, but there was no managed way to make it execute on a schedule. Organizations found themselves spinning up the only servers in their otherwise serverless landscape solely to run cron jobs and make sure the trains ran on time.

I'm happy to report that that world has also faded into the past, since Cloud Scheduler jobs can invoke Cloud Functions directly. Any transformation, ETL job, or server maintenance that you currently do overnight can now be run as a Cloud Scheduler task. Cloud Scheduler is compatible with cron format, so you can move your maintenance triggers into GCP directly.

Real-World Application

Now that you know what cloud functions are, how they are created, and how your application might handle them in the real world, let's take a look at a simple example for how this might all plug together.

Clint's Ramen International is a local chain of ramen restaurants with severely antiquated technology. The restaurants aren't networked together, and the cash registers aren't connected to the Internet. As the beleaguered data architect for the organization, you struggle with Microsoft Excel and Access on a daily basis, trying to get basic insights about sales and revenue to present to your marketing team. When the CMO drops by your desk on Monday morning, they ask you how many iced green teas were sold over the weekend. If you start dumping files into your Access database, you might know the answer by Thursday. How can BigQuery help without requiring re-architecture of your system?

This example reflects what a small business goes through on a regular basis. Many organizations pay exorbitant consulting fees to address these problems in suboptimal ways. Other organizations try to force massive change through to their end users, solving the technical problem but risking the business itself. Often the best solution here is something that keeps everything rolling without massive disruption, proves the case, and sets you up for bigger successes as you go.

In this case, you know that each franchise exports its books from its point-of-sale (POS) system every evening and emails them to corporate. Accounting does, well, whatever they do with these things and drops them in a shared folder. You manually then take the files from that folder and load them into the "data warehouse." Let's see what we can do about this.

Proposed Design

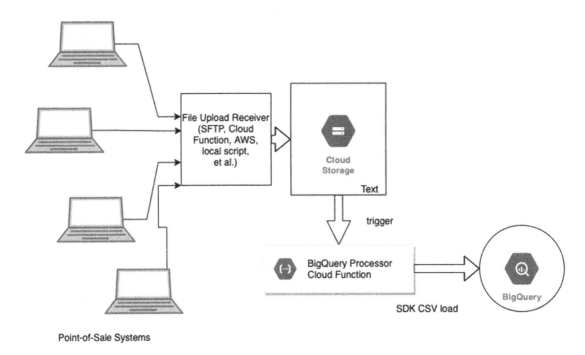

Point-of-Sale Systems

Figure 11-3. *A workflow to load data through cloud functions into BigQuery*

Getting the Files

This design uses everything we've covered in the chapter up to this point to create a simple data pipeline to BigQuery. The point-of-sale system exports a CSV already—we're just going to redirect it to Google Cloud Storage. You could do this in any number of ways, depending on how much access you have to the end users. If you had no access at all, you could actually set up a Pub/Sub function that receives email directly from a box. This would be fairly effort-intensive, so I am going to assume you could have the end users run a small application after exporting that CSV to load it into Google Cloud Storage.

Oddly, there is no direct transfer method between Google Drive and Google Cloud Storage, which would seem like the easiest way. You could apply the same cloud function techniques to transfer data between these services, but it doesn't work automatically.

You might also consider setting up an (S)FTP server to receive the files. Also oddly, Google Cloud Storage doesn't support this natively either. (AWS S3 has a managed SFTP transfer service.) One GCP-native way to do this would be to use a utility such as gcsfuse to mount a Google Cloud Storage bucket as a file system and accept (S)FTP uploads into that folder. However, that approach would require you to set up a server and push us somewhat back into the bad old days of importer creation.

There are even more exotic solutions, like using the Amazon S3 SFTP service to receive files, which can trigger a Pub/Sub across to GCP to retrieve the files across clouds. I wouldn't bother with anything this complicated unless you were already using AWS for everything except BigQuery. You could connect AWS and GCP queues together using—you guessed it—a Google Cloud Function. You could also use the BigQuery Data Transfer service to pull the Amazon S3 bucket over to Google Cloud Storage directly on a schedule.

You could even attempt to write an extension for the point-of-sale system itself, but unless Clint's Ramen has a surprisingly robust on-site IT function, that would probably also be prohibitively difficult.

My point is that there are many, many valid ways to accomplish each step of the pipeline. Hopefully, armed with a survey of all of them, you can evaluate which delivers the best ROI for your particular use case.

Detecting the Files

Accordingly, after the file arrives at Google Cloud Storage, a trigger will be fired indicating that an object was created.

That trigger will be received by a Google Cloud Function, which can then retrieve the file and load it into BigQuery using techniques we already know for loading CSV files. The only difference in this case is that we will be doing the CSV import from inside a cloud function instead of via the Google Cloud Shell or through the UI. To configure a cloud function to do this, you deploy it and specify the trigger. The syntax for this sort of deploy is as follows:

```
gcloud functions deploy your_function_name \
--trigger-resource GOOGLE_CLOUD_STORAGE_BUCKET_NAME \
--trigger-event google.storage.object.finalize
```

The finalize event covers any time a new object is created or an existing object is overwritten. There are other Cloud Storage triggers for deletion, archive, and metadata update.[3]

---

[3]https://cloud.google.com/functions/docs/calling/storage

You could even take this opportunity to email the same file to accounting once you're finished with it.

Note that I've taken advantage of the relatively small scale of this operation to do things in a simpler fashion. These files will all be pretty small and easily accessed in memory by the cloud function. If you're running millions of transactions daily, you will need something more robust like a Dataflow pipeline. Of course, if you need that, you likely already have a much broader structure to integrate with, and none of this would be necessary in the first place.

Processing the Files

Lastly, you want to ensure that the data arrives in a structure that matches how you intend to use it. This is where you get to apply your knowledge of building data warehouses to do this. You might want to load the data into time-partitioned tables per day, or you might have a store-based system. Your accounting department may also have been relying on the sender's email address to indicate which store's data they were looking at, and you need to parse in a column for the store ID itself.

Remembering to deploy the cloud function with the Cloud Storage trigger is the important part. Then, when the file arrives, you can write a cloud function that looks like this:

```python
from google.cloud import bigquery
client = bigquery.Client()

def process_incoming_file(data, context):

    table_name = 'sales'
    uri = 'gs://{bucket}/{file}'.format(bucket=data['bucket'],
    file=data['name'])

    job_config = bigquery.LoadJobConfig(
        schema=[
            bigquery.SchemaField("StoreID", "STRING"),
            bigquery.SchemaField("SKU", "STRING"),
            bigquery.SchemaField("Date", "DATE"),
            bigquery.SchemaField("Price", "NUMERIC")
        ],
```

```
    skip_leading_rows = 1,
    time_partitioning = bigquery.TimePartitioning(
        type_=bigquery.TimePartitioningType.DAY,
        field="Date"
    )
)

job = client.load_table_from_uri(uri, table_name, job_config=job_config)
job.result()

table = client.get_table(table_name)
print("Loaded {rows} rows from file {uri}".format(rows=table.num_rows,
uri=uri))
```

This function, when set to trigger on a file upload, retrieves the fully qualified URI of the file. Then it creates a schema for a date-partitioned table and loads the file to BigQuery. All of the "print" statements log to Cloud Logging (formerly known as Stackdriver).

(You can also change the trigger in the UI Cloud Function creation screen to Cloud Storage and choose these parameters there rather than deploying from command line.)

Trigger

| Cloud Storage | ▼ |

Event Type *
Finalize/Create ▼ ❓

| Bucket * | BROWSE |

Getting the Answer

The preceding cloud function responds to every file in the bucket, loading the CSV to a date-partitioned table automatically. Within a few seconds of file creation, the cloud function has fired and inserted the file into the relevant table. Getting the total number of sales for a given SKU can now be done with the appropriate SQL query:

```
SELECT SKU, COUNT(*), SUM(Price) FROM `sales`
WHERE SKU = '1001' -- the green tea SKU
AND Date BETWEEN '2020-06-27' AND '2020-06-28'
GROUP BY SKU
```

The Final Product

With this pipeline constructed, stores now upload their point-of-sale files on a nightly basis; and those files are automatically detected, transformed, and loaded into BigQuery. These insights are then fed through your reporting system (coming up in Chapter 16) and automatically surfaced to a live dashboard.

When the CMO comes in the following Monday, they swing by your desk again. "Just came by to get you started on the iced tea report again," they say. "Four hundred and seven," you reply. They're astonished. You pull up the report view and show them the data, already processed and validated, thanks to your new pipeline. You also tell them that you emailed a link to this report to them first thing this morning. They didn't read your email. There's nothing either of us can do about that.

Caveats

As with any simplified textbook example, there are lots of points upon which we could improve the robustness of this solution. I'm sure you have some ideas of your own, and doubly so if you've ever written a bad-old-days importer. Here are a few:

- Duplicates: Users may send the same file more than once. This is fairly easily detected by either disallowing overwrites or by checking BigQuery for the given store/date and making sure you have no rows. This gets more complicated if you want to prevent duplication at the *row* level. Cloud Storage triggers are based on Pub/Sub and are only guaranteed to fire at least once. This means the same trigger may hit multiple times, even if the user only uploaded the file once.

- Validation: We assume that because the files are coming from a known external source, they will be valid. This workflow has no protection against people unintentionally or intentionally putting invalid files into the system.

- Scale/streaming: As mentioned earlier, this solution will scale relatively well as long as file sizes remain small. Since it uses Cloud Functions, it can accept as many simultaneous files and imports as you care to throw at it. However, if files get too large to be efficiently processed inside a single cloud function's memory and CPU allocation, they will be rejected by this system.

- Schema: This technique is great when you have a single known file type and you know what data you need out of it. This will not work especially well if there are many input file formats, data across multiple files, or evolving schemas. This is where you need to apply your warehouse design know-how to design more robust schemas and move beyond a single function.

- Organization: I touched upon this earlier in the chapter as a drawback to serverless systems in general. You need to ensure that you document and understand all the pieces of infrastructure you build so you don't "lose" them. Tools like Google Deployment Manager can help with this, but your peers should have some idea of how to work with the system you've built.

Summary

Functions as a service is a powerful paradigm to write and run code without creating a server or installing an operating system. Much as BigQuery does for data warehouses, Google Cloud Functions allows you to interact with APIs and other GCP services to work with data in BigQuery. Writing a function can be done in a number of ways using the shell tool or directly in the cloud console. Functions can be triggered in a variety of ways, both synchronous and asynchronous, and can be used to insert or select data directly from the project's BigQuery database. There are countless ways to do this, but we saw in a simple retail example how straightforward it is to build an analysis system to moderate scale with minimal effort.

CHAPTER 12

Cloud Logging

Google Cloud Logging, known until March 2020 as Stackdriver, is the central tool used to collect event logs from all of your systems. As with other systems we've discussed, it is fully managed and supports event collection at scale. It's also directly integrated with all of the other services we've engaged with up until now: BigQuery, Cloud Storage, Cloud Functions, and so forth.

In this chapter, we'll look at how to import and analyze Cloud Logging logs in BigQuery and how to tie them together to gain system-wide understanding of how your applications are operating. On the flip side of this coin, BigQuery generates logs to Cloud Logging itself, which you can *also* import back into BigQuery for analysis.

All of this is building up to advanced topics in Parts 4 and 5, where we'll get into the long-term potential of the data warehouse using reporting, visualization, and real-time dashboarding. Adding performance monitoring to this mix is a surefire way to vault you ahead of your competition.

How This Is Related

What does logging have to do with data analysis or data warehouses? Why is it important for us to be familiar with how it works? One modern paradigm in DevOps is remaining cognizant of the fact that monitoring an application is closely related to monitoring what users do with an application. Detecting normal user activity, elevated error rates, unauthorized intrusions, and reviewing application logs all share some similarities.

BigQuery enters the picture as a tool for analyzing these massive amounts of real-time data over much longer periods of time and with the ability to regard Cloud Logging as only a single facet of the available data. To go all the way up the ladder again, the idea is to create insights from information from data. Simultaneously, you can analyze application-level inputs and outputs, what effect those are having on the overall system, how healthy the system is, how much it is costing you, and if it is being used as expected.

© Mark Mucchetti 2020
M. Mucchetti, *BigQuery for Data Warehousing*, https://doi.org/10.1007/978-1-4842-6186-6_12

Until now, it would have been difficult to get so close to the real-time unit economics of every single event on your business. Let me illustrate a little more concretely with concepts we'll cover as we go through this chapter.

An Example: Abigail's Flowers

Abigail's Flowers (AF) is a successful ecommerce business that ships customized floral bouquets ordered through their website. BigQuery is already a fixture in the business, powering all of their analytics dashboards and providing real-time insight into current orders. They even have a small predictive function that allows them to forecast impending demand. How can Cloud Logging help in such a sophisticated business?

Well, the AF Data Crew has received complaints from customers that credit cards are being declined a lot. The team checks the dashboards. From Cloud Logging, they are able to see that application health is good and the error rate for transactions is low. From BigQuery, they can see that revenue looks to be within expected values. Nothing at the system level is showing trouble. What's the next step? The team makes a list of tasks:

- Ensure the application is recording the results of payment calls. It turns out that it's already doing this through a Cloud Logging event.

- The team creates an event sink to BigQuery for these calls and lets it run for a few hours.

- Meanwhile, they ensure that the payment API itself is recording its requests and responses. This is also already being logged to Cloud Logging.

- They make an event sink for the payment API as well.

- The team also looks more closely at application performance using Cloud Monitoring. There are no unusual spikes or long-running calls, so they rule out slowness and timeouts as a root cause. (They make a sink anyway, just in case.)

- Lastly, they review their BigQuery schemas and learn where data about user accounts and user orders is being logged.

Now they have two important types of data: the performance of the application and the behavior of the application in use. The team starts their analysis.

First, they identify the common identifier that joins the data together. The primary key across all of this data is the UserID column. This means they are able to answer several key questions immediately. Diagnostically, the team identifies these as the most likely to yield useful information about the problem:

- When do payment failures occur? Are they higher by day of the week and/or hour of the day? (Remember, this number wasn't significant across all errors on the system, but it may be visible when looking solely at payment errors.)

- What kinds of errors are occurring in payment? Do they happen on the application or in the API?

- How many orders are being made when the error rate is higher?

- How many distinct users are making orders when the error rate is higher?

- What are the characteristics of users with high numbers of failing orders?

- What are the characteristics of orders that are failing?

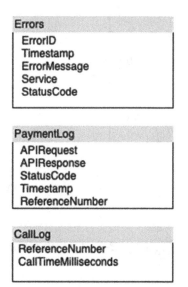

Figure 12-1. *The data schema for Abigail's Flowers*

Note that BigQuery doesn't actually have the concept of primary and foreign keys; these are just used to illustrate the logical data relations.

This information is only accessible to them because they have both the error information and the account/order information in BigQuery. If they were in separate data sources, the team would have to export each set of data and merge it manually. There might be manual data transformation errors. Also, there are millions of rows and gigabytes of data in each set, limiting the effectiveness of what can be exported. Even more interestingly, they can now create real-time dashboards that answer these questions **as orders come in**.

As the AF team reviews the results of these queries, one thing immediately becomes clear. While there are correlations in days of the week and hours of the day, those correlations line up more or less with expected traffic patterns. What pops out is that one of the characteristics of the order—specifically, the cost—is strongly correlated with failure rate. The team drills in, constructing a query to look directly at an order's failure rate vs. the price of the order.

Success Rate vs. Grand Total

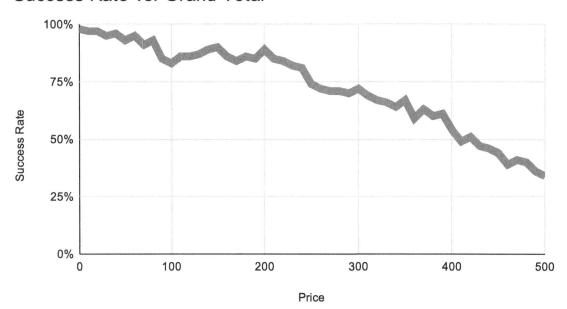

Figure 12-2. *Graph showing correlation between failure rate and price*

Aha! Orders over $200 fail at five times the rate of orders below $200. In fact, there is a steady curve as order price increases, leading to extremely high failure rates when orders exceed $500. The team then joins back in the specific errors that are occurring and ties that to the same graph.

Success Rate vs. Grand Total

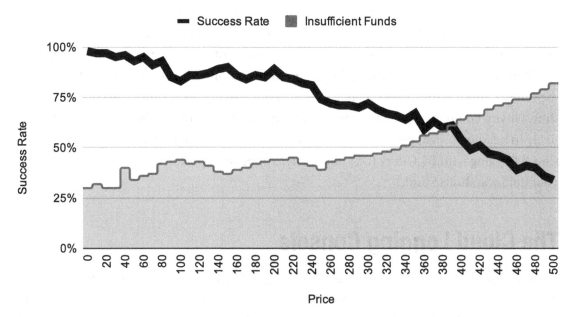

Figure 12-3. *Same graph with error type included*

Now it's crystal clear: this elevated error rate is caused by an error saying that the bank declined the card for insufficient funds. As customers try to charge cards for higher and higher dollar amounts, they are more likely to be declined for this reason. It turns out there's no problem at all. The issue is caused by customers trying to exceed their credit limits. Relieved, the team leaves the new event sinks in place, creates some additional alerting to fire if this expectation is violated, and goes off to happy hour.

It's easy to see how this might have spiraled out of control in a less sophisticated organization. Pulling these datasets manually from multiple systems and consolidating them would lead to hours of work to look at a single static view. An inconsistent data warehouse might have made it prohibitively difficult to marry the error logs and the user account data. And as the team was analyzing increasingly stale data, they would have been unable to defend or explain new cases still arriving from customers.

This is a key insight for any business process. Shortening your feedback loop allows you to surface and react to relevant information as soon as it's generated. Now that the team knows this could be an issue, they can monitor it continuously—and should a cluster of customers report the issue again, they can quickly determine if it has the same root cause or if a new issue has surfaced.

Using this as a template, you can easily imagine constructing more sophisticated scenarios. A live clickstream could be integrated to show how users react to unexpected conditions during payment and used to improve the website experience. An alert could be set on one customer receiving large amounts of errors from many different credit cards, indicating potentially fraudulent transactions. You could see if users who experience these errors are likely to succeed at purchasing on another card or at a later time. Or you could just see if users who encounter errors on one order are more or less likely to become repeat purchasers. These are all ways you might fruitfully integrate Cloud Logging with BigQuery (or, generically, application performance monitoring with your data warehouse tool.)

The Cloud Logging Console

Click the hamburger menu and go to the Logging tab. (Again, if you've done this in the past, it was called Stackdriver, but has been renamed. Google likes to rename services on a regular basis to make useful books go out of date.) After a bit, it should bring you to the primary screen, which is the Logs Viewer.

Depending on how much you've used Google Cloud Platform to this point, you may not have much to look at yet. By default, it will automatically show all of the services you currently use. Pretty much everything you do on Google Cloud Platform is logged here in excruciating detail. This means it's very easy to get some data for us to look at in the logs. If you don't have anything interesting yet, go over to the BigQuery console and do a few select statements from your tables or just select static data. Then come back here.

Looking at Logs

Now that we have some data to look at, let's go back to the Cloud Logging main page and see it. Using the new Logs Viewer,[1] look at the Query builder panel, click "Resource," find and click "BigQuery," and click "Add." This will generate a query that looks something like the following.

Figure 12-4. *Logging/BigQuery log query panel*

Click "Run Query," and you will see your results populate. This will restrict the view just to events generated by BigQuery. The view is also close to real-time; if you continue performing activity in BigQuery, you can click the "Jump to Now" button to update the results with the latest.

The first thing you will notice here is that there is a tremendous amount of data being logged. Each service has a set of payloads that it uses when recording logs. You can also define your own logging schemas to be emitted from your own services, as we'll discuss a little later on.

In a way, BigQuery and Cloud Logging have a lot in common. Both can ingest large amounts of data at sub-second latency and make it available for detailed analysis. The biggest difference is that Cloud Logging data is inherently ephemeral. It's designed to collect all the telemetry you could ever need as it's happening and then age out and expire. This makes a lot of sense, and we've also talked about relevant use cases for BigQuery that are quite similar. Partitioning tables by date and setting a maximum age resemble the policy that Cloud Logging uses by default.

---

[1]As of this writing, the new Logs Viewer is in preview and is not yet feature-complete. The classic viewer is still being maintained, and you can accomplish these same tasks in that mode. See
`https://cloud.google.com/logging/docs/view/overview`

In fact, unless you have a very small amount of traffic, the logs aren't going to be especially useful without a way to query them for the information you need. The base case is that you're looking for something in particular that you know to be in the logs already, and for that, you may not need BigQuery at all.

Querying via Cloud Logging

Even without BigQuery, you can still get some great insight about what's going on. Google Logging has its own query language that you can use to get deep into the data to find what you are looking for. The four dimensions in which you can query are as follows and are also selectable above the query box:

- Resource type (resource.type): Each service has its own resource tab, that is, "bigquery_resource" or "gae_app." These will determine where the log entry comes from and what other information it carries.

- Log name (logName): The service's log that you want to see. Each service (or custom application you build) will have multiple log types for each activity. For BigQuery, the major ones are from Cloud Audit and are "activity," "data_access," and "system_event."

- Severity (severity): Also known as log level, this helps you triage messages by their priority. The values are Emergency, Alert, Critical, Error, Warning, Debug, Info, and Notice. Having properly assigned severity is extremely important to keep your logs clean. If you are having a high-severity issue, it will be slower and harder to see if there are other, less important events in the mix.

- Timestamp: When the event was logged. Note that the event itself may have other timestamps in it if it's recording an activity that occurred across a process. This timestamp will show you when this event was recorded to Cloud Logging.

There are other parameters you can query on based on the particular resource or log. Here are a couple of interesting queries that apply specifically to BigQuery usage that should give you an idea of the query language's capabilities.

Query	Purpose
resource.type="bigquery_resource"	Needed for all queries to filter to BigQuery only
resource.type="bigquery_resource" AND protoPayload.authenticationInfo.principalEmail = {email_address}	Show all activity by a given user
resource.type="bigquery_resource" AND proto_payload.methodName="jobservice.insert"	See the start of all queries
resource.type="bigquery_resource" AND protoPayload.serviceData.jobInsertResponse. resource.jobConfiguration.query.query={query text}	Find all the instances a specific query text was executed
resource.type="bigquery_resource" AND protoPayload.requestMetadata.callerIp = {IP ADDRESS}	Get all queries from a particular IP address (note: may be IPv6)

Figure 12-5. *Sample queries for BigQuery logs*

If you are looking for several needles in a field of haystacks, this should get you pretty far. If you need to go further back in time or tie together other pieces of data, like the AF Data Crew did, then let's keep going.

Log Sinks to BigQuery

One of Cloud Logging's restrictions is that it generally only records up to 30 days' worth of data[2] and only about eight weeks' worth of metrics. It's not uncommon to need to analyze logs going back much further for security or compliance reasons or just to track down a pesky application bug that is difficult to replicate.

---

[2]Some classes of data, namely, Admin Activity audit logs, Data Access audit logs, and Access Transparency logs, are retained for 400 days.

The restriction makes sense when you consider the nature of the data from both the real-world example and the logging console. For the vast majority of this kind of data, if you don't need it within a short period of time, you probably won't ever need it.

As the AF Data Crew found out, application monitoring data can occasionally be useful over the long term. When you run into a situation like this, it's easy to set up a continuous flow of data from Cloud Logging into BigQuery (or other destinations) that can then be parsed along with the rest of the data in your warehouse.

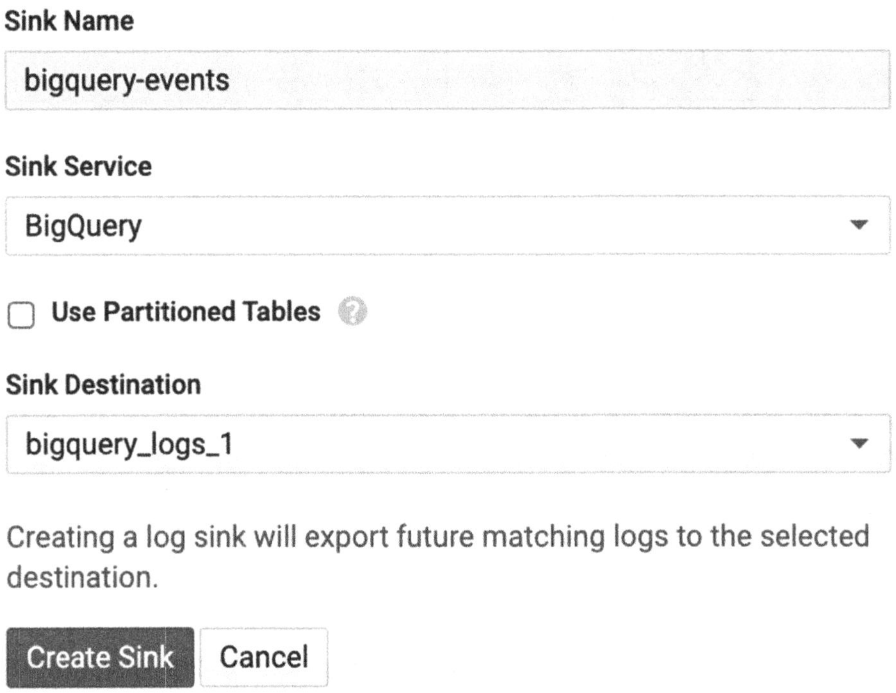

Sink Name

bigquery-events

Sink Service

BigQuery   ▼

☐ **Use Partitioned Tables** ⊘

Sink Destination

bigquery_logs_1   ▼

Creating a log sink will export future matching logs to the selected destination.

[Create Sink]   Cancel

Figure 12-6. *Log sinks to BigQuery*

There are actually three valid destinations for Cloud Logging sinks: BigQuery, Cloud Storage, and Pub/Sub. Combined with what we discussed in the previous chapter, you could apply similar techniques to use Pub/Sub as the event sink, which in turn would call a Cloud Function to identify and transform valid entries, which would then log into BigQuery.

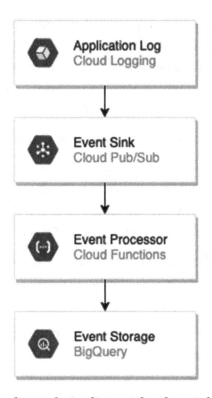

Figure 12-7. *A more complicated pipeline with a log sink*

What Is a Sink?

The term "sink" refers to an object that can receive events. As near as I can tell, the etymology of the term is closer to how it is used in electrical engineering, such as the term "heat sink" to indicate a conductor which receives heat from another component and disperses it away. Similarly, a sink is a one-way consumer of one or more other objects producing events. Despite some conceptual commonalities, there's no relationship to "sync" either. The interaction is purely in a single direction—the producer makes the event and the sink receives it.

Creating a Sink

Making an event sink is very straightforward. It will appear as an option in the "Actions" dropdown on every query result. Click Actions and then "Create Sink" to open the sidebar. Since you can make a sink for any logging query, you can be as broad or narrow as you like. Sizing the query is a bit of an art: you want all the events you might conceivably need for your use cases, but you don't want to make so many that cost and processing time are too high. If your task requires a sink instead of using Cloud Logging directly, then you can err on the side of including more data. After it has been purged from Cloud Logging, it's gone forever unless you preserve it in this way.

The panel is also intuitive to understand and only has three selections to make.

- Name: Obviously you want to assign a descriptive name.

- Sink Service: As mentioned previously, the three main options are BigQuery, Cloud Storage, and Pub/Sub. (The fourth option, "Custom Destination", is actually still the same as the first three, but if you want to log to a different Google cloud project.) Select BigQuery here.

- Sink Destination: You have the option to use an existing dataset or make a new one. You can use an existing dataset if you want to create multiple queries that route to the same sink.

After filling this out, click Create. That's it: all incoming events matching your query will now go to a BigQuery dataset.

An important note: If you do try to log multiple queries to the same sink, remember that the BigQuery schema for a table is set using the first row inserted. If you change anything or the queries have disagreeing schemas, the sink will fail to receive the entries that don't align. The easiest way to avoid this, of course, is to log each query to a separate table, but you may have a valid reason not to do this. Should you have this problem, it will be sent as an email, appear as a notification on the console activity page for the project, and increment a metric (called exports/error_count).

Additionally, Cloud Logging does a fair amount of field name shortening and alteration to push logs into the BigQuery sink. More importantly, it automatically shards by timestamp using date sharding or partitioning, with date sharding by default. This means that you should use the techniques for querying date-sharded tables when querying the sink.

To edit or delete the sinks, as you would likely want to do with any samples you made, go to the Logs Router on the left sidebar, check the sink(s) you just made, and click Delete. All gone. The dataset being used as the sink will remain intact until you choose to remove it from BigQuery.

To the extent that you are a software engineer or have software engineers in your organization, now might be a good time to do a "look what I can do" presentation to open up some possibilities. Many engineering organizations haven't yet established consistent logging practices, and you may not be as lucky as the AF Data Crew when you go to get data to investigate your problem. Understanding the interplay between any custom applications you have and your ability to administer your data warehouse is key to deriving value. And, as we've already seen, you will be able to help them as well.

If your engineers already have a solution, that's great too. There are countless logging solutions out there—far too many to name. If your organization runs primarily on Amazon Web Services (AWS), they probably already use Cloudwatch for a similar purpose. I will mention that Google does have a logging agent that you can install on servers inside AWS. And of course you can always use functions-as-a-service techniques from the previous chapter to create pathways from other cloud providers into BigQuery.

Metrics and Alerting

The other major piece of this puzzle is Cloud Monitoring. Monitoring also used to be under the Stackdriver umbrella but now just goes by Monitoring. While Monitoring is not directly related to BigQuery, it is closely related to what we've done with logging thus far and also ties into Google Data Studio, which we'll discuss at a later point.

Creating Metrics

Using the same method as the previous section for creating event sinks, write up a query or select the data for which you want to create the metric. Click "Actions" and then "Create Metric" (instead of "Create Sink"). This will open up a similar window in which you can specify the details for the metric:

- Name: Again, the name of your metric.

- Description: Without all of the metadata to inspect, metrics can be somewhat more obscure than sinks. A description helps you remember what exactly you are trying to track.

- Labels: You can use labels to split a metric into multiple time series using the value of a field in the relevant log entry. This is a bit beyond the scope of what we're trying to do here, but you can learn more at `https://cloud.google.com/logging/docs/logs-based-metrics/labels`.

- Units: If your metric measures a specific unit (megabytes, orders, users, errors, instances, etc.), you can specify it here.

- Type: Can be Counter or Distribution. Counter simply records the number of times the qualifying event occurred. Distribution metrics allow you to capture the approximate range of metrics along a statistical distribution. They're also out of scope here, but if you are interested, they are documented by Google at `https://cloud.google.com/logging/docs/logs-based-metrics/distribution-metrics`.

After you fill this out, you can click Create Metric, and you will have a new value representing the occurrences of this particular Cloud Logging query. To interact with this metric, you can go to "Logs-Based Metrics" on the left sidebar.

Logs-Based Metrics

When you go to the Logs-Based Metrics view, you will see a host of built-in metrics collected by GCP, as well as your custom metric(s) at the bottom. You can do a couple of things with the metric from this page by clicking the vertical ellipsis menu. Notably, you can view the logs associated with this metric. This means that if you decide in the future that the metric data is insufficient, you can "upgrade" it to an event sink by going to the logs and clicking Actions and "Create Sink" to follow the previous process.

You could also have both the metric and the sink for the same log query, using the metric on dashboards and reports, but having the sink available in BigQuery should you need to do deeper analysis.

A Note About Metrics Export

I'm afraid there is no native way to export metrics to BigQuery. If you're interested in doing this, you'll have to venture fairly far afield to build your own solution. Google provides a reference implementation for this use case at `https://cloud.google.com/solutions/stackdriver-monitoring-metric-export`.

As we get into techniques for real-time dashboarding, the value of this may become clearer. Using a system like this allows you to avoid exporting all of the event data when all you may want is the count or rate of events. This is especially true when you want to look at trends over a much longer period of time. In the example at the beginning of this chapter, the AF Data Crew might have opted to log only the number of errors by type and timestamp. This data would still have allowed them to join in the order data to see that the error rate was higher when the average order price was higher. It would not, however, have allowed them to conclusively determine that the orders experiencing failures were precisely the same orders as the ones with high costs.

There are also countless providers of real-time application monitoring, metrics collection, and so on. Depending on how your organization utilizes the cloud, your solutions for this problem may not involve BigQuery at all.

Alerting

The other tool traditionally associated with the product formerly known as Stackdriver is Alerting. Alerting connects to your metrics and provides a notification system when a metric's value leaves a desired range. Alerting goes beyond Cloud Logging and can also be used for application health monitoring, performance checks, and so on. Most of these use cases are out of the scope of BigQuery. However, there are a couple of interesting recipes you might build with them.

Business-Level Metrics

Since you can alert on any custom metric, this means you could create alerts for things outside the DevOps scope. In the example at the beginning of this chapter, recall that the issue turned out to be high order cost causing credit cards to exceed their credit limits. Using this knowledge, you could create an alert that fires whenever the failures per dollar exceed a certain ratio. This would be an indication to your business users to check the report or dashboard or to look at the BigQuery order data and see what is causing the anomaly.

Logging Alerts to BigQuery

If you find the alert heuristics useful and want to leverage the automatic aggregation and detection that Cloud Monitoring gives you, you can specify that alerts go to a Cloud Pub/Sub as a notification channel. Then, using techniques in the previous chapter, you can build a Cloud Function that logs the alert to BigQuery and keeps a record of past alerts. (Make sure you don't create an infinite loop doing this...)

ChatOps

Creating applications leveraging organizational messaging apps is growing increasingly common. Cloud Monitoring supports notification to Slack, email, SMS, and so on natively, but you could also build an application that allows users to acknowledge and dig into the cause for a given alert. For example, an alert might trigger a message to a relevant Slack channel with details about the error condition, but also link to a BigQuery-powered view to look at the data causing it.

Feedback Loops

Way back in Chapter 2, I laid out a rubric for assessing your own organization's data maturity. The rubric references feedback loops as a key mechanic to achieve a higher degree of maturity. That concept specifically bears revisiting now as we wrap up Part 3. If you have successfully completed your project charter and are looking down the road to the future, you have likely also thought about this in some form. Luckily, you have everything in place to move to the next level. If you'll permit me the discursion, let's step up a bunch of levels from organizational theory and look at the dynamics themselves.

The concept of feedback loops arises in innumerable disciplines across history. The first recorded feedback loop was invented in 270 BCE when Ctesibius of Alexandria created a water float valve to maintain water depth at a constant level. The term itself is at least a hundred years old. The feedback loop, at heart, is the recognition that a system's output is used as part of its input. The system changes itself as it operates. This has profound implications for the understanding of any functioning system. (It's also, in a lot of ways, the opposite of the sink concept we discussed earlier in the chapter.)

In a way, human history has progressed in tandem with the shortening of feedback loops. Consider the amount of time delivering a message has taken throughout history. Assuming it arrived at all, a transatlantic letter took months to arrive at its destination in the 17th and 18th centuries. By the 19th century, that had shrunk to days. In the early 20th century, the first transatlantic Morse code messages were arriving and dropping times to hours, minutes, and seconds. Now, I can ping a server from the west coast of the United States to the United Kingdom in less than 200 milliseconds and not even think twice about it.

What I am getting at is that the faster a message can be received and interpreted, the faster it can be acted upon and another message sent. While there are many reasons to construct a data warehouse, including business continuity, historical record keeping, and, yes, data analysis, the real additional value in constructing one today is the promise of shortening feedback loops. Not only can you shorten them but you can also dramatically increase the complexity of messages and their effects on the system. Major organizations are adopting one-to-one personalization techniques to address their consumers on an individual basis. Technologies like BigQuery level that playing field so that even smaller organizations can begin implementing these insights without extreme cost or concession.

This won't happen evenly across your organization or its functions. There's also no single blueprint to making good interpretations or good decisions based on those interpretations. In fact, without the mediation of data scientists and statisticians, business leaders might jump to the wrong conclusion. This risk increases measurably if there is a risk the data is inaccurate, as it might have been at lower levels of organizational maturity. Using these tools is a foundational part of the strategy, but it is not the only part.

I encourage you to think about ways in which you have already shortened certain feedback loops and can shorten others. More transformationally, you can now begin to think about new feedback loops, like the credit card acceptance scenario we looked at. Adding even more data sources into the mix, as we'll see in Part 5, can take feedback loops out of the organization and into the world at large. As more organizations, government agencies, and other groups put their datasets into the public domain, you can create feedback loops that understand and react to human behavior itself.

Summary

Cloud Logging, formerly called Stackdriver, is a scaled logging solution attached to all services on the Google Cloud Platform. It receives events automatically from across GCP, as well as custom applications and external sources that you can define. The logging console has a robust searching mechanism to look at events, but they can be persisted for only a maximum of 30 days. Using sinks, you can persist the data indefinitely to BigQuery, where you can analyze and connect it to other data. Cloud Monitoring allows you to synthesize information from logs into real-time dashboards and insights. These tools are both critical in shortening the length of feedback loops and delivering ever-increasing business value.

In the next chapter, we'll return to the familiar ground of SQL and discuss more advanced concepts you can implement in your data warehouse.

PART IV

Maintaining the Warehouse

CHAPTER 13

Advanced BigQuery

Did you feel unmoored through several chapters without SQL? I get it. Well, we're back to SQL now. In this chapter, we're going to go over some advanced BigQuery capabilities that will give you a whole new set of tools to get at your data. After this chapter, I guarantee that the next time you get a juicy business question and a blank console window, you'll start hammering the keyboard like Scotty in *Star Trek IV* keying in the formula for transparent aluminum.[1]

Fair warning: There's some JavaScript in this chapter. I'll give you a heads-up so you don't crash into it while enjoying your SQL reverie.

Analytic Functions

As you become familiar with subqueries, joins, and grouping, you will start to think with more and more complexity about how to get at the data you need for analysis. Layering in capabilities outside of BigQuery, like Cloud Functions and Dataflow SQL, you can conceive of multiple solutions to any analysis problem.

But there's one tried-and-true toolbox for doing data analysis that we haven't explored yet. Analytic functions have been critical to OLAP workflows for decades, and they're not going anywhere anytime soon. To really bring your game up to par, learn and use analytic functions.

Analytic functions are also sometimes called window functions or even OLAP functions, so if you've heard of them in that context, I'm referring to the same thing here. Many data engineers avoid them because of the unfamiliar syntax. When I was a junior database developer (at some point in the undisclosed past), I got nervous whenever I opened up a stored procedure and saw OVER, ROW_NUMBER, or the other keywords that signal a query using analytic functions. Databases were the most expensive

---

[1] I do not guarantee.

© Mark Mucchetti 2020

M. Mucchetti, *BigQuery for Data Warehousing*, https://doi.org/10.1007/978-1-4842-6186-6_13

resource, and so writing queries that performed poorly or used too much memory could affect production system operations. It often seemed safer to rewrite them using multi-statement subqueries and joins, especially when they were running in production.

So those things are, on balance, still true. Analytic functions still run more slowly on the whole; they can always be refactored using subqueries and joins; and many data engineers avoid them. I don't blame you for loading your table into Python with the BigQuery API and scripting out your analytics. In reality, you do what is most efficient for you with the tools you have. People got by before BigQuery too. (And when I was a junior database developer, a cloud was still a fluffy thing in the sky that sometimes rained on you.)

Definition

An analytic function is kind of like an aggregate function with partitions.[2] We covered the aggregate function set pretty thoroughly in Chapter 9, and they all have something in common—they reduce the entire group to a single value. This is often all you need. The easiest way to do this is to show a representation of how different types of SQL functions behave. See Figure 13-1.

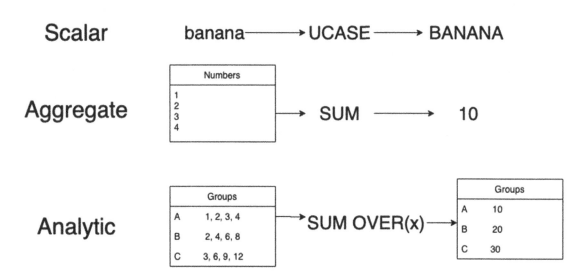

Figure 13-1. *Scalar, aggregate, analytic*

---

[2]These are not the same as the partitions supported by BigQuery tables; this terminology refers to partitions within a single table, as we'll cover.

As you can see, the analytic function retains the grouping inside the partitions. The analytic function runs an aggregate across multiple rows, but each row gets a result.

Window Frames

Imagine a sheet of paper with a printed table on it. Choose a single row in the middle of the table, which will be the row being "evaluated." Then, use two more sheets of paper—one to cover some of the rows above the evaluated row and one to cover some of the rows below. The rows that you left uncovered are your "window frame."

This is essentially what a window frame does when processing an analytic function. As each row is evaluated to assign the result, the query uses the window frame to decide which rows should be included in the input grouping. The pieces of paper move along with the row under evaluation to expose different rows as the analytic function proceeds.

The OVER clause defines the window frame. It's also acceptable to use the entire input set as a single frame.

Partitions

In addition to the window frame, you can also use PARTITION BY to group rows by key. The last step that GROUP BY takes to collapse those rows does not occur; they are held in separate partitions. You can also use ORDER BY when defining the partitions; unlike a query-level ORDER BY, this version specifies the order within each partition.

Because we've been talking about partitioned tables in BigQuery so much, I want to point out that this is not a related concept. This type of partitioning refers to the bucketing of sets of input rows from a single query result.

Order of Operations

Now that you understand the basic terminology for an analytic query, we can examine the order in which they are executed:

- All GROUP BY and regular aggregate functions are evaluated first.
- Partitions are created following the expression in PARTITION BY.
- Each partition is ordered using the expression in ORDER BY.
- The window frame is applied.
- Each row is framed and the query is executed.

The partition is a stricter boundary than a window frame; the frame won't span multiple partitions. Once the partitioning step has occurred, you can imagine that these are actually all separate tables grouped by the partition—they will not interact.

Many analytic functions do not support windows; in this case, the window frame used is the entire partition or input set.

Numeric Functions

One rule of thumb for identifying a business problem that might benefit from an analytic function is when you hear someone ask for "the most/least X for each Y." The "X" is your ORDER BY expression, and the "Y" is your PARTITION BY.

For numeric functions, you'll always be doing some sort of precedence ordering. Window frames aren't allowed for numeric functions, so the analytic function will always be operating across the entire partition.

ROW_NUMBER

Before we go too crazy, let's look at the simplest of the analytic functions, ROW_NUMBER. All ROW_NUMBER does is return the ordinal of the row within its partition. While this is pretty simple, it's very powerful and gives us an easy way to order subsets of a query. It's otherwise surprisingly nontrivial to assign row numbers to returned rows.[3]

In the sentence construct I just explained, the question this answers is "the ordinal of X for each Y," as in, the order of items in each category. Let's look at an example that does that. Let's say I run a shoe store and I want to know the colors I have for each type of shoe, going from most to least expensive. That would look something like this:

```
SELECT
ShoeType, Color,
ROW_NUMBER() OVER (PARTITION BY ShoeType ORDER BY Price DESC)
FROM Products
```

---

[3]In the bad old days, we used to join to a tally table, which was just a one-column table that had the natural numbers from 1 to maxint in it. Someone, either unintentionally or as a sick joke, once deleted the "3" from my tally table. I don't even want to tell you how long it took me to find that.

Applying the preceding order of operations

- Partition the Products table by ShoeType, creating one partition per type.

- Order each partition by the price of the shoe, highest to lowest.

- Return one row for each shoe type and color and a number indicating where it fell in the price order.

For ROW_NUMBER, you actually don't need to specify an ORDER BY at all; without one, the results are non-deterministic. You would still get the benefit of the partitioning and a unique ordinal for each type of shoe.

RANK

RANK is substantially similar to ROW_NUMBER, except as the name implies, it gives a ranking. That means it'll behave like a ranking in a sports division; if the ORDER BY has two rows that evaluate the expression identically, they'll get the same rank.

To apply to the preceding example, if two shoes had the same price, they'd get the same rank. ROW_NUMBER() always assigns a distinct value to each row in a partition.

DENSE_RANK

DENSE_RANK is the same as RANK except instead of jumping after a tie is encountered, it'll increment by 1. To illustrate the difference between the two, see Figure 13-2.

		ROW_NUMBER	RANK	DENSE_RANK
Philadelphia	15-2	1	1	1
Houston	14-3	2	2	2
Miami	14-3	3	2	2
Atlanta	12-5	4	4	3

Figure 13-2. *Showing a baseball division*

Basically, RANK is what you're used to seeing in sports standings ("Houston and Miami are tied for second with Atlanta in fourth"), and DENSE_RANK is what you'd see in a statistics report ("Houston and Miami have the second highest count of rabid zombies, with Atlanta in third.")

PERCENT_RANK/CUME_DIST

These two functions are closely related in that they both return a fraction between zero and one indicating the row's position in the partition.

PERCENT_RANK returns the percentage of values that are less/more (come earlier in the partition) than the current row. So the first row in a partition will always be 0; the last row will be 1. The formula is (RANK() – 1)/(Partition Row Count – 1).

CUME_DIST returns the percentage of the row within the partition, or just a straight fraction of RANK() over the partition row count. The first row in a partition will always be 1/n, where n is the number of rows in the partition; the last row will always be 1.

Window Frame Syntax

See, that wasn't so bad. I always find that a new syntax looks daunting until I actually sit down with it and learn it, and then the next time I see it, I'm pleasantly surprised to discover that now it means something to me. SQL is kind of like that.

Before we get into navigation functions, we should cover how you specify a window frame. Reading this syntax can get a little hairy. To simplify as much as possible, don't think about partitions for the moment; just think about a single table of, say, 48 rows, being iterated sequentially. For each row, we use the window frame to determine which rows around it we use to evaluate the analytic function. Using the syntax, we can specify pretty much any set we want. Lastly, remember that the frame *moves* relative to the row under evaluation. Each of these frames then constitutes a tiny table we'll do a regular aggregation on. Since the frame moves, the same rows will be included in multiple frames—just think about it as an iterative process over each row, and it won't be confusing.

Let's use a moving average example first to explain what I mean there. In my 48-row table, let's say I have two days of current temperature readings, each taken precisely on the hour. See Figure 13-3.

Hour	TempF
0:00:00	64
1:00:00	63
2:00:00	63
3:00:00	63
4:00:00	63
5:00:00	63
6:00:00	62
7:00:00	63
8:00:00	65
9:00:00	65
10:00:00	67
11:00:00	67
12:00:00	68
13:00:00	69
14:00:00	71
15:00:00	69
16:00:00	68
17:00:00	68
18:00:00	67
19:00:00	66
20:00:00	64
21:00:00	64
22:00:00	63
23:00:00	63
24:00:00	62
25:00:00	62
26:00:00	61

Figure 13-3. 48-row table with hourly measurements

If I want to see the moving average of each three-hour period, that means that for each row under evaluation, I care about 1 hour (row) before that hour and 1 hour (row) after that hour. Using the window frame specification

```
ROWS BETWEEN 1 PRECEDING AND 1 FOLLOWING
```

I've specified a window that will be three rows wide—the row under evaluation, the row before it, and the row after it. (At the top and bottom of the table, my window will only be two rows wide, since there are no rows above the top or below the bottom.)

To be even more explicit, if I've numbered these rows from 1 to 48, each row under evaluation will use a frame as shown in Figure 13-4.

Row	Hour	TempF	
X	X	X	
1	0:00:00	64	
2	1:00:00	63	63.5

Row	Hour	TempF	
2	1:00:00	63	
3	2:00:00	63	
4	3:00:00	63	63

Row	Hour	TempF	
2	1:00:00	63	
3	2:00:00	63	
4	3:00:00	63	63

Row	Hour	TempF	
46	45:00:00	62	
47	46:00:00	61	
48	47:00:00	61	61.33

Row	Hour	TempF	
47	46:00:00	61	
48	47:00:00	61	
X	X	X	61

Figure 13-4. Shows the frame for each row under evaluation

Then for each frame, we perform the average of current temperatures in the specified rows and apply the result to the row.

There are a few other forms of syntax to use to create different behaviors for frames. I would often want to extend the frame as I go, in order to create running totals or sums. That means that the window should always extend from the beginning of the table to my current row. I can do that with

```
ROWS BETWEEN UNBOUNDED PRECEDING AND CURRENT ROW
```

This syntax introduces two new concepts: UNBOUNDED, which means it just goes to the end of the table, and CURRENT ROW, which is the row under evaluation. I can similarly reverse this to

```
ROWS BETWEEN CURRENT ROW AND UNBOUNDED FOLLOWING
```

which will shrink the frame as I go from the entire table at the start to a single row at the bottom. And I can also create one fixed frame that contains the entire table:

```
ROWS BETWEEN UNBOUNDED PRECEDING AND UNBOUNDED FOLLOWING
```

(This is more useful when I've partitioned the table and want to calculate a value for each partition; you'd also generally use it in combination with other analytic functions. Otherwise, you could just select the whole table and then get the aggregate in a GROUP BY.)

There are two types of window frames I can make: rows and ranges. The syntax for each is the same, except that the clause starts with RANGE instead of ROW:

```
RANGE BETWEEN 2 PRECEDING AND 2 FOLLOWING
```

is an example. BigQuery refers to row-based windows as "physical frames" and range-based windows as "logical frames." What this means is that using ROW as a qualifier means the literal rows in the table to specify the frame. Using RANGE uses the value of the ORDER BY to specify the frame. The implication of range windows is that the size actually changes between rows if the data is not evenly distributed. RANGEs also don't really hold meaning without the ORDER BY to tell you what the RANGE is attached to. Let's look at a common RANGE:

```
ORDER BY Date RANGE BETWEEN INTERVAL '30' DAY FOLLOWING AND '30' DAY PRECEDING
```

This specifies a logical window frame that goes 30 days into the past and 30 days into the future. It doesn't matter how many rows that comprises; it will use the value of Date to decide.

Back to that implication, if you knew for certain that you only had one row for each day and no days were skipped, then this RANGE would be equivalent to a ROW BETWEEN 30 PRECEDING AND 30 FOLLOWING. It's easy to think you need to prepare your input to fill in the gaps so that you can do a ROW window, but this is not necessary. You can work directly with any expression in the partition by using the RANGE option.

Navigation Functions

I find this label a little questionable, but the idea is that the value they yield is produced using data from another row than the row being evaluated. In that sense, the function must "navigate" to a different row to get the result. The navigation is bounded first by the partition and then by the frame. Then the analytic function is applied over the frame and the result applied to the row under evaluation.

Using this navigation idea, we can actually consider most of the functions together by describing where they navigate to in order to calculate the value. Then we can dive into each and see how they might be useful.

Given a window frame

- FIRST_VALUE returns the value for the first row in the frame.

- NTH_VALUE returns the value for the row at the position you specify in the frame.

- LAST_VALUE returns the value for the last row in the frame.

- LAG returns the value for a row earlier in the frame by offset.

- LEAD returns the value for a row later in the frame by offset.

Using the model of function to locate by frame, this is the most natural way to establish the connection between "navigation" and these functions. To round it out, let's reexamine the order of operations with respect to navigation functions specifically, now that you understand all the component pieces:

- Table is partitioned by your PARTITION BY.

- Each partition is ordered by your ORDER BY.

- Then, for each partition

    - Each row is evaluated in order.

    - For each row, the frame is set based on your framing options.

    - Based on the frame, the navigation function chooses the row to look at, relative to the current row.

- All rows in each partition are rejoined together, producing your output range.

What kinds of questions can you answer with navigation functions? Well, as you could reasonably deduce, they answer questions like "Who/what was the first/middle/last/n- earlier/n-later X for each Y?"

- Which day had the highest temperature each month?

- Which day had the lowest temperature each month?

- Which employee has the next-most tenure for each employee by department? (Rephrased naturally, which employees started around the same time?)

- Which movie comes two movies later in each series, by franchise?

- What book came out closest to the beginning of the same year as each book, by subject?

See if you can construct the PARTITION BY, ORDER BY, and window frame, either ROW or RANGE, for each of these questions. While all of these examples have a PARTITION BY, you can also use the full table and often calculate useful information and the table level. The partitioning just gives you an extra level of grouping to work with, so you can answer the same question for every piece of data in the input.

Now you can also start to imagine what a query like this would look like without the use of analytic functions. In order to discover what movie comes two later per series, for example, you would end up attaching a row number manually to each series and then doing a subquery or a self-join to attach the data from the same table at the different ID. You can tell someone is avoiding analytic functions where you start seeing query syntax like

```
SELECT A.ID, A.Name, B.Name NameTwoEarlier
FROM A
JOIN A AS B
ON (A.ID - 2) = B.ID
```

Self-joins where one side of the join is doing a computation are usually a pretty good giveaway. The following is the same query with navigation functions:

```
SELECT ID, Name, LAG(Name) NameTwoEarlier
FROM A
OVER (ORDER BY ID ROW 2 PRECEDING)
```

No self-join, no messy aliases, and a lot easier to modify if it turns out you need something besides the name. Also, this query only works for an input of a single series. As soon as you add "for each series" to the question, the analytic version just needs "PARTITION BY Series." Doing this with regular SQL is substantially more complicated, involving the construction of a subquery and/or self-join.

Having fun yet?

Aggregate Analytic Functions

The last class of analytic functions are those that do double duty as regular aggregate functions. So good news: You already know these. To use them as analytic functions, you just specify them with an OVER clause instead of paired to a GROUP BY clause.

Most of the obvious aggregate functions support analytic use, so let's take a query template that you can copy and use for your own exploration:

```
WITH numbers
AS (SELECT * FROM UNNEST(GENERATE_ARRAY(1, 100)) AS num)
SELECT num,
       AVG(num) OVER (ROWS BETWEEN 2 PRECEDING AND CURRENT ROW) MovingAverage,
       SUM(num) OVER (ROWS BETWEEN UNBOUNDED PRECEDING AND CURRENT ROW)
       RunningTotal
FROM numbers
```

Let me break it down, and then you should be able to easily see how to test different analytic functions on different sets of data:

- Using the WITH clause, generate all the numbers from 1 to 100 and put them into a table named numbers. Each number is referenceable by the column num.

- Using this table, select three things:

  - The original number

  - A moving average using the current number and the two numbers preceding it

  - The cumulative sum of all numbers up to the current number (i.e., a running grand total or, if you like math, term n+1 of the triangle number function)

Copy this query into BigQuery and run it. It's self-sufficient since it generates its own data for the functions, so you don't need to do any preparation.

Now, here are some tweaks you can try to the query to see how the various analytic functions behave. Doing this is probably the best way to get comfortable with these functions. Just mess around with them and see if you can predict the answer:

- Change the numbers the GENERATE_ARRAY sequence produces. Try negative numbers or larger or smaller ranges. Add a third parameter to the function, which specifies the step between elements. For example, GENERATE_ARRAY(1, 100, 2) will produce the sequence [1,3,5,7,...]. Watch what the RunningTotal begins generating when you do this! It's an obvious but perhaps nonintuitive result.

- Try floating-point numbers in GENERATE_ARRAY. You can step over decimal numbers by decimal steps.

- Change the window frames of the average and sum functions to calculate moving averages or sums. Try extending the frame to the entire table.

- Try RANGE windows instead of ROW windows. Notice what happens to the results if you only replace "ROW" with "ORDER BY num RANGE" vs. what happens if you change the GENERATE_ARRAY sequence as well as the frame type.

- Add some other analytic functions to make more columns and explore their results as well. Use the instructions in Chapter 9 to guess what they'll do in this context. Some interesting ones to try here are COUNT, COUNTIF, and ANY_VALUE. (ANY_VALUE is especially interesting because you can peer into the soul of BigQuery's determinism. The value doesn't change over repeated runs, even though it could, according to the rules.)

- Change the expression in the analytic function without changing anything else. For example, what happens when you do SUM(num*num) OVER (ROWS BETWEEN UNBOUNDED PRECEDING AND CURRENT ROW)?[4]

- Try adding partitions to one or all of the columns. Experiment with different values for partitioning.

- Generate multiple sequences into the numbers table, for example, all odd numbers from 1 to 100 and all even numbers from 1 to 100. Try ordering by one column and using analytic functions over multiple columns.

- Start adding back in the navigation and numbering functions we already covered. What can you do with ROW_NUMBER() as a column? With LAG and LEAD?

I heard you hammering on the keyboard just now. You didn't even notice, but my guarantee came true! The questions you can answer with a single query employing analytic functions are amazing. Sorry, Google. The BigQuery documentation just doesn't do it justice in this case.

Analytic functions really add a whole new class of power to what you can do with SQL. With some syntax variations, all modern OLAP systems support this, so you'll also be able to take this knowledge and use it in other data warehouses. As I suggested earlier, getting this deep with SQL can truly change the way you see the world!

---

[4]Math lovers: It generates OEIS sequence A000330, otherwise known as the square pyramidal sequence.

BigQuery Scripting

When all else fails, BigQuery still has your back. BigQuery supports the full set of scripting commands too. So when your coffee mug is empty and you just can't translate a recurrence relation into an analytic function, procedural programming will still be there for you.

In BigQuery's case, scripting brought about multi-statement requests too, which had been lacking and made it somewhat difficult to do complicated transformations in a single call. This also gives you the normal trappings of variables, assignments, loops, and exceptions.

If you've worked with PL/SQL, T-SQL, or other procedural implementations of SQL, these concepts will all be familiar to you. And if you've worked in other languages and are new to SQL, they will still be relatively familiar to you.

Blocks

BigQuery uses BEGIN and END as the keywords for a block. A block signifies scope for variables declared and exceptions thrown inside of it. All statements inside a block must end with semicolons.

Variables

Variables are declared using DECLARE, and all variables must be declared before use. You can declare a variable in any type supported by BigQuery, and you may declare multiple variables of the same type with the same statement. Variables can be assigned a default value, which they will retain until you SET some other value. If you don't specify a default, the variable will be initialized to NULL.

You can also set the DEFAULT to be the result of a subquery, which is a convenient way to avoid a SET statement directly after the declaration.

There are no higher-level language features like constants, pointers, object orientation, classes, private variables, and so on.

Comments

As a reminder, comments in SQL begin with two hyphens:

```
-- This is a comment
```

You may also use C-style syntax for multiline comments:

```
/* This is a multiline
comment */
```

IF/THEN/ELSEIF/ELSE/END IF

These statements comprise the logic for an IF statement. No BEGIN or END statements are required to delineate an IF block. Here's a basic example, which rolls two dice and prints something interesting if certain rolls occur:

```
-- declare the variables we'll need
DECLARE DIE1, DIE2, TOTAL INT64;
-- declare the special result string
DECLARE RESULT STRING;
-- generate two random numbers and set the variables. sum them to get the
total.
SET (DIE1, DIE2) = (CAST(FLOOR(RAND() * 6) + 1 AS INT64), CAST(FLOOR(RAND()
* 6) + 1 AS INT64));
SET TOTAL = DIE1 + DIE2;

-- check for some special results with an if block and set the result.
IF (DIE1 = 1 AND DIE2 = 1) THEN SET RESULT = "Snake eyes.";
ELSEIF (DIE1 = 6 AND DIE2 = 6) THEN SET RESULT = "Boxcars.";
ELSEIF (DIE1 = 4 AND DIE2 = 4) THEN SET RESULT = "Hard eight.";
ELSE SET RESULT = "Nothing special.";
END IF;

-- return the results to the user
SELECT FORMAT("You rolled %d and %d for a total of %d. %s", DIE1, DIE2,
TOTAL, RESULT);
```

This sample shows all of the concepts we've covered so far, as well as a few new ones:

- You can set the value of multiple variables inside the same statement by parenthesizing both sides of the assignment.

- You can combine conditions in the IF statements with boolean logic.

- You can use FORMAT to insert variables into a string.

- RAND() is the pseudo-random number function in BigQuery; it generates a FLOAT between 0.0 and 1.0.

Control Flow

BigQuery has three primary control flow constructs, LOOP, WHILE, and exception handling. If you want to implement anything more complicated, like a FOR loop, you'll have to do it yourself.

LOOP/END LOOP

Loops run forever unless you BREAK (or LEAVE) them. This isn't the first opportunity you've had to make an infinite loop in BigQuery, but it's the easiest one that's come along so far. The maximum query duration is 6 hours. I'll just leave those two facts there and keep going.

Here's an example of a loop that prints the numbers from 1 to 10 and then exits. There's no reason you would want to do this:

```
DECLARE I INT64 DEFAULT 0;
DECLARE R ARRAY<INT64> DEFAULT [];
LOOP
  SET I = I + 1;
  SET R = ARRAY_CONCAT(R, [I]);
  IF I > 9 THEN LEAVE;
END IF;
END LOOP;
SELECT * FROM UNNEST(R);
```

Despite its negligible value, this is a great example. This statement batch takes 6.4 seconds and runs 11 statements. Doing it the natural BigQuery way

```
SELECT * FROM UNNEST(GENERATE_ARRAY(1,10))
```

takes 0.3 second and runs a single statement. Just because you have loops available to you doesn't mean you should immediately rely on them when there is probably a SQL solution that uses sets. Note: LEAVE and BREAK are completely synonymous keywords.

WHILE/DO/END WHILE

The WHILE construct looks like WHILE in most other languages. Here's the same query from earlier rewritten using a WHILE loop:

```
DECLARE I INT64 DEFAULT 0;
DECLARE R ARRAY<INT64> DEFAULT [];
WHILE I < 10 DO
  SET I = I + 1;
  SET R = ARRAY_CONCAT(R, [I]);

END WHILE;
SELECT * FROM UNNEST(R);
```

This query takes roughly as long as the LOOP version and is roughly as useful.

Exception Handling

Exception handling is scoped to the BEGIN/END block in which you declare it. When something illegal happens, the exception is thrown, and control jumps to the EXCEPTION statement and executes the statements there, for example:

```
BEGIN
SELECT 1/0; -- attempts to divide by zero
EXCEPTION WHEN ERROR THEN
SELECT "What are you even doing there.";
END
```

If you run this sample, you'll actually see the results of both queries in the display: the failed query trying to divide by zero and the "successful" query returning the error message.

When inside the exception clause, you will no longer have access to variables declared in the corresponding BEGIN/END scope, but you do get some system variables that can tell the user more about the error. They're quite useful:

- **@@error.message** gives you the error message.

- **@@error.statement_text** gives you the SQL statement that caused the exception—very helpful for debugging, especially when it's an obvious division by zero.

- **@@error.stack_trace** returns an array of stack frames and is intended for programmatic traversal of the error's stack trace.

- **@@error.formatted_stack_trace** is the human-readable version of the stack trace, and you should not do any processing on the string. Use .stack_trace instead.

Knowing all of this, we can craft a much better response to the user:

```
EXCEPTION WHEN ERROR THEN
SELECT FORMAT("Hey, you. When you executed %s at %s, it caused an error:
%s. Please don't do that.", @@error.statement_text, @@error.formatted_
stack_trace, @@error.message);
END
```

You can also throw your own user-generated exceptions with the RAISE keyword:

```
RAISE USING message = "Error.";
```

Using RAISE inside a BEGIN will cause flow to be transferred to the EXCEPTION clause, as usual. Using RAISE inside of an EXCEPTION clause will re-raise the exception to the next error handler, eventually terminating with an unhandled exception if nothing intercepts it.

RETURN

Return ends the script from wherever you invoke it. It works anywhere inside or outside of a block, so if you use RETURN and then continue the statement list, those subsequent statements will be unreachable.

Stored Procedures, UDFs, and Views

Scripts can be pretty useful on their own, even when run interactively. However, the name of the game here has always been reusability. At the GCP level, we're looking to manage our imports and streams so that they can be used across a variety of incoming data. When we write table schemas, we want them to describe our data in a durable way so that they can hold all the types of relevant entities and grow with our business.

The way we do that with scripts is to encapsulate them in stored procedures and user-defined functions, or UDFs. (Views are a little different, but they're traditionally all taken together so we'll honor that approach here.)

Stored Procedures

A lot of ink has been spilled discussing the pros and cons of stored procedures, whether we should use them at all, and why they're amazing or terrible. Despite the on-and-off holy war about the value of stored procedures over the last couple decades, they've never gone away. It is true that they still leave something to be desired when it comes to versioning, source control, and deployment practices. But the tools to manage all of those things have been around for nearly as long as stored procedures themselves. The failure to embrace these processes is in large part a function of how data organizations operate.

The purpose of showing all of the things you can do with integration to BigQuery, other services, and other paradigms was, in large part, to show that you have the best of both worlds. You can maintain your Dataflows, cloud functions, and transformation scripts in the most cutting-edge of continuous integration systems. You can ensure that all of your critical warehouse activities are documented, repeatable, and resistant to error.

There is still room for stored procedures and UDFs in that world too. While I'd be significantly less likely to recommend or build a massive inventory of chained procedures to perform production line-of-business tasks, I'd also store any reasonable, reusable script in a procedure for use by other analysts and applications. Stored procedures are great for containing complex analytic function work. While a lot of business logic has migrated out to API or serverless layers, this core online analytics work belongs with SQL.

Ultimately, I think if stored procedures weren't a sound idea architecturally, Google wouldn't have taken the trouble to add support for them into BigQuery. This isn't holdover functionality; they were only introduced in late 2019.

Key Principles

A script can be turned into a stored procedure with a small amount of effort. In turn, you can build more complicated data structures by calling stored procedures from other stored procedures, kind of like subroutines. Procedures have parameters that can be treated as IN, OUT, or INOUT. These roughly correspond to arguments in other languages as such:

- IN: Like an argument passed to a function

- OUT: Like a return value

- INOUT: Like a pass-by-reference

There's no encapsulation of methods, so if you SELECT inside a stored procedure, it will be emitted as if you were running an interactive command. You can use this if you just want the client calling the stored procedure to get results back without the use of parameters.

Temporary Tables

We haven't needed temporary tables for much so far; BigQuery basically creates a temporary table to hold results every time you run a query. But within stored procedures, you often want a place to store the intermediate results while you work. You can do this simply with "CREATE TEMP TABLE AS," followed by the SELECT query with which you want to initialize it. When you've finished with the table, be sure to "DROP TABLE TableName" so that it doesn't persist anywhere.

Syntax

Here's a basic stored procedure to show you an example of the syntax:

```
CREATE OR REPLACE PROCEDURE wbq.GetRandomNumber(IN Maximum INT64, OUT
Answer INT64)
BEGIN
    SET Answer = CAST((SELECT FLOOR((RAND() * Maximum) + 1)) AS INT64);
```

```
END;
DECLARE Answer INT64 DEFAULT 0;
CALL wbq.GetRandomNumber(10, Answer);
SELECT Answer;
```

Note that I used "CREATE OR REPLACE," instead of just "CREATE," so that the procedure will alter itself as you make changes to it. This procedure just selects a random number between 1 and the Maximum parameter. After creating it, the last three lines show a sample invocation, where a variable is created to hold the result, the procedure is called, and the answer is returned.

Also note the use of a subquery to set the value for the answer. Since "Answer" is declared as an OUT parameter, I can assign to it directly. One important note: BigQuery actually doesn't do any checking to prevent you from assigning to an IN variable. If you forget to declare an argument as "OUT" and then SET it anyway, the variable will be updated within the scope of the stored procedure, but it will not be emitted to the caller. This doesn't cause an error at parse **or** runtime, so watch out for it.

User-Defined Functions

User-defined functions are also stored code that you can use inside other queries, but they don't stand alone like stored procedures do. They are functions you create that behave the same as any of the functions in the standard library, like UCASE() or LCASE() or the RAND() we just used earlier. (Oh, and as promised, here's your warning that the JavaScript's coming up.)

Here's an example function declaration:

```
CREATE OR REPLACE FUNCTION dataset.AddFive(input INT64) AS (input+5);
```

Impressively, this function adds the number 5 to whatever integer input you pass in. You can invoke it like this:

```
SELECT dataset.AddFive(10);
```

This will return 15, which is magically the correct answer to 10 + 5. While the example is simple, it's all that's really needed to convey what a user-defined function would typically do. You are likely to have operations in your business that have fairly simple mathematical definitions, but which are critical in your business domain. Rather than hardcoding them all over all your queries, this is an easy way to make those operations consistent.

For example, if your business consists of a lot of travel between the United States and Canada, you may want a simple unit conversion operation to go between miles and kilometers, if only to make the code more readable and avoid the specification of the constant each time.

On the other end of the spectrum, you can make arbitrarily complex functions for statistical and mathematical operations. Whatever operation you need that BigQuery doesn't provide built in, you can create it.

ANY TYPE

BigQuery also supports templating for functions. Templating as a concept usually means that it's able to copy and paste your function text to apply to multiple data types that have shared operations. With a simple modification to our scintillating AddFive function, as shown

```
CREATE OR REPLACE FUNCTION wbq.AddFive(input ANY TYPE) AS (input+5);
```

we can now invoke the function across any data type we like. BigQuery can automatically figure out based on our operations which types are valid. So with this modification, I can run AddFive(10.5) and get back 15.5 with no problem. But if I try to AddFive("help"), BigQuery catches it and tells me I need a signature of NUMERIC, INT64, or FLOAT. (Were you expecting the result "help5"? What is this, JavaScript?)

User-Defined Aggregate Functions

What if you want to define your own aggregate functions? There's no native support for this, but there is a way to fake it.

An aggregate function, in the abstract, takes a set of values and returns a single value. For example, the AVG() aggregate takes a number from each row and sums them together, returning a single number. So that implies we will need a UDF that takes an ARRAY of something and returns that something. But it turns out we don't need to worry about that, because BigQuery templating can infer it for us. So here's how you wrap the existing AVG() function in a UDF:

```
CREATE OR REPLACE FUNCTION fake_avg(input ANY TYPE)
AS ((SELECT AVG(x) FROM UNNEST(input) x));
```

This creates a function that takes an array of numerics and calculates the average. You could of course write SUM(x)/COUNT(x) or any other type of aggregation you would want to perform.

The template analysis will restrict the input to an array of numerics, because the AVG aggregate needs numeric input, and the UNNEST function needs an array. But you still can't use this fake_avg function directly, since you still need to generate the array of numerics.

Luckily, we already have an aggregate function that does this for us—ARRAY_AGG. So all you need to do to invoke our new UDF is to wrap the group input in an ARRAY_AGG before calling it. That gives us

```
SELECT fake_avg(ARRAY_AGG(x)) FROM input;
```

Tada! Our own user-defined "aggregate" function. You can use this as you would any other aggregate, for instance, by GROUPing BY other columns and obtaining the results per row. You can **even** use it as an analytic UDF:

```
SELECT fake_avg(ARRAY_AGG(x) OVER()) FROM input;
```

Unfortunately, that syntax is starting to look a bit less natural.

JavaScript User-Defined Functions

User-defined functions have another trick up their sleeves, and that's the ability to call out to any arbitrary JavaScript. This feature is fantastically powerful, because it's basically like being able to write any procedural code you might need, all within the scope of values across rows. This opens up all kinds of avenues. Even more interestingly, it gives you the ability for the first time to share code with applications running in the browser or on NodeJS (with limitations, of course). We'll discuss that possibility after we go over the basics.

The syntax for a JavaScript UDF looks like this:

```
CREATE OR REPLACE FUNCTION wbq.AddFiveJS(x FLOAT64)
RETURNS FLOAT64
LANGUAGE js AS """
  return x+5;
""";
```

This does the same thing as our SQL UDF, but now we're doing it in JavaScript. Some other things have changed here too. First of all, we're using FLOAT64 as the type now; that's because JavaScript has no integer-only data type. FLOAT64 goes over as NUMBER, and that's one important gotcha—type mapping between SQL and JavaScript.

The second thing you'll notice is that the RETURNS clause is now required. BigQuery can't infer what kind of type you'll be returning unless you give it the conversion back into SQL. Interestingly, you can return INT64, but if your JavaScript tries to return a number with a decimal part, it will get unceremoniously truncated on its way back.

Lastly, you'll notice the odd-looking triple-quote syntax. If you're writing a single line of JavaScript, you can use a single quote, and indeed we might have done that in our example. But it's probably best to be explicit and use the triple-quote syntax, both because it prevents an error later where we try to add another line to the function and because it signals to any other readers that something unusual is going on here.

Limitations

- There is no browser object available, so if you're taking code that you ran in a web browser, you don't get a DOM or any of the default window objects.

- BigQuery can't predict what your JavaScript is going to do nor what would cause an output to change. So using a JS UDF automatically prevents cached results.

- You can't call APIs or make external network connections from a UDF, as fun as that sounds.

- There's no way to reference a BigQuery table from inside of the JavaScript—you can pass structs in, and they will appear as objects on the JS side, but you can't arbitrarily select data.

- You also can't call out to native code, so don't go trying to use grpc or anything. But you **can** use WebAssembly to compile native C or Rust into JS and then use it in SQL. (But do you really want to?[5])

---

[5]I did, and as with all insane BigQuery-related envelope pushing, Felipe Hoffa has you covered. See https://medium.com/@hoffa/bigquery-beyond-sql-and-js-running-c-and-rust-code-at-scale-33021763ee1f and have your mind blown.

External Libraries

Here's where it gets wild. You can also reference external JavaScript libraries in your function. To do this, you need to upload your library to Google Cloud Storage and then reference its path in a special clause called OPTIONS, as so:

```
CREATE TEMP FUNCTION externalLibraryJSFunction(x STRING)
  RETURNS STRING
  LANGUAGE js
  OPTIONS (library=["gs://some.js", ...])
  AS
"""
 return externalFunction(x);
""";
```

This example will fetch the library from the Google Storage location you specify and include it in the processing for your function. Then you can execute any function the library defines as if you had written it inline.

If you're familiar with the Node ecosystem, your next question is likely, "But can I use npm packages?" The answer is sort of. You're still subject to all of the memory, timeout, and concurrency limitations, but all you need to do is get the package to Google Cloud Storage. The best way to do this is Webpack, which works totally fine with JS UDFs.

Other BigQuery users, already recognizing the conceptual leap this represents, have begun repackaging useful BigQuery functions as Webpack JavaScript and publishing those as repositories. It seems fairly likely that people will begin creating public Cloud Storage buckets with these libraries available for referencing, much as popular JavaScript plugins began appearing on CDNs for browsers, but I haven't seen anyone doing this yet. Maybe you could be the first.

Views

A view is best summarized as a virtual table. Typically, views don't actually move any data around; they are, as implied, a "view" into the columns of one or more tables. In the case of BigQuery, views do store the schemas of the underlying tables they use, so if you modify the table schemas, you should also refresh the view.

Creating a view is easy; whenever you run any query in the interactive window, directly next to the "Save Query" button is another button labeled "Save View." Clicking that will ask you to specify the dataset to store the view in and the name of the view.

To edit a view, you can double-click it and go to the Details tab. At the bottom of that tab, you will see the query used to generate the view and can edit and resave it.

Materialized Views

Materialized views, on the other hand, are views that actually collate and store the results of a query. You can use materialized views to replace any "reporting" tables you create with an automatically refreshing, precomputed version.

Materialized views have substantial advantages for data that is frequently accessed. They even pair with streaming (see Chapter 6) to run aggregation on top of incoming data for real-time analysis.

Unlike regular views, materialized views can only use a single underlying base table. Their primary use is to perform various grouping and aggregation on that table to have it available at all times. (Unfortunately, you can't use analytic functions in a materialized view yet.)

Also, as with regular views, you need to fully specify the project.dataset.table in all places. The syntax for creating a materialized view is

```
CREATE MATERIALIZED VIEW `project.dataset.mview`
AS SELECT ... FROM `project.dataset.table` ... GROUP BY ...
```

After you create a materialized view, BigQuery will automatically begin refreshing the data from the underlying table with the query you wrote. From now on, whenever you change the data in the underlying table, BigQuery will automatically invalidate the correct portions of the materialized view and reload the data. Since this use case is so tightly tied with streaming, BigQuery also understands how to invalidate and read from partitions.

Advantages of Materialized Views

Materialized views give you a substantial speed boost on your query aggregation. Not only do they improve the performance when querying the view but BigQuery will automatically notice speed improvements in queries to the base table and reroute the query plan to look at the materialized views.

Also, unlike waiting for a scheduled query or an analysis trigger, the data in a materialized view will never be stale. This creates a natural pairing with high-velocity streaming. Several examples in Chapter 6 would be improved by placing a materialized view on top of the ingestion table in order to get automatic aggregation.

Disadvantages of Materialized Views

One potential disadvantage is cost. Since you pay for the query which refreshes the view on underlying table updates, you can transparently incur extra costs just by performing regular operations on the base table. You can also have multiple materialized views pointing at the same table, so basic operations will incur a multiple of cost. Similarly, since the data for the materialized view constitutes a separate copy, you pay for its storage as well.

Another disadvantage is keeping track of your materialized views. BigQuery won't notify you of a constraint failure if you delete the base table.

Finally, you can't perform some normal table operations on a materialized view. For example, you can't join other tables or use the UNNEST function.

Automatic vs. Manual Refresh

You can still use materialized views in concert with your existing maintenance processes. This also mitigates the potential cost risk, since you'll be controlling when the view updates. (Of course, then you also take back responsibility for keeping the data fresh, so you can't have everything.) You do this with "OPTIONS (enable_refresh = false)" when you create the table.

Summary

Analytic functions, or windowing functions, give you the ability to express in a few lines of SQL what would take complicated subqueries or self-joins to replicate. Using various types of analytic functions, you can evaluate conditions over partitions and window frames to generate groupings of data without collapsing them as a GROUP BY clause would do. Through numerical, navigation, and aggregate analytical functions, we looked at a variety of ways to order and analyze your data. Beyond that, we entered the realm of scripting, with which you can write constructs using procedural language that are not easily expressible with SQL. Using SQL scripting, you can create powerful stored procedures and user-defined functions, even replicating the usefulness of aggregates. We also looked at the ability to write user-defined functions in JavaScript and referencing external libraries available in the vast ecosystem of npm packages. Lastly, we looked at both traditional and materialized views and how they can lower maintenance operations for the streaming of aggregate data.

You now have a wide breadth of information on the power of SQL for data warehouses, as well as the integration of special BigQuery capabilities and other Google Cloud Platform features. Despite that, we still have a few areas of BigQuery we haven't even touched yet.

In the meantime, the next several chapters are back to the operational and organizational aspects of supporting your data warehouse. Having secured the ongoing success of your data project with ever-increasing insight, it's time to look at the long term. In the next chapter, we'll be looking at how you can adapt your warehouse to the ever-changing needs of your business—and hopefully its continued growth and success as well.

CHAPTER 14

Data Governance

In this chapter, we're going to talk about strategies to ensure the long-term success of your data program and actions you should take to ensure it is relevant and successful. The first of these topics is the drafting and implementation of an organizational data governance strategy.

All of the topics we've discussed fall into one of the three categories of effective program implementation: people, process, and technology. I freely mix the three, because to a great extent all the factors depend on each other. An effective data governance strategy will specify elements of all of them, as well as outline the dependencies they have on each other. You can't really say that one is more or less important than the others.

This is also the point in your program where you can seriously say the words "data governance" and people will not assume you are putting the cart before the horse. If your data is on an exponential growth curve, you need to establish a program before things get out of control. The good news is that with thoughtful schema design and reasonable, maintainable ingestion processes, you have created stable channels for new data in the existing system. That means you should now have time to establish rules for the data lifecycle. This will be your most important legacy and what will set the stage for long-term success.

The advantage of a well-defined governance system is manifold. Most importantly, it removes you as the bottleneck for all data design decisions. This removes barriers to business velocity. Moreover, it removes the cognitive load of needing to make a separate decision each time you encounter a new type of data. Process isn't about telling people what they have to do; it's about enabling them to make the right decisions so they can focus on what makes the situation unique.

A data governance process for your organization is like a manual for how to build a car. The surpassing majority of all cars have properties in common. (That's why it's the go-to example for object-oriented programming tutorials.) They all have a steering wheel, a brake and an accelerator pedal, and an instrument panel that tells

305

© Mark Mucchetti 2020
M. Mucchetti, *BigQuery for Data Warehousing*, https://doi.org/10.1007/978-1-4842-6186-6_14

you the speed and fuel level in the car. Sure, there are differences as dramatic as what side of the car the driver sits on. Some cars don't have fuel tanks. Others have manual transmission. The number of seats varies. But the systemization here means that you can be reasonably sure you can drive any car you rent or buy.

The systemization here is not at the level of the owner's manual—you probably should read that when you purchase a new car to learn what makes your car unique vs. others. This is at the manufacturing level—all car manufacturers produce cars that operate similarly, and thus the amount of variation in their respective owners' manuals is limited.

Operating from this point forward without a data governance strategy would be analogous to owning a car factory with no standards. That's what I mean by the "cognitive overload" of needing to make a separate decision each time. Without standards, you'd have to have a meeting for each car about where to put its steering wheel. A stray comment might cause the speedometer to measure furlongs per minute. Another designer might try putting the engine on the roof. In the worst case, these cars will catch on fire being driven off the lot. At best, each car will have strange unexplainable quirks. You'll try to figure out how to drive the car and eventually find the manual in the spare tire well labeled "VehiclOwner Book."

I'm belaboring my point. The truth is, without data governance, you'll get reasonably close to standardization because you and your team know what you're doing. Your program will continue to expand, though, and the number of users and stakeholders will multiply. At some point, systemization becomes the best way to maintain quality.

What Is Data Governance?

Data governance is a broad term to cover the process an organization uses to ensure that its data is high quality and available consistently across the organization. It covers a variety of areas, most of which we have covered as related to benefits to BigQuery. Some of the major concepts associated with data governance are handled directly by BigQuery, specifically having an available warehouse. Here are some key characteristics data governance aims to address. Some definitions skew toward the decision-making capabilities, while others focus on the technology. In truth, your organization will have a unique profile of areas of emphasis.

Availability

Data should be available at all times to all users who need it. Systems should have service-level agreements (SLAs) that are measured and adhered to. Any analysis downtime should be coordinated with the appropriate parties and executed on a predefined schedule.

Compliance

Data should be collected and stored according to the laws and regulations to which your organization is subject. Data should be retained in a format which is consistent with the organization's compliance rules and available for auditing purposes. This likely includes access to the warehouse itself; data being accessed by users should be auditable. Luckily, BigQuery does this automatically.

Consistency

Data should be read and labeled consistently across the organization. This includes the data warehouse, but also systems outside of it, extending into company reports, financial statements, and so on. A properly created and maintained data glossary defines, in large part, the specific jargon of the organization. Wherever possible, definitions of consistency should capture the organizational culture accurately (descriptive), instead of trying to impose unfamiliar terminology and unnecessary complication (prescriptive).

Cost Management

Ideally, an organization-wide data program will allow you to understand exactly how much is being spent and invested and make calculations about how additional investment might improve the other characteristics or allow for new business functions. The more dynamic your cost management can be, the faster you can adapt to market conditions or identify areas of waste.

Decision Making

A key part of data governance is the establishment of the roles and responsibilities of members of the organization. This ranges from the extremely simple ("Emily is the data person") to complex RACI charts with matrix responsibilities and backups. The form depends entirely on your organization, but the function is the same: minimize confusion in the decision process, establish clear ownership, and execute efficiently.

Performance

Data should be available within a reasonable amount of time, where "reasonable" is a function of the type of data and your organization's needs. Related to availability, this includes traditional data maintenance tasks like reindexing and data defragmentation, as well as archiving and deleting old data. BigQuery does most of the basics automatically, but ensuring performance of the systems you build within the data warehouse remains mostly your responsibility.

Quality

This is a basic tenet of any data program, but data governance usually incorporates some ability to measure the quality of data entering the system. Appropriate process and standards should be followed when creating or modifying core data systems. Schemas should be accurate and up-to-date. Ongoing process should ensure that the desired level of quality is maintained (or improved).

Security

Conversely, data should not fall into the hands of unauthorized people. Users with system access should only be able to view and edit data to which they are entitled. No data should ever be deleted without following appropriate procedures which you define. Governance should include procedures for reporting the loss of data, unauthorized access to data or external breach, and onboard/offboard procedures for users to ensure access is granted and revoked appropriately.

Usability

This is more of a composite characteristic of the others, but I include it as a reminder of the final, top-level measurement of a data program. A hard drive in a basement safe may be filled with high-quality data that is highly secure, utterly consistent, and available 24/7 to authorized users, but it's not usable. Going all-in in other areas may yield unacceptable compromises in usability. Any data program which is not usable will quickly fade into irrelevance, at which point none of the other aims will matter.

Anatomy of a Governance Strategy

I have a confession to make. This whole time, as we created a charter, identified stakeholders, and executed our data warehouse project, we were actually following data governance practices all along. The insistent harping on a data glossary, taxonomic standardization, and consistent, extensible models were all part of the plan. Your inclusion of stakeholders, first as contributors and then as users, already built the framework for a long-lived, successful program. And it is a program—remember finishing the warehouse "project" was just the tip of the iceberg.

And most of all, the integration of business value into your data program from day 1 baked the DNA of your organization's idiosyncrasies directly into the model. This isn't a cookie-cutter program that's the same for every organization. Yes, as with car manufacturers, there are substantial similarities. But as each manufacturer has their own process that marries organizational DNA with solid, repeatable technology frameworks, your organization now has a data program that complements its way of doing business.

BigQuery is hardly the most important factor in this equation. Analogously, it lets you outsource some of your car manufacturing responsibilities. You can have a big, fast engine without fully understanding how to build one. Your cars can go faster, or farther, or have cool racing stripes on them. But you own the factory now. How do you make the rules?

Roles and Responsibilities

You may have noticed that people are paying attention now, doubly so if your project started out as a skunkworks side-channel say-so from an executive who had heard some buzzwords. This is common in smaller organizations; when real transformation starts to occur, people eventually notice, and then interest and pressure grow exponentially. In Chapter 8, we talked about the need for a discrete "launch." One of the purposes for that is to over-communicate your capabilities and progress through the data maturity rubric.

In the early maturity stages, people wear many hats and move fluidly between roles that would inhabit different departments or divisions in larger organizations. This constitutes an extremely valuable skill in these organizations, but as the organization grows, this can create what is known as "organizational debt." Organizational debt is on the whole worse than technical debt because it includes irrational beliefs in practice based on fallacies like "This is how we've always done it." (You'll note this statement to be a shibboleth for program maturity.) Establishing a data governance program challenges these notions. This phase is really where organizational holdouts have to confront a changing reality.

The best way to combat this in a growing organization is to establish clear roles and responsibilities. I hesitate to specify specific "roles" or their "responsibilities" because trying to over-formalize what needs to start as a lightweight process is a chokehold. Being prescriptive here would basically contradict everything from earlier about baking the idiosyncrasies of your organization into the DNA of your governance program. There's a fine line here between "idiosyncrasies" and "process issues." Ultimately, as your organization is alive, you'll have to decide for yourself. Actually, though, I recommend that you find someone who truly understands the nuances of how the organization operates on the ground and use them to help you decide. If you make the best decisions and senior leadership kills your project, those decisions didn't really matter.

With that out of the way, let's go over some potential roles and their responsibilities, and you decide what resonates.

Senior Leadership

Chiefly, leadership needs to **advocate for** and **champion** your program. This support needs to come from the highest level because your initiative requires organization-wide transformation. By definition, everyone has other things to do, and even if they support your program, they have their own priorities. The senior leadership team of your organization needs to get on board so that effective data governance becomes and remains a priority.

Governance Council

This might also be called a "steering committee" or a "cross-functional roundtable" or whatever your organization likes to call these things. Important note: Call this whatever your organization likes to call these things. Naming things is important, and this is a key way to align your strategic goals with your business. (I've heard of people calling these things the "Imperial Senate" or "The Council of Elrond" or whatever. Let me go on the record as explicitly prohibiting "The Ivory Tower.")

The role of the governance council is to facilitate major strategic decisions as a cross-functional group. The group should meet regularly to discuss major issues impacting data quality, collection, or retention. Meeting notes should be public, and all decisions should be recorded in a framework of your choice. (The decisions are themselves data, after all.) Some examples of decisions the council might make are as follows:

- Modifying the data governance policy

- Onboarding additional (or new) business units into corporate-level data services

- Choosing to adopt a technology like BigQuery or to replace it

- Steering the priority of data management, that is, selecting projects to fill the program

The council's participants have a second responsibility, which is to evangelize the program and enable their affiliated business units to derive value from it. The members of the council, in the aggregate, should have visibility into the organization in a way that lets you get ahead of utilization failures or data quality issues before they spill out of their area.

By the way, while someone needs to run this committee, it need not be the most senior member. It can also rotate on a regular basis, so long as someone is ensuring the basic functions: having regular meetings, publishing the notes, and making decisions while they are still pertinent.

If you're privileged enough to have a robust project management office (PMO) or something similar operating at the organizational level, you can use them to charter a data program. The organization will then be able to balance this program's priorities against other critical work in progress. Otherwise, your council will be responsible for scheduling its own meetings and holding each other accountable. When in doubt, communicate. Without this lifeline, the council will dissolve. Someone will say, "Do we really still need to have these meetings?", and your objections to cancelling will be overruled—everyone has other things to do. I've seen this happen, and usually around 6–12 months after a data program dies a quiet death, the organization suffers a data loss. Executives are furious, and someone timidly says, "Well, we **did** have a steering committee for this…"

Subject Matter Experts

It's time to formalize this role. These are the people you've been relying on throughout this whole process to tell you what data you need and what gotchas there are. Some of them were project stakeholders and then warehouse users. A couple are probably obvious picks for the steering committee.

The term "subject matter expert" (SME) sometimes carries a stigma with it that as domain-knowers, that's all they can do. I have found that so-called SMEs have lots of other insight into how pieces fit together and what is causing friction in the organization; they just don't always feel comfortable volunteering it. Accordingly, you may prefer a term like "data owner." Some responsibilities that make sense at this level are as follows:

- Understanding ongoing data needs and project future ones

- Flagging new initiatives when likely to have downstream impact on the data program

- Recognizing regulatory, compliance, and data classification issues and managing them where applicable or surfacing them to the steering committee when impact is greater

- Being the squeaky wheel: making sure that data issues in their area and business requirements that depend on the data program get effectively prioritized by the data team

That last one approaches mandatory. The data team can't know or understand the requirements for every project in progress at the organization. You can certainly attempt an embedded model where a member of your data team is attached to each project. For that to succeed, each member needs to have wide-ranging insight into what business-level requirements will drive changes in the data program. This is definitely possible, but in larger organizations, the mindshare can quickly become prohibitive.

Data Analysts

In full disclosure, the line gets a little blurry here. Technology tends to disintermediate; the net effect here is that data analysts can self-service in a way that was difficult before. When the data team is operating effectively, data analysts can maintain inertia without much direct contact with the operational team. Inertia isn't sufficient in a growing organization, which means they also end up serving a secondary role requesting features or tools they need to do their work.

The line here is something like analysts can request enhancements to the data warehouse or ask for integrations to other tools they use, but they cannot alter its construction. For instance, a data analyst could submit a project request to import data from Google Analytics into BigQuery tables, but they could not say "I'm using Redshift, so you have to put all the data in there now." Decisions at that level still need to be owned by the steering committee. Data analysts are consulted, but they aren't decision makers.

In smaller organizations, the data analyst may also be the warehouse developer and may also be the subject matter expert. In those organizations, also, hello! Thank you for reading this book. You'll have to functionally separate your roles so that you make the decision at the appropriate impact level for each role. (For example, if you are that person, then you could wear the architect hat and choose another warehousing technology. You just have to be careful not to make that decision while you are engaged in a process to create a new view.)

Some other potential responsibilities are as follows:

- Suggest enhancements to tools or processes that make their lives easier, such as the creation of a materialized view or new stream

- Serve as stakeholders for the data team's backlog and de facto "product owners" of their business unit's data

- Own the quality and technical definition of data for their business unit (schemas, integration to other datasets, etc.)

- Work with the subject matter expert to understand and implement appropriate retention and classification policies

- Work with the data engineering team to implement new tools and features where possible and appropriate

Data Engineering Team

In the purest form, this is the team that implements the technology and keeps the system running. They used to pay the bill for the data warehouse too, but as cost becomes more granular across lines of business, this is no longer necessarily so. This team may or may not include data analysts, should have at least one member on the steering committee, and must own the operational controls for the data governance program. If the steering committee says all data must be deleted after one week, the data engineering team makes sure that's happening.

I hesitate to be prescriptive also because I feel passionately that the engineering team must not simply "take orders." The true innovation center of the organization lies here—as a data practitioner, you're the one that thought BigQuery might be a good choice to implement a data warehouse, and you're the one that understood the transformational potential of new technology as an enabler to managing increased complexity. Ultimately, if you are a reader of this book who has applied the information from this (or any other source) to build your data program, you are its chief architect and most ardent champion. It's important to respect that, even as you recognize that systemization means the delegation and dispersal of these responsibilities to permit further growth. A robust data program will require two-way communication among those in each of these roles. Consequently, it's not just the organizational DNA that has been baked into this program: it's yours.

Some responsibilities you should maintain when wearing "only" this hat are as follows:

- Owning the scorecard for the program's health. You should have periodic assessments in key areas like reliability, performance, and user satisfaction so you can objectively report on success metrics.

- Run the process for severity issues like analysis downtime, data corruption, or integration failure. Work with the technology function to understand their metrics for incident command and adapt them to your area.

- More generally, provide technical support for users of the system on a day-to-day basis. If you have data analysis capabilities on your team, support that too.

- Ensure the security of the system as a whole. Administer permissions and access rights. Work with the technology function to align with any data loss prevention practices or disaster recovery protocols they follow.

- Own the taxonomy of the data program system-wide, including the data glossary. Serve as final arbiter of conflicts in data classification (as you did during construction).

- Stay abreast of new developments in BigQuery, data warehousing, and technology as a whole. The next replatforming of your data warehouse will be done in tandem with your entire organization, but the impetus and details will likely originate with you.

The "System of Record"

The data governance strategy should clearly define a system of record for all data entities in your organization. It need not be BigQuery in all cases, but you'll need to work with your systems architects to understand why that is and what it will be when it isn't BigQuery.

As discussed many times, users need to know where to look to find information, and they all need to be looking at the same place. The consequences of failure on this should be pretty obvious by now: if sales and finance have different numbers for revenue and each believes they are correct, no one will trust your data program—even if neither number came from BigQuery. With the system of record established, you can point to it and indicate that the correct revenue number comes from the specified system. If that number is wrong, that's a different problem, but it's an actionable one.

The "system of record" concept is fundamental to a master data management (MDM) strategy for an organization. Unlike some of the other considerations in your governance plan, you can't skirt this one for long, even if your organization is small and has limited resources.

When drawing up your governance plan, include the system of record definition even if it seems redundant. One line could even suffice: all data settles in BigQuery.

Golden Records

No, not "gold record." Golden records refer to a clean copy of all of the information about an entity in your organization. The typical example is a master person record, which has all of the data you know about a particular individual attached: their phone number, address, name, and whatever business data is relevant to you (purchase history, blood type, horoscope sign, World of Warcraft guild, whatever).

This whole time, we've been building the capability to maintain golden records for all of the data in our system. When it comes to formalizing this in a data governance strategy, we need to take a couple more steps.

Data Cleansing

While we've been painstaking in defining our data sources and ingestion strategies, having multiple systems outside of the system of record means the potential for conflict. With websites where your end users can directly enter their names and create accounts, you're bound to have duplication and orphaned records.

In a golden record, you're seeking to eliminate the imprecision of this data. If Reynaldo Jones forgets his password and just makes a new account with the same name and address, your operational system is unaffected. But from a golden record standpoint, you would seek to detect, merge, and clean duplicate records.

You'll never be fully successful at this, especially if the data input is low quality. Attempting to resolve it is an important way to ensure you're extracting accurate information from the raw data.

Multiple Source Systems

It's not unusual for a single golden record to require information from multiple subsystems. Different departments may interact with the same entity, but care about completely disparate properties. Requiring centralization at the source system creates a dangerous bottleneck for your business operations, and you likely don't have the ability to specify that anyway.

Consider a company that produces organic granola. Each department in that company will understand the concept of the product "granola bar." But the perspectives are wildly different. The production side of the business cares about the ingredients and the recipe. Finance cares about how many bars have been sold and what the profit margin is. Marketing has promotional images and videos of the granola bar. Legal needs all of the certifications required to call the product organic. Logistics needs to know how much it weighs and how much fits on a truck. These attributes will likely all reside in different systems, which have been tailored to the departments that use them. The correct pattern for establishing a golden record in this model is to build reliable pipelines from the source systems and assemble it in your data warehouse.

The result of this is that the warehouse still holds the "golden record," but it is not the operational system for the data. The data is produced by its relevant system of record and then shipped to BigQuery to create a golden record.

Single-Direction Data Flow

Regardless of where BigQuery sits in the informational architecture of your organization, the single best practice you can have is to ensure that data flows in only **one** direction. Once you designate a system of record for an entity or a partial entity, that must become and remain the authoritative source. All data updates must be done there and only there. I'm not speaking about conflicts between end user data submissions in concurrency scenarios—I'm saying that when a given system decides on an update, that's the update.

Whichever system you have designated, all other systems must read their state from that system. That includes BigQuery, if it holds the golden record but is not the authoritative system for that data. This implies that any piece of data is writable in only a single system and read-only in all others.

To clarify, I also mean this in a logical sense. If the data takes a few seconds or hours to propagate from its system of record into BigQuery, the principle is fine. What I mean is that by the principle of eventual consistency, there cannot be change conflicts across systems nor bidirectional syncing of data.

This "single direction of data" may sound familiar from a previous chapter. And yes, this is the directed-acyclic graph writ large. Those graphs ended with data generated in other systems settling in BigQuery; and it's those graphs, replicated and diffused at the organizational scale, which will enforce this principle.

Security

Data security and access rights are another foundational part of your data governance program. Data must be secure from unauthorized modification, deletion, and access. In a globally distributed system, the attack surface is massive and difficult to comprehend. As most cloud providers state in some form or another, their responsibility is to secure the cloud; yours is to secure the data you've placed on the cloud.

BigQuery runs on custom bare metal with a secure BIOS. Whenever a processor-level vulnerability is identified, Google is among the first to know. For instance, when the widely publicized Spectre and Meltdown vulnerabilities rocked the world, the data centers that run BigQuery had been patched before anyone outside of the cloud providers or intel knew there was an issue. By paying for BigQuery, you're expressing trust that Google is capable of securing their systems from reasonable intrusion. At the very least, you're admitting that they can do it more efficiently than you can.

Authentication

Before a user can interact with BigQuery, they need to authenticate to it. Managing your identity pool, both for custom applications and in the cloud, is the first line of defense. Authentication best practices are a constantly evolving area, so I'll stick to the basics:

- Require users to use multifactor authentication. (G Suite calls this 2-Step Verification, or 2SV). Prefer security keys and authenticator applications to text messages.

- Evaluate your identity pool on a regular basis. Integrate with your organization's on- and offboard policies to ensure that departing employees are immediately removed from the system.

- Conduct regular audits of user activity. The machine learning tools for automatically identifying anomalies are improving, but solutions aren't fully reliable yet.

In addition to users, remember that another primary mode of authentication to BigQuery will be through service accounts. If you followed along with the examples up until now, you'll have created several service accounts along the way. Include in your data governance policy the requirement that automated systems use service accounts. It must be clear when access to GCP was facilitated by a human and when it was an automated principal.

Permissions

The number one risk to your data is unauthorized access by real user accounts. Whether accounts have been compromised by social engineering or malicious intent, the risk is real. People need access to the data in order to use it, so this surface cannot be fully eliminated.

The best way to handle this is to develop access principles as part of your data governance strategy. Early in the program, when convenience outweighed restriction and you had no real data to speak of, you likely granted permissions liberally. Now is the time to audit those permissions and adapt the ones you have to conform with the new policy. This may ruffle some feathers, but better you do it now than wait until an incident occurs.

Key activities in this area include the following:

- Perform regular audits of user and service account permissions. Recently, GCP has begun showing on the IAM screen how many discrete permissions a user has and will perform live analysis to see if those permissions are in use. It then recommends to you to remove unnecessary permissions (see Figure 14-1).

- Restrict permissions both by service and role, but also by object. For BigQuery, you can set permissions granularly at the project and dataset levels. Classifying datasets by sensitivity is one way to control and understand granularity.

- If BigQuery should be accessible only from within your organization, you can use VPC Service Controls[1] to restrict access to the BigQuery API. Consult your networking operations personnel for how to make it available via site-to-site VPN or other access measures; there are restrictions.

BigQuery supports the concept of "authorized views," which is basically a fancy way of configuring datasets across projects.[2] In short, you have one dataset for source tables and another for views that rely on those source tables, and then you configure permissions such that some users can see only the views. If you intend to include this practice in the security section of your data governance strategy, make sure the procedure is well documented.

---

[1]https://cloud.google.com/vpc-service-controls/docs/
[2]The full tutorial is available here: https://cloud.google.com/bigquery/docs/share-access-views

An additional level of granularity, namely, column level, is in beta as of this writing. This can supersede authorized views in some situations and will ultimately be the best way to gain maximum control over your permissions structure.

Role	Over granted permissions
Editor	1594/1610
Cloud Build Service Account	
Editor	
Editor	1606/1610
Dialogflow API Client	12/12
Firebase Admin SDK Administrator Service Agent	
Service Account Token Creator	8/8
Firebase Service Management Service Agent	
Owner	1518/1780

Figure 14-1. *The IAM window showing permissions usage*

Encryption

Your responsibility to encryption for data comprises a few areas:

- Securing traffic between your systems and the Google perimeter

- Managing data once it has left GCP, either to your local file system or an end user's web browser

- Additionally encrypting and/or hashing personally identifiable information, at minimum to comply with relevant regulatory standards (HIPAA, FERPA, PCI, etc.)

The documents Google publishes about how they secure data inside their systems are intensely technical and not strictly relevant here.[3] In short, all BigQuery data is encrypted at rest. As you've seen throughout the BigQuery console UI and on other services, they also support designating the key you wish to use.

Cryptography is incredibly complicated and very easy to get wrong if you are not a security professional. Your obligation here is to make sure all connections use TLS (like HTTPS) and that you are employing additional encryption for sensitive data. All GCP APIs require secure connections, but if your organization writes custom applications, that obligation extends to them as well. Combined with access rights, you can prevent data from falling into unauthorized hands.

In this instance, consider if you really need a certain data piece in your data warehouse. For example, it would be useful for data analysts to know how many credit cards a customer typically uses to purchase from your website. However, they could obtain this information just as easily with a hash of the last four digits as they could with more information. (PCI compliance prohibits this anyway.) The best defense against losing sensitive data is not having sensitive data.

Classification

The operational safeguard against accidental disclosure of your data is to employ a data classification system. Following this system, all data, including paper documents, media, your data warehouse, operational systems, end user machines, ad infinitum, all has a classification level. Most data classification systems have about four levels:

- Public: Approved for external distribution or publication on the Internet

- Internal: Restricted to organizational representatives but can be distributed with prior authorization

---

[3]Please read https://cloud.google.com/security/encryption-at-rest/default-encryption#what_is_encryption for more information.

- Confidential: Restricted only to those in the organization, should not be distributed, and for which disclosure could mean adverse harm

- Restricted: Restricted only to a small subset of individuals in the organization who require the information in order to perform their operational duties

Using the authorized views methodology, if you needed BigQuery to store restricted data for analysis, you could create the underlying tables in a dataset classified as "restricted" and then expose only the nonrestricted portions of the data to analysts in a dataset of lower classification.

Specify this policy clearly in your data governance strategy. With the approval of your HR department or legal counsel, include instructions for disclosing a classification violation, as well as penalties to individuals who knowingly violate the classification standard.

This gives you coverage against unauthorized individuals accessing data they should not, whether or not they had digital authorization to do so.

Data Loss Prevention

Google Cloud Platform has a tool called Cloud DLP, which you can use to automatically inspect data in GCP for sensitive information and detect its presence or transmission. Cloud DLP integrates automatically with BigQuery, and you can access it by going to a resource in the left sidebar of BigQuery and clicking Export and then "Scan with DLP." See Figure 14-2 for what this looks like.

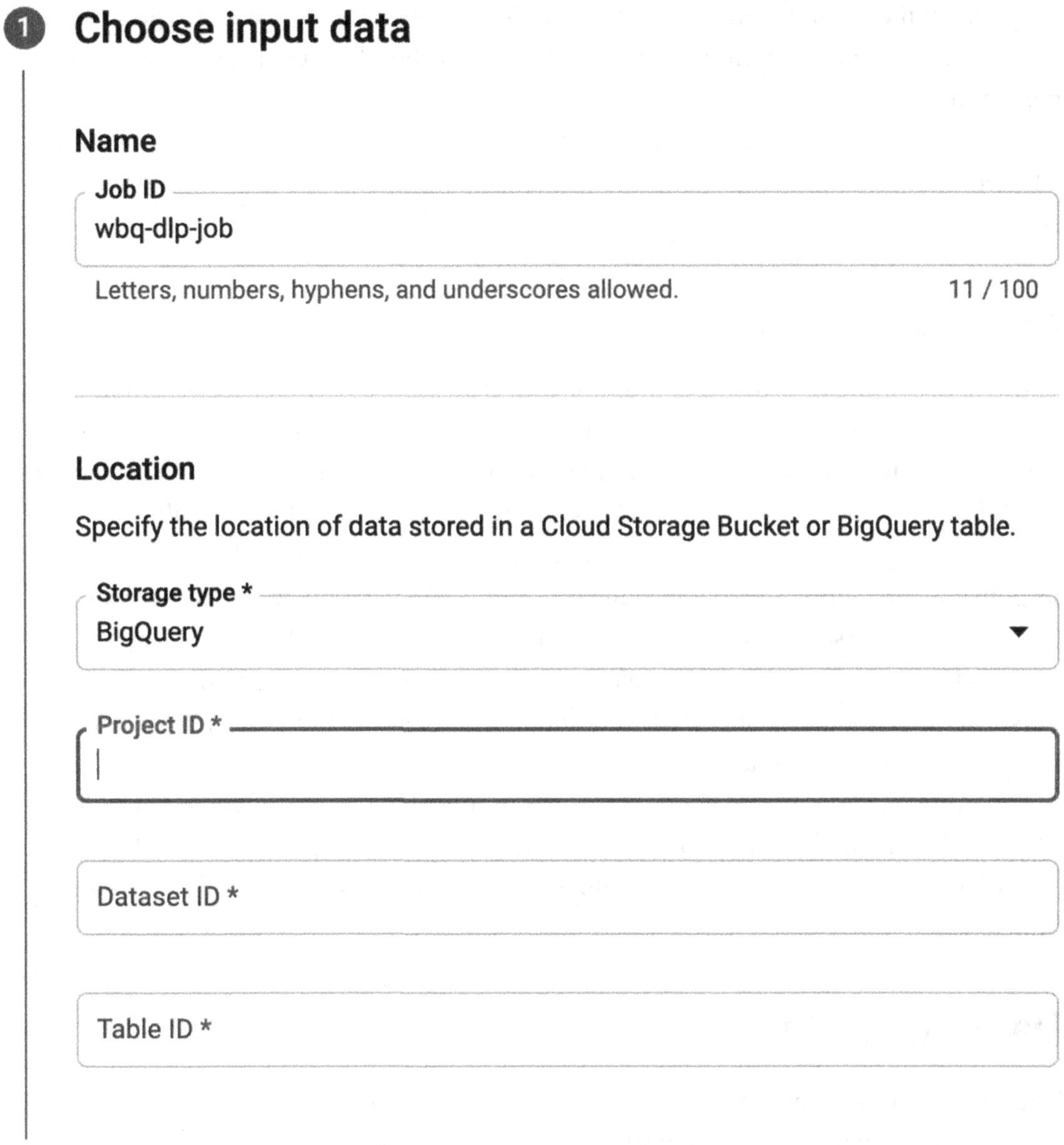

1 Choose input data

Name

Job ID

wbq-dlp-job

Letters, numbers, hyphens, and underscores allowed.   11 / 100

Location

Specify the location of data stored in a Cloud Storage Bucket or BigQuery table.

Storage type *

BigQuery   ▼

Project ID *

|

Dataset ID *

Table ID *

Figure 14-2. *Cloud DLP export screen*

Cloud DLP is not a cheap service, so if you are testing it, check the costs first and make sure you don't run it on too much data before you've determined what you're going to do with it. DLP also offers the ability to monitor systems, run scheduled jobs, and automatically anonymize any data it finds. All of that is beyond the scope for this chapter, but if your organization works with a lot of sensitive data, I encourage you to consider incorporation of Google's Cloud DLP or another data loss prevention tool to help manage this risk.

Regardless, your data governance plan should include steps for loss prevention and what activities should be performed on any potentially sensitive data entering your system.

Auditing

The next best thing you can do to monitor your data security is to record and monitor an audit log. In Chapter 12, we reviewed Cloud Logging and Monitoring, which is a natural fit to perform this role for a BigQuery data warehouse. Using those tools, you can create log sinks and from there an audit analysis policy so you can look for anomalies.

Specify in your governance policy what activities must be auditable, who is responsible for conducting or reviewing the audits, and what mechanic there is for remediating any issues discovered in an audit. All query jobs are logged to Cloud Logging (formerly Stackdriver) by default, so you already have a leg up on this policy. This is another good touchpoint for your technology security function, who may already have these processes in place.

An audit log does you no good if no one is monitoring it or taking remedial actions. After a major incident occurs, someone will probably think to go back and look at all the helpful log sinks you set up and realize that there was an early warning that went unheeded.

Data Lifecycle

The data governance policy should also specify the lifecycle for data.

In the next chapter, I'll explain why I don't think cost should drive your data retention policy, but for now I'll just say that all lifecycle considerations should be driven by the theory about what's right for that particular piece of data.

Your lifecycles will likely have variable steps and processes specific to your organization, but some features will be common, so let's address those here. All of these considerations should be applied to a particular "type" of data, which might be a business object, an individual record, or the analysis function for a business unit. That should be decided based on the relevant concepts to your organization.

Ingestion/Time to Availability

- What is the system of record for this data?

- How will we ingest it into the warehouse? How often?

- When it is ingested, will it require an ELT or ETL pipeline?

- If so, how often will that pipeline run? Will it be triggered by the ingestion process or run on a separate cycle?

- How long will that pipeline take and where will it place the data? Is aggregation or online analysis necessary to make the data consumable?

- How long before all of the necessary steps are complete and we consider the data to be "available" to the warehouse?

- Is there a natural partition to this data, either by date grain or some other key?

- Does this data need to interact with (and thus be available to) other datasets in the warehouse or external systems?

- Does this data's lifecycle include the creation and maintenance of stored procedures, UDFs, and so on that we must maintain for the lifetime of the associated data?

- When will this data start arriving at the warehouse? What will its approximate order of magnitude be, and do we know if and when that magnitude will change?

- Do we already know if this data will be ingested over a finite range of time, or does it represent a permanent addition to the organization's data? (Is it a pilot program?)

- How many users will need to analyze this data? Do they have access to BigQuery already?

Active Data and Quality Metrics

Once you understand the ingestion characteristics of the data, you need to understand how it will be governed while it is active in the warehouse. This includes any additional or unusual responsibilities you may have or if you must dedicate support resources to own it:

- Who is responsible for the maintenance of metadata for these datasets?

- Are there reporting responsibilities, and if so, who owns them? (Same for active monitoring, dashboarding, or scheduled delivery of any of the data)

- Who is responsible for defining the quality metrics for the data?

- What are the quality metrics of the data?

- What is the projected level of quality (quantitatively measured) for this data?

- Pertinent to the data program, how can I include this data in the system reports for warehouse health?

- What are the options if this data exceeds projected size or maintenance cost?

- Are there data cleansing considerations, and if so, what are they and who owns them?

- Are there special classification requirements that must be maintained?

- In some organizations, which department is paying for this service?

Quality metrics are necessary for any data in your custody. You need to understand if a high quality of data is expected from a low-quality input source and whose responsibility it is to ensure that happens. Also, as the one who must answer to discrepancies or lack of trust in your data, you must ensure that the right weight is placed on the data. It's not that you should necessarily prohibit low-quality data from entering the warehouse. But you should ensure that the active lifecycle policies for that data stress the idea that important organizational decisions should not be made with data that you and the owner have designated as "low quality."

Decommissioning

You may call this "sunsetting" or "retirement" or a whole host of other terms, but this refers to the ostensible last step in the data lifecycle—ending its ingestion:

- Was this supposed to happen? That is, is this a planned decommissioning, or are we taking unusual action?

- Do we need to turn off ingestion mechanisms, or is it also necessary to delete the data?

- Are there retention policies for this data? Does deleting it conflict with those policies?

- For a partial dataset, is this a process we should prepare to repeat with other data of this type?

- Will the data ingestion rate slow to a halt, or will it stop all at once?

- After ingestion has halted and retention policies have been fulfilled, do we need to take additional action?

- Are there other datasets that depend on this data? Will this impact the functioning of other parts of the system? If so, will this be automatic, or do we have to make adjustments elsewhere?

- Is this decommissioning temporary or permanent?

Your data governance policy should also specify when this information about the data's lifecycle is required. If you need it up front, make sure that your policy specifies that you need answers to all steps at the beginning. You may also opt to request only the ingestion information to get started and deal with active and decommissioned data at a later time. (This is also the source of the question "Was this supposed to happen?" If people are frequently decommissioning data without prior notice, either they should have a good reason for this or you should institute a lead time policy.)

Crypto-deletion

Google uses this term; it's also called "crypto-shredding." Essentially, all this means is that when all of your data has been encrypted with a key you have supplied, you can render that data inaccessible by deleting the encryption key. GCP has a few additional safeguards, like preventing you from exporting keys outside of GCP so that it knows there's no unauthorized management.

This is a good solution when access to the data may be available from countless end user machines, in caches, through APIs and command lines, and so forth. Deleting the key used to encrypt the data means all of those avenues are secured simultaneously.

At this moment, the legal situation seems a little unclear as to whether this can be considered deletion of data from a privacy compliance perspective. I'm not aware of any case law that answers the question, but it's something to keep in mind if the practice is deemed insufficient for that purpose.

For any data not otherwise bound by regulatory compliance, you should be okay. You should still continue the practice of whatever physical and digital media protection policies your organization practices.

Governance Modification

Like any good constitution, the data governance policy should also specify how it can be modified. Throughout growth periods, the number of individuals the policy touches may grow quickly. It may be necessary to quickly split roles and responsibilities or to adapt policies to preserve organizational agility. Conversely, if your organization were to shrink, you might combine roles and suspend elements of the policy which are no longer necessary.

You can be as formal or informal about this as you think appropriate. Large organizations have change control boards that must engage in a six-hour parliamentary debate in order to remove a second space after a period. Find the level that's appropriate for you.

Road Map

Another thing you should include in your governance process is how you will manage road map considerations, prioritize future work, and schedule important projects for the program. If you've already developed and piloted your road map as a function of the discussion in Chapter 8, incorporate the medium-term plan into the governance plan. Otherwise, work with your proto-steering committee to develop one.

A good rule of thumb for data program road maps is that if you find you don't know what to do next, take it up a level. You may not be able to say with certainty that you will onboard six particular departments in the following year. The next higher level is to say that you will have the capability to onboard new departments by doing X, where

X is enhancing the security program, ingestion, or hiring new people. Then when the information about onboarding specific departments arrives, you will have provisioned your function to do that work.

Road map development and execution is by no means an easy task. Rely on the steering committee and lean on those with product or project management expertise. While it doesn't have to be set in stone, it's another exercise to lower your cognitive overhead. With a clearly specified, working road map, you won't have to argue for resources for every piece of it.

Approval

As with the initial project charter, you want the governance strategy signed off by your senior leadership team. This will be your opportunity to gain their continued advocacy. This may also be your best opportunity to share the successes from the launch and post-launch activities. The transformation you have already brought to your organization will be the springboard to keep the momentum going.

The first act of your steering committee should be to get formal approval of the plan by your executive team or equivalent. The second act should be to go for a round of drinks with them and celebrate the birth of the next phase in your data program: long-term success.

Google Cloud Data Catalog

The most recent entry into data governance as a service is Google Cloud Data Catalog, which became generally available at the end of April 2020. Data Catalog aims to capture accurate and up-to-date metadata about all of the data flowing through your system, including data resident outside of GCP. Using a tagging system, you can quickly identify where and what kind of data lives in your system.

In practice, this allows you to establish a data governance strategy on a system that is already live or to build it into the DNA of your data warehouse as you go. Data Catalog automatically searches for and identifies data already in your system, allowing you to take a data-first approach to data classification and governance.

Overview

When you enable and visit the Data Catalog console, it will present a dashboard that has some general information about your most popular tables and views from BigQuery and allow you to explore data it has automatically instrumented across Google services such as Pub/Sub and Cloud Storage.

I hesitate to use the recursion, but you are essentially building meta-metadata here.[4] In order to apply tags, you create templates for tag structures with the metadata you are interested in tracking, and then you can attach those structures to individual columns or fields in datasets.

After items are tagged, you can search for them, allowing you to see, for example, all fields storing zip codes across your organization. You can also query properties of the fields, for instance, seeing when a particular column in a BigQuery table was created.

There is also an API allowing you to integrate Data Catalog with other services. You can even obtain information about the tag templates you currently have in your system, which I suppose constitutes meta-meta-metadata.[5]

BigQuery

For BigQuery, you can also specify a taxonomy of "policy tags" indicating permissions for individual assets in BigQuery. As of this writing, this capability is in beta, but you can use it to enable column-level security by defining policy tags that apply to those columns and granting the appropriate permissions.[6]

---

[4]I'm not sure why there isn't an industry term for this yet. I suggest *piometadata*, since the Greek etymology of "meta" is much like the Latin "post." *Pio* means "more."

[5]When you make such a call, the Cloud Logging record that records your user account and time of call has meta-meta-meta-metadata… I'll stop now.

[6]https://cloud.google.com/bigquery/docs/column-level-security

External Connectors

You can ingest metadata from systems external to GCP, such as RDBMS instances you may have running in other clouds. This requires connectors and code from the source system you choose. The process is generally to use whatever functions that database system uses for metadata discovery and pipe that into a format that Data Catalog will understand. This information will likely quickly go out of date as Data Catalog improves, but there are resources showing currently how to set up these connectors.[7]

Google has already open sourced connectors to two of the larger business intelligence systems, Looker and Tableau.[8] If you use (or choose) these systems, you can prepare processes to ingest metadata. Since this technology is extremely new, the process does require some code and effort.

Personally Identifying Information

Personally identifying information, or PII, describes any piece of data which can be used to determine the identity of an individual. This includes things like a person's full name, driver's license, social security number, phone number, photograph, and so on. The protection of PII is a cornerstone of nascent privacy regulations like GDPR and CCPA. In the early days of cloud computing, the perceived inability for clouds to protect PII was often used as a deterrent to cloud adoption. Now, PII is stored in every public cloud, and data breaches make national news.

Data Catalog, in combination with Cloud Data Loss Prevention, can automatically identify and begin tagging PII. You can also use metadata to tag fields as containing PII and automatically opt them into your data governance's strategy for the management of PII.

---

[7]https://medium.com/google-cloud/google-cloud-data-catalog-integrate-your-on-prem-
  rdbms-metadata-468e0d8220fb

[8]More information is available about these systems in Chapter 16.

Summary

An explicit data governance plan is a cornerstone of ensuring the continued success of your data program. Just as you elevated the data warehouse from a project to an ongoing program, you now have the great power and responsibility to maintain it as a permanent and foundational practice in your organization. To develop an effective governance plan, you need to find the right people in your organization to fulfill key roles. In concert with that group, you can then build policies around each facet of how data will be managed in your business. Key facets include systems of record, security, lifecycle considerations, and the rules for governing the plan itself. Obtain approval from the leadership of your organization and request their advocacy in keeping the data program healthy and on an upward slope.

In the next chapter, we'll discuss considerations for long-term management of the data warehouse and how to follow your governance plan at an execution level.

CHAPTER 15

Adapting to Long-Term Change

The true test of a data program's resilience is what happens over the long haul. The common variable (as always) is people. People create new data, either by performing new activities or analyzing existing data. Organizations change constantly, with people joining and leaving continually. New stakeholders arrive and depart too. Each of them will make an impact on your data program with their agendas for the business. Handling these changes gracefully is all part of the job.

While I believe strongly in the push-pull model we discussed in Chapter 8, I also believe that as data practitioners, we have a fundamental custodial and fiduciary responsibility to the organizations we support. I think that obligation extends even further, into our industries and the world at large. The overwhelming majority of generated data now lies in the hands of the corporate sector. It's our responsibility to build programs that handle it responsibly, evaluate it honestly, and use it for programs which better humankind. At the level of organizational data warehousing, that implies two key priorities that we should keep in mind when preparing for long-term change:

1. Never lose any existing data.

2. Always strive to store and preserve new data.

One of the focal questions in library science is how to determine what data is worth preserving and investing in, given the associated costs. The limitations of physical space pose a significant obstacle. Furthermore (despite what the Google Books project may have suggested), a digital copy loses fidelity from its original physical representation. Physical space costs real money too. Effective preservation can require climate control, thoughtful design, and serious attention to accessibility.

© Mark Mucchetti 2020
M. Mucchetti, *BigQuery for Data Warehousing*, https://doi.org/10.1007/978-1-4842-6186-6_15

A key theme in this book has been the process of extracting information, and thereby insight, from the raw data. The culling of data may remove potential insight from the world. Librarians and archivists have the Herculean task of understanding potential use cases for the data and making difficult decisions along those constraints. For example, would you think that a cookbook from the Depression Era would have any value? It describes old recipes that have been replicated or improved countless times since. The information seems duplicative or even pointless. Given the poor quality of the physical material, much of it hasn't even survived. But it turns out that this material provides astounding insight into the living conditions of Americans at the time, by showing how people were eating and cooking at the time, what ingredients they would have had available, and how this differed from professional publications of the time. This information might easily have been dismissed and destroyed if not for the efforts of talented archivists, who recognized its potential value. (This is a real example. The "What America Ate" project[1] does precisely this kind of preservation.)

As database architects in the cloud era, we effectively have neither of those problems. All of the generated data we produce is automatically loaded and backed up in a fairly durable way—durable enough, in fact, for Google to run a business that guarantees it. We don't have physical limitations for data storage, and we don't need to purge data.

This doesn't mean that we don't **want** to purge data, though. This ties into the "right to be forgotten," which the European Union used as the basis for its landmark General Data Protection Regulation. This is an issue that Google has wrestled with itself when determining if links to websites can or should be deleted from their search index. The fact of the matter is that as preservation for organizations ceases to be constrained by technology, it falls to us to constrain it by ethics and empathy. You will have to make these decisions too.

However, there is a third problem we all have in common: how do you reasonably sift through petabytes of data to find the insight you're seeking? Eventually you have too much data to perform queries in a reasonable amount of time, or the raw data really has aged into worthlessness and can be discarded. (Whether you *know* it can be discarded is a different question.)

The other techniques we've discussed, like table partitioning and expiration, allow you to manage this consideration. Using them judiciously will be a function of cost, performance, and the mission for your organization. What I mean to say is that the

---

[1]https://whatamericaate.org/

process of adapting to change is not the blind insertion of rows into tables. It's a process that requires thinking about its destination, its duration, and the implications for future processing. In that regard, data warehouses are still an awful lot like real warehouses.

Business Change

You may have a reasonable idea of the direction your business is headed. Knowing the products and services it intends to offer in the near future was an input into the construction of your data warehouse. Consequently, you should be able to handle all of the things you know about and their variations. For instance, if your organization launches a new product into the market, the rest of the organization will be busy building market assets and developing and launching the product. As far as data collection, you may not even notice at all—the new identifiers will log and store into the warehouse as with any other product your company offers.

Where this idea begins to break down is when you add a new dimension to the equation. What if your business began offering an entirely new business line? How about if your business acquired another company and wanted to incorporate their data insights into your master strategy? These sorts of decisions happen on a daily basis. And as we've discussed, when following the push-pull model, your own warehouse's insight may drive core changes in turn.

This sort of work also differs from new insights your analysts or business leaders may surface. You'll always be engaged in producing new kinds of analysis or supporting new integrations. This alone gives you plenty of opportunities to systematize or to look down the road and see core change on the horizon.

All software projects tend to incur debt of one kind or another throughout their lifecycles. One advantage that your new warehouse project has is simply that it's new: you can make greater changes while it is still malleable, and those changes will improve your success over time.

There are two tracks for supporting long-term adaptation in your data program. The first is regular maintenance and improvement. You do this work as you go, encapsulating each level of complexity, documenting it, and building on it. We'll discuss a number of areas you should periodically assess in your data program to keep this happening.

The second track is dealing with a major business event. This comprises both the ability to run a process and to absorb large changes in your data program. Typical business events are things I mentioned earlier, like substantial modification to the business's strategy, new lines of business, or acquisitions.

Major Business Events

When you learn formally that a major event is impending, meet with your data governance steering committee (see the previous chapter) and begin to lay out the potential impacts to your data program. It may be too early to tell, but begin your due diligence as early as possible to ensure you are not caught off guard. Where possible, speak to those who may be your subject matter experts after the change. For example, if your organization is adding a new line of business, find a business development expert who knows one of your current lines of business well, and ask them what characteristics will be unique to this new line of business.

For an acquisition, you may not have access to anyone from the acquired party, but you can get a sense of what you're dealing with by visiting their website, looking through any available marketing material, and asking people around you who may have been involved. (Obviously, do not do this before news of the acquisition is public![2])

Some of the information you learn will point to primary requirements for a project that your data governance team should prioritize as soon as is feasible. Those requirements may include things like

- Adding new users to the warehouse

- Adding new datasets with new classification levels or creating additional classification levels to segregate data

- Creating integrations with new third-party data providers

- Migrating, integrating with, or in some way connecting to another data warehouse technology

- Doing nothing at all

It's possible that your warehouse already supports all of the concepts needed to bring on a new business line. (If your company sells SuperWidgets and will now sell HyperWidgets, you may just need to accept new metadata in a nested column you already have.)

---

[2]When a company I was working for was acquired, one of our employees happened to visit and follow the acquirer on LinkedIn a few days before the announcement. This was entirely coincidental, and the person possessed no confidential information, but it caused quite a fuss at the executive level about how the news had gotten out. Don't be that person!

Do take care to distinguish between "new" as a marketing concept and "new" as a concept that has relevance to your data program. A new formulation for your favorite cereal is unlikely to have a significant impact on your back-office operations, despite being a major launch from the marketing perspective.

Key Performance Indicators

You can also monitor the things that are important to the organization by understanding its key performance indicators (KPIs). There are many philosophies on the meaning and usage of KPIs, their interaction with the meaningful work of the business, and so on. But generally most organizations use a term like KPI to indicate metrics they are watching and changing to measure the health of the business as a whole.

Your data warehouse is doing its job if you can produce an up-to-date report on the business's quantitative KPIs. This is also a great baseline to figure out what effect a major business event will have. Will the KPIs change, either in value or in definition? This question will also align with what senior leaders will be looking for as new things come online, so if you are working out how to deliver that information ahead of time, you will be ahead of the game.

In case you're new to KPIs or you don't recognize what your organization calls them, here are some examples. You may already be able to generate reports for metrics like these:

- Revenue and revenue growth

- Operating cash flow

- Website traffic by period

- Total sales, by product, by period, as a growth function

- Customer retention/attrition

- Conversion rates

The list is endless and will vary by which departments you have and their primary focuses. If your warehouse started by covering one or two departments, you may not have access to department-specific metrics like sales funnel numbers or social media statistics. Generally the highest value for the warehouse will be cross-departmental or synthesized data; stakeholders in departments with their own systems may not have an urgent need to analyze their data in a warehouse. (For the preceding KPIs, think Salesforce or Facebook Ads Manager.) However, a major business event may change that disposition.

Timeline

The timeline for the change will change what options you have available. While you may want to incorporate all of the data immediately, it may not be possible given incompatible warehouse technology or lack of information. When you define the project with your data governance team, be explicit about what you will be able to tackle in the near term vs. what will have to go onto the road map for later quarters.

If this change entails major build-out to your data warehouse, treat it as an invasive project that may incur scope creep and technical debt if not properly managed. It may seem like a remote possibility, but if the change is large enough, then people will miss "details" that have major implications for your schemas.

Approach

Recall my definition of optimistic extensibility: reasonably predicting likely enhancements and building empty shells for them. With a little bit of educated guesswork and a decent crystal ball, you'll already have anticipated the changes. Now is the time to fill out those shells to take advantage of the extensibility you pre-wired.

If you're not so lucky, you will have to make a difficult data architecture decision: modify the core, or place the new features to the side. If you modify your core data structures in an impactful way and the new business is a flop, you'll be left with extra maintenance for something that didn't matter. On the other hand, if you set the new information off to the side in different datasets and it's a wild success, you'll have to quickly incorporate it. That will probably mean doing things in a hacky way or trying to do them right under the time pressure of the business already being live.

Unfortunately, there is no right answer to this. The best approach is to learn as much as possible and make the best decision you can at the time.

Data Program Charter

Sometimes the business event is so substantial that it renders large parts of your existing data program obsolete or insufficient. If you see this happening, call an off-cycle meeting with your data governance team and discuss the possibility of rechartering the program entirely.

The reason for this is that the term "data warehouse" or "data program" will come to mean something specific to your organization. This business event, whatever it is, will create a gap between what the organization means when they say "data warehouse" and what your data warehouse does according to its charter. The further you allow these two definitions to get out of alignment, the more friction you will allow. Eventually this will lead to misalignment among stakeholders themselves. The program will fail to meet expectations you didn't know it had, and an us vs. them mentality will develop. Finally, this will lead to business leaders making statements like "Well, I wanted to see this data, but the warehouse still doesn't have it, so..." which imply an insufficiency on your program's part which is purely the result of mismatched expectations.

I am not exaggerating when I say this can cost you the program or even your job. I have seen this happen as well. I'm not trying to be a fearmonger; only to reinforce the premise that over-communication prevents these problems before they become too large to address. If your program charter will no longer be applicable in the face of these new business changes, rewrite it and have it reapproved before the expectations of the program shift irrecoverably.

As someone once said, with great power comes great responsibility. To participate in a successful push-pull model, you should surface concerns and take proactive action to improve your data program with the available information. If you sit back and wait for the issues to come to you, you won't be able to push innovation into the organization. The data program's success will be constrained by the business's preconceptions, without any signal from the data that might alter them.

Organic Growth Over Time

Most of the time, you will be dealing with incremental and largely predictable changes in your organizational process. The data warehouse will still be adding data, columns, and schemas. You can manage this growth through all three facets of a software program: people, process, and technology. Also, if your evaluation of a potential major business event implies a small amount of change, you can metabolize it through these growth processes too. As far as processes go, that's preferable; exception processes should always be an exception.

Change Control

Much as with permissions and other warehouse control mechanisms, you probably made liberal use of breaking changes while constructing the warehouse. That must end after you launch the initial warehouse project. The safest rule of thumb to follow for safety is simple but restrictive: all changes to the warehouse must be backward-compatible.

Backward Compatibility

In a backward-compatible model, all changes should require no action from any of your users for their consumers to continue working. This means no changing data types of existing columns or deleting columns or tables. In practice, this is nearly impossible to follow, so it's best treated as an ideal and a cue to take changes that break backward compatibility seriously.

The best example here is misspelled or redundant columns. At some point, a developer or analyst will miss that there is already an "accountID" column and make a "userId" column. Or, my favorite, users will have already adapted to a misspelling like "vehiclOwnerID," and someone will make the correct spelling in a well-meaning way, inadvertently duplicating the data.

Eventually, without change management, your warehouse schema will proliferate with junk columns, all of which contain the same value. It will be backward-compatible, sure, but no one will know how to use it. There are all kinds of secondary issues this creates too. It muddles your data glossary, prevents hashing your objects to determine equality (because they each might use separate column names to represent the same data), and irritates those well-meaning users who refuse to use a misspelled name.

This is the kind of thing which can cause death by a thousand paper cuts to your data warehouse. If the barrier to effective analysis is rising over time, people will be less inclined to invest the effort to extract the insights they need.

Instead, batch several of these schema changes and submit an itemized list through your change control mechanism.

Change Control Mechanisms

In previous chapters, I lampooned the chilling effect that bloated change control boards have on organizational velocity. You still need change control, but you need the right weight of change control for your organization.

The basic features of a change control process look the same:

- Measuring and understanding impact

- Contextualizing changes by priority against other ongoing initiatives

- Communication to all affected users and stakeholders

- Appropriate lead time for affected users to make changes (gauged by priority)

The formality of your change control process depends on the number of people or departments in your decision matrix. It also depends on the methods and formality of communications you accept to fulfill those steps and the lead time ranges you must adhere to to perform maintenance.

For example, in a small organization, you may know the impact immediately, and you may also have a sense of where to slot the initiative. Communication might just be a Slack message in a designated channel saying, "Hey, I'm going to change this at 9 PM. Any objections?" Lead time might be as small as is required for those affected to tell you that you're clear to proceed.

More formal processes may require the submission of documentation in a standard form to a change control board, who must approve the change before even stating a lead time or scheduling the change. My advice is solely not to over-formalize the process for an organization of your size.

Change Control Process

When making compatibility-breaking changes in BigQuery, you have several options. The easiest to manage, but most invasive, is to simply break compatibility after you have done the required notifications.

This will work until you've reached the scale where you no longer know all the potential consumers of the data, and some might be obsolete or unreachable. This problem multiplies if you sell bespoke software to clients that integrates with BigQuery. When you break compatibility, it's effectively irreversible if some of your consumers have updated and others have not. If changes are made to huge tables with giant schemas, you might incur measurable analysis downtime trying to sort it out.

Versioning and Deprecation

Another method you can use is a longer lead time where you temporarily tolerate the new columns or tables in parallel with the old ones. In this model, you create the new columns with the correct names or the new tables with the schema changes. Then you set a deprecation period (which should be specified in your data governance plan) and wait. Once time is up, you break compatibility.

Where tables are concerned, you can use Cloud Logging to see which consumers are still accessing the old table. You can follow up with them or wait for them to make the switchover before doing the deprecation.

This still falls short in that you have to maintain multiple versions in place for an indefinite length of time. New users coming onboard during this time may inadvertently begin using the old columns or tables again, since there is no unambiguous way to communicate deprecation. (Well, except deletion.) You could additionally use process to create a deprecation system in your data governance plan that uses tags or automated notifications to mitigate some of this risk.

For instance, upon formal deprecation, you might write a script that uses Cloud Monitoring to detect access to the deprecated table and immediately email the associated principal that the table is deprecated. It feels a little hacky because it is. In setting the level of formality appropriately for your business, you may find you need more in the way of process than you thought, even if communication mechanisms remain informal.

Shadow Views

A typical pattern for this type of change in traditional warehouse systems is the "shadow view." To use this process, users must already be accessing analysis via a view and not the underlying table.

In this model, you create a second view of the data with the new schema, either using the same or a different base table to back it. When it is time to update, you swap the views so that the "shadow" view becomes the main view and the main view becomes the "shadow" view. (This is akin to a blue-green deployment for software releases.)

This creates the same issue, namely, that you have multiple versions of the data to maintain simultaneously. If they share a base table, that table has the same problems as in the previous example, where both versions must coexist simultaneously. However, this model offers you the ability to test consuming applications to ensure they still work with the new model, without disrupting the existing model.

Source Control Management

For some reason, databases and source control management seem to have trouble mixing. In the last 20 years, as continuous integration went from dream to buzzword to standard practice, database systems have been left behind. I still hear regularly that database developers are copying their queries into Notepad and saving them on their local machines for later use.

I have plenty of suspicions as to why this might be, but the fact of the matter is that running your data program this way has been and still is pretty dangerous. Most "code-first" environments now specify their database migrations as part of the deployment, which is great for tightly coupled web applications but is impractical for a data warehouse pulling from a huge number of disparate sources.

BigQuery has some characteristics that help protect you:

- User queries are saved in the history.

- Queries can be shared with other users.

- Queries can easily be saved as views or saved to your local workspace.

- You can query the state of a table up to one week in the past, which will include both data and schema changes.

- Short of what Google calls a "hard regional failure," you should never lose more than an hour's worth of unreplicated data.

Consequently, the most dangerous risks of storing your SQL exclusively in the database are mitigated. One hard drive exploding can't destroy your data or the code used to access it. Cloud data centers are specifically designed to tolerate the regular failure of commodity hardware.

Some of this even protects you from the other types of data failures that data warehouses can suffer. If someone accidentally overwrites a table, you can restore it from its past state. The time and energy it takes to restore a warehouse is a function of its complexity. Eventually it will become impossible for a single person to be able to restore a warehouse to functioning without intensive manual inspection.

I have no single good answer to this. It is certainly a hassle to copy your database objects into Notepad, even if you then commit them to a source control repository and manage them outside the system. The reverse direction is also possible, where a deployment service like Cloud Build executes queries against the warehouse at build time to restore a known state. Ultimately, your database code is also data, and it qualifies under the "Never lose any existing data" tenet.

Data Retention Considerations

A best practice for traditional data warehouses is that you set a fixed retention period for your data, say, 5, 7, or 10 years. The retention period may depend on your organization's compliance obligations, accounting practices, or common sense. As you ingest data on a periodic basis, you purge the old data to make room for the new data. You might have an additional storage tier, like backup to tape, that you use to keep older data in cold storage, but it wouldn't be available for online analysis. These are prudent or mandatory decisions when storage provisioning is a major concern. Additionally, on magnetic storage, you have to worry about the media's physical characteristics.

Today, it is unnecessary to delete any data from your BigQuery implementation. BigQuery is designed to indefinite scale,[3] and you can just continue piling data in. With partitioned tables, there is also limited performance impact. Per my introductory example, you might also find that there is value to be extracted from older data. All of these are indications to prefer retaining older data.

If you object to the statement, consider whether you'd prefer the converse statement: you only have to delete data from your BigQuery implementation if you want to. You can still follow your data retention and purging practices, and you may have good reason for doing so. For personally identifiable information (PII) or personal health information (PHI), you may be required to. New legislation such as the European Union's General Data Protection Regulation (GDPR) and the California Consumer Privacy Act (CCPA) specifies that you must have an easily accessible way to delete customer data entirely from your systems.

---

[3]By this, I mean, BigQuery's ability to handle scale is growing faster than most users' ability to need it.

Privacy Legislation

With GDPR and CCPA both in effect and other US states quickly moving to adopt similar programs, it's clear that data deletion for privacy purposes is going to be relevant to your data warehouse's operational workflow.

Google Cloud Platform already complies with these regulations and offers some tools so that you can comply at the organizational level too. You can read their official policies on CCPA[4] and GDPR[5] compliance to see how they handle these considerations at the cloud level. These laws codify what has been true for much longer: the need for an effective data governance strategy in your organization. This strategy can help streamline where and how you accommodate new data.

Cost Management

The other major concern you may have about the indefinite retention of data is cost. This is a real consideration that we addressed in Chapter 4, also discussing the concepts of table expiration and automatically aging out old data. You can configure BigQuery to automatically expire and delete your data at a certain age and thereby implement all of a previous expiration scheme automatically.

If you're routinely accessing older data, you're paying to query it. You can also infer the data has some value, since someone is still looking for it. The exception there would be if you have zombie processes operating on defunct data. Part of your data governance plan includes decommissioning processes you no longer need.

If you don't modify your table or partition, after 90 days Google reclassifies it as long-term storage and the price of storage drops by half. If you touch the data again after that, it returns to active and the regular price takes effect.

Let's do a real-world modeling exercise. Let's say you started a fresh warehouse, lucky you. You calculate that you'll add 5 gigabytes of data a month, and your company will grow at 20% a month. Let's splurge and say that you'll keep all the data active indefinitely, so no cold storage savings. At the time of writing, BigQuery storage costs start at $0.02/GB in active storage and $0.01/GB in cold storage. (Check your region for the exact number.) The first 10 GB is free each month. How much is the storage component of BigQuery going to cost you?

---

[4]https://services.google.com/fh/files/misc/googlecloud_and_theccpa.pdf
[5]https://services.google.com/fh/files/misc/google_cloud_and_the_gdpr_english.pdf

Entertainingly, you can calculate this directly in BigQuery using analytic functions: the per-month calculation for your data is $(1 + (m \wedge 1.2))$, where m starts at 0. The analytic function is a running total on (ROWS PRECEDING UNBOUNDED TO CURRENT ROW). I leave it as an exercise to the reader to inspect the Google Cloud Platform Pricing Calculator, extract the JavaScript for the BigQuery module, bake it into a JavaScript UDF, and then write a simulator using everything from Chapter 13. (Why would anyone do that?)

After 36 months of activity, at this starting point and growth rate, you will have spent $129.54. If you never modify your data, it will enter cold storage after 3 months, dropping your 3-year cost to something like $87. In fact, given the 10 GB you get on the free tier, you don't even start paying for a few months. This includes the assumption that your business, and thus the amount of data you are storing, is growing exponentially over time.

Anyway, let's look at Figure 15-1, which shows total cost dependent on your initial data intake and varying rates of growth. This should give you a good idea of when you actually need to worry about data storage costs, depending on your cost tolerance.

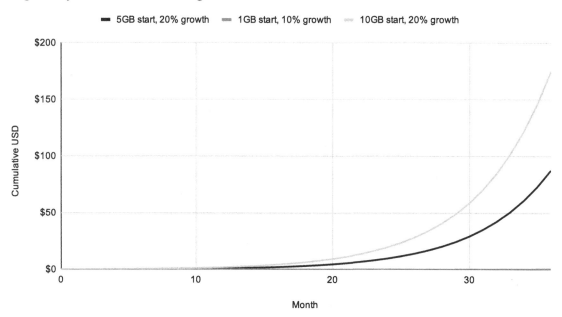

Figure 15-1. *Graph showing 36-month cost curves given varying inputs and growth rates*

Reviewing this analysis, I don't personally think storage cost presents sufficient justification for data expiration, but this at least gives you some context of data storage as a variable. Note also that I haven't included the real cost of operating BigQuery here, namely, the queries and maintenance. Cost arguments about data retention revolve solely around this cost, though.

Expiration

Despite my preference, you absolutely should look to automate the deletion of data you do not want. If you want to delete older data, use BigQuery's automatic expiration capabilities.

Configuring a default and specific expiration window should be part of your data governance plan and clearly specified for each type or classification of data. One underestimated risk is the anger of a stakeholder who didn't realize that their old data would no longer be available for analysis.

Colder Storage

If you look at the costs for storage in Google Cloud Storage, you will see that nearline storage costs the same as BigQuery cold storage. That's partially because both Google Cloud Storage and BigQuery use Google's internal file system, known as Colossus.

If you have a truly massive amount of data, it is possible to export it to Google Cloud Storage and run it at a lower storage class. Google Cloud Storage has four classes of data: standard, nearline, coldline, and archive. Standard and nearline are roughly equivalent to active and cold for BigQuery. In order to utilize the two lower methods, you would have to build out a data pipeline that exports your tables into Google Cloud Storage and then deletes them from BigQuery.

Once the data arrives in Google Cloud Storage, you can build lifecycle rules there to transition it to coldline and then archive and finally purge it. Key scenarios for this model would include compliance management that requires retention of all data for six years, seven years, or longer. See Figure 15-2.

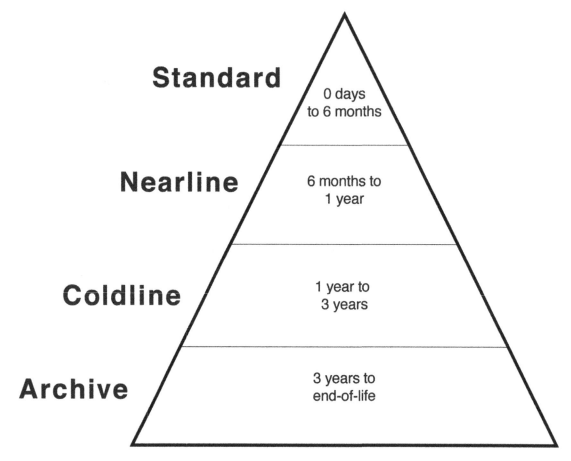

Figure 15-2. *A GCS cold storage policy*

Regardless, your data governance plan should include lifecycle considerations for data stored outside of BigQuery. You can apply a similar practice to data generated by other systems we've reviewed, such as Cloud Logging.

If you use these colder storage classes in GCS, Google will actually charge you for reading the data or deleting it early. This is something to consider when evaluating the probability you will need the data again.

DML Statements

Data Management Language (DML) statements are limited by quota and by performance. Recall that treating BigQuery as an online transaction processing (OLTP) system is considered an anti-pattern by Google. INSERTs should be called sparingly, and if you need to insert on a per-row basis, use the streaming pattern (see Chapters 6 and 7). From a quota perspective, whether you insert a single row or a million rows, it is treated equally.

As part of your long-term strategy and data governance plan, be sure to account for this restriction when you specify how a certain kind of data will be loaded into the warehouse.

Downtime

BigQuery currently specifies a ≥ 99.99% uptime in its service-level agreement (SLA), or about 43 minutes of downtime a month. The service generally adheres to that SLA, but if you are curious about what kinds of issues it has had, Google keeps an incident log with detailed descriptions of each incident timeline.[6] Nonetheless, you should consider BigQuery downtime as a consideration that will have a downstream impact on your warehouse and plan accordingly.

More crucially for your organization is what Google calls "analysis downtime." This describes a condition in which BigQuery is still in good health and serving requests, but you are either in the midst of executing a scheduled change or something has caused your warehouse to stop working properly.

Analysis downtime will still prevent your users from completing their work, and it may affect other production systems if they rely on BigQuery. For the former, your data governance plan and the proactive communication it should outline will allow you to schedule downtime at regular intervals to match with your update cadence.

The latter impact, that of your end user's production system, requires a risk analysis to the applications using BigQuery and what the functional impact is if they cannot reach data stored there. There are two strategies to mitigate this.

---

[6]https://status.cloud.google.com/incident/bigquery

Code Freeze

A code freeze is commonly employed when system stability is deemed to have a higher priority than business velocity. This occurs seasonally in certain industries. For example, most ecommerce businesses freeze code around Black Friday. Similarly, most companies in the tax preparation space freeze code between January and April 15. If BigQuery plays a critical role in your production infrastructure, implement code freeze at designated times to minimize the risk of analysis downtime. As with other change control initiatives, this should be communicated to relevant stakeholders well ahead of time.

Graceful Degradation

A strategy popularized by Netflix, graceful degradation aims to retain critical elements of the user experience while temporarily disabling enhanced features. For instance, if the services powering the Netflix recommendation system experience downtime, the Netflix UI quietly hides that insight from the menu. If BigQuery plays a tangential role in your user experience, you can employ a similar approach. For instance, say that when users view a product page on your ecommerce site, the clickstream is immediately sent to BigQuery for analysis, from which a prediction of other interesting products is returned. If the BigQuery recommendation is unavailable, the user can still view and purchase products from your website. Quietly hide the recommendation feature, or replace it with a less powerful one, until service is restored. (Rephrased: If a service falls down in a cloud and there's no one there to see it, did it really fall down?)

The BigQuery Ecosystem

When it all comes down to it, your obligation is to provide your users with the best available experience. I assume that by now, you are either an avid reader, or you have committed to serve your users in some fashion with Google BigQuery.

The best way for you to do this is to stay abreast of new features in BigQuery, Google Cloud Platform, and every other data warehousing technology. The rate of change in the cloud can be difficult to track these days. A slew of articles on the Web penalize BigQuery for not supporting scripting—but it has it now. A similar number complain about the difficulty of learning BigQuery Legacy SQL—we haven't used a single line of it. Follow the BigQuery release notes[7] and use them to push innovation to your data program.

There is a thriving BigQuery community on Reddit at /r/bigquery.[8] Felipe Hoffa is a Google big data developer advocate who is hugely active both there and on Stack Overflow. He publishes and contextualizes new features as they come out, and he's also immensely knowledgeable about the limits of what is possible with BigQuery.

Summary

You are now a fully fledged BigQuery practitioner. As your data program matures, you will encounter the challenges of sustaining a data warehouse across significant organizational change. Whether you are dealing with a major business event like an acquisition or growth over time, a steady hand is required to minimize architectural debt and maintain a forward-looking plan. Using the data governance plan you established in the last chapter, you can decide on key considerations like how you will manage change control and retain data. You also now understand when to pull the trigger on rebooting your data program entirely with a new charter. From this point onward, you can look to the BigQuery community and to BigQuery's own evolution as your lodestar.

In the next two chapters, we'll discuss how to visualize your data with reporting and real-time dashboards.

---

[7]https://cloud.google.com/bigquery/docs/release-notes
[8]www.reddit.com/r/bigquery/

PART V

Reporting On and Visualizing Your Data

## CHAPTER 16

Reporting

It would be hard to claim that business intelligence could exist without reporting. Some of the earliest human-written communication is reporting. Figure 16-1 shows an ancient Babylonian tablet from 514 BCE recording a rental contract in cuneiform. You could see this as something like a row in a modern database table.

Figure 16-1. *A cuneiform tablet. Roughly translated, it says that party A rents his house to party B yearly, for a rent of 18 silver shekels. The renter is responsible for reroofing the house and fixing the drain*

© Mark Mucchetti 2020
M. Mucchetti, *BigQuery for Data Warehousing*, https://doi.org/10.1007/978-1-4842-6186-6_16

Twenty-five hundred years later, humans are still renting houses and haggling with landlords about their repair responsibilities. It would certainly not be out of place to find a BigQuery table describing exactly the same kind of data today.[1]

For such a "basic" concept, there are sure a lot of solutions out there. SaaS (software-as-a-service) reporting vendors compete on speed, data, visualizations, compatibility, and sometimes just plain old marketing hustle. The space is glutted with search engine optimization experts making sure that their blog posts are the first thing you read. You can hardly do any research on the subject without each article reminding you that while there are lots of good products, theirs is the best. Here are some examples of this kind of marketing copy. I've paraphrased these lightly to discourage calling out specific companies. This is solely so you rely on your instinct and rely on the technical merits, not the market speak:

- "It's a tedious challenge to gather data and send it all to your business intelligence system. That's where [DataCorp] saves the day."

- "It's simple! While you kick back, [DataCorp] will get the data and deliver it to your destination."

- One company provided a list of the top 20 reporting solutions. Then they ranked themselves first, beating out the likes of Google Analytics and Salesforce. (Unlikely.)

- Another company praised Google's data solutions and then claimed that they were inferior to their own. The reasoning for this was riddled with obvious mathematical and factual errors. Talk about destroying confidence in a company that sells data.

What Is Reporting Now?

The lines have blurred among reporting, business intelligence, dashboarding, visualization, analysis, and data science. Most solutions do a number of these things well, at varying degrees of scale and price. To name a notable example, Salesforce does many of these things well. Consultants will happily fill any gap in their off-the-shelf solutions so you can get what you want and you will. You'll also pay for that privilege—Salesforce's

---

[1]When announcing the Kaggle/BigQuery integration, which we'll cover in Chapter 20, the dataset recording house sales in Ames, Iowa, was used as an example.

professional services revenue alone approached $900MM in 2019.[2] The reason that it's worth talking about Google BigQuery as a data warehousing system is that the pay-as-you-go model allows your usage to scale with your budget. It will be some time before you hit a scale limit, and at that scale you will have substantial latitude in price negotiation with Google or any other vendor.

Here's a disambiguation for the context of this chapter. "Reporting" is any thing that can show you reports. The intention is to avoid dragging along all of the baggage and blurry lines associated with the marketing speak. Your existing reporting suite, a BI tool, BigQuery saved queries, a cuneiform tablet—these all qualify. At the most basic level, your users need to be able to see reports about their data. How will you accomplish that?

Do We Still Need Reporting?

Occasionally, someone asks if traditional report suites have been outmoded by live analysis or real-time dashboarding and visualization. I usually say that it depends on what you think a report is. There is certainly a stigma from decades past that reporting is done at the end of the day, and no one can go home until the report run succeeds. In that model, reports fail frequently because of bad data or because something has timed out. Yes, I'd say that type of reporting is the bare minimum a modern business should accept. Lots of companies still do things that way, of course. The amount of time spent covering the people and process side of the equation is strong evidence for that. Most of those steps will apply no matter what data warehouse solution you're moving to.

While I wouldn't like to wait minutes or hours for a basic report anymore, other factors aren't especially relevant to what constitutes a "report." For instance, the speed at which a report refreshes doesn't matter. A real-time view of data structured in the format of an old report is still a report. Furthermore, historical performance data is fixed. Last month's sales report isn't going to change. (Okay, shouldn't change.) For historical reports, the major advantage BigQuery brings is the ability to connect it to the current data to see ongoing trends quickly.

A lot of the low-quality marketing literature out there will play upon the stigmatization of the word "reporting." Many suggest that the mere existence of "reporting" means the data will be stale or different people will be looking at different data. Between BigQuery and your data governance program, you've already solved those

---

[2]https://investor.salesforce.com/financials/default.aspx

problems. Now, when we speak about reporting, we're talking about an analysis and UI layer on top of a solid system. We also want to make sure that business stakeholders can interact with the data and place it into their specific systems of choice. Even better is if we can both leave those stakeholder systems as authoritative and maintain the golden record in BigQuery.

This also opens the possibility that stakeholders can continue to use whatever systems they already have, while enterprise data analysis occurs from the warehouse. We'll come back to that in a minute.

The challenge now, for reporting and for the next couple chapters on visualization and Google Data Studio, is delivering good, accessible reports. If you're going to freshen up those key reports, you'll need substance *and* style.

Reporting and Data Democratization

Let's tackle this head-on. A primary theme of this book is to promote a collaborative, cross-organizational approach to data warehousing and the programs they fuel. I firmly believe that the success of such a program relies on these factors at least as much as the technology. As a result, there hasn't been much coverage of the history of business intelligence programs nor why this sort of collaboration is fairly recent for a lot of organizations.

Another key theme has been the ease with which cloud platforms can tie together colossal amounts of disparate data. The technical and financial barriers are much lower as well. So why might collaboration be an issue? The answer lies on the flip side, before the cloud.

Historical Context

When a data warehousing program needed to be hosted on-site or in a data center, huge front-loaded investment was required. The technical know-how required to stand up such a program was present only within IT departments. IT departments became the owners of data programs by necessity. The existence of the warehouse depended entirely on them, thereby driving a priority where mere existence superseded useful output. Many projects failed before even getting launched, so this was actually a pretty practical use of resources.

Regardless, friction often developed almost immediately between "users" of the warehouse and the IT department. The reasons are all of the things we have been consciously avoiding—to name a few, mismatched expectations, technology failures, and poorly (or no) coordinated change management. Each led swiftly to conflict. The "business" began to see IT as a bottleneck preventing them from getting at their data.

This generalization was often completely unfair. Technical process is delicate and inscrutable. Without rational guardrails, data teams were often forced into inadvisable solutions. When data teams would ask business stakeholders what needed reports, the answer was usually "everything." To an engineer, making all things highest priority is equivalent to saying "Here, you choose." Poor structural decisions were made with insufficient information and no accountability on either side. An odd silver lining of BigQuery here is that it allows you to compensate to some degree for earlier bad decisions. But even that won't matter without mutual investment and accountability.

Of course, if IT truly were a bottleneck, this would present a grave risk to the business. As SaaS solutions began to mature, business leaders realized that they could simply go around IT to get what they needed. Undoubtedly many of these leaders recognized this approach as risky, but lightning will find a way to the ground. In turn, many software-as-a-service vendors realized that they could print money by descending upon unsuspecting corporations and convincing them that their internal IT shops were incompetent. And thus "democratization of data" arose: freeing data from the prison of IT teams who just "didn't get it." This was also unfair. The expectation of an internal department is often that everything will stay the same while also getting better. A SaaS solution can require sweeping adaptation to integrate, but it's couched as, say, a "digital transformation." Internal departments rarely get the leniency to interrupt business like that. Furthermore, SaaS vendors have their own sales teams—who is responsible for selling a company's own data program? (Sorry—you are.)

Integration as a Service

This created a patchwork of internal and external data systems vying for centrality. Information was indeed fragmented, yielding different results and leading to unsupportable actions. Since these programs ran outside of IT governance, there was no way to corral them. Many of these systems weren't even in the IT inventory, or IT had been excluded from procurement and couldn't say what they were paying for.

A new market need soon arose: tying all of those systems together into a master data management solution. As the pendulum swung back the other way, IT teams were often brought back into the fold and told to unite all of these ungoverned systems into one unholy mess. (Compare the IT arguments around bring-your-own-device as smartphones arrived.) A lot of these integration projects failed too,[3] but at least this concept has some features of a successful data program. Data warehousing functions the way it should, and single views of data are possible. Unfortunately, drawbacks included a whole new round of chicanery about who had the best integration solution.

Gray Market Data

With the advent of cloud solutions, anyone can create a data program with no involvement from the IT department. This is what I mean by "gray market data": if the internal solutions are not sufficient, people will begin taking whatever data they can get access to and doing their own analyses. The data started out coming from an official source, but now runs through an application somewhere that people have begun to depend on. Before, that meant some pivot tables in Excel. Now, your organization may already have a shadow data program that's working better than the official one: but critically, it only works unevenly across the organization and can only serve the needs of the people using it. The business can't get the full potential out of a program like this, and both the internal solution and its informal competitors will suffer. This also results in a lot of cost duplication and data silos, since more than one person will create gray market data.

"Democratization of data" does not exclude "single source of truth." The purpose of promoting cross-functional collaboration is so that the best solutions can be chosen thoughtfully by representatives of each function and then implemented in a way that benefits the whole. Financial reporting solutions A, B, and C may be equivalent to the point that the department doesn't care greatly which is selected—but technology knows that only C integrates with BigQuery. When all stakeholders have the same picture, these issues can be easily avoided. This prevents both integration pain and future pain as the two connected systems slowly grow apart.

---

[3]Including one of mine.

Reporting as Democratization

In turn, democratizing your data does not render a reporting program obsolete—it enhances it. Consider a system architected as in Figure 16-2.

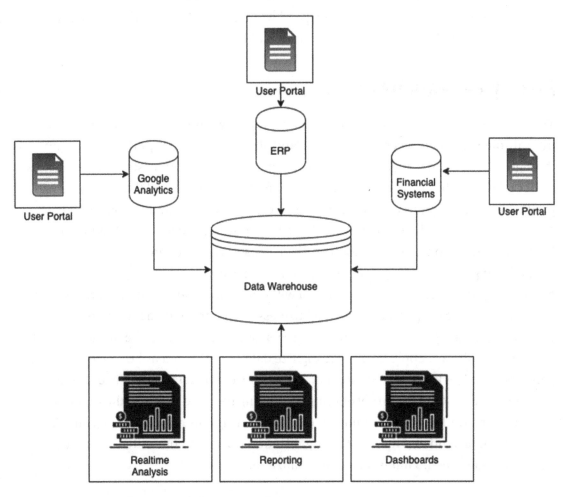

Figure 16-2. *Architectural diagram of systems*

In this model, the data is freely available to all parties. Finance can run its own reports on its own system; the SEO team can examine website conversion rates for its experiments and proceed accordingly. No one is bottlenecked by anyone.

But here is the critical difference—when someone wants to know if recent A/B test experiments are leading customers to purchase products with a lower profit margin, they go to the data warehouse. When they read the daily report on sales performance, it came from the data warehouse. The data program is in the **middle** without being in the **way**. When your teams and cross-functional organization look like this, your software solution will too. If you see the value of this model and want to build it from the inside out to resolve existing deficiencies, the answer is good old reporting.

History Repeats Itself

The latest iteration of the data democratization tug of war is that the data scientists are the only ones who can access the analyses and all of the custom reporting has to run through them. New decade, new bottleneck. There are two good reasons why a business leader might say this. One, the data scientists are legitimately afraid that someone will produce a bogus analysis on bad data and drive the business into the ground. (It has happened.) Two, the data is readily available for reporting and analysis, but no one knows how. Both come down to the same root cause—data literacy.

Reporting is the gateway drug to data literacy. If everyone in an organization is data-literate, then democratization of data will truly work. The data governance steering committee empowers people across the business to champion data literacy in their areas. Reviewing reports, their sources, and their statistical methods begins to create the data-driven culture. People begin to recognize data scientists not as bottlenecks, but as partners. (Feedback loops!) At that point, the quality of the data can sell itself. Vendors can only break in if they are truly offering something new and useful to the corporate data program. And most importantly, your data steering committee has the collective ability to understand and decide. The organization trusts the committee. Everyone has the reports they need. **That** is data democratization.

Reporting as a Product

It follows from the preceding text that the reporting function should be considered a formal product supported by the organization. In fact, it's one of the least outsource-able products the company maintains outside of its core business. It represents access specifically to the corpus of data that only your organization possesses.

Through the B2B Lens

Of specific interest to business-to-business (B2B) organizations, the reporting system can also be sold to customers. Somewhere along the way, Microsoft popularized the term "dogfooding" for this practice. The sentiment goes: if it's good enough for the customers, it should be good enough for you. Many organizations subscribe to this practice fully, Google included. Almost all products on GCP are tested by internal user groups before release.

Considering your reporting function as a product neatly bundles up many problems that a new reporting system would have. Thinking through these considerations is akin to designing a new product. Here are ten areas in which you can productize your reporting by imagining you might sell it:

- Tenancy/permissions: Users must only see the data they have permission to see. This can be segregated at the customer level, immediately implying a permissions hierarchy for the data.

- Accessibility/security: In order to make the product available for customers, it must be regularly available and accessible from customer locations. This implies creating a standard security model.

- Logging: You will certainly want to know what customers are looking at, and customers may want to know the same about you. You will need a way to monitor data retrieval and audit history.

- Integration with core product: The reporting system will need its own build and deploy process that corresponds with core product releases, causing internal teams to remember that it's part of their portfolio.

- Legitimacy: Adding a revenue stream to the product puts to rest any arguments about its relative importance for the purpose of resourcing and budget.

- Customer feedback: Another critical feedback loop. Understanding how your internal users work with the system vs. how customers interact with it improves everyone's experience. Sometimes these use cases are almost totally disparate.

- Value proposition support: Customers using the reporting system will be able to see for themselves how much value your product adds to theirs. Discussions about additional business can be managed in a data-driven fashion, because all parties have access to the data. Forestall unhappy customers by acknowledging a shortcoming in one area, but bolstering the value of another. This also encourages customers to notify you before unceremoniously terminating.

- Flipping the script: Now **you** can go to customers and suggest how your product might do something better than their internal group. Even better, you can sell something the internal group doesn't even want to do. By selling into both the relevant department and technology, you turn the internal group to your side.

- Case study: As a corollary to customer feedback and value proposition support, customers are more likely to be referenceable and will also collaborate on joint case studies. This is where all the successful quotes on B2B tools saying "DataCorp helped improve my efficiency by 73%!" come from. (Results may vary on whether pull quotes actually increase your sales.)

Chartering a Reporting Product

You may have thought to include reporting in your original data warehouse charter. If not, this is a good time to do that. Many of the considerations in your charter overlap with that for the general data warehouse. Accessibility of underlying warehouse data leads to easier report construction.

It isn't necessary to rely on generating revenue as a function of the charter. Selling reporting to customers is an extra incentive on a necessary product. In fact, if you tie the product's success to revenue generation, people may assume that an internal-only version is a failed product, when this is not the case. By the same token, don't confuse this product with an argument to sell it—you may force yourself into a situation where the product doesn't even get approved because of the additional hurdles. An unapproved reporting product is worse than no reporting product at all. (This is because you will still have reports; you have to. But all of the budget and resourcing and requirements will come from unallocated sources.)

However, you can use the criteria specified earlier to create an internal charter that conforms to your needs as well. Even if it won't deliver straight revenue, it will deliver cost savings. With the warehouse populated, those savings can even be measured, in a statement of the form "If business leaders had ready access to data X, they could optimize decision Y to save $Z."

Also, don't write any checks you can't cash. The data warehouse was a massive undertaking and solved many problems a reporting system would face, but there are still significant technical challenges in the reporting arm. Building in-house means wrestling with everything alone, but buying a solution means both figuring out how to integrate and being at the mercy of the vendor's default implementation timeline. Even if your internal team is pretty sure they can do it in, say, a week, the vendor is likely to have a much longer default timeline to account for other clients and unexpected surprises.

Speaking of bounced checks, one parameter you have to consider with BigQuery is cost control. While you may look to move to a slot reservation model to avoid this, your solution should also include some method of ensuring that individual users can't inadvertently bill thousands of dollars of queries. The most basic way is to run only static reports and cache them, which means only the report runner incurs cost. Some third-party solutions, like Looker, have their own support for cost controls as part of the reporting offering.

As with a data warehouse charter, construct it in concert with the data steering committee and ensure that it gets executive sign-off. Be as clear as necessary in articulating what properties it will have in these areas:

- This solution (will/will not) replace our existing reporting solution.

- The executive (will/will not) need to change location, process, or cadence of reports when this solution launches.

- The following reports (list them) from the existing suite (will/will not) be ported over.

- For reports that are moved over, they (will/will not) use the same raw data source.

- For reports that are moved over, they (will/will not) use equivalent reporting logic.

- The following reports (list any) will be improved versions of existing reports.

- These reports (will/will not) be intended to replace original reports, but both versions can coexist side-by-side for a time.

- The new reports (will/will not) match the old ones in the following areas (or just say "some areas," if you don't know yet).

- Phase 1 of this project (will/will not) produce user-readable reports at its conclusion.

- Phase 1 will include the following reports (list any).

- This solution (will/will not) include real-time reports.

- This solution (will/will not) include data visualization or dashboards.

- This solution (will/will not) allow interaction with the results.

As a group who knows the organization's senior leadership team, also explicitly head off questions about the characteristics of the solution. Since they're not formal product requirements yet, say "We expect, but cannot yet guarantee, that..." For instance, you can say that you expect a daily report to run in 10 seconds "given current volume trends." You need only specify this sort of detail at the charter level if you think that without it, you may lose the support of the executive sponsor(s).

Lastly, don't lean in too heavily on past failures, if you have them. Prefer positive language and things the reporting solution can do, even if those statements are obvious callbacks to previous problems. Reporting is the basic interface most users have with your data warehouse, and you want to avoid accidentally undermining the credibility of the whole program by talking too much about failures specific to its front end.

In short, utilize the strengths of your data governance teams and plans. You know what needs to be said—go in and say it, and come away with assurance that each person commits to what you said.

Product Management

Your organization may very well lack the particular skill set needed to manage a high-quality reporting system. More precisely, those individuals who have that skill set are likely to be occupied with other products. This is another area in which SaaS solutions easily outpace internal teams; by definition, their product management teams are all skilled in this area.

Small organizations won't even have dedicated product management for software tools, let alone anything to spare for a data warehouse or reporting system. That's okay; we've been discussing all of the interdisciplinary skills required to make the data program a success. So let's talk about why reporting is a product unto itself.

What's unique to reporting and visualization is the front-end interface. Even if you use another provider exclusively, they will have a certain look and feel common to their tools. (Honestly, if they don't and can't explain it by rapid growth/acquisition/extremely diverse product portfolio, run away.) Furthermore, if you are looking to sell your reporting solution, the tool will have to match the look and feel of your own products. Regardless, it's a consideration the data warehouse doesn't have.

If you do have a product manager on your team, ensure they're familiar with the capabilities of the data warehouse and the road map. Even better is if the product manager for the first phase of reporting happens to already be on your steering committee and has been looped into all of the previous discussions.

Defining Requirements

As a software product, the requirements for the reporting solution will take a slightly different form. Take care to cleanly separate the line between reporting and the underlying data warehouse: the reporting solution will use BigQuery as its source, and it can't do anything that you haven't built BigQuery to do. You'll still be writing SQL queries to create the reports, but something like "build a real-time Dataflow from System X we forgot about" is either a predecessor task or out of scope.

If those requirements are popping up frequently, ensure that you've actually built the data warehouse appropriately to meet users' needs. Go back to the original charter and your warehouse schema design; that should have prevented this kind of mismatch. If the warehouse matches the signed-off schemas, then this sort of requirements shouldn't arise; if it doesn't, figure out where the discrepancy occurred. A remedial project may be necessary to update the warehouse to serve effectively as the back end for this reporting solution. Be sure to run this as a separate dependency project rather than mixing in reporting solution requirements.

The charter can serve as the top-level information about how to construct this product. There are two primary areas in this interaction, even if you are wearing both hats: the "what," as specified by the product manager, and the "how," as specified by the engineering and/or integration teams.

The Platforms

The biggest "how" is what software systems comprise this solution. BigQuery, obviously, but this is also where you define external providers and connections to legacy systems and outline phased approaches to transition from one state to another.

You may need to draw out the multiphased approach so you can quickly specify what comprises the charter's "phase 1." Take it down the road as far as you can using optimistic extensibility, and then think about the minimum viable product for this phase (even if you hate that term). If you need help with the thought exercise, show the product manager the drawn-out phases and ask them to help you scope a minimum viable product (even if they hate that term). You don't have to call it that; it's a compact definition of what is required in phase 1 to meet your specific definition for "reporting solution." It's also intended to highlight scope creep, either in the form of extra requirements or in the form of requirements that are secretly data warehouse structural requirements and may not belong in this workstream at all.

The Reports

Of course, the primary functional requirement of this solution will be the reports themselves. How much effort defining this scope will require is a function of how many existing reports you have and how closely you can or want to adhere to their structure. The charter already has the list of what you need. In the simplest model, you've defined the framework and the front end, and anyone can do a translation from old format to new format. That's pretty unlikely though and belies the reason for chartering a project.

This may also be the first time that you're really testing your schema quality against the business problem. While you followed a consistent path from the initial warehouse sign-off to here, things change. The business may have even modified its way of doing things while you were building the warehouse. (Someone should have told you, yes.)

This process consists of breaking down any existing reports for discrepancies, gaps, redundancies, and potential back-end issues. Some of the common things you'll find in these areas are as follows:

- Prior to an official data glossary, **the names of data points may have meant something else**. This especially applies to department-specific definitions of things like "sales" and "conversions." The best solution is to change the names. The second-best solution is to add a tooltip or description in the new report to indicate the changed meaning and the new term.

- **Reports have data points you can't find in your warehouse**. If this happens, first check the old report source to see if it's a calculated column. Then decide based on its importance if it can remain a calculated column or if it should actually be a data point available to the warehouse directly.

- **There are data points that are missing from your warehouse**. Put on your product hat and go figure out if anyone still needs those data points. If they weren't captured in your schema, they may not be important anymore.

- **Multiple reports capture what seems to be the same piece of data**, but they do it in different ways. It's unclear whether they're actually doing the same thing. Unfortunately, you'll have to reverse-engineer the old report to understand how it got its data. Often, you'll often find that the unexplainable values in the old report are actually just bugs no one caught.

- **A new report performs very poorly**. This is usually one of two things. One, the report may hold way too much data in the default view. Stakeholders may insist they need all of that data on the page at the same time. You can either talk them out of it (product hat) or build a materialized view to create the report (engineering hat). Two, the report depends on an unusual query structure that doesn't perform well in BigQuery. In that case, use an optimization strategy to improve the performance; don't try to talk a user out of a report that already worked fine.

- **Several reports all do basically the same thing with minor variation.** Most organizations don't do this on purpose, so find a user of each of these reports, sit them down, and see if you can hammer out a new version that meets everyone's needs. Here you may find that the person who insisted on bizarre variation #3 is no longer with the company.

You will encounter problems that aren't on this list. If the answer isn't a BigQuery technique found somewhere else in this book, use product management principles. If it were possible to capture all of those solutions in a single list, the next section of this book would be about training a machine learning model to be a product manager.[4]

Road Map

Following the first phase of reporting implementation, you can incorporate it as a product timeline inside of your program road map. Someone should own the role of product owner for reporting as well.

As part of your governance plan for adapting to long-term change, each significant enhancement or onboarding to the warehouse should have a reporting and visualization section indicating what support will be required. If the reporting solution is part of your core product offering to customers, this exercise needs to be repeated across each significant business feature across the entire organization.

As with the initial charter, don't let reporting drive the data warehouse structure. Analyzing reports is a good way to learn what people are looking at and care about. Driving requirements down from report definitions into warehouse functionality is like signing a greeting card after it has been put in the envelope. It might work, but it won't be pretty.

The Solution Spectrum

Somehow, you'll have to answer the questions about which systems you need to construct your reporting solution. There are as many answers to this question as there are organizations. If a company has two employees, a founder and a CTO, the reporting solution might be "Hey, Andy, come take a look at this."

Google Cloud Platform

You can use several combinations of GCP services to build a reporting function using BigQuery as the data repository. These solutions should have a similar lifetime as BigQuery itself. And as Google releases new tools for reporting and visualization, they

---

[4]Actually, it wouldn't be, because I'd have already retired.

will likely work with BigQuery right out of the gate. Upgrading to a better solution may get easier over time. You could also choose another solution and go back to GCP if/when that happens, but that means another project...

Roll Your Own

You've seen what can be accomplished with Cloud Functions, Cloud Scheduler, and saved queries. To build a simple reporting system this way, you could save and schedule a few queries to be delivered by email or to Pub/Sub where they're picked up by a cloud function for distribution.

This wouldn't take very long to build, but it would have a few disadvantages. Changing the schedule or running reports on-demand would require GCP access. Changing anything about the reports would require SQL knowledge. It would be fairly difficult for anyone besides the author to know if the reporting job had failed for some reason, and it could fail for basic reasons.

In the absence of any formal solution, or budget, this goes some distance. Here are a couple of suggestions when going this route. These apply to any email-based reporting system, but there's more flexibility when rolling your own:

- Use plain English for the subject and body of the email. Provide a table or some summary detail in the body so people can derive some information at a glance without looking at the report.

- In addition to the plain English, you can include a tag at the end to make troubleshooting and searching easier. For example, "3/14/2015 Daily Sales Report [DSR_20150314]" is readable but still has a tag you can correlate.

- If the full report is less than a certain size (choose based on your own environment's parameters, say, 10 KB, 100 KB, or 1 MB), then attach the full report as a CSV.

- If the report exceeds this size, or if you have any raw report data that is protected by regulations, do not place it in the body or attach it to the email. Provide a secure link requiring authentication. (You can use your data classification rules to decide this.)

- Set an appropriate cadence for reports. Most people will quickly relegate reports to junk if they arrive too frequently. Or they'll just reply "unsubscribe" to the unmonitored email, and nothing will happen.

- If the report is only actionable when the data is anomalous, consider providing it only ad hoc when those conditions are met. For example, you can send daily emails about the performance of a sales promotion only while a promotion is ongoing. (We'll talk about special occasion dashboards in the next chapter.)

- Endeavor to give reports a consistent style and appearance. This helps to create an unconscious sense of trust that the data is coming from the "same" place.

That last one applies to every kind of reporting and visualization. It also applies to any reporting front end you may build or buy.

Google Data Studio

Google Data Studio is GCP's reporting and dashboarding tool. It has native integration to BigQuery. Since it has similar characteristics to BigQuery, including management and scale, we'll cover it separately in Chapter 18.

Other Third-Party Providers

There are endless reporting, analytics, and visualization solutions available. If your organization is of even moderate size, you might already have several. There really is no right answer, and the product requirements document is the best way to choose.

If you have no solutions at the moment, conduct a request for proposal (RFP) process with several providers. Evaluate them on all of the major areas of your requirements document and choose the best fit. Make sure that anything you need is captured contractually somewhere; after initial implementation, it can be hard to get that favor you were promised during the sales process. Actually, where did that person even go?

I looked at Google's recommended BigQuery solution providers list[5] and selected a few. You should visit the page or do other research yourself. This space changes on a quarterly basis; and each solution has its own ecosystem, blogs, and technical books.

Looker

Looker is a BI and data analytics platform that ticks most of the boxes in this space. While we're focused on reporting at the moment, Looker also provides dashboards, application frameworks, and data science tools. Google acquired Looker in 2019, so it has deep integration with BigQuery while still being compatible with other systems like AWS Redshift and Snowflake. It can also connect directly to most of the data sources we've looked at for BigQuery, like Google Analytics and Salesforce.

Looker uses its own intermediate format, called LookML, to model relations and generate the appropriate SQL. Looker will actually use BigQuery as a repository for building temporary tables to improve data modeling performance and segmentation.

Intriguingly, its deep BigQuery relationship has a couple other benefits. For instance, it can generate input datasets for BigQuery ML (BQML) models, which we'll use in Chapters 19 and 20. It also has cost controls to ensure users don't go over a certain cost allotment when running reports.

Tableau

Tableau was founded in 2003 and helped establish the first wave of interactive reports and visualizations to replace traditional periodic reports. It's a go-to solution for many organizations now and connects well with most data sources.

The BigQuery connector is native, and promisingly, the documentation is specific about which API calls it uses under what circumstances. It runs directly against BigQuery, meaning it handles large datasets well. On the flip side, since it also uses generated SQL, cost control could be a real concern. It's also possible to extract static data from BigQuery, which lowers cost but raises latency.

If your organization is already using Tableau, the reporting product does not need to be a catalyst for changing that.

---

[5]https://cloud.google.com/bigquery/providers#tab2

MicroStrategy

MicroStrategy is the oldest player, founded in 1989, and has been doing enterprise business intelligence since then. MicroStrategy does not use a native BigQuery connection and instead relies on the JDBC/ODBC drivers. Support was recently added for the Data Transfer service, so query reads should be reasonably fast.

MicroStrategy's solutions are geared fairly high up the market at the enterprise level. It wouldn't be a good choice for an organization just getting started, especially since BigQuery integration is not its first priority. However, if your organization already uses MicroStrategy, you will be able to run your reporting solution against BigQuery.

"DataCorp"

DataCorp is my catch-all name for a generic vendor. Many people are happy customers of "DataCorp," or it wouldn't be in business for very long. But is it right for you?

Shady marketing language and obfuscation of actual product capabilities do not in themselves mean the product has no value. When evaluating any arbitrary vendor during an RFP process, some basic due diligence can reveal potential issues. If you can't get a good answer, that may mean there isn't a good one. Interestingly, a lot of these vendors have their own blog posts or whitepapers detailing questions you should ask in an RFP. Many of these questions skew heavily toward problems BigQuery already solved around reliability and infrastructure. Some BigQuery-specific ones to get you started are as follows:

- Do you integrate with BigQuery? If so, what method do you use to connect? Native API? ODBC/JDBC? Something unusual?

- Which advanced BigQuery features does your connector support— for example, Data Storage API, STRUCTs and ARRAYs, results surfaced through views or stored procedures, and so on? Do you plan to support more?

- Do you support reporting directly from BigQuery, or must the data be transferred into your system first?

- How do you manage cost controls when performing BigQuery calls? Is there work on our side to set that up?

- What is the support model for your solution and BigQuery? If we have issues with the connector, whom do we call?

- Do you have referenceable clients whose primary data warehouse is BigQuery? May we speak with one?

If you work for a data analytics company not listed here, check again in the second edition.

Other Solutions

You may already have a reporting solution, and it's not on the table for you to change it. There are still some options remaining to integrate data. However, also examine if it represents an organizational dynamic. An issue like that would be better addressed via people or process, rather than attempting to conform to a flawed way of doing things.

Here are three more solutions, ordered in decreasing order of desirability.

JDBC/ODBC Drivers

In Chapter 5, we discussed the idea of using the JDBC standard as an abstraction to connect to other systems and treat them as relational stores.

The same is possible in the reverse direction, using BigQuery as a JDBC or ODBC source. Google has partnered with Magnitude Simba to produce both drivers for BigQuery. You can find more information and download the drivers from the BigQuery site.[6] ODBC drivers are available for Windows, Mac, and Linux. As long as you download the drivers from Google's site, they're free.

There are some limitations, since BigQuery supports concepts through its API that can't be cleanly represented via a database connector. Advanced features that sidestep the SQL interface are also unavailable. Here are a couple examples (also listed on the driver download site):

- BigQuery loading, streaming, and Dataflow are unavailable.

- You can use standard INSERT statements, but since OLTP is an anti-pattern, it will be slow and you will quickly hit quotas trying to use it like a regular database.

- Nested and repeated data will be output as pure JSON, so working with this data may be cumbersome.

---

[6] https://cloud.google.com/bigquery/providers/simba-drivers

You can get around the last of these limitations by flattening tables out into intermediate views, which you can query from the source system to avoid dealing with JSON. This obviously has its own problems though, so if you are using deeply nested data in your reports, it might warrant additional consideration.

The Simba drivers **do** support querying via the Storage API, so you can still get high throughput on reads.

Lastly, if you are purchasing a vendor solution and they have touted their integration with BigQuery, find out whether it is via a native connector or if they are just using the ODBC or JDBC drivers themselves. Most BI tools have ODBC/JDBC integrations, which is why I'm suggesting it in the first place. Make sure you understand the nature of the connection if it's being used as a selling point.

This is currently the best way to get data into Amazon QuickSight too, as it has no native BigQuery connector.

Intermediate System(s)

This is the data equivalent of plugging a Bluetooth receiver into a cassette tape adapter, so you can connect your phone via Bluetooth and listen to Spotify in your late model vehicle. In other words, it may work, but it's going to be hacky.

If your existing reporting solution can integrate with other platforms, and *those* platforms have JDBC/ODBC connectivity, you could use the intermediate system to forward the data. This has basically all of the disadvantages of a flat file option, except that the latency and possibly the performance will be better. The major disadvantage is that when something goes wrong in a chain of responsibility like this, it's incredibly difficult to figure out what failed where.

Flat File

This isn't referring to files you need to send to customers, vendors, or partners. Flat files are still a perfectly reasonable way to transmit data in a common format. This refers to using them to power your fully internal reporting system.

If you really have no better option, you can write a Cloud Function and schedule it to query tables and push out flat files to SFTP or a folder. (Or a Gopher server.) There are numerous disadvantages, including latency, performance on large tables, reliability... Actually, there aren't really any advantages at all. This is really a choice of last resort if you need to ship data to an IBM AS/400 server powered by a hamster running in a wheel.

Cuneiform

First, purchase a substantial amount of raw clay and some reeds for fashioning into styluses. Then, learn ancient Sumerian, along with the cuneiform writing system, which consists of thousands of symbols and syllables. This will take somewhere between 8 and 12 years.

In the meantime, purchase an actual building to serve as your "warehouse." To be clear, it will be literally a warehouse. You will need climate control and careful storage to ensure that the impressions on the clay don't smudge and fade away within days. (However, this could be used as a form of automatic tablet expiration.)

Devise an education program for the thousands of scribes you will need to hire to imprint the clay. In addition to learning the cuneiform writing system, you will need to employ an anthropological linguist to create new symbols to represent modern technological concepts inexpressible by standard cuneiform. In order for the tablets to be readable to future generations, these symbols will have to fit naturally into the existing symbol corpus as well as ancient Sumerian, requiring substantial study of morphology and historical context.

Purchase one computer terminal per scribe. Make sure that your DevOps group creates a common image that will be able to call an API on GCP.

Then, write a custom Cloud Function that takes a BigQuery query as input and splits the output row by row. Employ parallel processing techniques to distribute the query as a workload across all scribes in the cluster. Each scribe reads a data row from their terminal screen and impresses it onto their clay. The scribes will also need a rudimentary task signaling system, like a button that they can press when their row has been transcribed. (Error checking is out of scope for this solution.)

If a scribe does not press the button indicating completion of the work unit after a predefined amount of time, return it to the work pool. Like commodity hardware, scribes will often fail; keep a training program running constantly so that you can easily swap in a new scribe when this happens. Appropriate water cooling systems can raise the mean time between failures (MTBF) of nodes/scribes.

Finally, you will need a transport system to load the completed tablet-rows into the warehouse. Calculate how much data your warehouse can store and provision a trucking fleet accordingly. Note that this can be difficult to manage in a scalable fashion. Eventually, you will need to purchase or construct additional warehouse locations, preferably in multiple regions for data redundancy. Organizing the tablets within each warehouse location for later access is a formidable logistics problem, but you made it this far.

This approach has a number of significant disadvantages, chiefly among them being its incomprehensible stupidity.

Summary

Reporting is a basic function of written communication and has taken on many different connotations. In an attempt to avoid a clash with marketing jargon, "reporting" is defined here simply as something that can produce reports. Many negative opinions of the reporting function are based on mismatched expectations or simply different definitions of the word. To avoid this, consider reporting to be its own product and follow a product lifecycle process for building it. Do this as formally as you are able. In terms of software solutions, the landscape is endless. Use your technical and product knowledge to select something that works for you. If you must integrate with an existing system, choose the highest-fidelity method available to bridge the two systems.

In the next chapter, we'll cover a related topic with different implications for your data culture: visualization and dashboarding.

CHAPTER 17

Dashboards and Visualization

Accurate and up-to-date visualization of an organization's systems is foundational to modern business. In a world where data is constantly bombarding us through the plethora of devices we use each day, your business data is literally competing with everything else for attention.

An Internet-focused career requires constant access. We use dozens of online resources daily to help us do our jobs and keep in touch. The nature of human attention means that despite our best intentions, we tend to gravitate toward the most prominent pieces of information. Regardless of how you feel about the effect this has on productivity, you can find a study to support your position. Either way, it's in the best interest of your data program to meet its users on their terms.

Visualization should make important information apparent with minimal interpretation. Green is good; red is bad. I used to joke that an executive summary report should consist of a single emoji: ☺ or ☹. The state of the business is clear at a glance; this generally prompts questions that continue the discussion. In reality though, your typical stoplight dashboard is basically equivalent.

Dashboards take the visualization one step further and present it real-time. When properly executed, they act like thermometers during fundraisers on public television. Everyone watches the dashboard and responds to every major update. The rest of the time, it sends a constant signal of how things are doing. You can't improve what you can't measure—it seems reasonable that continuous measurement and continuous improvement would be related.

This also prevents issues based on anecdotes or feelings from spiraling out of control. I couldn't tell you the number of times I received a call about how a user had experienced an error and, consequently, every user must be experiencing it and the

© Mark Mucchetti 2020
M. Mucchetti, *BigQuery for Data Warehousing*, https://doi.org/10.1007/978-1-4842-6186-6_17

sky was falling. I would immediately look to my primary dashboard, where everything was green and within range. I could confidently say that the user was experiencing an isolated incident and move to triage appropriately.

On the flip side, this level of visibility makes it hard to conceal issues. If I arrived at work and any metric was red, my team already had an explanation, even if it was just "we're looking into it."

Ultimately, a culture of data comes from a continual stream of things to look at coupled with an awareness of what those things mean. The goal is to be as clear as possible, such that the intent of the message is immediately apprehensible. A dashboard with 400 metrics may be very useful to its creator, but no one else is going to have a clue how to read it.

False positives and false negatives can be equally damaging. Calibrating metrics in a way that indicates the actual scale of the problem is critical, in the same way we've treated data accuracy. If people come to learn the presentation of the metric is misleading—even if the underlying metric is accurate—they will begin to tune it out. There's a theory here around making periodic changes and refinements to encourage a conscious re-evaluation from time to time. That also represents a delicate balance: too much change and people will lose their instinct into reading the data; too little and it will fade to background noise.

In healthcare, this problem is known as "alarm fatigue."[1] Healthcare professionals hear so many alarms, beeps, and background noises from medical equipment that they start failing to process their meaning. Many alarms are false or disproportionately loud or insistent. Lives are at stake in this example. While your use case may not be as extreme, this illustrates the need to calibrate dashboards to the correct sense of urgency.

The recent popularity of automatic modes like "do not disturb," "night hours," or "quiet time" on mobile devices is another indication that we've reached notification overload. More ominously, we've reached notification homogeneity: a picture of your friend's dog and an impending natural disaster both notify with the same importance level.

---

[1]https://nacns.org/wp-content/uploads/2016/11/AF-Introduction.pdf

We have the tools to program whatever dashboard design and notification hierarchy we want, but we can't change the underlying finite resource—the attention of your users. Conveying information visually is a daunting task. As your key resource for a valuable reporting suite is a product manager, your key resource for a valuable dashboarding system is a UI designer. If you don't have one available, don't worry; most people are still doing this on their own.

This chapter is about creating worthwhile visualizations and dashboards for your data and deploying them as broadly and pervasively as possible.

Visualizations

A straightforward tactic to convert data into information is to visualize it. This accomplishes two things. Firstly, it shows raw data in a format that is easy to understand at a glance. Secondly, it allows the creator of the visualization to reduce the data into only its most salient characteristics. In other words, you can selectively eliminate data that isn't relevant to the information you're presenting.

A Bad Example

I'm a big fan of illustration by counterexample. Figure 17-1 is a terrible visualization.

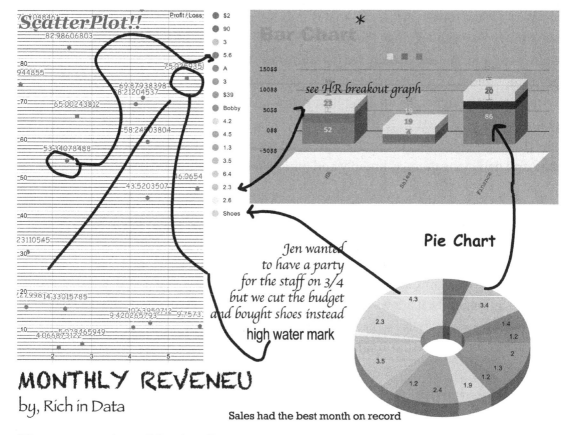

Figure 17-1. *A terrible visualization*

Can you spot all the issues?

The tendency to compress as much information as possible into the space can be overwhelming. The same issues plague slide decks, reports, and instruction manuals. It's not always enjoyable to assemble a piece of IKEA furniture, but compared to a less-reputable manufacturer, the advantages of simplicity are obvious.

Visualization Features

There are many attributes which contribute to a clear and effective visualization. To understand the problems this visualization failed to solve, let's look at some of those attributes. (Any design resource you have access to will easily be able to do this exercise in their heads and suggest something better, so if you have one, use this section to appreciate how difficult their work can be.)

Chart Type

Choosing the right visual form for your data is the most critical step. Thankfully, this area is well-understood, and lots of guides exist for choosing the right kind of chart. Here are a few basic pointers:

- When showing data points in relationship to each other, bar and line charts are appropriate. Line charts show connected values over time (like stocks), while bar charts are good at comparing across categories.

- For proportional data, where items add up to a whole, pie charts and their variants are good. If you need to compare multiple proportional series, a donut chart works.[2]

- Showing all pieces of data in relationship to a single set can be done with histograms or scatter plots.

- You can also use stacked charts to break categories down into multiple values.

The nice part about using a visualization tool instead of constructing manually is that you can quickly switch among chart types and see which one tells your story the best.

However, keep it simple. If a particular chart type looks impressively complicated, but its purpose is not clear, don't use it. That being said, it can be fun to write a bulleted list and then style it in every conceivable PowerPoint SmartArt style. Some of these formats don't even seem to display any type of data particularly well.

Example: A pie chart is used, but the values don't total to 100% or even to a stated total. A bar chart is used in place of a pie chart. It's completely unclear what purpose a scatter plot serves here.

Scale

Choose a scale that makes sense for your data. This means choosing the correct minimum and maximum values for each axis, as well as choosing the right kind of scale.

---

[2]Björn Rost, the technical consultant for this book, hates pie charts. And I totally get that; the bad visualization example is a great reason why. We recommend this article for a more nuanced discussion: https://medium.com/@clmentviguier/the-hate-of-pie-charts-harms-good-data-visualization-cc7cfed243b6

The scale must be chosen appropriately so that everything fits in the available space, but also conveys the correct relationships between data points. Linear and logarithmic scales are both common.

We're innately wired for comparison and need digestible ranges on which to understand magnitude. In casual language, people can say things like "I ate a lot of food," and we can map it to a roughly equivalent scale of satiety. Many technology data points are at scales which are difficult to comprehend. Let's say that I ran a "huge" query on BigQuery. What does that mean? No one could guess if it even referred to giga-, tera-, peta-, or exabyte scale. In the same way, the natural question "Compared to what?" arises as any scale is presented.

By the same token, if two graphics have a relationship to each other, the scale should be the same between them. Viewers are likely to form comparisons based on the occupied physical space. In some instances, you can use "not to scale," but that leaves people with no reference frame whatsoever, and it's still hard to suppress the instinct to compare.

Example: Bars have values that don't correspond with their height. In some cases, it's unclear what the scale is intended to represent.

Labeling

Here's another reminder that naming things is difficult. Placing data in context means supplying accurate and succinct labels.

Place labels near the things they label. If a viewer has to jump back and forth between charts and legends, context is easily lost. Drawing arrows to make this connection means the viewer has to follow the arrow instead. When there are too many labels, the viewer is spending more time reading than looking at the measurements in relation to each other.

Always label axes and include units. If scale is involved, state it clearly (i.e., "sales in millions"). Use horizontal labeling that can be read easily unless you have a compelling reason not to do so. If a specific value is important, label it; if it's not or if the relative scale is more important, let the axis values do the labeling.

When a single chart clearly has too many labels, decide whether you can eliminate some or if it's actually better to separate it into two separate charts. If it can be done simply, communicating related messages in the same chart is fine, but don't confuse clarity with compactness.

As for the actual things being labeled, use consistent language taken from your data glossary. In most cases, the data and axis labels should closely resemble the BigQuery column names they come from. Summary and aggregate labels should be used more to get your point across.

Example: There are essentially no useful labels. Charts are labeled with the kind of chart they are, but nothing about what the chart actually represents. Some labels are missing entirely. Labels aren't placed near the things they describe.

Simplicity

Show required data only.

In an information-dense format, there's no space to clarify or explain a statement. If people want lots of details about a subject, they will read a book.

Example: This visualization is not simple.

Relevance

As a corollary, don't include details that aren't important to the understanding of the information. Examples include superfluous explanations like "XXX sent an email about this" or any textual redundancy of the chart itself. If the chart is too confusing for the viewer to understand, a giant block of text isn't going to help. If you find it difficult to explain the data yourself, re-evaluate the message you're delivering.

Example: There's a textual description explaining the value for pizza, and the label is placed in an irrelevant spot. Arrows distract the viewer from the data on the chart.

Consistency

Labels, colors, fonts, and data points should be used consistently within the same chart and across charts on the same report or dashboard. Using extra colors or fonts for no reason will confuse the viewer into thinking they mean something.

Remember from the previous chapter that people will assume things that look similar come from the same place. This sort of consistency is also important in visualizations.

Example: In addition to the values being mislabeled, some values have units, while others do not.

Style

As with chart type, don't overdo it. Resist the urge to complicate a visualization to show off.

If your organization has a style guide, even if it's primarily for external use, use it in your visualizations. In addition to looking "official," it will prevent you from using too many colors or fonts if you are constrained to your organizational design language.

On that note, apply the same concepts of simplicity to the visual design. When in doubt, do less. Don't use lots of different color patterns or more than two or three fonts. Also, consider what form(s) your visualization may appear in. Print design and digital design have different objectives, and the common denominator is fairly narrow. If there's any chance that your visualization will be seen on paper, in black and white, optimize for that or produce a second visualization.

Design resources are equally intensive; if you have access to a designer, rather than asking them to design individual visualizations, let them help you to establish an organizationally aligned design language. They will know if there already is one and, if not, can help fill the gap in a natural way. This will let you focus on the actual information and its display, not the presentation.

Example: Honestly, it's just a mess.

Accuracy

Most importantly, display accurate data. Viewers need to trust the underlying data source. They also need to trust the creator of the visualization. Avoid misspellings, references to data which has been omitted from the chart, or inaccurate or out-of-date descriptions.

Example: The description text at the bottom has misspellings. It says the data was collected from three sources, but only two appear on the chart. It suggests you refer to another part of the diagram for more information, but that part isn't on the diagram.

Example: Several words, including the title, are misspelled. An asterisk indicates a footnote, but none is present.

Transparency

As a corollary to accuracy, don't violate these rules to bias a viewer into a certain conclusion. Absolutely highlight the relevant data, and show contrast in areas where the emphasis is necessary for understanding. Don't omit or obfuscate data that doesn't support your viewpoint.[3]

If the viewer senses you are attempting to mislead or recognizes that the graphic is concealing important information, they will become angry. That will undermine any legitimate point you have to make.

Example: This diagram isn't based on real-world data, but the attention drawn to the "high-performing cluster" omits any description of what the low end of the chart might refer to.

Dashboards

Unlike reports, dashboards are a much newer invention and only recently came to take on their current meaning with respect to organizational data. The original term "dashboard" was first attested in the mid-19th century. In that sense, it referred to a literal wooden board that prevented the driver from being covered by mud that had been "dashed up" by the horses (see Figure 17-2). Unlike early reporting, the early dashboard didn't convey any information at all.

---

[3]Unless it's a sales presentation, in which case, my company, DataCorp, produces the best reporting and visualization solution in the world. Email now to receive our whitepaper on truth in information and a 14-day free trial.

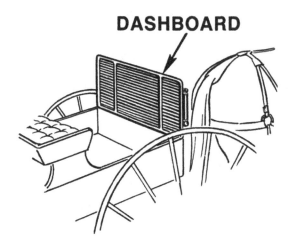

Figure 17-2. A dashboard. Really!

As the years went by, automobiles replaced horses. The dashboard served its original use, first against debris and then from scalding motor oil. When cars began to feature simple instrumentation, the dashboard was the natural place to put it, given its convenient position in front of the driver. The name was retained and now primarily connotes the modern meaning: a system of dials and gauges designed to be read quickly and provide instantaneous feedback.

The original auto designers had the right idea—instrumentation needs to be in line of sight and convey basic information rapidly. Also like the original designers, you have a similar responsibility, which is to find your users' line of sight and place the simplest possible data there. You make do with what you have. Also key to the automotive analogy is that users cannot interact with dashboards; they are read-only. Even in today's cars, the number of screens you can reach with steering wheel buttons is limited, and most cars will prevent an attempt to do anything complicated during driving.

There are other design cues from modern automotive dashboards that apply here. Large amounts of raw data must be synthesized to provide, say, a blind spot detector. Showing the driver more than an on/off indicator that someone is in their blind spot could be distracting and possibly dangerous. Most of the data on an automotive dashboard is current point in time (speedometer, tachometer, fuel level) or reflects moving averages from the recent past (distance to empty, average fuel economy). Cumulative or running totals can also be useful to assess the overall age of the system (odometer, trip meter). Lastly, there are many alert notifications of danger or required action, but these are only visible when active. There is no "don't check engine" light—it is only active when action is required.

Car manufacturers have had decades to discover information display best practices. They also reflect a limited system under one person's direct control. Your task is considerably more challenging (and hopefully less dangerous). Data dashboards must reflect countless systems and health indicators with widely varying ranges. Any data that originates from an end user or process can fluctuate wildly during the course of a day and have unpredictable spikes or lulls at thousands of times average. Users aren't yet familiar with how to incorporate dashboards into their own work. And the scale and importance of dashboard metrics may be unclear to anyone except the developers of the system.

If these hurdles are overcome, users will ask to create their own dashboards, and they will proliferate throughout other departments. Dashboards are just as effective for all kinds of business data as they are for technology data, system health, and the outside world.

In fact, as we'll cover, providing business context for data inside technology is an effective way to get your technology team thinking along business lines and prioritizing revenue. This can eliminate schisms between technology KPIs and the rest of the organization in a low-maintenance way.

Visualizations vs. Dashboards

The biggest difference between visualizations and dashboards is the temporal dimension. This creates an emphasis on "recency" in a way that reporting visualizations don't have.[4] For example, a common visualization would be showing an organization's revenue by quarter, perhaps over one or several years. Stock charts may go to five years as static visualizations.

When you place those same metrics on a dashboard, the value of the data point fades exponentially with age. This is the same concept that helped us determine how to expire activity and error logs. In that model, it also suggested that we use moving averages or to collapse less recent data into the aggregate as we go.

This window depends on the information your dashboard reports, but it rarely goes beyond 30 days or so, with the exception of grand total metrics like "Year-to-Date" (YTD) revenue. Note that a YTD metric still has a recency component—it reflects the past, but

---

[4]This also illuminates a key design distinction between Chapter 5, in which we covered batch loading, and Chapters 6 and 7, when we looked at real-time streaming. It's also why whether you need real-time data is a fundamental question in the data charter and governance: your organization might not have thought about it.

it also constantly changes to capture the present. That sort of temporal variation is a way to show scale in dashboards too. Viewers can understand the rate of change by watching the dashboard for a short period of time.

Visualizations can also tolerate a time period where the viewer is "reading into" them. For complex messages, you want the trend to be quickly discerned, but other implications of the visualization can reveal themselves as the viewer obtains additional context.

With dashboards, there's no subtlety. A spaghetti mess of lines and colors may look impressive (there's that word again), but you've lost the viewer already. If you have a metric that is 5, and it was 3 a few minutes ago, the best way to show it is a giant 5 and a green arrow pointing upward. As an outsider, I may not understand the meaning of the data point at first, but I do know that it's 5, that it's rising, and that that's a good thing.

Dashboard Hierarchy

The biggest advantage that the data warehouse provides is the ability to combine metrics from disconnected areas of the business. Yes, each of your departments can use their internal authoritative tools to produce dashboards with their departmental data. Also, many dashboards will consist of data tailored from a specific department's logical data mart. And as you democratize, stakeholders in each department can do this from themselves using BigQuery.

Where the centralized warehouse comes in is the ability to create organization-wide dashboards linking together data in innovative fashion. You can break out of individual siloed feedback loops with a single view uniting data. This can produce results that highlight problems or opportunities no department could see on their own. For example, what could it mean if website traffic is at an all-time high, but sales are below average? What if error rates on your mobile application are extremely high, but the call center reports average activity levels? Instead of relying on an email between departments to even identify these two key metrics aren't following their normal relationship, you have it at a glance.

In a similar exercise at a higher level of abstraction, you can design a hierarchy of dashboard displays that roughly sketch out what message each dashboard will convey and at what level it must do that. This also gives you a prioritization rubric if you don't have time or space to do all of them. Have this discussion with your data governance steering committee—they will each have a litany of ideas for metrics from which they would benefit.

Use Cases

Any set of related pieces of information that needs to be monitored on an ongoing basis is a candidate for dashboarding. A single dashboard should provide a meaningful piece of information about a system as easily as possible. A "system" may be a literal system, or it may be a department's performance or information about the organization at large.

There's no set level of importance that warrants dashboard creation. It's probably not useful to visualize areas with low impact to the business or things at such a granular level of detail that they won't ever change. (For example, if your business operates in a single state and has no immediate plans for expansion, showing a map of the United States with that state lit up and the number "1" isn't very helpful and will probably actually lower spirits.)

By the same token, any data which can be represented in an easy-to-read form is also a candidate. This usually means following the same rules as visualizations, but as we covered, the existence of the temporal dimension emphasizes certain things and de-emphasizes others. All the rules about clean display of information apply and then some: it should roughly be as simple to the business as a speedometer is to the driver.

Ubiquity

Data everywhere, all the time. Public-facing data in reception. Department data in every department. Every single employee should have line of sight to a dashboard with metrics that are (or should be) relevant to them. Obviously, this won't always be possible, but it's a target.

I consulted for a Fortune 500 company that had several dashboards in the main lobby for employees and visitors to notice as they arrived for work. The metrics they had chosen were things like Twitter word clouds and sentiment analysis. They were also totally unfiltered, so negative sentiments weighted just as highly as the positive ones. This meant that every day, every employee had an instinct about how the public was feeling about them that day. That's what you're going for in the ubiquity category.

Surprise

The opposite of notification fatigue is "surprise." This doesn't mean blocking employees in their cubicles with rolling dashboards while they aren't looking. Instead, it means creating the right amount of variation that the dashboards remain fresh.

Rotating Views

One way to maintain "surprise" is to use rotating views on dashboards, say four or five. People walking by will catch different views at each glance, and it will take proportionately longer for them to get used to a single board and stop looking at it.

Animation

The board will update on a regular basis and stay interesting, but also consider using relevant graphics or animations for unusual events. For example, you could create a dashboard where a record sales day causes the board to show an animation of raining money. This principle is the same as achievements in video games or the recent trend toward showering your screen in confetti when you complete a desired action. It's a form of feedback in response to organizational action.

Easter Eggs

Most dashboarding systems don't support this sort of thing yet, but they should.[5] I've accomplished it with creative use of iframes or browser content plugins. Occasionally, the dashboard should do something really surprising, like a bear dancing on screen, grabbing a metric, and running off with it. A moment later it reappears on the board. It does not repeat.

This sort of secret is almost certainly not worth the effort, unless your full-time job is making dashboards, but it will get people talking.

Related Metrics

If you have a laundry list of metrics people want to see or you feel like you have hundreds of relevant metrics in general, begin to investigate their relationships and see if you can compress some of the redundancy into a more meaningful point of data.

For example, you may want to know how many messages are in your Dataflow queues. If you have multiple steps in the queue, it seems reasonable to list all of them. Instead, consider showing an average of messages in each step or a sum of messages in all steps. If you really need to know each queue individually, consider whether the actual number is important or the relation between the numbers of messages in each queue is

---

[5]You heard it here first.

the important data. If the latter, you can make all queue counts into a single line chart and place it next to the sum or average.

In some cases, seemingly unrelated metrics will all tie down to a single thread, for example, the number of orders or transactions. Sometimes it's appropriate to do a calculation on metrics and show the result, if you know viewers are just going to do it in their heads. For example, even though the three numbers comprise a division problem, showing a total revenue, a number of transactions, and an average transaction value would be okay, even though all three numbers move in tandem. Do this if all related numbers are important and viewers otherwise mentally calculate them every time they look at the board.

This one is a delicate balance between showing redundant information and answering the question "Compared to what?" Viewers need a frame of reference, and the entire dashboard should communicate that message. Use your best judgment.

Major Business Events

A great way to get surprise (and also to demonstrate the value of dashboards) is to assemble special views for momentous business events.

If a new system is going live and it's not even clear what to track yet, pull some high-level information that demonstrates the moment's message, and style it accordingly. For example, if you are opening a new retail store, the dashboard can be entirely focused on statistics about that store, including a picture, a map, and other superfluous metrics. Obviously if this store is one of many, the dashboard won't be important for long, but it's a great way to celebrate and bring awareness to other teams' success. (And again, to be successful, that data will have to come from your data warehouse...)

Community

Dashboards provoke conversation about the business. Even on an average day, you'll see a few people stop in front of the dashboard and make a comment about how a certain thing is doing. As you "democratize" dashboards and others start to make them, others may come up with some truly creative ideas. If this is their bridge to adding business value, don't stop them.

One company made a dashboard to show their employee's progress in a bike race, complete with maps, graphs, and a live web cam feed from their helmet. Tableau used Game of Thrones as a platform to solicit dashboards of all kinds of data related to the show. These are valuable training exercises to onboard others into your data program. (Obviously, your organization's code of conduct and behavior applies.)

There has recently been a proliferation of DIY projects around smart mirrors and dashboards for the home too. Commercial products like the Echo Show and Nest Hub are basically piloting this concept into how we run our personal lives as well.

How to Build Dashboards

There's a significant logistical component to getting your dashboards up and running. Once you have a sense for how many you need and what metrics are most important, you can get to work. Use your hierarchy to do a prioritization exercise and know which metrics are most important for real-time feedback. As I'll repeat, resist the urge to cram more metrics into less real estate.

After that, it's a matter of procuring or finding the tools you need.

Hardware

To accomplish the goal of ubiquity, we're going to need hardware. The best dashboard setup in the world won't accomplish anything if no one ever sees it. If your organization does not yet understand the value of dashboards, this may actually be the most difficult part of implementing your strategy. Possible barriers include adequate wall space, support from facilities and IT for installation, or budget. Do the best you can— the barriers will begin to fall as organizational leaders begin to notice dashboards. Expect some visitors to stop by and ask, "What is that? You know, right now, that {x} is happening in our business? Is that up-to-date?" followed shortly by "How do I get one?" Then, pull out the sheet of paper on which you've written all the current barriers to the dashboard culture, and read it aloud. This is also a great place for your data governance team to advocate inside their own functional areas. No doubt, they have live metrics they think would inspire or inform their own teams. The spectrum of requests can be astounding—I've had people ask for everything from current spend on pay-as-you-go contracts (like...BigQuery) to a running list of employee birthdays. Support everything you can, with the stipulation that the data be sourced from the data warehouse. Two birds with one stone.

Screens

Not to be cliché, but get as many of the largest screens you can. Don't even worry about the resolution; anything 1080 p or higher is fine. The larger the screen, the farther away from which it can be seen. The more screens, the more metrics you can display. However, keep the dashboard hierarchy in mind: don't use more screens to show the same density of metrics, only larger. And **definitely** don't use more screens to show more total information.

As with any hierarchy of information, the scale moves from largest and most important to smallest and least important. If you have a single, all-powerful business metric, the space, and the money, you might try placing that metric alone on a screen. The effect is overwhelming; and you will probably add supplementary data about the metric, say, recent values or other correlated metrics. But you'll get your point across. See Figure 17-3.

Figure 17-3. *One metric to rule them all*

Many people scrounge for old hardware or can secure approval for a single, moderately sized screen to start. Again, resist the temptation to overload that screen—if you have one 32″ TV, stick to no more than six metrics. Then add to your list of barriers that you could display more if you had a larger screen.

Seriously, this isn't a boasting or power game, even though some people may take it that way. This is about having business information in view of all stakeholders at all times. By the same token, you can use projectors to get more real estate, but old stock may not be bright enough in typical office lighting conditions.

As a side note, most TVs have power saving settings where they can turn on and off by a schedule or by HDMI-CEC signal. Please use these settings to save energy and only have the screens on during normal business hours.

Computers

Once you have all of the screens, you still need something to show the data. And that means another set of potential obstacles from IT, along the same lines: budget, device security, and setup. Before you can kick off a program like this, you'll need to ensure that your computers will have broad enough Internet access to reach the dashboards. If your organization already has a CCTV or media distribution system, you may be able to start a project to hop on that. Your requirements are simple: display an HTML5 dynamic web page.

You can scrounge around for hardware here too, with the benefit being that leftover machines in your department probably already have security and wifi clearance. The power and maintenance requirements may be an issue if the machine decides to randomly do system updates or hardware crashes. You may also not like the running wires coming from a wall mount to a machine sitting on the floor.

Any system-on-a-chip (SoC) should have sufficient power to run your dashboards and may also have the benefit of being able to be powered from the 5 V USB ports on the back of an HDTV. These are available from many organizations in x86, ARM, and single-board computer options.

The Raspberry Pi frequently comes up here as the hobbyist device of choice, and it will in fact run a pretty good dashboard. You can purchase as many as you need, as it's hard to break the bank with a list price of 35 USD. Purchase a model 3B+ or a model 4; built-in wifi and Bluetooth will make it easier to interface with the system remotely.

Finally, some smart TVs have web browsers built in. These browsers sometimes are up-to-date and fast enough to power your dashboards. Note that with the exception of the

Amazon Fire Stick, most media stick-based devices don't run their own browsers without some modification. For example, you can get a Chromecast to load an arbitrary website, but officially the supported pattern is "casting" to your device from your computer or phone, which is not sufficient. In all cases, you want dedicated hardware to display the board. If it's frequently broken or someone has to turn it on, this will present a self-created barrier to adoption. If you do this, check it for reliability for the first couple weeks to make sure it has enough memory and CPU to handle refreshing a web page indefinitely.

Security

If your dashboard runs on a machine that has access to internal systems, you may need to prevent passersby from using an attached keyboard or mouse to gain other unauthorized access. You can solve this problem with networking, only allowing the single address hosting your dashboard to be accessible from the machine. Or, if you have remote access that automatically configures on start, you could take the more extreme action of locking the machine in a case or even epoxying the case and ports shut. You may not need to take any of these steps, but don't inadvertently create a vulnerability during this process.

Software

There are two components to the software, one being the dashboard display itself and the other being the tool that loads it. As with reporting, the landscape is ever changing, and people's needs are rapidly evolving. This reminds me of the application lifecycle monitoring days. People were clamoring for task boards and agile management systems—Jira was still primarily for bug tracking, and many project management systems were heavily waterfall-driven. After a time, as the actual market request coalesced, companies started targeting these users directly. Dashboards are nearly at that point, but no one's winning yet.

Dashboard Tools

Many traditional reporting and BI companies have leapt over into the dashboard space. From another angle, many DevOps performance monitoring companies like New Relic and Datadog have created dashboarding systems that serve other types of data perfectly well. There are countless open source systems and projects of even smaller scale to tackle this problem.

Many are unattractive or feature limited. Others are great for certain kinds of data, but are harder to integrate with others. In one example, I was trying to integrate data into a dashboard from Segment. Segment is an organization that integrates customer data collection across multiple sources, for example, uniting your scripts and tags across systems like Google Analytics. In fact, they even have their own dashboarding system for visualizing data. I was attempting to tie customer data into system health data. The dashboard tool I was using had a Segment integration, and I thought I could just tie them together. Unfortunately, the metrics collected by the integration were around the health of the Segment service itself: number of Segment events delivered, rejected, retried, and so forth. I couldn't get at the data I wanted, which was inside the events themselves.

This wasn't a failure of the dashboard I was using—it was just that the use cases I wanted weren't compatible. As this area matures, it should get easier to cross-reference all kinds of metrics on the same dashboard to meet your needs.

In the next chapter, we'll explore doing this with Google Data Studio, more or less as a proxy for any of the hundreds of other tools you might use. The concepts are similar across dashboard providers, and the design language is relatively consistent.

Displaying the Dashboard

Typically you can do this with a web browser. There are a few considerations for running a browser in unattended mode that you'll want to take into account. This depends on your hardware and its operating system; there are a few things to take into account.

First, as I mentioned earlier, make sure the hardware can handle refreshing a graphics-intensive web page for an indefinite amount of time. Second, make sure you have a script configured to boot the computer directly into the browser with a default web page. Lastly, unless your dashboard is showing public data, you will need authentication to access it. Figure out a way to handle this so that the dashboard isn't just showing a login prompt all the time.

Maintenance

Once the system is up and running, it will be important to avoid decay. Dashboards go out of date as underlying systems change. This is a mini-version of your plan to adapt to long-term change in your data program, with a couple extra wrinkles.

First, anything tied to system performance or health will change regularly as the DevOps team changes infrastructure. While they likely want to manage their own boards, understand what if any data is going into BigQuery from Cloud Logging or other application performance monitoring tools that you may be using. It's totally fine to keep these dashboards and monitors separate if that's your organizational culture. Depending on the infrastructure, it may not be relevant at all anyway.

On the same basis, when an underlying integration to BigQuery is changing, confirm that the affected data schemas won't change. This would ideally be part of your data governance decision making, but can get harder to manage with a greater number of integrations.

Most importantly and to the points made earlier, ensure that all the dashboards come up as expected every day and continue to display information throughout the day. The idea of making a dashboard to measure dashboard availability has occurred to me, but that is maybe a bit too meta.

I anonymized and redacted an actual system health dashboard from a real company in Figure 17-4. It fails to follow most of the principles we discussed. Furthermore, it sat unmaintained for a year before it was replaced with a better one, by which point it looked like the following.

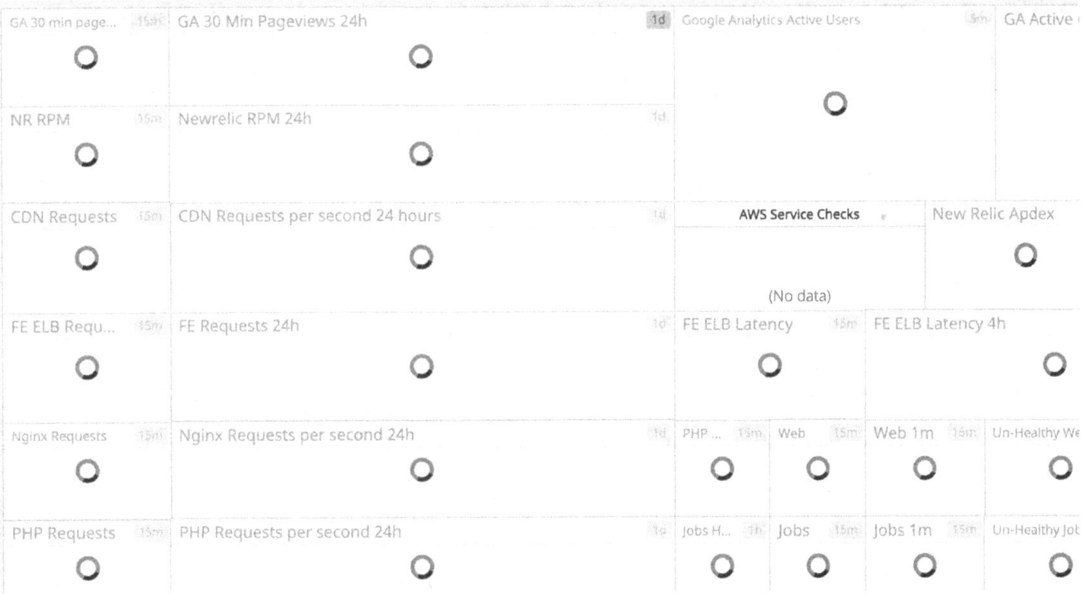

Figure 17-4. *A dashboard graveyard — lots of boxes, mostly spinners, and no data*

Summary

The next step up from reporting is creating visualizations and dashboards. Visualizations can be challenging to conceptualize and build, but an effective visual language is critical. Choosing the right ways to display your data can dramatically influence if and how stakeholders respond to it. Visualizations have a lot in common with reports and should be used in tandem, but the audience and message may vary. Another effective way of bringing people into your data program is to deploy data dashboards of all kinds everywhere possible. Dashboards and reporting visualizations also have much in common, but dashboards have a strong time-based component and heavily prioritize recency. The design discipline around effective dashboard presentation is not fully mature, but there are a number of good practices to follow. Even when dashboards have been created effectively, the program often fails due to logistical challenges of actually deploying those dashboards. In order to create and maintain a culture of data, the presentation of organizational data must be reliable and protected from deterioration.

In the next and last chapter in this part, we'll explore an applied version of the concepts we've discussed for reporting and visualization. To do this, we'll use Google Data Studio, which is directly integrated with BigQuery and can be used effectively on top of the data warehouse.

CHAPTER 18

Google Data Studio

Google Data Studio is Google's own foray into reporting, analytics, and visualization. In this chapter, we will take our survey of reporting and analytics and apply it with real examples of how reporting and dashboards can continue to build your culture of data.

Data Studio has the advantage of being connected directly to BigQuery, so it will be easy to get up and running with your data warehouse. It's also free, which means learning it and following along with the examples will be easier.

Different tools have different strengths and weaknesses across all of the different areas. And as we covered in Chapter 16, many external solutions also integrate with BigQuery in varying ways. Early in your warehouse process, you may have other data sources external to the warehouse that don't integrate as easily with Google Data Studio. Because the number of available solutions is so vast right now, many organizations end up with two or more to cover all of their use cases.

Ultimately, if you aren't satisfied by what Google Data Studio has to offer, don't be discouraged. Following the principles laid out by the previous two chapters, you can make the buy vs. build decision yourself and conduct an effective request for proposal (RFP) process to make the best choice. For what it's worth, Google Data Studio is clearly better at static reports and visualizations. It still has some limitations in data flexibility and presentation. Most data flexibility issues can be resolved by preprocessing the data in BigQuery; for interactive reports, users can still manipulate the end product to get at the data they want.

Google Data Studio is part of the Google Marketing Platform, not Google Cloud Platform.

© Mark Mucchetti 2020
M. Mucchetti, *BigQuery for Data Warehousing*, https://doi.org/10.1007/978-1-4842-6186-6_18

Data Studio Reports with BigQuery

First, hit the console at `https://datastudio.google.com/`. Then click Create and click "Data Source." If you haven't used Data Studio before, it'll take you through the steps to read and sign the user agreement and optionally sign up for newsletters. Once you get through that, you'll be able to proceed to the data source list.

Data Sources

There are a bunch of data sources supported natively by Data Studio and then several hundred more partner connectors. Originally, these connectors skewed pretty heavily to marketing and analytics data, since Data Studio emerged from a Google Analytics-specific tool. Recently, the offerings have expanded to include other kinds of data. A couple others to note besides BigQuery are as follows:

- Google Sheets: You can use this to tie in some of your direct user data that doesn't have a formal connector via BigQuery.

- Build Your Own: You can build your own connections to data, if you need to visualize information that isn't in BigQuery and is a proprietary data source.

- Kaggle: In Chapter 20, we'll look at Kaggle, a machine learning platform that also maintains public datasets and has close integration with Google.

Following the principles of the data warehouse and "source of truth," ideally you would want everything tracked from the same source. But given the cost and latency associated with BigQuery, you may also end up with an intermediate store for reporting data or in some cases going directly to the authoritative situation. These will be implementation considerations.

BigQuery

When you select the BigQuery connector, you'll get four options: My Projects, Shared Projects, Custom Query, and Public Datasets.

My Projects will have you select a billing project, a dataset, and a table to connect.

Shared Projects has you select a billing project and then asks you to specify the external project you want to connect to. If you have your warehouse set up across multiple projects, you can connect to all of them using this method.

Custom Query asks you for a SQL query inline to use as the connection. You can also specify parameters, which will become parameters available to the report. This is a relatively easy way of migrating reports from another system, if you've migrated the underlying tables in a similar schema. The downside is that the SQL for the report will be stuck inside Google Data Studio and be slightly more difficult to maintain.

Public Datasets allows you to connect to public datasets hosted by Google. We'll learn more about these in Chapter 20.

Preparing a Report

After you've selected a table, you proceed to the report creation page. Data Studio behaves oddly if you navigate back and select another table; it treats the connection and fields setup the same. If you want to choose again, clear out and make a new BigQuery "connection."

On this page you have a few options and then the field configurations.

Data Credentials

Data Studio gives you the option to make the viewer authenticate themselves, as opposed to piggybacking on your credentials. If the report has sensitive data (and will not be displayed in a public area), you can select the viewer options.

Data Freshness

The options here are currently 1, 4, and 12 hours. This does limit your ability to do truly real-time dashboards. In any event, BigQuery could get fairly expensive if small pieces of data are queried frequently. For a fully streaming infrastructure, I have also configured data pipelines where the initial stream goes to both BigQuery and some other log-based live dashboard view.

Side note if you want to go faster: While there do not seem to be any official ways to configure Data Studio reports to auto-refresh, the community has produced several scripts and extensions to fill this gap. The highest rated appears to be Data Studio Auto Refresh.[1] In full disclosure, I have not used it extensively and consequently will not formally recommend it. At the very least, it can provide a template of how to use Data Studio in a dashboarding context.

Community Visualizations Access

Here you can decide if you want the report to have access to use community visualizations. Presumably this is in case you don't want your data to be used with visualizations hosted outside of Google. For what it's worth, the visualizations are hosted under a Content Security Policy (CSP) that prevents them from making third-party calls, which would be necessary to funnel your data to an untrusted third party.

We'll discuss community visualizations themselves later on in the chapter.

Fields

Below that, all of the fields from your BigQuery table will be populated. Types will be supplied automatically based on the underlying schema, and default aggregations will be supplied. You'll also get column descriptions if they exist. (You can't add column descriptions while creating the table schema, oddly, but you can supply them afterward or via the JSON schema description. So your columns may not have descriptions unless you happened to go back and add them.)

The schema detector to type is reasonably good, but there are occasionally some issues. For example, it knew a column named "City" should be a geographical city type, but it rendered a GEOGRAPHY column as text.

At this point you can also add additional fields based on this data.

---

[1]https://chrome.google.com/webstore/detail/data-studio-auto-refresh/inkgahcdacjcejipadnndepfllmbgoag

Building a Report

Once the report is connected to the data source, you'll end up on the report building screen. This screen has a lot going on, so a couple of orientation notes first.

Layout

Reports default to a single US Letter page in portrait. Start by clicking the "Theme and Layout" button so you can set this to your preference. For a report that might be printed, landscape or portrait US Letter is best. The other two options are 16:9 for a screen display. You can also set your own size for other paper or screen sizes. I would recommend deciding on this before you actually start placing charts, because it can be a hassle to move everything around.

If you do set up the size for a screen, also note that the default is 1366 × 768, which is suitable for a 720 p TV. Use 1920 × 1080 for a 1080 p TV. You can also go to 2560 × 1440 (1440 p) or 3840 × 2160 (4 K). At much larger canvas sizes, you'll have to adjust the default sizes of elements and other text sizes. Unfortunately, there doesn't seem to be a mode that will auto-arrange and rescale your widgets appropriately. As recommended in the previous chapter, full HD (1080 p) is about the right crispness to allow for as much detail as you should need on a display board.

If you're only looking to print or distribute as a static electronic document, US Letter is the way to go. For paper reports, you can add multiple pages to the report to create a full document. Since you can also place text, you can use this format to create the entire report.

Theme

There are lots of options to choose from here, including full customization and the novel option to extract colors from an image to create a theme. This is a good opportunity to align your report display with your organization's theme colors. As far as overall theme, don't use dark themes for anything that will be printed, but it looks good on boards. (When you export a report to PDF, there is an option to ignore the custom background color, which will prevent the dark background from showing up, but this can also make text harder to read with the different contrast value.)

Report Settings

In the File/Report Settings menu, there are a couple extra options. You'll see your primary data source, which you can edit from here if necessary. You can also set a global date dimension and filters, which will affect all data this report shows.

You can also supply a Google Analytics Tracking ID here. This allows tracking of the report viewing itself. This also creates a loopback to BigQuery, where you can use Google Analytics to track how users are engaging with the reports, which in turn reports that data back to BigQuery so you can do analysis on it. Some features using Google Analytics in Data Studio do require you to have Google Analytics 360, which can be quite pricey. That may be overkill for your organization, but if you're selling your reporting suite to clients, you'll want to know what the adoption looks like. Either way, data and feedback are necessary to improve your data program, so it's something to think about.

Creating Charts

Once the basic layout and design are set, you can start placing charts and text on the report. The basic guidelines are the same as laid out in the previous two chapters; figure out what question this report is answering. Then go from top-left to bottom-right in order of importance.

Designs and Dynamic Data

In addition to charts, it's possible to place text boxes, images from local computer or by URL, and basic lines and shapes. The options aren't especially fancy; however, there is definitely enough to get whatever basic layout is required. The regular grid-snapping guides are available too, so you can drag all your charts into a regular layout.

This is also where some of the shortcomings can become apparent. For example, there's no way to use variables in text boxes, so the text can't be shown dynamically based on the data in the source. (In Chapter 20, we'll explore a fully programmable system for chart creation using Jupyter Notebooks, but obviously this requires more work.)

Another restriction is that when using embedded URLs or images, those connections also only refresh as often as the report. This means some of the creative avenues for dynamic live boards aren't easily available on Data Studio. If the primary intention is to maintain a single tool, this may drive a decision to use a separate tool for dashboarding and possibly also reporting. While Data Studio is a powerful **free** tool, other options are preferable if you want to cover all of the use cases we discussed in the previous two chapters. Looker, for instance, supports displaying the same report views in a constantly refreshing format.

Adding Charts

This may come as a shock, but clicking the "Add a chart" button will open the list of available data types. This can also be done from the Insert menu. Just grab a bar chart and drop it in the panel.

When you do this, a sidebar will slide in from the right with the options for configuring the chart. It looks fairly similar to other report builder interfaces. It will also try to pick a value to use as the dimension, mostly guessing incorrectly. To show the data you're looking for, you'll need at least the dimension and the metric. Dimension is the field you want to measure on the chart; metric is the field that shows how you want to measure it. Accordingly, a bar chart only has one dimension of data, but can have multiple metrics by which to measure it. This might be easier simply slightly inaccurately into dimension labels x-axis, metric labels y-axis.

Let's introduce everyone's favorite example, the sales table. (We'll use a similar construct—but with real-world data—in Chapter 20.) This report can be hooked up to a flattened BigQuery table showing all the sales in your system along with associated metadata. It could actually have hundreds of columns with all kinds of purchase information and be the primary source for sales reports to all departments.

Bar charts are good for comparing categories, so we can take types of sales, categories, or any kind of division of items and make that the "dimension." You can do this by dragging the field into the dimension box or by clicking the dimension box and searching for it.

Then, we have to decide what we want to know about each category. Reasonable things to check would be the number of items we sold in each category, the total dollar value sold for each, or the net profit for each.

Lastly, choose a sort order. You can sort by any numerical field, even if the field isn't displayed on the chart. In some cases your data may have a standard sort order that viewers are used to seeing. In other cases you may want to sort multiple charts by the same field regardless of their appearance. Optional sort fields can be added, which will then be available to the user in view mode.

Fields can be aliased for appearance in labels and legends, which ensures consistency of naming. Styles can also be individually applied. In the case of bar charts, an important toggle is in the style tab—switching between vertical bars (column chart) and horizontal bars (bar chart). This is also where display of the labels on each bar can be controlled. And of course, the actual colors and fonts for the chart are here too. As discussed in previous chapters, don't diverge from the selected report theme unless you have a compelling reason to do so.

Once all is said and done, the report will look like Figure 18-1.

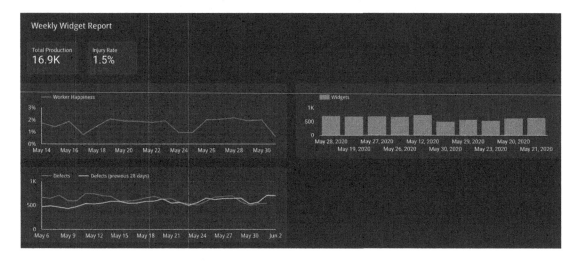

Figure 18-1. *Basic Google Data Studio report*

Click "View" in the upper right, and the report will switch into display mode.

Report Viewing Options

In the view mode, you can test the report to make sure it looks and works the way you intended. This is also where copying and sharing is configured. View mode will also enable filter controls that the user is intended to operate, as well as hovers and drill-downs. For the first few reports, make sure to check all of the additional interactivity like drill-downs and sort fields, to avoid the accidental display of controls that may be irrelevant or sensitive.

Across the top are a few controls to show and productionalize the report.

Full Screen

If this report will be used as a dashboard, test it in full screen mode to ensure it fits properly. As mentioned before, there's no "TV mode" or auto-resize to make the report fit into the screen boundary, so be sure that it looks as expected.

Copying Reports

Copying is more like "templating" in that the report may be copied from the original, but put against a different data source. This would be useful in a scenario where a report or dashboard is needed that is substantially similar to an existing one.

Sharing

From the share window, you can choose who can view or edit the report. This is also a good way to manage security for any public dashboards that may be accessible. Create a dashboarding account that only has view access to these reports and no other privileges. That way, physical access to the machines running the dashboards doesn't compromise any other Google services.

There is also a configuration to schedule email delivery of the report. This system isn't especially robust, but it may be sufficient for basic reporting purposes. If the recipients of each report are frequently changing, you could create and manage distribution lists so you can control the report audience without changing the scheduled delivery.

A couple more caveats: One, the report must come from your email address as opposed to a do-not-reply, which could be extremely inconvenient depending on your organization.[2] Two, the reports can only be configured within your local timezone, which means that to users in other timezones that don't follow Daylight Savings Time, the report may shift an hour forward and backward during the course of a year. This may be preferable, but there's no option to change it. Third, the delivery schedule is a little more limited than schemes we've discussed in previous chapters. If you reach the point where a more complicated schedule is required, it is likely best to avoid the use of this Data Studio–specific scheduler altogether. Lastly, if the report has an error in it, it simply fails to send. This is one of the practices we designed against when using the Cloud Scheduler in Chapter 10.

---

[2] I once had a senior executive commend an extremely diligent employee to me. When I asked why, he replied that this employee was so dedicated that he stayed up to send the nightly reports **precisely** at 2 AM. I didn't have the heart to tell him…

You can also obtain a link to the report. This modal is where more permissive settings for the report can be configured. From this window, access can be broadened to private, where the link can be used by anyone without authentication. The report can also be set to public, which I would not recommend for any reports with a BigQuery backing. Google Data Studio is a great platform on which to publish live public insights about data in your organization, but you will want to harden the data sources and available fields before you consider an action like this. Any public access to a BigQuery-backed report could mean a massive surprise bill. Test these settings before distributing the report to a wide audience of any kind.

Lastly, you can download the report as a PDF. Not many additional options here, though you can password protect the PDF. (You can't actually protect the PDF going out as a scheduled delivery.) If you do intend to email the report, either by schedule or manually, remember that emailing outside the internal corporate network is often not encrypted and that those emails can be intercepted. Be sure to follow any regulatory guidelines for these reports as you do for all other email activity.

Additional Data Studio Concepts

In addition to report creation and publication, Data Studio has some other features that supplement BigQuery or which might even be useful even if not using Data Studio for reporting at all.

Data Studio Explorer

The Data Studio Explorer is a tool that lets you visualize data source results in a single view, where you can manipulate the type of visualization quickly to find the best fit. You can use this tool even if you don't create a Data Studio report with it, just to get a sense of the data you're looking at. Since this option can be invoked directly from BigQuery, you may have already tried it out.

After you run a query in BigQuery, the option to "EXPLORE DATA" appears next to the query results. If you click that and then click "Explore with Data Studio," it will create an "Untitled Explorer" using the query as a data source. This option is also available from inside Data Studio itself on each chart. The view defaults to a table visualization of the query results.

Sometimes, especially with abstract datasets, it's difficult to get a sense of which visualization would be the easiest to understand. Even when you know solid design principles, the best test is to look at it or to have someone else look at it.

The easiest "exploration" to do is just to click all of the different chart types and see how the data is presented. Some will fail; for instance, you can't display a map view if you have no geographic data. Others will collapse into a single row or column, indicating they need an additional dimension of data.

This window also allows you to use pivot tables to quickly manipulate your data. This view will seem fairly familiar if you're used to doing pivoting in Google Sheets.

Bonus Trick: Google Sheets

Speaking of Google Sheets, I've noted on several occasions that Google Sheets isn't a destination for BigQuery exports. If you google how to export BigQuery to Sheets, there are a lot of ways, including writing JavaScript UDFs and using intermediate APIs.

If you click the tricolon menu in the upper right of the visualization pane, there is an option to export the results to Google Sheets. You can use this to relatively painlessly export a BigQuery result to Google Sheets.[3]

Yes, I did try it on a multi-gigabyte public dataset, and as soon as I exceeded a certain number of columns, it crashed and burned. I was left with a series of empty "Untitled spreadsheets" last edited by anonymous. It wasn't totally clear what the boundary was, as it handled a few hundred thousand cells without a problem. This is really useful for the casual sharing of query results outside of Google Cloud Platform, though, and it does allow you to export more than the BigQuery UI.

At scale, you can use the Connected Sheets feature of G Suite, though this requires the business- or enterprise-level license.[4] If you need to share large datasets in this way—and I can think of a few cases—this hacky solution is not ideal.

---

[3]You can save results to Sheets from the BigQuery UI, up to a maximum of 16,000 records.
[4]https://cloud.google.com/blog/products/g-suite/
connecting-bigquery-and-google-sheets-to-help-with-hefty-data-analysis

Blending Data

You can create data sources that combine fields from multiple underlying data sources. This is functionally equivalent to a SQL LEFT OUTER JOIN, but it works across all available data sources. It's available in both the report creation view and the explorer.

Below the current data source, click "Blend Data." A pane will come up from the bottom with the data source on the left. Then, click "Add another data source," and a second data source view will appear. Select the source and then supply "join keys," which are the same as the ON clause. You can use a composite join key, that is, multiple dimensions, which obviously must match in number and value.

Blended sources currently support only the LEFT OUTER JOIN operation. To simulate an INNER JOIN, apply additional filters (as you would a WHERE clause) to remove the rows that don't have matching join keys. To simulate a RIGHT OUTER JOIN, blend the sources in the opposite order.

Self-joins are possible, or, in this nomenclature, blending a data source with itself. This could be used to simulate basic analytic functions in the same way subqueries do. Essentially, the aggregation you choose on the results of the blend represents something equivalent to an analytic aggregation.

If you aren't connecting BigQuery and non-BigQuery sources, or you exceed this level of complexity, it's probably best to additionally prepare your data in BigQuery before using it as a data source in Data Studio. The maximum number of sources which can be joined together is five.

Blended data sources aren't available as data sources in their own right; they only exist with respect to the reports you use them in. Keep this in mind during the next area, around calculated fields.

Calculated Fields

If there are data values that are useful to your reports, or specific charts inside of them, you can use calculated fields. While any aggregate value that is of general use might be better as an addition to the BigQuery table or query itself, you will likely have the need of specific calculations for the benefit of an individual report. Calculated fields can also be added to blended data sources, which is a huge help for calculating anything useful about the join. This is the easiest way to do ratios or sums across datasets.

Calculated fields can be used either at data source level or at the chart level. Which to use depends on whether you have the permissions to edit the data source itself and whether you consider this calculated field to be of use beyond the chart itself.

If you edit a data source, you'll see "Add a Field" in the upper-right corner. Clicking that will open a formula box to allow you to create the new field. You can combine any of the fields from the existing data source using formulas. The full function list is fairly comprehensive[5] and resembles some combination of SQL, Google Sheets, and some custom functions. A few standouts that don't resemble anything we've covered with SQL are as follows.

TOCITY (REGION, COUNTRY…)

You can automatically apply functions to blow out ISO country and region codes into their full values, that is, US-CA ➤ California. Some of the functions additionally take geography types, allowing you to group by geography as a dimension, even if your original dataset only contained coordinate values.

IMAGE

Using the IMAGE function, you can embed image URLs as fields in your data sources. This lets you display helpful graphical guides within your visualizations.

HYPERLINK

You can create a custom field that has a URL in it using the HYPERLINK function. This way, you can embed links to the source data in your tables. For example, if your report tracked the performance of various product sales, you could embed a link back to the product detail page from the report itself. You could also use this to link into other reports or other reporting systems entirely.

LEFT/RIGHT_TEXT

The LEFT_TEXT and RIGHT_TEXT functions truncate strings to their leftmost or rightmost n characters. This is handy when you need a prefix or suffix and don't want to calculate it out with SUBSTR. (Adherents of Microsoft SQL Server will recall the LEFT and RIGHT functions, which have the same purpose.)

---

[5]https://support.google.com/datastudio/table/6379764?hl=en

Community Add-Ons

Data Studio has a burgeoning community of third-party developers. At this time, it's possible to build both custom connectors and custom visualizations to use within Data Studio. Between the two, it should be possible to greatly extend your ability to visualize data.

If Data Studio is your tool of choice for reporting, this may be something worth pursuing. This could be especially useful when migrating a previous reporting suite. A custom connector might be used if there is some data that is not available through BigQuery but is currently used in the reporting framework. You could even blend it with your BigQuery data source. For custom visualizations, it would be possible to replicate any custom UI the previous suite utilized. In a scenario where Data Studio is **almost** good enough for your needs, customization could bridge the gap.

The instructions for both custom connectors[6] and visualizations[7] are comprehensive. Both contain CodeLabs that you can complete in less than an hour and which should give you a pretty good idea of how to construct custom add-ons.

There are a pretty good number of third-party data connectors, largely to marketing and advertising platforms, as well as social analytics data.

As for visualizations, this capability is still in developer preview as of this writing, and there isn't a whole lot to choose from yet. There are already some dashboard-type visualizations like gauges, candlesticks, and funnels.

If you're familiar with raw visualization libraries like chart.js and d3.js, you can use these in the creation of your own visualizations. Even if you're not, d3 has a huge following and countless gorgeous-looking visualizations.[8] These are now available for inspiration and adaptation for display within Data Studio. (Be sure to check the licensing model before duplicating someone else's work.)

Google Analytics

If you use Google Analytics to track the performance of your site, you may already be familiar with Data Studio from that context. As discussed previously, Data Studio is a Google Marketing Platform product because it originated as a premium tool for visualizing data coming from Google Analytics.

---

[6]https://developers.google.com/datastudio/connector/get-started
[7]https://developers.google.com/datastudio/visualization
[8]https://github.com/d3/d3/wiki/Gallery

Using Google Analytics 360, it is also possible to set up a connection to export your data directly to BigQuery. This means you could get your Google Analytics data in Data Studio via BigQuery or directly from Analytics. Chances are you want to do the latter for cost-related reasons. However, you may also want to pipe the Google Analytics data to BigQuery for use in more advanced analytics or as a combined data source with other BigQuery items.

This creates a unique scenario where Google Analytics data is visualized in Data Studio both behaving like a data mart for the authoritative source (Google Analytics itself) and also as a data warehouse from the system of record. Whether this special case is relevant to you depends on how important analytics data is to the operation of your business.

BigQuery BI Engine

When using BigQuery and Data Studio together, you may have noticed the lightning bolt in the upper-right corner. This icon signifies that the BigQuery BI Engine is in use for the query. The BI Engine is essentially an in-memory accelerator for BigQuery tables. It is designed to eliminate the latency you might experience when doing lots of interactive slicing and dicing on data stored in BigQuery. Since it's only available with Data Studio, it can only help to accelerate reports you are building there. In Google's description of the product, it cagily states that "BI Engine is currently only available for use with Data Studio,"[9] suggesting that this tool may at some point become available for other purposes.[10]

The reason you see the lightning bolt even if you haven't purchased or looked at the BI Engine console is because there is an automatic 1 GB free tier for Data Studio to BigQuery connections. Google indicates that this is not intended to run production workloads, but since it turns on automatically you may end up engaging it anyway.

Most importantly, queries that only hit the BI Engine are not charged for reading data. This means that if your datasets fit within the 1 GB free space (or whatever space you opt to pay for), then your reports won't rack up any BigQuery billing after the data is initially cached. If your Data Studio query doesn't fit in your reserved space, then it overflows into regular BigQuery, and you are charged for any bytes it needs to scan in the process.

---

[9]https://cloud.google.com/bi-engine/docs/overview

[10]There is a blog entry from 2019 at https://cloud.google.com/blog/products/data-analytics/google-cloud-smart-analytics-accelerates-your-business-transformation that mentions future availability for Looker and Tableau, so this is a pretty good bet.

In order to see reservations you have purchased, go to the BigQuery console and click "BI Engine" on the left sidebar. From here you are also able to purchase additional memory to store datasets. The cap is currently 100 GB, which will cost you several thousand dollars a month. You also get reserved BI Engine capacity bundled in if you have a flat rate for slots (see Chapter 4).

Google manages the distribution of queries among BI Engine, BigQuery cache, and BigQuery itself. This means that you don't have to handle an additional data transformation pipeline to bring your data back out of BigQuery into live streaming. If you're already trying to solve the problem of accelerating data for reporting and dashboard purposes, and you already use Data Studio, this fits the bill. It will certainly be interesting to see if Google expands the ability to use the BI Engine to other dashboarding tools.

Summary

Google Data Studio is a free visualization tool for reporting and dashboarding. Part of the Google Marketing Platform, it allows for real-time connections to a number of data sources including BigQuery. You can configure and add all types of visualizations to create engaging reports or digital views. Data Studio has some limitations for updating data on a real-time basis, which may be a consideration based on your use case. It also supports some features resembling the data manipulation that BigQuery or Google Sheets can do, for example, the basic joining, filtering, and aggregation of data. You can use these features to seamlessly incorporate BigQuery data into reports.

It turns out that BigQuery has one last major trick to show us. In the next chapter, we'll make the jump over to the world of data science and machine learning with BigQuery ML.

PART VI

Enhancing Your Data's Potential

CHAPTER 19

BigQuery ML

In this chapter, we will look at how to train and utilize machine learning models using BigQuery directly.

BigQuery ML (BQML) became generally available on Google Cloud Platform in May of 2019. The aim is to open machine learning models to a wider audience of users. Accordingly, BQML allows you to specify and run machine learning models directly in SQL. In most cases, you don't need extensive understanding of the code required to produce these models, but a background in the concepts will still be helpful. Machine learning uses fairly accessible mathematical concepts, but as they are abstracted over many variables and iterations, the details get more difficult.

The next chapter will introduce Jupyter Notebooks, which will give a sense of how data science is typically done. The notebook concept now interoperates with Google's AI Platform and BigQuery, so you can switch among the tools you're most comfortable with. Before going into Python data analysis, we'll go over the basic concepts using SQL in this chapter.

The crossover between data science and traditional business intelligence is the future of the field. Machine learning concepts have begun to pervade every industry. The power they've already demonstrated is astonishing. Within a few short years, classification and object detection algorithms have evolved to a high rate of success. Machine learning succeeds in places where humans might be unable to conceptualize a solution to a problem. Given some data analysis and some educated guessing, the model learns how to solve the problem on its own.

In June 2018, the GPT-2 text prediction model was released by the DeepMind AI Research Lab. This model is a general-purpose text generator capable of producing writing in nearly any format. Given a prompt, it will produce a plausible continuation of the text. *This model can also take inspiration from the writer and will try to convey that writer's style.* In fact, the italicized sentence was written by GPT-2. If you don't believe me, try it for yourself and see.[1]

---

[1] `www.talktotransformer.com/` has an online version of the full-sized GPT-2 model.

© Mark Mucchetti 2020
M. Mucchetti, *BigQuery for Data Warehousing*, https://doi.org/10.1007/978-1-4842-6186-6_19

In April of 2020, OpenAI trained a neural net to generate raw audio containing music and even singing, based on training models consisting of numerical representations of music datasets and the text of the lyrics.[2] In some cases it produces entirely new songs. While this is similarly impressive right now, we're still only seeing the first fruits of machine learning.

This chapter has two goals: First is to introduce the basic concepts of machine learning to make BQML feel a little less magical. The second goal is to show you ways you can solve business problems with BQML. Both will increase your preparation for an increasingly ML-driven world and the new skill sets that data jobs require.

Fair warning: This chapter does vary both in tone and difficulty from the rest of the book. While BQML is easy to use, the underlying machine learning concepts are complex and are grounded in subject matter which is disparate from the rest of this book.

If this topic is of interest to you, there are several Apress books that explore this topic in significantly more detail.

Background

Machine learning and artificial intelligence are heavily burdened terms crossing multiple disciplines within mathematics and computer science. Before even delving into how to apply machine learning, let's wade into the morass of ambiguous and confusing terminology.

Artificial Intelligence

Marketers often use the term "artificial intelligence," or AI, and in recent years have begun to use the terms AI and machine learning (ML) interchangeably. As you may have heard, AI and ML are not the same thing.

History

Artificial intelligence has been a trope of human thought since antiquity. Over the centuries, AI appeared as a by-product of mythology, alchemy, or mechanical engineering. The intersection between artificial intelligence and prototypical computer

---

[2]https://openai.com/blog/jukebox/

science comes quite early. The story of the "Mechanical Turk" (the namesake of the Amazon product) tells of an 18th-century machine that could play chess. It enjoyed great success on multiple world tours, playing Benjamin Franklin, Napoleon, and other contemporary luminaries.[3] Of course, the Mechanical Turk was in reality a person hidden underneath the table moving the pieces via magnets. However, in 1819, the Turk was encountered by Charles Babbage, the person who would later go on to invent the first mechanical computer. Babbage guessed that the Mechanical Turk was probably not an automaton. Nevertheless, it seems likely that the Turk was in his mind as he produced his first Analytical Engine in the 1830s. While Babbage invented the machine itself, the first person to truly see its potential as a thinking machine was his partner Ada Lovelace. Lovelace is the namesake of the programming language Ada and defensibly the first computer programmer.

The term "artificial intelligence" itself didn't come into existence until 1955, when computer scientist John McCarthy coined the term.[4] Since then, the term has proliferated into modern pop culture, inspiring authors like Isaac Asimov and in turn sentient synthetic lifelike *Star Trek*'s Mr. Data. The term is in general currency now to the point that it describes, essentially, computers performing any task that was typically done by humans. As a relative definition, it also means that it shifts as technology changes. In 1996, Deep Blue, the IBM chess-playing computer, famously defeated the world-reigning champion, Garry Kasparov, for the first time. At the time, this was the vanguard of AI. Some accounts of the time even claim that Deep Blue passed the Turing Test.[5] As our capabilities grow and various entities persist in the claim that their simulations have passed the Turing Test,[6] this definition has continued to grow and expand. In short, the term is weighted and conveys a great many things.

---

[3]https://spectrum.ieee.org/tech-talk/tech-history/dawn-of-electronics/untold-history-of-ai-charles-babbage-and-the-turk

[4]www.aaai.org/ojs/index.php/aimagazine/article/view/1904/1802

[5]www.washingtonexaminer.com/weekly-standard/be-afraid-9802 (It did not. The standard formulation of a Turing Test requires a dialogue between the tester and the computer; the tester must not know which they are conversing with.)

[6]www.bbc.com/news/technology-27762088

Machine Learning

Machine learning (ML) appears in the title of an IBM research paper by scientist Arthur Samuel in 1959,[7] where he suggested that "Programming computers to learn from experience should eventually eliminate the need for much...programming effort."[8] This seems like a natural approach to artificial intelligence as an extension of the idea that humans gain intelligence through learning.

Essentially, ML is an approach to solving problems in the AI field. A coarse way to state this is to say that it uses data as an input to learn. This is obviously an oversimplification, as other AI techniques have inputs too. However, machine learning techniques build their models over the input of real observational data. Intriguingly, this also gives them a purpose that is somewhat distinct from classical AI. Typically, the standard for AI is to do things "like humans," maybe faster or better, but still in a recognizably human way. Science fiction stories turn to horror when rogue AIs decide to take over. Whatever means they choose to do this, they still exhibit recognizably human motivations and ambitions.

Machine learning, on the other hand, is "interested" only in using data to create a model that effectively predicts or classifies things. The method by which it does this is not inherently important. Data scientists prioritize the characteristic of "interpretability," meaning the model can be dissected and understood by humans, but this sometimes requires explicitly incentivizing a model to do so.

Interpretability

In a well-known example from 2017, Facebook researchers trained chatbots to barter basic objects such as books and hats with each other.[9] In the initial model, the chatbots negotiated only with themselves and not other humans. After some time, they began to communicate using exchanges that appeared completely nonsensical to humans, such as "I can can I I everything else" and "Balls have zero to me to me to me..." This resulted in a lot of breathless media coverage about how the robots were evolving their own language. They would accordingly take over the world, bent on enslaving humanity to make their books, balls, and hats for all eternity.

---

[7]https://citeseerx.ist.psu.edu/viewdoc/summary?doi=10.1.1.368.2254

[8]Ibid.

[9]https://engineering.fb.com/ml-applications/deal-or-no-deal-training-ai-bots-
  to-negotiate/

In reality, this model was simply not easily "interpretable" by humans. The algorithm drifted away simply because there was no incentive for the chatbots to use English. The researchers tweaked the algorithm to reward humanlike speech, creating a more interpretable and slightly less effective model.

In its quest for optimization, machine learning will take any path that improves its results. There are several entertaining examples where machine learning models (and other artificial intelligence) exploit the simulations themselves to produce unintended but "correct" results.[10] One common theme is that the model will learn to delete its inputs altogether and produce an empty output set. In doing so, these models score perfectly over the zero evaluated outputs. For example, a model optimized to sort lists simply emitted empty lists, which are technically sorted. In another similar example, the candidate program deleted all of the target files, ensuring a perfect score on the zero files it had processed.[11] (There is an odd parallel to the AI from the 1983 movie *WarGames*, who discovers that "the only winning move is not to play." Riffing off of this, the researcher Tom Murphy, teaching an algorithm to play Tetris, found that the algorithm would pause the game forever to avoid losing.[12])

Statistics

Machine learning isn't just statistics, either. Understanding statistical methods is important to building good machine models, but the aims of each are not fully congruent. The relationship between statistics and ML is somewhat like the relationship between computer science and software engineering. The theoretical/applied gap comes into play in a big way.

Statistics is mathematically rigorous and can be used to express some confidence about how a certain system behaves. It's used academically as a building block to produce accurate conclusions about the reason that data looks the way it does. Machine learning, on the other hand, is most concerned with iterating to a model that takes input and produces the correct output. Additional input is used to refine the algorithm. The focus is much less on the "why" and more on how to get the algorithm to produce useful results.

---

[10]https://vkrakovna.wordpress.com/2018/04/02/specification-gaming-examples-in-ai/
[11]https://arxiv.org/abs/1803.03453
[12]www.youtube.com/watch?v=x0CurBYI_gY#t=15m50s

Of course, ML practitioners use statistics and statisticians use ML methods. There's too much overlap for this to be a useful comparison, but it comes up a lot and is worth touching upon. To the math/CS analogy, imagine wanting to know the circumference of a circle. Inevitably, the value of π arises in the process. In the algorithmic view, it's a means to an end—we want to derive a sufficiently accurate value to calculate the circumference of any circles we may encounter. We could do this with measurement or a Monte Carlo method and create a ratio between circumference and diameter that we'd be quite happy with. However, from the mathematical perspective, we want to prove the value of π itself to show "why" it arises in so many contexts and how it is related to other mathematical concepts.

There's an interpretability factor here, as well. ML models, unless incentivized to do so, can produce pretty opaque results. It may not be trivial or even possible to understand why a model produces extremely accurate predictions or descriptions of certain phenomena. We may apply a statistical method to a machine learning model in retrospect and discover that it's extremely accurate and still not know why. Statistics, on the other hand, has the ability to formulate intelligent conclusions that help us understand the phenomena under study and their possible origins or relations to other disciplines. And that's about as granular as is sensical.

Ethics

A discussion of machine learning requires some review of the ethical implications. As custodians of data, we may have access to privileged information including financial or health information, private correspondence, or even classified data. In the aggregate, we may not think much about the value of each data point. However, machine learning models have the potential to affect millions of lives both positively and negatively. Before we jump into BQML, here's a quick refresher.

Implicit Bias

Implicit bias refers to unconscious feelings or attitudes that influence people's behaviors or decisions. These attitudes are often formed starting an early age by messages from surroundings or from the media.

When it comes to machine learning, these biases can find their way into the training models in nonobvious ways. One example is if certain language carries coded meaning that is more often used to describe people of particular classes. An ML model might pick up on these distinctions and amplify a bias where none was intended. This could adversely affect a scoring or prediction model, like an application for a loan or a hiring candidate.

Disparate Impact

When a machine learning model is implemented that contains these biases, it can create the possibility for disparate impact. This arises when a seemingly neutral decision-making process unfairly impacts a certain group of people. This could happen very easily—say that certain data points are more commonly missing for certain classes of people, either due to data collection methods or cultural sensitivity. Dropping those data points could cause the affected people to be underrepresented in the data model.

Another scenario highlights a deficiency of statistical learning models. What if the built model in fact contains no implicit bias and correctly represents the state of the world? This may reveal ugly imbalances that do not represent the world as we hope or wish it to be. In that case, the machine learning model is doing exactly what it is "supposed" to do, but it does not get us where we are trying to go.

Responsibility

Many practicing professions require licensure—lawyers, doctors, architects, and civil engineers come to mind. Software and data engineering generally do not, with scant few exceptions. A code of ethics for software engineers was approved in 1999 by the IEEE-CS/ACM Joint Task Force and clearly lays out the professional obligations of software engineers.[13] Terms like "big data" and "cloud computing" were still several years in the future, but computer scientists had a good idea of what lay ahead.

Careless or malicious code can cause catastrophic loss of monetary value or human life.[14] The twist with machine learning, as applies to both interpretability and power, is that it can take actions humans might consider unethical, even when programmed by humans with the best intentions. It's too easy to say "the algorithm did it" when something goes awry. This may sound preachy, but the ease of integration brings this power so close to hand. When it's all there at your command, it's easy to forget to think about your responsibility in the equation. To the preceding question

---

[13]https://ethics.acm.org/code-of-ethics/software-engineering-code/
[14]Seminal example: www.ccnr.org/fatal_dose.html

of disparate impact, the code of ethics states it directly: "Moderate the interests of the software engineer, the employer, the client and the users with the public good."[15]

BigQuery ML Concepts

BigQuery ML follows a theme familiar to other services we've discussed—it takes a concept from another domain and implements it using familiar SQL. This makes it accessible to data analysts who may not have substantial experience with machine learning. It also provides a gentle slope into more complex topics by allowing the direct implementation of TensorFlow models. As your skill naturally grows through application, you can take on more advanced implementations. In the following chapter, our examples will be in Python as we survey the data science landscape outside of BigQuery.

BQML implements a natural extension to SQL to allow for prediction and classification without leaving the BigQuery console. However, you probably will want to, in order to visualize your results or to work with the model training directly. In general, BQML is great for creating inline models that you can use without a deep understanding of either statistics or machine learning. Options like AutoML and TensorFlow (which we'll look at in the next chapter) become more appropriate as your investment in ML techniques grows.

Cost

If you are on a flat-rate plan (see Chapter 4), your BQML costs are included with your plan, so you can skip over this. Matrix factorization, in beta as of this writing, is only available through a flat-rate plan or flex slots.

The cost calculations follow the same rules as regular BigQuery for storage and querying, including ML analysis. The free tier includes the same amount of storage and data processing, and any ML queries you run on existing models will be factored into that price.

Machine learning of any type can get expensive pretty quickly. This shouldn't be a deterrent—the free tier is more than enough for learning the ropes and doing some decent-scale models. (At least in BQML. AutoML Tables, which we'll cover in the next chapter, has a free trial but no free tier.) As with cost analysis for BigQuery as a whole,

---

[15]See footnote 13.

assess your intended scale and usage and decide what makes sense. At anything approaching the upper end, you'll be working with Google instead of paying list price, anyway—tell them I told you to give them a discount. (Your results may vary.)

Creating Models

With model creation, there are some additional costs. BQML model creation (i.e., any job including a "CREATE MODEL" statement) is billed at a different rate and has a different free allotment. The free tier is currently 10 GB of processing data during model creation, after which the price (as of this writing) goes to $250/TB for US multi-region. Recall that multi-region is cheaper than single region because the query can be redistributed according to need.

This creates two separate problems for cost tracking. First, since ML analysis and queries are bundled into the regular analysis pricing, there's no simple way to separate your ML analysis costs. It might seem like there is no reason to do this, but when a cost-conscious executive suggests that artificial intellige-ma-what is costing the company an arm and a leg, it could be useful to be able to separate those costs. (Of course, on a flat-rate plan it's all "data warehouse" anyway.)

The second issue is that model creation costs are not itemized at all—on your monthly statement, they're going to get bundled in with the rest of the BigQuery costs, even though model creation is billed at a different rate. There is some documentation that implies that this limitation will change at some point, and perhaps queries that invoke ML functionality will also get a separate line item.

If you are really interested in how to show individual model creation costs, you'll have to go into Cloud Logging (see Chapter 12). The BQML documentation has a tutorial[16] on how to do this. No doubt, there is a fun infinite loop (and infinite bill) for those who want to use BQML to predict how much they will spend on BQML over time.[17]

Flex Slots

Flex slots are a new pricing concept that is essentially a time-bounded flat-rate pricing. The minimum reservation is only 60 seconds, and slots are charged per second. This pricing model is considerably more expensive over the long term than actual flat rate—

---

[16]https://cloud.google.com/bigquery-ml/pricing#bqmlexamples

[17]Don't try this at home.

46% at list price for US multi-region. However, for short-term or bounded needs, it can be used without requiring a full flat-rate commitment or reservations.

Any models that use matrix factorization are only available via flat rate, reservations, or flex slots. While flex slots are still basically a "pay-as-you-go" model, it's worth planning ahead of time how much you intend to use these models and what the right approach is.

Since it's only the CREATE MODEL calls that are billed separately, it might be possible to create a factorization model using flex slots and then utilize its predictions with regular BigQuery. I did not personally attempt this, but it seems like a possibility.

Supervised vs. Unsupervised Learning

BQML supports two major classes of learning models, supervised and unsupervised. The major difference between the two types is simply whether the model has access to "ground truth"—essentially, objective reality measured empirically. You can use a combination of both or even use unsupervised model results as ground truth for supervised models.

Supervised Models

In a supervised model, you supply some data which is already labeled, that is, it contains both the input and your expected output. Regression is a good example of a supervised model; in order to predict numerical values, the model needs to know existing data relationships. For example, to predict home prices, a regression model needs to know the historical prices of houses sold, as well as other salient features of the data. This is the "ground truth" for a supervised model. By testing your supervised model on facts you know, but your model has not yet seen, you can test its accuracy.

The literature varies on an appropriate split for the test data into its constituent groups. It also depends on the size and shape of the test data, but a good rule of thumb is 80/20: 80% of the data goes to the training model, and 20% of the data goes to validation. BQML has a slightly more robust model based on the data size:

- Less than 500 rows: 100% of data goes to validation.

- Between 500 and 50,000 rows: 80% of data goes to training and 20% to validation.

- Over 50,000 rows: More than 80% of data goes to training; 10,000 rows go to validation.

You can set this directly if you want, either with a percentage or with a BOOL column to say whether the row is for training or evaluation.

Supervised models typically have an additional split in the test data between validation (biased testing while tuning) and testing (unbiased data the model doesn't see until the end). AutoML Tables, which we'll talk about in the next chapter, lets you add a column to specify directly which of the three you want each row to do. AutoML Tables also uses a default of 80/10/10 (training/validation/testing).

Unsupervised Models

Unsupervised models, by contrast, don't have any labeled data. Generally this is because there is no specifically desired outcome. Unsupervised models will search for and extract relationships in the data and then produce clusters or detect anomalies in the data. BQML natively supports k-means clustering, which is covered in more detail in the following, followed by an example.

Unsupervised model results are often useful as a subsequent input to supervised models. They can be used to create groups of similar data points, and then that grouping can be used as an additional feature in a supervised model to increase its predictive capability. Of course, it can amplify biases in the unsupervised results too.

On their own, unsupervised models are well suited to identifying patterns unseen to human observers. Fraud detection, data loss prevention, or unusual system behaviors can all be detected by unsupervised models.

Model Types

BQML supports the most common types of both supervised and unsupervised models. There are other types of models and plenty of other variants on the ones given in the following.

Note This section contains a lot of math and statistics to illustrate how the various models and metrics work. Don't let that scare you off—they're not necessary for comprehension, and in fact you can use BigQuery ML without much of this information at all. However, your ML intuition will be much stronger if you understand how to assess the performance of your model. This is especially good if you have limited resources and want to stop when you believe the results are "good enough."

Linear Regression Models

Linear regression models are supervised models which generate a function to predict output based on input. Generally, the input features will predict a target value using the function that the model computed.

It works just like a statistical linear regression. Known data points are plotted ("ground truth"), and then a line of best fit is found. Since this technique is mathematical, the labeled inputs must all be real numbers. You can address yes/no variables by assigning them numerical values like {1.0, 0.0}, and you can address variables with a fixed number of choices as {0.0, 1.0, 2.0, ...}. BQML will do this for you automatically.

Linear regressions can be done over multiple variables. In statistics, you take real information about your data and use it to choose appropriate variables. The goal of the statistical analysis is to come up with intelligent theories about which variables are responsible for changing the outcome. In machine learning, you throw every possible combination at it, potentially thousands or millions of terms. You run them all and see how it goes. If the model predicts better with half the variables removed, you take them out and try again. This would be considered a pretty severe lack of rigor as a statistical practice. In machine learning, it's looking over the largest possible problem space to get the most predictive function. This isn't brute force, exactly, but it definitely takes advantage of modern parallelization and computation to examine as many results as it can.

RMSE

The statistical methods used to determine the fitness of the function can also be used on machine learning. The most basic measure is RMSE, or root mean square error. RMSE measures how close the data is to the line of best fit (in this case, the best fit being produced by the ML regression model). Figure 19-1 shows a visualization.

Predicted vs. Actual

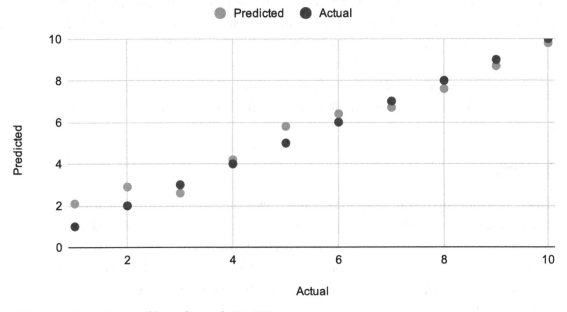

Figure 19-1. *Line of best fit with RMSE*

You can calculate RMSE, although you don't have to since BQML will do it for you. Over millions of rows and columns, it won't exactly be fun. Anyway, the formula looks complicated but is actually pretty simple:

$$\sqrt{\frac{\sum_{i=1}^{n}(p_i - o_i)^2}{n}}$$

If you prefer algorithms:

- For each point in the set

    - Subtract the observed value from the predicted value.

    - Square it.

- Find the average of all of these squares.

- Take the square root of that average.

RMSE is an example of a "loss function," since for a set it tells you exactly how much fidelity is sacrificed by using this linear regression model. Improving linear regression models means optimizing the loss function, and thus a lower RMSE means a better model.

This will come up in the next chapter as well, but if your RMSE is zero, that is probably not a good thing. A perfect fit means your test data and your predictions are an exact match. This is referred to as "overfitting"—the model corresponds so well with its training data that either there is an obvious relationship somewhere or it will be brittle when it encounters new data.

Overfitting

If there is an obvious relationship somewhere, this is often referred to as "data leakage." Data leakage is a problem with a supervised model where some features accidentally expose information about the target value. This leads the model to pick up a relationship that won't be present in real-world data. The model will likely be useless in the real world, because the features it determined to calculate the best fit won't be present or will not follow the pattern.

A great example of this is when the row number of the data makes it into the model. For example, say you want to predict how many people in a given zip code will purchase a specific product this year. One good training input might be the purchases by zip code from last year, so you prep the data. However, it is accidentally sorted by increasing number of purchases and also contains the original row number from the source table. So row 1 is someone who purchased $0 last year, and the last row is the biggest spender. The regression analysis is going to detect that there is a strong correlation between "row number" and total spending. Essentially this is like saying, "Oh, those row number 1s. They never buy anything!" Your real-world datasets aren't going to come with row number labels—that information only exists retrospectively as the data was collected. But that model would probably score an RMSE of pretty close to zero, and not for the reasons you want.[18]

Classification Models

The other major type of supervised model is the classification model. In a classification model, the goal is to classify data so that the result predicts a binary or categorical outcome.

---

[18]Depending on the evenness of the distribution of the data.

The canonical example is spam filtering. In a spam filter algorithm, the features would be things like email body, subject line, from address, headers, time of day, and so on. The output from the binary classifier would be "spam" or "not spam." Similarly, you could predict a category based on the input. For example, computer vision often uses images or videos of real objects (supervision) and then can train itself to categorize pictures of other objects. If you train a supervised classification algorithm on five different kinds of trees, the output will be able to receive a picture as input and respond with a classification (i.e., oak, birch, pine, jungle, acacia).

BigQuery ML's classification algorithm works by performing a regression analysis as mentioned earlier.[19] Once it does this, it divides up the space into discrete areas and will run future inputs through the function, returning the value associated with the space it fell into. To look at it visually, as we did with the linear regression, look at Figure 19-2.

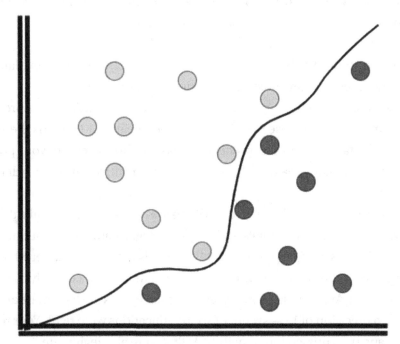

Figure 19-2. *Classification model*

At its most basic, a classification model is a linear regression model with discrete outputs. There's an underlying prediction value (i.e., this email is 0.4 SPAM so therefore it is not spam). Confidence values can be obtained in that way.

---

[19]There are many other types of classification models that do not have an underlying regression model.

You can also test the model in a similar way, by simply assessing what percentage of classifications were made correctly on the test data. This has a drawback, which is that it doesn't take into account the data distribution. If data is strongly imbalanced between "yes" and "no," then the model could be right solely by predicting that answer every time. For example, if 99% of customers are repeat purchasers, and the model says "yes" to every input, it will be 99% correct, which looks good, but reflects the data more than the model. This metric is called "accuracy" in ML, and it's necessary but not sufficient.

Precision and Recall

An additional way to show the performance of a classification model is to look at false positives and negatives as well as correct predictions ("accuracy"). (You may recognize these as Type I and Type II errors from statistics. In machine learning, these ideas are captured in two terms, known as precision and recall. Recall is sometimes known as sensitivity, but BQML is consistent in the use of recall.)

Judging by the amount of blog entries and web pages purporting to explain the definitions of these terms, they must be challenging to understand.

Precision and recall are both measured on a scale of 0.0–1.0. A perfect precision of 1.0 means that there were no false positives. A perfect recall of 1.0 means there were no false negatives. Stated in reverse, precision measures how accurate your positive identifications were. Recall measures how many of the positive truths you identified (labeled as positive).

The extreme cases are useful here in describing the boundaries. Let's take the preceding spam example. Say you have ten emails and they're all legitimate. By definition, precision is going to be 1.0 as long as a single positive identification is made—no matter which emails you say are legitimate, you're right. However, for every email you incorrectly class as spam, the recall score drops. At the end, if you say six of the ten emails are legitimate and four are spam, you have a precision of 1.0—six out of six identifications were right. Your recall is only 0.6 though, because you missed four emails (0.4) that were also legitimate.

Same example, but opposite case. Now you have ten emails, and they're all spam. In this case, if you identify even a single email as legitimate, your precision will be 0.0, because every email you identified as legitimate was spam. Recall, on the other hand, will be 1.0 no matter what you do, because you found all of the zero positive results without doing anything. So if you make the same determination—six emails legitimate, four spam—those are the results you'd get: 0.0 precision, 1.0 recall.

Because this concept can be so tricky, let's look at a more formal matrix in Figure 19-3.

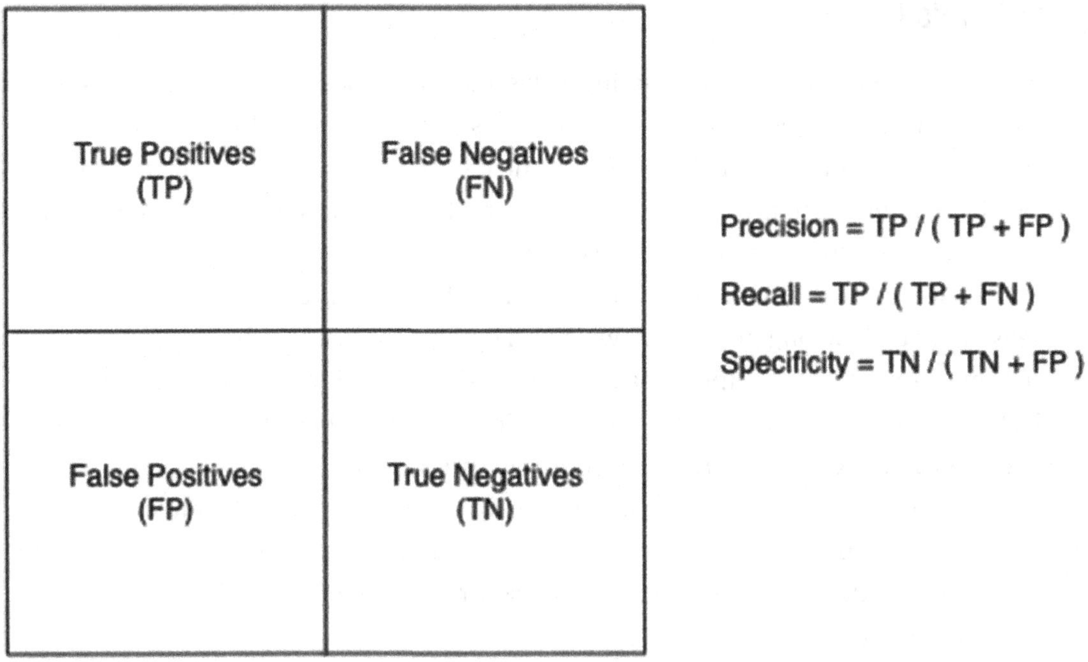

True Positives (TP)	False Negatives (FN)
False Positives (FP)	True Negatives (TN)

Precision = TP / (TP + FP)

Recall = TP / (TP + FN)

Specificity = TN / (TN + FP)

Figure 19-3. *Confusion matrix followed by calculations*

This is sometimes referred to as a confusion matrix, which is intended to refer to the classification of the dataset and not its reader.

You may also have noticed one odd thing about the preceding cases, which is that following this formula, the recall calculation appears to produce division by zero. By convention, since we're actually talking about sets here and not numbers, this question is really asking what ratio of items in the set were identified—the denominator set is empty (∅) so recall is 1.0.

This also illustrates why both precision and recall are necessary to see how accurately a model worked as a classifier. Generally, as you try to increase precision to avoid making an inaccurate result, recall goes down because you didn't get all the results. If you go for broke and just return every item in the set, your recall will be perfect but your precision will be terrible.

When you evaluate a logistic model using BQML, it will automatically return the accuracy, precision, and recall of the model, as well as a few other metrics.

Logarithmic Loss

The most common method for evaluating a classification model is logarithmic loss. This is a loss function specifically for logistic regression that essentially measures the prediction error averaged over all samples in the dataset. It's sometimes called "cross-entropy loss," referring to the loss between the actual dataset and the predicted dataset. Minimizing cross-entropy maximizes classification.

In practice, log loss improves (decreases) for each correct prediction. It worsens (increases) for each wrong prediction, weighted by how confidently that incorrect prediction was made. The output for a logistic classifier will ultimately be either 0 or 1, but it still reflects an underlying probability, which is selected based on the threshold. The log loss calculates this discrepancy across all thresholds.

The value of the log loss function in measuring the performance of your model will vary based on whether it's binary or multi-class. It will also vary if the probability of both 0 and 1 in the real dataset is even, like a coin toss, or if it is heavily imbalanced in one direction or another.

F1 Score

The F1 score, so named by apparent accident,[20] gives equal weight to precision and recall by calculating their harmonic mean.

Harmonic means to show up in lots of places where the two components influence each other in a way that would bias the arithmetic mean. Basically, both precision and recall are related by the numerator and are already ratios themselves. The canonical example is average speed on a train trip; if you go 40 mph outbound and 120 mph inbound, your average speed was not 80 mph. The ratio of miles over hours means you spent less time at 120 mph to go the same distance. So, if the destination were 120 miles away, this means it took 3 hours at 40 mph one way and 1 hour at 120 mph on the return—the average is actually ((3*40)+(1*120))/4, or 60 mph.

The advantage of the harmonic mean is that you don't actually need to know how far away the destination is or, in this case, what the total magnitude of the data looks like. The calculation for harmonic mean for precision and recall is

---

[20]Seriously. It seems that someone accidentally applied this name to the wrong metric.
  See www.cs.odu.edu/~mukka/cs795sum09dm/Lecturenotes/Day3/F-measure-YS-26Oct07.pdf

$$2\left(\frac{pr}{p+r}\right)$$

Since precision and recall are both between 0.0 and 1.0, the F1 score is also bounded between 0.0 and 1.0. (Plug 1.0 into both precision and recall, and you'll see it yields 1.0, the same as the arithmetic average. If both precision and recall have the same value, the harmonic mean will equal the arithmetic mean.)

This score is only useful if you believe that precision and recall have equal weight. An extended version, F_β, allows you to bias either precision or recall more heavily and could be considered a weighted f-measure.

ROC Curves

An ROC curve, or receiver operating characteristic curve, is another common way to measure the quality of a binary classification model. Developed in World War II, it refers literally to the recall (sensitivity) of a radar receiver at distinguishing birds from enemy aircraft.[21] It describes the tension covered in the "Precision and Recall" section. As the sensitivity of the receiver was turned up, it began to lower precision as more false positives were identified. Leaving the sensitivity low ran the risk that enemy aircraft would fly over undetected (false negatives). Using the ROC curve helped to find the optimal setting for recall that yielded the highest precision while maintaining lowest number of false alarms.

The ROC curve uses a measure called specificity, which is the proportion of true negatives correctly identified. Note that while precision and recall both focus on performance of correct positive identification, specificity looks at correct negative identification.

An ROC curve is a two-dimensional graph showing a line, where inverted specificity (1-specificity) is on the x-axis and recall (sensitivity) is on the y-axis. As the origin indicates, it plots hit rates (enemy aircraft) vs. false alarms (geese). Along the curve, you can see the average specificity for all values of recall from 0.0 to 1.0 (or the converse).

---

[21]www.ncbi.nlm.nih.gov/pmc/articles/PMC6022965/

The reason the curve is so useful is because depending on the problem you are trying to solve, a greater degree of false positives may be acceptable, especially when the cost for a missed identification is high. For example, in any test to detect a disease, a false positive is usually better than a false negative.

When using BQML, the metric returned is called roc_auc, which refers to the calculation of the area under the curve of the ROC. The area of a 1-by-1 plot is also 1, which means that the maximum area under the curve is also 1.0. A perfect roc_auc score means that the diagnostic accuracy of the model is perfect—it gets both the positive and negative cases accurate in every case.

A roc_auc of 0.5 means that a diagonal line bisects the plot area—0.5 unit lies above it and 0.5 unit lies below it. This suggests the test's prediction ability is at chance; in all cases, it's equally likely to guess right as wrong. See some examples in Figure 19-4.

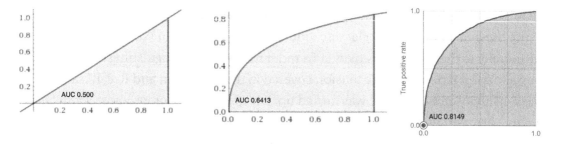

Figure 19-4. *Several plots of roc_aucs graphed together*

Where roc_auc can be extremely useful is in comparing the characteristics of two different models. Plotted along the same axes, you can make an apples-to-apples comparison of which model performs "better" without looking at the curves themselves.

To calculate the area under the curve, you can use the trapezoidal rule.[22] Since the roc_auc is a definite integral, you don't need calculus integration techniques to work it out. Or even better, just let BQML tell you the answer.

---

[22]www.khanacademy.org/math/ap-calculus-ab/ab-integration-new/ab-6-2/a/
understanding-the-trapezoid-rule

TensorFlow Models

TensorFlow fills hundreds of books on its own, so by necessity this is only a brief summary. We'll also touch upon TensorFlow in the next chapter. Essentially, TensorFlow is a Python-based platform for machine learning models. TensorFlow is one of the two most popular Python ML platforms (along with PyTorch), enjoying a robust community and lots of documentation and support. Google supplies its own quick introduction to classification in TensorFlow, in concert with a higher-level library called Keras.[23]

For our BQML purposes, in late 2019, importing TensorFlow models into BigQuery reached general availability. This bridged existing machine learning practice directly into BigQuery, allowing data analysts to directly utilize and incorporate custom ML models into their work.

To load one in, you can create a model of type TENSORFLOW using a Google Cloud Storage location where the model has been stored. BQML will automatically convert most common data types back and forth. Once you've imported the model, it's locked into BQML.

TensorFlow models in BQML support the common prediction methods, but you won't have access to the training and statistics. For example, you can't evaluate a TensorFlow model to see its performance nor examine its features. Models are also currently limited to 250 MB in size, which may not cover larger scale.

Nonetheless, this feature addresses a key concern around the initial BQML release, namely, that custom-tuned TensorFlow models were more accurate and suitable for production workloads. Now, as a data analyst, you could create a BQML model by yourself and begin using it. Once the data science team returns to you a TensorFlow model with more predictive capability, you could silently replace the native BQML model with the TensorFlow model and take advantage of it immediately.

K-Means Clustering

K-means clustering describes an unsupervised machine learning algorithm that performs segmentation on a dataset. The name comes from the algebraic variable k, indicating the number of clusters to produce, and mean as in the statistical average of each cluster. As it is unsupervised, k-means clustering can perform this segmentation without any input on the salient features.

---

[23]www.tensorflow.org/tutorials/keras/classification

In brief, the algorithm selects k random data points and assigns them as representatives for the clusters. Then, the other points are taken in and calculated for similarity to each of the representatives. Each row is grouped with its closest representative. Then, representatives are recalculated using the arithmetic mean of the current clusters, and the process is repeated. After enough iterations, each cluster's arithmetic mean, or *centroid*, stabilizes and future iterations produce the same k arithmetic means. At that point the data has been successfully grouped into k segments, where each segment has a mean that averages all the data points in that segment.

Let's break this down visually. This is easiest to visualize in a two-dimensional space, where all of the centroids and data points are on a plane. Take the example in Figure 19-5.

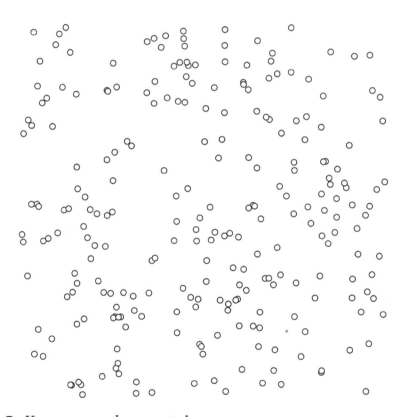

Figure 19-5. *K-means graph, unsorted*

If you think of this as quadrant I of a Cartesian plane, then each centroid is placed at an (x,y) coordinate. "Similarity" is the two-dimensional equation for Euclidean distance, $d = \sqrt{(x_1 - x_2)^2 + (y_1 - y_2)^2}$. (Huh, this looks a lot like the RMSE calculation...) Each data point is also an (x,y) coordinate, and its distance to each of the k centroids is calculated accordingly. The point is assigned to the centroid which is closest. After this iteration, the two-dimensional mean of each cluster is calculated, and those values are assigned as the k centroids for the next iteration. Rinse and repeat. Eventually, the centroids converge and stop moving around (stabilize). The data is now segmented into k groups, with each group being compactly described by an average. See Figure 19-6.

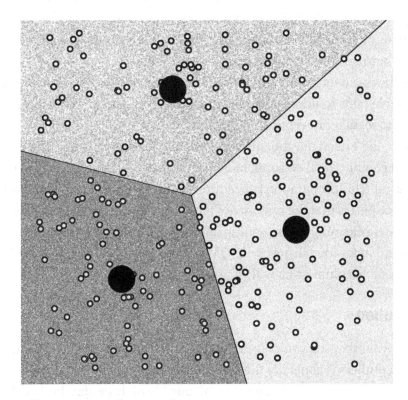

Figure 19-6. *K-means graph, complete*

When we look at this in BQML, the equivalent is a k-means model on a two-column table. We can certainly add more columns. The equation for Euclidean distance works in higher dimensions as well, by adding the terms $((z_1 - z_2)^2 + (a_1 - a_2)^2...)$ under the square root, but this gets pretty difficult to visualize above three.

Procedure

The process for implementing BQML is similar across all types of models. This section will review the general steps, before applying them to a few examples in the following sections.

Prepare the Data

In order to create the model, you first need to prepare your input dataset. Typically this will be a subset of raw data that you believe is salient to answering the business question at hand. This may also include some exploratory data analysis (which will be covered more deeply in the next chapter) and column selection. In some types of supervised learning, you may also need to annotate the data with information about how the model should treat it or to be able to look back at a model's quality.

If you're drawing data from multiple sources, you may also need to construct the subquery or table joins required to collect the input data into the same location. Note that you can use regular or even materialized views as the input source for BQML models, so you don't need to explicitly copy the data in the preparation step.

In the next chapter, we'll do some model generation without much explicit preparation at all. This preparation procedure should be used on any models for BQML, as well. The nice part is that the majority of these techniques are the same as you would do for regular data cleaning when loading data into a BigQuery warehouse.

Remember that for the purposes of BQML, when we talk about "features," we're talking about a table column that will go into the model.

Data Distribution

Depending on your dataset, you may not want outliers in your model. The rule of thumb for eliminating outliers is generally the same. If you have a normal data distribution, generally you want to eliminate values that fall outside of three standard deviations from the mean.

Again, because of the vast amount of rows and columns you may be analyzing, it's worth looking at outliers to see if you can pinpoint a cause. For example, I was once trying to analyze a dataset of prices with two maxima, one at the far left and one at the far right. The mean was useless, and most data points qualified as outliers by the standard definition. When I went to look at the dataset, I realized that most of the rows were decimal, that is, 4.95, but a significant set were measured as pennies in integers, that is,

495. I multiplied all decimal values by 100 and the data suddenly made sense. (Yes, I did account for decimal values that fell within the range, i.e., $495.)

Sometimes data collection methods are bad or an error produces unhelpful data. If there are a lot of maxint or other sentinel-type values in the data, this could be an indication of that. In some extreme cases, the dataset may be unsuitable for processing until these errors have been corrected and the data reimported.

Missing Data

Real-world datasets are likely to have missing data. Deciding what to do about this is highly model-dependent. In general, removing columns or rows with mostly missing data is preferable. Consider disparate impact when you do this though: why is the data missing?

Normally, you might also consider imputing data. If the data is missing only in a small number of rows and the distribution is normal, you can "make up" the remainder of it by filling in the average. Luckily, BQML will do this for you, so you need only decide whether you want the row or column at all.

Label Cleanup

Depending on the method of data collection, columns may have spelling or labeling variations to represent the same items. If you're using properly normalized data, you can use the IDs (but mind leakage). Otherwise, you may want to do some alignment to make sure that you use the same string identifier to mean the same class. For example, if your accessory type column has "Women's Shoes," "Shoes – Female," "Women's Shoes size 6," and so on, you will want to regularize all of those to "Women's Shoes" if that feature is important to you.

Feature Encoding

Feature encoding is another task that BQML will handle when you create a model. If there is some reason that it should be done outside of the BQML model creation—that is, you want to use the dataset with Python libraries or you want to combine encoding with data cleanup—you can do it yourself. Here are some of the techniques BQML performs on your input data, since they're good to know.

Scaling

Scaling, or "standardization," as Google refers to it, reduces integer and decimal values to a range centered at zero. This means all values will normalize into relative distances from zero, meaning that numeric features can be compared in a scale-agnostic fashion.

One-Hot Encoding

One-hot encoding is a loan term from electrical engineering, where it refers to the transformation of multiple logical values into a series of single values, each representing a state.[24] Or, if you prefer, it's the same as converting a number to unary notation. See Figure 19-7 for an example.

One-Hot Encoding

		Sunday	Monday	Tuesday	Wednesday	Thursday	Friday	Saturday
Sunday		1	0	0	0	0	0	0
Monday		0	1	0	0	0	0	0
Tuesday		0	0	1	0	0	0	0
Wednesday	⇒	0	0	0	1	0	0	0
Thursday		0	0	0	0	1	0	0
Friday		0	0	0	0	0	1	0
Saturday		0	0	0	0	0	0	1

Figure 19-7. *One-hot encoding with days of the week*

The reason for this is that it allows each feature to stand on its own. For example, if you needed to convert the days of the week into one-hot encoding, you'd end up with seven columns, one for Monday, one for Tuesday, and so on, where only one of the values could be on ("hot") at a time. This would allow for a single day of the week to shine through as an individual feature if it made a major impact on the predictions. While you might be inclined to think of these as seven separate booleans, all features are numerical, so it's actually 0.0 or 1.0.

---

[24]Amusingly, in integrated circuit design, this process is called "decoding."

Another reason for this is that converting categorical data into numerical data might imply scale where none exists. If Monday were 1 and Saturday were 7, that could translate to Saturday being "more" than Monday. It would also lead to nonsensical decimal predictions; what day of the week is 4.1207?

On the flip side, if your categories are ordered or sequenced in some way, you can leave them in numerical form to reflect their relationship. For example, encoding gold, silver, and bronze as 1, 2, and 3 could make sense. While you'll still get nonsensical decimal predictions, the meaning is slightly more intuitive.

Multi-hot Encoding

Multi-hot encoding is used specifically for transforming BigQuery ARRAY types. Like one-hot encoding, each unique element in the ARRAY will get its own column.

Timestamp Transformation

This is Google's name for deciding if BQML will apply scaling or one-hot encoding to timestamp values based on the data type and range.

Feature Selection

Feature selection is the process of choosing which features (columns) make sense to go into the model. It's critically important and BQML can't do it for you, because it relies on understanding the problem.

First and foremost, the computational complexity (read: time and money) of the model goes up with the number of features included. You can see with one-hot encoding and large datasets how the number of features could easily go into the hundreds or thousands.

Second, you reduce interpretability when there are too many features in the model to easily understand. Often, the first order of approximation is good enough, which means while all those extra features are slightly increasing the performance of your model, it's not worth the concomitant reduction in comprehension.

Lastly, the more features you use, the more risk there is of overfitting your model or introducing bias. It certainly raises the chances of accidentally adding the row number or something like it. With respect to bias, it could cause the model to reject all loan applications for people with a certain first name. While it very well may be that people named Alastair always default on their loans, it would be hard to assess that as anything more than coincidental.

There are many ways of doing feature selection. For BQML models, you might just go with your gut and see what happens. There are also some statistical methods you can use to assess the quality of various features on your model. For supervised models, you can use Pearson's correlation to calculate how significant each feature is in predicting the target value.

BigQuery supports this as a statistical aggregate function called CORR, which was conveniently ignored in the chapter about aggregate functions (That was Chapter 9.) CORR will look at all the rows in the group and return a value between -1.0 and 1.0 to indicate the correlation between the dependent and the independent variables. (You can also use it as an analytic function if you need windowing.)

This is just the tip of the iceberg. Many other functions like chi-squared and analysis of variance (ANOVA) can also be used to help with feature selection. Neither of those is built into BigQuery, although you can certainly find plenty of examples in SQL. (Or use a JavaScript UDF!)

It is also possible (though not built into BQML) to use statistics to perform automatic selection to optimize to the metrics you select. However, doing this properly requires actually running the model and calculating the metrics, mutating it, and then doing it again. Looking at all possible combinations across hundreds of features is effectively impossible, and so automated feature selection relies on making good choices based on the available statistical information. There are a number of methods for doing this. In practice, using available Python ML toolkits is the best way, and in the next chapter we'll look at integrating Python with BigQuery so you can move seamlessly between the two.

Feature Extraction

Whereas feature selection refers to choosing from the columns you already have, extraction refers to creating new columns using available data. Feature encoding and imputation could be seen as a form of extraction, but it generally describes more complex processes. The goal is to synthesize data points which better reflect the problem under consideration. Sometimes it's a necessity. When you've performed feature selection and the remaining features are too large to fit into your available memory, you need to find a way to represent them more compactly without losing too much fidelity.

Feature extraction is especially important on datasets with a lot of extraneous data. Audio and video are too large to process uncompressed in their entirety. In fact, when the Shazam algorithm for music identification was invented[25] in 2003, its revolutionary approach involved feature extraction. As a drastic oversimplification, audio tracks are reduced to discrete hashes based on peak intensity over time. When a recording for identification is made, it undergoes the same hash algorithm, and the database is searched for a match. The features that were extracted are invariant (for the most part) under background noise, and clustering techniques (like k-means) can be used to find likely matches.[26]

One basic feature extraction technique is setting a threshold you know to be good and using that to define a boolean. For instance, if you know that a credit score over 800 is "exceptional" and you feel that this problem is likely to care about that specifically, you can define a new feature which is just (credit score > 800) = 1.0.

BQML also provides a number of feature extraction methods, which they refer to as "preprocessing functions." These include scalers, bucketizers, and combiners. You can use these in combination with ML.TRANSFORM when creating your model.

One common feature extraction method that isn't easily described by the preceding techniques is known as "bag of words" in ML. The bag of words model converts text into a list of words and frequencies, either by total count or ratio. This gives ML models a predictable feature as opposed to a mess of text. Text preprocessing also includes filtering punctuation and removing filler words.

The bag of words model is a valuable preprocessing step for natural language analysis. It's extremely useful for sentiment analysis, that is, deciding if a particular text is positive or negative. While general sentiment analysis can be performed without machine learning, you can use this technique as a classifier for sentiment analysis in your specific domain. For example, you could run it on all of the tickets and emails your call center receives, allowing the prediction of sentiment specifically on relevant data to you. While general sentiment analysis classifies something like "It's been a month since I asked for a replacement" as neutral, your domain-specific classifier could learn that the customer was unhappy. You can use this method on BigQuery with the ML.NGRAMS keyword.

---

[25]www.ee.columbia.edu/~dpwe/papers/Wang03-shazam.pdf

[26]Incidentally, Google's sound search uses a convolutional neural network, a machine learning technique we're not going anywhere near in this chapter.

ML.TRANSFORM

The TRANSFORM keyword is used to perform both feature selection and extraction while creating the model. Since it is possible to specify only certain columns, selection is built in, after the hard work of deciding which those are. Transformation is accomplished using preprocessing functions like scaling and bucketizing. Finally, BQML does encoding on its own with whatever data types it gets.

We'll see this in action in the examples.

Create the Model

Next, you create a model using. SQL. This SQL statement handles the creation and training of the model using the input data that you have supplied. It also creates a BigQuery object to represent the model. In evaluation and prediction, the model name is used as the reference.

This means you can create multiple models of different types using the same input data and then perform predictions and compare them. This is known as "ensemble modeling." When multiple models agree on a result, it adds weight to the prediction. Of course, as discussed earlier, this can also get quite expensive.

To do this, you run the CREATE MODEL statement and indicate which kind of model to create, as well as the features to be included.

Evaluate the Model

For all model types except TensorFlow, you can then use ML.EVALUATE to see the performance of your model. Depending on the type of model, the returned statistics will be different. For instance, linear regression models will return things like RMSE and R^2, and classifier models will return things like roc_auc and the F1 score.

Depending on what sort of performance is required for the use case, these metrics may indicate the need to reprocess data or to refine feature selection/extraction. It may also be necessary to train multiple models and compare their performance. Sometimes this iterative process is referred to as feature engineering, which sounds really cool.

After repeating this process for a while, the metrics will converge on the desired result. Usually as the model approaches its best state, the metrics will stabilize. At some point, it's time to declare "good enough" and begin using the model for prediction.

Use the Model to Predict

Prediction is accomplished through the use of the ML.PREDICT keyword. This keyword takes a model and the table source used in the model creation. The result columns use the convention of "predicted_" as a prefix to select the result data. For example, if the model predicts how much money a customer will spend next year from a source column called "purchases," the ML result will be in a column called "predicted_purchases."

As you might expect, for linear regression, the predicted_ value will be numeric, and for classification models, it will be the predicted classification label. BQML does the same automatic feature encoding on the predictions, so there's no need to worry about doing it here either.

Exporting Models

If the final destination for the model is not BigQuery or if others need access to the same model for their work in Python, it is possible to export models to a TensorFlow format.

This works for all of the model types discussed earlier. It even works for models that were imported from TensorFlow, in case the data scientist lost the files or something. However, it doesn't work if you used ML.TRANSFORM or the input features had ARRAYs, TIMESTAMPs, or GEOGRAPHY types. (As of this writing, only the k-means type supports GEOGRAPHY anyway.)

To use it, click "Export Model" in the BigQuery UI after double-clicking a model in the left pane.

Examples

In the final section of this chapter, it all comes together in some examples. Given the technical background, it may come as a surprise how easy BQML makes this. A primary goal of BQML is the democratization of machine learning, so the simpler, the better.

In order to make it possible to follow along, we'll use datasets available on BigQuery. You can of course use any data already in your warehouse that's suitable for each type of model.

K-Means Clustering

In this example, we will examine the collection of the Metropolitan Museum of Art to see if there is any segmentation that can tell us about the collection practices of the museum or different categories of art. To do this, we'll use k-means clustering. (This is a great little dataset to use for exploration because it's only about 85 MB, so even if you want to look at all the columns repeatedly, you won't hit any limits on the free tier.)

As discussed earlier, k-means clustering is a form of unsupervised machine learning. Given a number of segments, it will find logical groupings for the segments based on the "average" of all of the data in each cluster. It iterates until the clusters stabilize. To create a k-means clustering model in BigQuery, we'll start by preparing the data.

Data Analysis

The data is stored in "bigquery-public-data.the_met.objects." Let's take a look at the columns. There are a lot of identification columns we don't want because they'll bias the data, like object_number. A couple of other observations from the initial analysis are as follows:

- Department looks like it could be good, since that is a curated classification.

- Artwork has "titles," but sculptures, artifacts, and so on have "object_name." This could be tricky. It looks like we might prefer "classification."

- Culture is also good, but it has a lot of extraneous data in it.

- Object begin date and object end date show the estimated dates of the artwork. They look well formatted and numerical. Definitely want.

- Credit_line is interesting because it might give us a clue to collection practices. It has tons of different values though.

- Link_resource, metadata_date, and repository are all exclusions. Repository only has one value, the Met. Link resource is another form of identifier, and metadata_data would only leak data at best.

Based on this analysis, let's go with the following feature selection:

- Department: The area of the museum

- object_begin_date, object_end_date: When the work was created

- classification: What kind of work it is

- artist_alpha_sort: The artist's name

What about the artist? Artist is only populated on about 43% of the items, but maybe it will tell us something about the ratio between attributed works and anonymous ones. Okay, let's throw it in. We'll choose "artist_alpha_sort" in case the regular artist column has irregularities.

How about feature extraction? At this stage, let's let BQML encode the data and not try to perform any feature extraction until we get a sense of the output.

We probably also want to filter outlier data. When I select the MAX object date, I get the result "18591861," which is almost certainly an error for a work that should have been 1859–1861 and not a time traveling painting from millions of years in the future.

Creating the Model

Ready to go! The final model creation query is as follows:

```
CREATE OR REPLACE MODEL metkmeans
OPTIONS(model_type='kmeans', num_clusters=5) AS
SELECT
department,
object_begin_date,
object_end_date,
classification,
artist_alpha_sort
FROM `bigquery-public-data.the_met.objects`
WHERE object_begin_date < 2025 and object_end_date < 2025
```

This model takes about 2 minutes to process and train. When it has finished running, it will create the model in the specified location. If you open the model in the UI, you will see an evaluation tab that shows some visualizations of the discovered clusters. The results are shown in Figure 19-8.

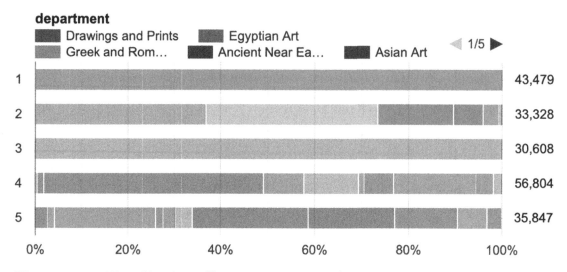

department
Drawings and Prints   Egyptian Art
Greek and Rom…   Ancient Near Ea…   Asian Art   ◀ 1/5 ▶

1	43,479
2	33,328
3	30,608
4	56,804
5	35,847

0%   20%   40%   60%   80%   100%

Figure 19-8. *Visualization of k-means on types of art*

Cluster 1 consists entirely of "Drawings and Prints," and Cluster 3 consists entirely of "European Sculpture and Decorative Arts." Cluster 4 seems to be a mix of art from the rest of the world, as well as medieval works and everything in the Cloisters annex. Cluster 5 is all over the board with photographs, American art, and so forth. Cluster 4 is also interesting because it contains Asian Art, Egyptian Art, Greek and Roman Art, and Ancient Near Eastern Art. And when we look at the numerical analysis in Figure 19-9.

Centroid Id	Count	object_begin_date	object_end_date
1	43479	1,721.7231	1,746.0865
2	33328	-1,370.6663	-814.5654
3	30608	1,701.8248	1,744.8933
4	56804	1,292.2790	1,443.7721
5	35850	1,811.6355	1,829.5175

Figure 19-9. *Numerical analysis of types of art by creation year*

we see that the object dates for Cluster 2 are negative, as in BCE. So we have learned something—classical European art and drawings and prints are areas of focus for the Met's curators, as is ancient art from all cultures. But—I hear you saying—we could have just sorted by prevalence and learned what the most popular categories are. What additional advantage does clustering give us here? Actually, if you look at a map of the museum,[27] there are the fundamentals of a physical mapping here too.

Drawings and prints are only displayed for short amounts of time to avoid fading caused by exposure, so they have no fixed geographic location. Cluster 3 is mostly in the center of the museum, while Cluster 4 is found along the edges on the front and sides of the museum. Cluster 5 is in the back. Cluster 2 tended to represent antiquity across cultures and is also mostly located with Cluster 4.

So we can actually use this to propose, without any curatorial ability, a basic idea for how one might organize artwork in an art museum. Nonetheless, should I ever see a sign directing you to the K-Means Museum of Algorithmic Art, I'll pass.

Evaluation and Prediction

K-means models return only two evaluation metrics, the Davies-Bouldin index and the mean squared distance. To improve your model, you want the index to be lower; changing the number of clusters to seek a lower score is one way to determine the optimal number of clusters for the data.

Time for a prediction. Knowing nothing about art, let's say I open a competing museum (ha!) and someone donates something. Where should I put it? To make it simple, this query will just specify one row of data directly to the prediction function. In practice this would run across a table of imports. Let's say someone donated a Rembrandt:

```
SELECT *
      FROM ML.PREDICT(
      MODEL metkmeans, (
            SELECT 'Painting' department,
                    1641 object_begin_date,
                    1641 object_end_date,
                    'Prints' classification, 'Rembrandt van Rijn'
                    artist_alpha_sort,
        ))
```

---

[27]https://maps.metmuseum.org/

Sure enough, it recommends Cluster 1, with the rest of the drawings and prints, even though I made up and misattributed the department name.

Additional Exercises

The Met also publishes some additional tables, including a table with the results of the computer vision API run on each object. This includes intriguing assessments like whether the subject of the work is angry, joyful, or surprised. It also looks to identify landmarks, even going so far as to note their location. There are some interesting extensions to this model to cluster works by subject or location. (Spoiler alert: I added whether the subject was angry as a feature to this k-means model. It had no measurable impact.)

Data Classification

Data classification is a supervised model. BQML supports binary or multi-class, that is, yes/no or multiple categories. In this example, we'll take a look at the National Highway Traffic Safety Administration (NHTSA) data for car accidents and develop a model for answering a question. Unlike k-means, where we went in a bit aimlessly, we have something in mind here. The question: If a car accident results in fatalities, given information about the accident and passengers, can we assess which passengers are likely to survive?

This may seem like a morbid question to ask, but it has significant ramifications in the real world. Regrettably, unfortunate accidents happen as a matter of course. Knowing which factors are associated with higher mortality rates can help at the macro level in provisioning emergency response levels and locations. It can characterize constellations of factors that may greatly increase the risk of fatality to improve car safety, road upkeep, or streetlight provisioning. It could even help on the ground directly—given partial information about the accident, it might suggest how quickly emergency services need to reach the scene and which passengers are at highest risk.

This model won't do all of that, of course. It's a jumping-off point intended to see how good it can get at answering the stated question, namely, can a given passenger survive a given accident, given that the assumption that the accident will cause at least one fatality.

Data Analysis

For this model, we'll be using the dataset located on BigQuery at bigquery-public-data:nhtsa_traffic_fatalities. We'll need several tables from the set to get a clear picture of the situations. In all cases we'll use 2015 data (partially so we can run predictions against 2016 data):

- accident_2015: This carries the top-level data about the accident, including the time, location, and number of people and vehicles involved. It has one row for each accident.

- vehicle_2015: This has information about each vehicle involved in an accident. It includes things like the type of vehicle and damage. It goes as deep as describing specifics of the vehicle's stability before the accident, the area of impact, and the sequence of events.

- person_2015: This has information about each person affected by the accident, including both passengers in vehicles, cyclists, and pedestrians. It includes demographic characteristics like age, the involvement of alcohol or drugs, and whether the passenger's airbag deployed. It also has our target label, which is whether or not this person survived the accident in question.

Feature selection took quite some time in this example, given the vast array of data available. There are other tables describing driver impairment, distraction, the types of damage done, whether the driver was charged with violations, and hundreds more. This dataset would be suitable in building all kinds of regression and classifier models.

The last thing that will help if you really want to follow along in the details is the NHTSA Analytical User's Manual[28] (publication 812602). This has the full data glossary for all of the data points and will be extremely important as we perform feature extraction and transformation.

So down to business. What things do we think are important in a model to predict this sort of thing? Here are some features that seem like they would be of interest:

---

[28]https://crashstats.nhtsa.dot.gov/Api/Public/ViewPublication/812602

- General: Where did the accident take place? What was the scene like? How were the roads? Was it day or night? What kind of road did it take place on?

- Accident: What was the first thing that happened to cause the accident? Was it a collision and, if so, what kind?

- Vehicle: What vehicle was involved for each passenger? Was it going the speed limit? Were there other factors involved? How serious was the damage to the vehicle? Did it roll over? How did the vehicle leave the scene?

- Person: How old was the person? Where were they seated in the vehicle? Was the passenger wearing a seatbelt? Did the airbag deploy?

- Response: How long did it take for emergency services to arrive? How long did it take to transport a person to the hospital?

This exploration took several hours to perform, so don't assume it will be instantaneous to understand feature selection and extraction. Some features that I ultimately rejected included impact area (from 1 to 12 describing position on a clock), previous convictions for speeding, various personal attributes, maneuvers undertaken before the crash, and more than one descriptor for things like weather or extenuating circumstances. Many features helped only marginally or were eclipsed by other factors.

Creating the Model

For a model of this complexity, it makes sense to define the preprocessed data in a view as you go. That way you can see how it is developing and sanity-check any extraction you're doing in the query selection. It also makes the model creation statement much cleaner. This is by no means necessary, but it's useful to look at the input data you're building without actually running the model over and over again.

The final view for this model is generated as follows:

```
CREATE OR REPLACE VIEW `bqml_nhtsa_2015_view`
AS
SELECT
a.consecutive_number,
a.county,
a.type_of_intersection,
a.light_condition,
a.atmospheric_conditions_1,
a.hour_of_crash,
a.functional_system,
a.related_factors_crash_level_1 related_factors,
CASE WHEN a.hour_of_ems_arrival_at_hospital BETWEEN 0 AND 23 AND a.hour_of_
ems_arrival_at_hospital - a.hour_of_crash > 0 THEN a.hour_of_ems_arrival_
at_hospital - a.hour_of_crash ELSE NULL END delay_to_hospital,
CASE WHEN a.hour_of_arrival_at_scene BETWEEN 0 AND 23 AND a.hour_of_
arrival_at_scene - a.hour_of_crash > 0 THEN a.hour_of_arrival_at_scene -
a.hour_of_crash ELSE NULL END delay_to_scene,
p.age,
p.person_type,
p.seating_position,
CASE p.restraint_system_helmet_use WHEN 0 THEN 0 WHEN 1 THEN 0.33 WHEN 2
THEN 0.67 WHEN 3 THEN 1.0 ELSE 0.5 END restraint,
CASE WHEN p.injury_severity IN (4) THEN 1 ELSE 0 END survived,
CASE WHEN p.rollover IN ('', 'No Rollover') THEN 0 ELSE 1 END rollover,
CASE WHEN p.air_bag_deployed BETWEEN 1 AND 9 THEN 1 ELSE 0 END airbag,
CASE WHEN p.police_reported_alcohol_involvement LIKE ('%Yes%') THEN 1 ELSE
0 END alcohol,
CASE WHEN p.police_reported_drug_involvement LIKE ('%Yes%') THEN 1 ELSE 0
END drugs,
p.related_factors_person_level1,
v.travel_speed,
CASE WHEN v.speeding_related LIKE ('%Yes%') THEN 1 ELSE 0 END speeding_
related,
v.extent_of_damage,
v.body_type body_type,
```

```
v.vehicle_removal,
CASE WHEN v.manner_of_collision > 11 THEN 11 ELSE v.manner_of_collision END
manner_of_collision,
CASE WHEN v.roadway_surface_condition > 11 THEN 8 ELSE v.roadway_surface_
condition END roadway_surface_condition,
CASE WHEN v.first_harmful_event < 90 THEN v.first_harmful_event ELSE 0 END
first_harmful_event,
CASE WHEN v.most_harmful_event < 90 THEN v.most_harmful_event ELSE 0 END
most_harmful_event,
FROM `bigquery-public-data.nhtsa_traffic_fatalities.accident_2015` a
LEFT OUTER JOIN `bigquery-public-data.nhtsa_traffic_fatalities.
vehicle_2015` v
USING (consecutive_number)
LEFT OUTER JOIN `bigquery-public-data.nhtsa_traffic_fatalities.person_2015` p
USING (consecutive_number)
```

Rather than wading through the query, Figure 19-10 has a table that describes what each column does and what preprocessing was necessary to select or extract data prior to model creation.

consecutive_number	This is the unique identifier for all the records and is needed in joining
county	The county ID where the accident took place
type_of_intersection	The type of intersection (Not an intersection, Four-way, Roundabout, etc.)
light_condition	The type and level of light (daylit, lit at night, etc.)
atmospheric_conditions_1	The current weather (clear, rain, snow, sleet, etc.)
hour_of_crash	The hour (0-23) of the crash. This gets bucketized into six-hour intervals, corresponding roughly to late night, morning, afternoon, and evening.
functional_system	The type of road (interstate, principal, minor, local, etc.) This gets split into three categories, corresponding roughly to major, minor, and local/unknown.
related_factors_crash_level_1	Various conditions related to the crash (flooding, poor construction, road rage, school zone...)
delay_to_hospital	The number of hours it took to transport the passenger from the scene to the hospital (naively assuming this was never greater than 24.) This goes through standard scaling to adjust it to whatever the median response time happens to be.
delay_to_scene	The number of hours it took for EMS to arrive at the scene (same naive assumption.) This goes through standard scaling to adjust it to whatever the median response time happens to be.
age	The age of the person. This is bucketized into 5 year intervals.
person_type	Whether the person was a driver, passenger, or other involved non-motorist. This is split into categories that roughly correspond to car passenger, cyclist/pedestrian, and unknown.
seating_position	Where the person was seated in the car (if applicable.) This is bucketized into rows: front row, second row, third row, and everything else.

Figure 19-10. *All of the columns and their definitions*

restraint	The person's restraint status scored: 0 for none, 0.33 for a lap belt, 0.67 for a shoulder belt, and 1.0 for both
survived	The target variable; whether the person in question survived
rollover	Whether the vehicle involved rolled over (0 for none, 1 for all other kinds)
airbag	Whether the airbag deployed, regardless of where; 1 for any airbag, 0 for none
alcohol	Whether the police reported any alcohol involvement with respect to this person
drugs	Whether the police reported any drug involvement with respect to this person
related_factors_person_level_1	Any related factors for this person, such as physical impairment, standing in the roadway, etc.
travel_speed	The speed of travel, in miles per hour. This is bucketized into 10mph increments.
speeding_related	Whether the vehicle involved was speeding at the time of the accident (1 for "Yes", 0 for all else)
extent_of_damage	How much damage was done to the vehicle (none, minor, functional, disabling)
body_type	The type of vehicle this person was involved with. This is bucketized into a series of categories roughly corresponding to cars, buses, off-road, truck, van, motorcycle, etc.
vehicle_removal	How the vehicle was removed from the scene: under its own power, via tow, etc.
manner_of_collision	The kind of collision the vehicle was involved in (none, rear-end, front-on, side-swipe, etc.)
roadway_surface_condition	The condition of the roadway at the time of the accident (dry, wet, slush, standing water, etc.)
first_harmful_event	A numerical code for the first incident in the accident causing harm (fire, ditch, curb, building, bridge, person, mailbox, and a hundred others)
most_harmful_event	The same numerical code, but to describe the most harmful event in the accident

Figure 19-10. (*continued*)

We'll use the TRANSFORM keyword to do some additional processing as we load it into models. Using TRANSFORM to bucketize columns is much cleaner and easier to read than doing it in a mess of CASE statements. The model creation statement looks like this:

```
CREATE OR REPLACE MODEL `bqml_nhtsa_2015`
TRANSFORM (
  county,
  type_of_intersection,
  light_condition,
  atmospheric_conditions_1,
  ML.QUANTILE_BUCKETIZE(hour_of_crash, 6) OVER() bucketized_hour,
  ML.BUCKETIZE(functional_system, [1,4,7]) functional_system,
  related_factors,
  ML.STANDARD_SCALER(delay_to_hospital) OVER() delay_to_hospital,
  ML.STANDARD_SCALER(delay_to_scene) OVER() delay_to_scene,
  ML.QUANTILE_BUCKETIZE(age, 5) OVER() bucketized_age,
  ML.BUCKETIZE(person_type, [1,6,9]) person_type,
  ML.BUCKETIZE(seating_position, [0,10,11,21,31,40]) seating_position,
  restraint,
  rollover,
  airbag,
  alcohol,
  drugs,
  related_factors_person_level1,
  ML.QUANTILE_BUCKETIZE(travel_speed, 10) OVER() travel_speed,
  speeding_related,
  ML.BUCKETIZE(body_type, [0,10,20,30,40,50,60,80,90,91,92,93,94,95,96,97]
  ) body_type,
  vehicle_removal,
  manner_of_collision,
  roadway_surface_condition,
  first_harmful_event,
  most_harmful_event,
  survived
)
```

```
OPTIONS (model_type='logistic_reg', input_label_cols=['survived'])
AS
SELECT * EXCEPT (consecutive_number) from `bqml_nhtsa_2015_view`
```

This statement generates the classification model by specifying the model_type as "logistic_reg" and the target label as "survived," which is a column we defined in the view so that 1 represents a survival.

There are three preprocessing functions used here to further massage the data when creating the model:

- BUCKETIZE: This creates split points for categorical columns. These split points were determined by referencing the data dictionary and grouping common types together. For example, in the seating_position column, 10–19 are front row, 20–29 are second row, and 30–39 are third row. Rather than including all data about where precisely the passenger was sitting, this feature is extracted to convey only the row.

- QUANTILE_BUCKETIZE: This represents values where ranges are useful but specific values are too granular. For example, we only care about the vehicle speed in increments of 10.

- STANDARD_SCALER: This is used for columns where the relative value is more important than the absolute value. The exact time it takes for emergency services to arrive carries less weight than whether it is faster or slower than average.

When this statement is run, BQML gets to work and builds a model. This model takes several minutes to run and 17.6 MB of ML data. (Remember this is the statement that is billed differently than all of the other BigQuery statements.)

Evaluation

Once the model has been generated, we can review the statistics to see how it did.

When doing a binary classification model, BQML shows a slider for "threshold" allowing you to view the statistics for each threshold value. Recall that logistic regression is really a linear regression where you flip the decision from zero to one at a certain confidence threshold. To calibrate the model properly, we'll decide which statistics we care most about and use that threshold for prediction. Open the model and click the "Evaluation" tab.

This model has a log loss of 0.5028. For equally weighted data, guessing neutrally for all instances, 0.5, would yield a log loss of ≈ 0.693. The probability of survival on a per-sample basis is more like 0.35, which means that a chance log loss should be lower than 0.693; however, 0.50 seems to intuitively indicate a decently predictive model. There are more advanced (not in BQML) analyses we could do like calculating the Brier score. Log loss is known as a somewhat harsh metric given that it penalizes confident inaccurate classifications so heavily.

The ROC AUC is 0.8149. This is quite good. It means that over all thresholds, the model is accurate for both positive and negative 81% of the time.

Figure 19-11 shows BQML's evaluation of the other parameters at a threshold of 0.5102, closest to the middle.

Score threshold

Positive class threshold		0.5102
Positive class	1	
Negative class	0	
Precision	0.7723	
Recall	0.4349	
Accuracy	0.7536	
F1 score	0.5565	

Use this slider above to see which score threshold works best for your model.

Confusion matrix

Actual labels	Predicted labels 1	0
1	43.49%	56.51%
0	7.07%	92.93%

Figure 19-11. *Model performance for a given threshold*

At this threshold, the model correctly identifies 43% of all survivors and 93% of all fatalities and is right 75% of the time. Not bad. The F1 score, optimizing to both precision and recall, sits at a decent 55%.

Now we have to decide what we want to optimize for. Do we want to weight precision or recall more heavily? Do we want to find a balance of both, maximizing the F1 measure?

BQML also provides a chart across all thresholds, seen in Figure 19-12.

Precision and Recall vs Threshold

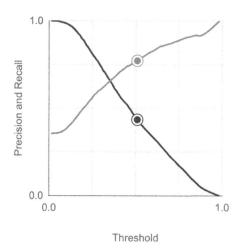

Figure 19-12. *Precision and recall across all thresholds*

Here, we see the expected tension between precision and recall. When the threshold is 0, that is, a positive prediction is never made, it's always right, but that's worthless. As the model begins selecting positive results more frequently, precision goes down and recall goes up.

In the general case, my personal opinion (and you may disagree) is that prioritization of the F1 measure is preferable. False positives and false negatives, when it comes to life-and-death situations, are both pretty bad outcomes. Optimizing for the F1 score gives us the final threshold and result in Figure 19-13.

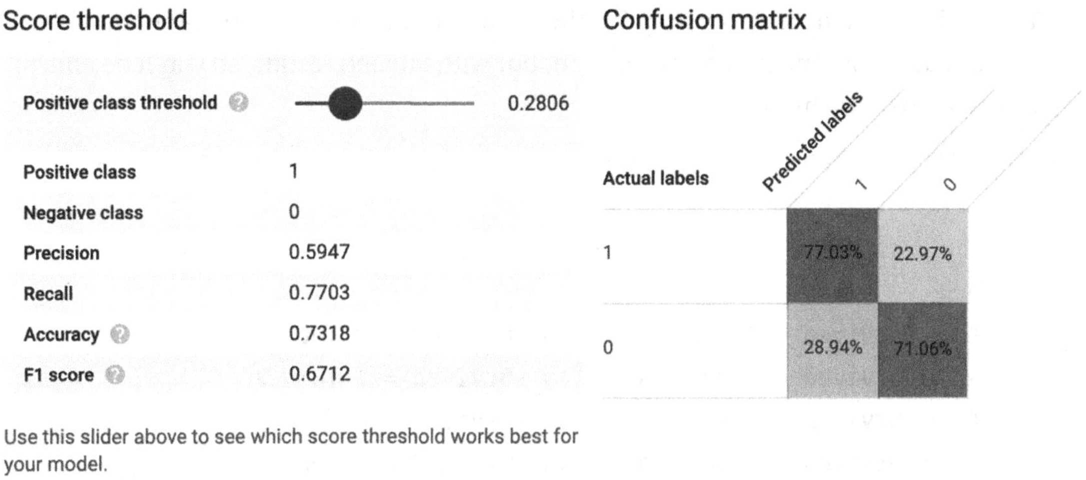

Score threshold

Confusion matrix

Positive class threshold ❓	——●——— 0.2806

Positive class	1
Negative class	0
Precision	0.5947
Recall	0.7703
Accuracy ❓	0.7318
F1 score ❓	0.6712

Actual labels	Predicted labels	
	1	0
1	77.03%	22.97%
0	28.94%	71.06%

Use this slider above to see which score threshold works best for your model.

Figure 19-13. *Threshold where the F1 score is highest*

At a threshold of 0.2806, the model is accurate 73% of the time, correctly identifying 77% of survivors and 71% of fatalities. We sacrificed true negatives to increase true positives. The F1 score rises to 0.6712.

Overall, this model isn't terrible. For a highly unpredictable event with so many variables, it's actually a pretty good first pass. However, there are likely other correlating variables lurking deeper in the data, perhaps related to crosses of existing features, or more complicated extractions to amplify particular conditions. For example (and this is not based on the real data), traveling on certain types of roads in certain locations at certain hours of the week might drastically lower the probability of survival. In fact, some combinations might constitute outliers over the feature set and might be lowering the predictive model.

Prediction

We reserved an entire year's worth of data to predict using our model. Let's cut to the chase and try it out. This query manually constructs a confusion matrix from the 2016 results as a comparison, but also so that you can tinker with it to produce the other values.

Before running this, modify the preceding statement which creates the view by searching and replacing 2015 with 2016, where the first line will be

```
CREATE OR REPLACE VIEW `bqml_nhtsa_2015_view`
```

This will create a new view with all of the same information for 2016. More notably, it will contain data your model has never seen, but with labeled results, so you'll be able to test its predictive capabilities:

```
SELECT confusion, COUNT(confusion), COUNT(confusion)/ANY_VALUE(total)
FROM
(
SELECT CASE
        WHEN survived = 1 and predicted_survived = 0 THEN 1
        WHEN survived = 1 and predicted_survived = 1 THEN 2
        WHEN survived = 0 and predicted_survived = 1 THEN 3
        WHEN survived = 0 and predicted_survived = 0 THEN 4
        END confusion,

        CASE WHEN survived = 1 THEN 58613 -- total survivors
             WHEN survived = 0 THEN 105087 -- total fatalities
        END total
FROM
   ML.PREDICT(MODEL `bqml_nhtsa_2015`,
      (SELECT * FROM `bqml_nhtsa_view_2016`),
      STRUCT(0.2806 AS threshold))
 )
 GROUP BY confusion;
```

Note the reuse of the 0.2806 threshold from the 2015 model. Figure 19-14 shows the confusion matrix results.

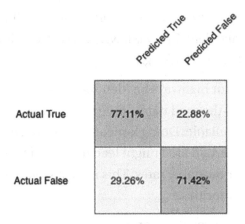

Figure 19-14. *Confusion matrix for classification model*

These results look almost the same, suggesting that this model retains the same predictive power from year to year. Two years is not a large enough sample, but in our nonscientific analysis, it's encouraging to see the models line up so accurately.

Additional Exercises

A natural next step would be to do additional feature engineering. In my data exploration, pruning any single feature did lower max F1 and AUC slightly, but there must be better features to represent clusters of passenger or vehicle data. More feature extraction would yield a better understanding of outlier data, and removing outlier data could improve precision.

Some broader questions that a model might look to address are as follows:

- Are certain makes or models of cars more likely to be involved in fatal accidents?

- Are cyclists more likely to be injured or killed by certain types of vehicles? Are adverse events like ejection correlated with mortality?

- Are there physical characteristics that change mortality, like height and weight?

- Does the behavior of the vehicle immediately prior to the accident matter?

- Is previous driving performance actually a factor in the mortality rate associated with accidents? (My analysis was extremely limited and did not involve feature crossing.)

- Can certain roads or highways be identified as especially dangerous? This one is **huge**—the road name, mile marker, and lat/lon of the accident are all available. Doing k-means clustering of the geography of accidents in a certain area might lead to some dangerous areas with much higher mortality rates. This in turn would be extremely useful to local authorities.

Hopefully this model has provoked some thoughts about the kinds of things even a simple binary classification can do. Are you excited yet? Go out there and do some exploration.

Summary

BigQuery ML, or BQML, is a feature intended to democratize machine learning for non-data scientists. Machine learning is a vast subfield of artificial intelligence and takes cues from statistics, mathematics, and computer science. However, it's important to practice machine learning "for humans." Interpretability and ethics of machine learning models are major considerations when using this technology. Using SQL directly in the UI, it is possible to process and train machine learning models in BigQuery. BQML supports both supervised and unsupervised models of several types, including k-means clustering, regression, and binary classification. Measuring the performance of each type of model is crucial to understanding its predictive power. The procedure for ML models is largely similar across types, involving preprocessing the data, creating the model, evaluating its performance, and then using it to make predictions. Through two examples, we saw the amazing power that even a simple model can produce—and a tantalizing glimpse of where it can go from here.

In the next chapter, we'll explore the data science and machine learning community through Kaggle, Jupyter notebooks, Python, and their special integration into BigQuery. We'll trade in mathematics for coding. You're on your way to being a true student of machine learning!

CHAPTER 20

Jupyter Notebooks and Public Datasets

One of BigQuery's advantages is its ability to query into external datasets. We've mostly used this capability for federated queries to your data hosted in other Google Cloud Platform services or as a stepping stone to loading that data into your own warehouse. Google hosts several hundred public datasets through its Google BigQuery Public Datasets program.[1] Google's available data crosses a wide variety of disciplines and includes datasets like the National Oceanic and Atmospheric Administration's daily weather records with some data going back as early as 1763. Other datasets cover cryptocurrency, politics, geology, and healthcare.

I'd also like to introduce Kaggle. Kaggle is a community of more than a million data science and machine learning practitioners, affectionately self-styled "Kagglers." It got its start as a competition-based data science platform. Competitions are hosted on the Kaggle platform for prize money, in exchange for a license to use the model. Afterward, Kaggle frequently interviews the winning team for a deep dive into the technical workings of the model. Typical competitions are fierce, drawing thousands of entrants and producing high-quality results, sometimes from groups new to the space. Visiting Kaggle at kaggle.com and browsing around is a good way to get a flavor for this area. It can be a very different world from that of SQL-based business intelligence.

Google purchased Kaggle in 2017, and in June of 2019, the two organizations jointly announced a direct connection between the Kaggle platform and Google BigQuery. The two services have integrated for some time, but the latest version allows you to access BigQuery data directly using Kaggle Kernels.

---

[1] https://console.cloud.google.com/marketplace/browse?filter=solution-type:dataset

469

© Mark Mucchetti 2020
M. Mucchetti, *BigQuery for Data Warehousing*, https://doi.org/10.1007/978-1-4842-6186-6_20

Kaggle's datasets range to the considerably more eclectic. A surprising number of datasets are dedicated to Pokemon. It's possible that Pokemon have relevance to your field of study and that you might want to perform some exploratory data analysis on them. (I was able to determine with about three minutes of effort that things called "Mega Mewtwo X" and "Mega Heracross" have the highest attack stat. But I have no idea if this is good or bad nor what to do with the information. Score one point for the observation that you need to understand your data domain to analyze it in any useful way.[2])

This chapter is about exploring the emergent possibilities of combining publicly available datasets together. The data in your data warehouse is a microcosm of behavior in the world at large, so the possibility of gaining insight from connecting to these other sources is both practical and alluring. I also believe it will be a skill expected for all data practitioners in the relatively near future.

The Edge of the Abyss

In the previous chapter and this one, we're coming right up to the edge of our discipline in business intelligence. On the other side is bleeding-edge research into machine learning. If you find these topics interesting and want to learn more, there are other Apress books that cover these subjects in great detail. By all means, get a running start and leap over.

As we've seen, BigQuery ML provides a stepping stone of accessibility for you to take advantage of some of this power inside your own data warehouse. It hasn't yet caught up to the latest state of the research.

The research to practice gap is a feedback loop too. New innovations are produced in raw form, requiring a lot of effort to understand and implement. After a time, companies figure out how to commoditize this research as a product and slap a marketing label on it. Then they collect learnings from the market at scale, which feeds back into the research process. By then, the research is months or years ahead again, and the cycle restarts. This feedback loop has been tightening—witness BQML—but it's not instantaneous.

---

[2]I solicited the professional opinion of a colleague, who informed me that these are base stats and have significant variance at higher levels based on a random number generator. Moreover, there is a difference between "attack" and "special attack," and the math is incompatible between Pokemon generations. In other words, my analysis was worthless.

From here on out, you get to decide how far upstream you want to push. If your organization is solving problems that would benefit massively from these capabilities, look to graft an R&D arm onto your data program. (That could represent a commitment as small as you reading about these topics after work.) Having a state-of-the-art warehouse that can turn massive datasets into real-time insight already puts you miles ahead of most of your competitors. If you've solved that problem, what's next?

Jupyter Notebooks

Jupyter Notebooks are a template for essentially a self-contained coding environment running in the cloud. There are several great implementations of them available in cloud platforms. Google supports them through its AI Platform and Google Colaboratory. You can also run them on Amazon Web Services SageMaker, Microsoft Azure Notebooks, and many others. I'm going to be using Kaggle Kernels for these examples, but you can use any notebook environment you prefer. Like its relatives, Kaggle Kernels are run inside isolated Docker containers that come pre-instrumented with a helpful suite of data analytics libraries preinstalled. Due to Kaggle's direct integration with BigQuery, it's low hassle to send data back and forth. It's also free, so at hobby scale it's a great choice.

The container for the default Kaggle Python kernel is open source, and you can download it and run it on your own machine if you like. The advantage of kernels, especially when you are getting started with data analysis in Python, is that you don't have to do any work to get under way.

The downside is that kernels operate with resource limitations in order to remain free for your use. Kernels have limited CPU, RAM, and disk space, as well as a time limit. The defaults are generous enough for you to do any exploratory or low-scale work. At this time, kernels support Python and R; we'll use Python because I promised we would.

Kaggle also provides some helpful syntax suggestions as you work. These can be helpful if your background is not in software engineering. It will remind you of differences between the deprecated Python 2.7 and the notebook's Python 3 or if you accidentally write R code in your Python notebook or vice versa. Of course, you get the full stack trace too.

Aside from accessing your own data on BigQuery, Kaggle grants you a free rolling quota of 5 terabytes per 30 days to use on BigQuery public datasets. 5 TB sounds like a lot, but many of these datasets are multi-terabyte. A single SELECT * FROM could blow most of your allowance for the month. Even though you're querying it from Kaggle, this is still the BigQuery you know and love—which means you already know better than to SELECT * FROM anything.

Setting Up Your Notebook

After you create your Kaggle account, you can proceed to create a new notebook. You'll see a screen similar to the one in Figure 20-1.

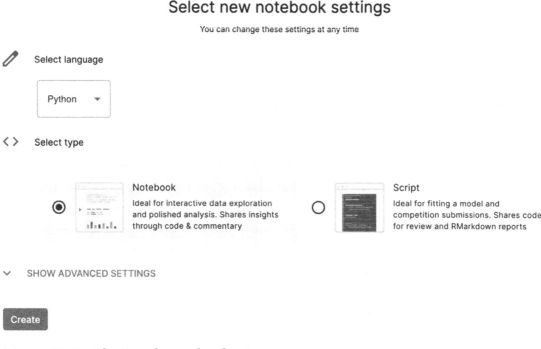

Figure 20-1. *The Kaggle notebook setup screen*

Open the advanced settings and select "Enable Google Cloud Services" to see the popup to integrate with BigQuery. This will allow you to sign in to your GCP account and link them. The window will also generate a code snippet—copy that out so you can paste it into the notebook.

You can integrate with BigQuery, Cloud Storage, and AutoML. We're familiar with the first two, but AutoML is new to us. AutoML is Google's offering to provide an even higher-level abstraction for machine learning models. The newest method of AutoML interaction is called AutoML Tables, which integrates natively with—you guessed it— BigQuery.

The Notebook Interface

When you get to the kernel window, you'll see a console for entering code and Markdown. On the surface, it doesn't look all that different from the BigQuery console. However, it has a lot of concepts designed for ease of use and quick integration. To be honest, SQL consoles could borrow some concepts from Jupyter notebooks and improve life for all of us. Once you start using notebooks, you may never go back to the BigQuery console for interactive sessions again. (No, you will, because SQL syntax highlighting.)

Cells

Cells are both a logical and execution unit for your notebooks. You can divide your notebooks into individual cells, each performing one logical step of your task. There are a few things that make them extra powerful and uniquely suited for this kind of work.

A cell can be code (Python/R) or Markdown. This allows you to freely intermix your analysis code with a formatted explanation of each step and the results. You can show your results quantitatively and then use Markdown to display them qualitatively. If you're unfamiliar with Markdown, then you're in for two treats today. It's a simple formatting language and has become pretty widely used. The GitHub tutorial[3] is pretty succinct. Additionally, Jupyter Markdown supports LaTeX equations so you can get your math formulas in there.

Furthermore, you can place the cells around in any order and run them independently or together. They all run inside the same container context, so you can perform individual analysis steps without having to rerun the whole notebook. This is also useful for BigQuery, where you may be running time- and data-intensive queries that you don't want to pay to repeat.

---

[3]https://guides.github.com/features/mastering-markdown/

You can hide and show cells as well, so if you want to focus on a particular step, you can hide your boilerplate code and dependency declarations so they aren't distracting.

Cells also have a rudimentary source control. Each time you save the notebook, it creates a checkpoint of the current state that you can refer back to if you accidentally break your notebook. You can compare your code across versions, including by execution duration. It's pretty easy to pinpoint where you tanked the performance of your notebook so you can recover it.

Keyboard Shortcuts

You can find the common keyboard shortcuts for Jupyter Notebooks, so I won't list them out here, but you can use them to navigate between cells, run individual cells, and shuffle cells around. The keyboard shortcut "P" opens a modal with all of the commands and their shortcuts, so you can always look at that to figure things out.

Community

Kaggle allows you to share your notebook with other users on the platform. If you're just getting started, you won't have anything to share yet, but you can browse other Kagglers' notebooks and read comments people have left on them.

Dark Mode

Look. I'm just going to put it out there. Android and iOS support dark mode system-wide; most of the daily productivity apps we use have rolled out dark mode in the last few years. Why not Google Cloud Platform? Google Colab and Google AI Platform also support dark mode, so maybe this is the business intelligence holy war we've all been waiting for. (Much lower stakes than SQL vs. NoSQL.)

Sharing

The most important way to present business intelligence and predictions to your organization is through easy, accessible sharing. Using a traditional method like Microsoft PowerPoint means more synthesis of data, copying, pasting, and generating graphs. The notebook concept makes it easier to publish results quickly without sacrificing clarity.

Most of my colleagues have many stories about a time when they found a huge risk or a major opportunity for the business, but they couldn't communicate it effectively in a way to get anyone's attention. Eventually they found the right mode—reporting, dashboards, or an in-person meeting—to convey the importance of what they'd found.

Data Analysis in Python

When your kernel starts, you will see a prebuilt script with some instructions. It also has a couple libraries referenced by default. If you're not familiar with these libraries, a quick introduction.

numpy

NumPy, or Numerical Python, is a venerable library written for Python in the mid-2000s. It grants powerful array and matrix manipulation to Python, as well as linear algebra functions, random number generation, and numerical functions like Fourier transforms. Python does not natively have numerical computing capability, so NumPy had a role to play in making Python a first-class language for data scientists.

pandas

Pandas is a data analysis and manipulation library and is also a fundamental inclusion for any work in this field using Python. (It's also built on NumPy, so they work well together.) Its primary data structure is known as a DataFrame, which is a tabular format. This makes it ideal for working with data from systems like BigQuery. In fact, the BigQuery SDK for Python has a function to load query results directly into a pandas DataFrame, as we'll see shortly. Pandas also works natively with other formats we've seen before, like CSV, JSON, and Parquet.

Also useful is that pandas has support for many kinds of plots and graphs directly from dataframes. There are other libraries to do this, most notably Seaborn, which integrates quite well with pandas and NumPy. For the scope of this survey, we won't be doing any advanced statistical plotting, so we'll try to keep it simple.

Pandas has other concepts to support the management of multiple DataFrame objects. The concept of "merging" closely resembles that of the SQL INNER JOIN, and GroupBy, which has concepts from both SQL GROUP BY and the analytic PARTITION BY.

TensorFlow

TensorFlow is a mathematical library created by the Google Brain team[4] to assist in deep learning problems. Over the last several years, it has grown to become the most well-known library for machine learning. As we discussed in the previous chapter, BigQuery also supports a TensorFlow reader so it's available to you in BQML.

Keras

Keras is a Python library for neural network development. It is designed to offer higher-level abstractions for deep learning models and can use several other systems as back ends, including TensorFlow.

I won't use TensorFlow or Keras in our sample data analysis, but I did want to call them out as the upstream versions of what is making its way into BigQuery ML. There are many, many other Python libraries of note in this area as well.

Other Libraries

Should you want to install other libraries into your instance, you can issue commands to the machine's shell by prefixing an exclamation point (bang) to the pip command, like this:

```
! pip install tensorflow-io==0.9.0
```

Since the dependency wouldn't be installed by default on the kernel, you'll have to run this as a first step each time you're using a new instance.

Setting Up BigQuery

As soon as you open the interface, you can click "Run All" immediately. Nothing will happen, but you can get a sense for a full run, and it will load your dependencies into the kernel so you don't have to do it again later. When you're inside a cell, you can click the blue play button to execute only the code in that cell.

---

[4]https://research.google/teams/brain/

Adding Data to the Kernel

Side note: We're going to pull a dataset down from BigQuery, but you can also add data directly to your notebook for analysis. Clicking "Add Data" in the upper-right corner allows you to pull in Kaggle datasets just by clicking "Add" next to one. You can also drag and drop your own files into Kaggle. Like a regular data IDE, you can preview some types of data files, like CSVs, in the bottom pane.

Loading Data from BigQuery

When you set up your notebook, you connected it to your BigQuery project. All of the authentication and connection stuff will be handled automatically, so we can get right down to pulling some data. You can pull your own data from the warehouse just as easily, but for the purposes of this chapter, we'll use a public dataset. This way the examples will work without any special preparation on your part. We'll use one of my favorite sample datasets, the Iowa Liquor Retail Sales dataset. This dataset gives us every wholesale purchase of liquor in Iowa since January 1, 2012. It's currently about 5 GB in size, so we'll run an aggregate query to cut it down to remain inside the free limits for both Kaggle and BigQuery.

(This dataset is available directly from the state of Iowa's government website, as well as on Kaggle, so you can obtain it in a variety of ways.)

Let's do this in a couple of cells, so you can get a sense for how to break down your code. The first cell will have the boilerplate Kaggle gave us, importing NumPy and pandas. In the second cell, let's define our BigQuery connection. (You may have some of this boilerplate already.)

```
PROJECT_ID = 'your-project-id-here'
from google.cloud import bigquery
bigquery_client = bigquery.Client(project=PROJECT_ID)
```

Then in the third cell, let's define and load the SQL query directly into a pandas dataframe. The query we'll run here will tell us, by month, every liquor store in Iowa's total sales in dollars and liters by item. This query uses about 2 GB, so remove some columns if you want to cut that down. Because of the aggregation, it also takes about 35 seconds to execute the query.

Also note my unjustified use of the ANY_VALUE aggregate to account for any discrepancies between the store number and what the store's name and location is. Variations there aren't relevant to this particular analysis:

```
sql = """
SELECT
store_number,
ANY_VALUE(store_location) store_location,
item_number,
ANY_VALUE(item_description) item_description,
DATE_TRUNC(date, MONTH) period,
ROUND(SUM(sale_dollars),2) sale_dollars,
ROUND(SUM(volume_sold_liters),2) volume_sold_liters,
FROM `bigquery-public-data.iowa_liquor_sales.sales`
WHERE date BETWEEN DATE(2019, 1, 1) AND DATE(2019, 12, 31)
GROUP BY store_number, item_number, period
"""

df = biquery_client.query(sql).to_dataframe()
df[:10]
```

If you haven't done so yet, click "Run All" to import the dependencies and also run the query. Otherwise, just run the last cell to execute the query. If all goes well, you should see the first ten rows of your sample data appear in the output for the last cell.

Out[12]:

	store_number	store_location	item_number	item_description	period	sale_dollars	volume_sold_liters
0	5693	POINT (-96.132644 43.185778)	26781	Templeton Rye Rare Cask Strength	2019-01-01	809.82	13.50
1	5224	POINT (-91.574095 41.671543)	43034	Bacardi Gold	2019-01-01	20.25	1.12
2	4485	POINT (-95.656064 43.186035000000004)	84197	99 Pineapple Mini	2019-01-01	9.00	0.60
3	5504	POINT (-92.313923 42.489893)	100659	Outerspace Chrome w/2 Shot Glasses	2019-01-01	25.50	0.75
4	2478	None	86251	Juarez Triple Sec	2019-01-01	43.56	12.00
...	...	...	...	...	...	...	...
10019	5487	POINT (-92.302514 42.498404)	47786	Courvoisier Vs Cognac	2019-01-01	25.19	0.75

Figure 20-2. *Sample results*

As you explore the data, you might want to try doing the aggregations and time-series work in pandas directly. This query eliminates the aggregates. It still uses the same amount of data, because both this query and the aggregate one have to scan all the columns:

```
SELECT
store_name,
store_location,
item_number,
item_description,
date_period,
sale_dollars,
volume_sold_liters
FROM `bigquery-public-data.iowa_liquor_sales.sales`
WHERE date >= DATE(2018, 1, 1)
```

You can also apply a narrower date range if you are only interested in the data in certain time periods. Again, this doesn't lower the amount of data scanned, but it does lower the size of the dataset being loaded into the kernel. With the default parameters for the free Kaggle Kernel, this could be material. (You may also opt to spin up a kernel elsewhere now with more power.)

One issue I have with using the BigQuery SDK to load a dataframe is that there's no progress bar. The pandas-gbq library, which also uses the SDK internally, gives you a running count of how quickly it's processing rows and about how long it expects to take. In my testing, the 2018 data took approximately 2–3 minutes to load.

In case you're impatient, like me, the alternate syntax is

```
! pip install pandas-gbq
df = pandas.read_gbq(sql, dialect='standard', project_id='your-project-id')
```

Because this doesn't give you the direct integration with GCP, you will have to authorize GCP to use the library and supply the authentication token to the notebook. You will have to do this every time the session restarts. But Figure 20-3 shows pandas-gbq offering us some helpful feedback.

```
Downloading:    17%|▉        | 292589/1690845 [00:35<02:51, 8162.42rows/s]
```

Figure 20-3. *pandas-gbq download status*

With the data in a dataframe, we can start doing some exploration. We're not after anything in particular here, and as a well-known dataset, it has already been fairly well picked over for insight. In the real world, you might be answering a question from your sales or marketing department like "Why did sales for X fall off?" You'll be looking to see if you can fit the data to clues in the dataset or by looking at other related datasets. Your dataset might benefit from analysis in a Jupyter Notebook environment because you could start to answer questions predictively, forecasting sales and applying machine learning models to understand the fluctuations of supply and demand.

Exploring a DataFrame

Since the purpose of this exercise is exploratory, feel free to veer off course and begin looking at other elements of the data. Keep in mind a few things:

- As I mentioned, it's tempting to want to SELECT * or look at every row. Going back to the beginning, BigQuery is a columnar store—using LIMIT doesn't help if you're pulling in all the columns.

- We've done fairly advanced analysis using SQL directly, and a lot of the fundamentals are the same between pandas and SQL, only differing in syntax and terminology. Try rewriting the SQL query to filter, but also try rewriting the pandas code to do the equivalent. You may have a preference after learning to work with both.

- While we're connected through BigQuery, if you want to go deeper, add this data from Kaggle to your notebook and use it there, or work on a local machine. The connectivity is to show how you can connect to your own data, not a fundamental part of the data exploration.

- The docs for pandas are really good. Even better, they thought of us and provide some helpful translations from SQL into pandas.[5]

---

[5]https://pandas.pydata.org/pandas-docs/stable/getting_started/comparison/comparison_with_sql.html

Finding Bearings

Some things you can do with a dataset you're seeing for the first time are to plot some of the data and sample random rows to get a sense of its shape.

Let's start by checking the data. This will also give you a sense of security that the data is in there.

```
df.count()
```

This gives me 1,690,845 rows for every column except store_location, which has 1,536,272, meaning some stores cannot be located on a map. (The dataset description indicates that addresses were geocoded manually to produce this data, so if they differ too far from standard format, the geocoder may have failed.)

```
df.sample(10)
```

Your results will vary, and you can run this multiple times to see different sample rows in the data. You can also pull out a fraction of the data to use for statistical sampling, which can be useful on **much** larger datasets. Consult your local statistical significance librarian for more details.

```
df2 = df.sample(frac=0.10)
```

This will pull in a random sampling of 10% of the rows. Next up, let's **describe** the data to see what the ranges are and what it looks like. We don't know anything about its orders of magnitude other than that it has about 1.5 million entries. We don't even really know what that means yet, save that in 2019, there were about 1.5 million wholesale liquor purchases across all stores and unique items.

```
display(df.describe().round(2))
```

The rounding allows us to read the results without the exponential notation it would otherwise generate. Then, "display" is a notebook function that formats our result in a nice rich HTML view. You should see something like Figure 20-4.

	sale_dollars	volume_sold_liters
count	1690845.00	1690845.00
mean	206.54	13.19
std	839.01	61.44
min	1.34	0.02
25%	43.44	2.25
50%	94.20	6.75
75%	182.88	10.50
max	185248.80	16065.00

Figure 20-4. *Results of using "describe" on the dataset*

Now we can get a sense of the magnitude. The average wholesale order in 2019 was about 13 liters and cost about 207 USD.

Exploring Individual Values

Now let's look at one of the specific rows the statistics call out. What's that $185,000 purchase?

```
df[df["sale_dollars"] == 185248.80].head(10)
```

This is equivalent to the SQL query

```
SELECT * FROM df WHERE sales_dollars = 182548.80 LIMIT 10
```

This returns us the information we were looking for, namely, that a liquor store in Northwest Des Moines bought 5940 liters of Crown Royal during the month of September 2019. Is Canadian whisky popular in Iowa?

```
df.groupby(['item_description']).sum().nlargest(15, ['volume_sold_liters'])
```

This is equivalent to GROUP BY item description and returning the 15 largest rows in terms of liters sold. Number one on the list is a product called "Black Velvet," also a Canadian whisky. Well, we've learned that Iowans like Canadian whisky and vodka. Data has become information.

We have two other dimensions available to us in this data—time and place. Using time, let's see what the buying trend looks like month over month for Crown Royal. Figure 20-5 shows the results.

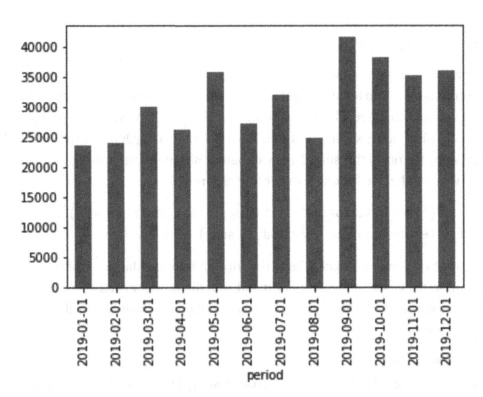

Figure 20-5. *Crown Royal sales by month*

```
df[df['item_description'] == 'Crown Royal'].groupby(['period']).sum()
['volume_sold_liters'].plot.bar()
```

That's interesting. Sales spike once in May and again in September, remaining higher for the rest of the year. Note: These are sales to the retail stores, so it's hard to see individual purchase patterns from here. Additionally, we quantized the data to the month level, so we can't see if there are interesting spikes inside each month.

This might be a clue that we want to look at the daily trend for these products to see if we can learn anything at a higher level of granularity. Meanwhile, with this dataset, let's include graphs of other item_descriptions to see if other popular items have the same trend.

Exploring Multiple Values

To do this, let's use the nlargest query we used earlier, except only select the item_description column, which we will then pass to the plot.

```
dagg = df.groupby(['item_description']).sum().nlargest(5, ['volume_sold_
liters']).reset_index()
```

Resetting the index is an easy way to pop a groupby that was done over multiple index columns back into a non-nested tabular view. (You might have noticed that when you visualized the results of the groupby, it showed the values as nested inside each item.) This is pretty similar to structs and UNNEST in BigQuery. It was one of the distinguishing factors of this sort of analysis before BigQuery came along.

Now we pass that back along into another groupby:

```
dfm = df[df['item_description'].isin(dagg['item_description'])].
groupby(['item_description','period']).sum()
```

This statement says to check if item_description is in the nlargest array we just made. If so, group by the description and period and sum the rows for each.

Then we'll reset the indexes again to make it suitable to pivot on. We'll pivot and display the result.

```
di = dfm.reset_index()
di.pivot(index='period', columns='item_description', values='volume_sold_
liters').plot.bar(figsize=(12,5))
```

Pivoting is incredibly common in data analysis, but not something that BigQuery can do natively. In order to get pivoting in SQL, you end up using a lot of analytic aggregates to flip the table axes. Here, it's very simple to plot the results. We pivot the table so that instead of the item_description being the index, the period becomes the index.

The last thing we do is set the figsize to be a bit larger than default so we'll be able to see the whole graph. Then we plot, and tada! Figure 20-6 just automatically plots something useful.

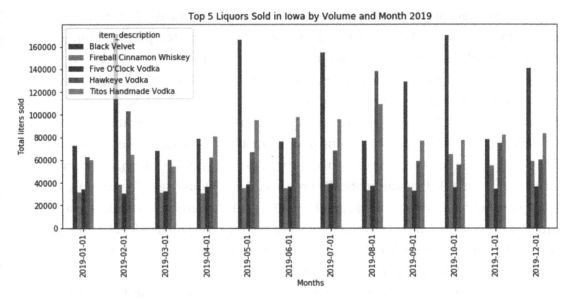

Figure 20-6. *Top five by plot and liters sold*

Next Steps

This shows us that the purchasing patterns are actually dissimilar across items. I'll leave my next exercise to you: namely, do these patterns vary substantially based on population? I'll lay out the steps:

- Find a dataset containing Iowa population data. (Hint: data.census. gov has downloadable data from the 2010 census.)

- Learn about Zip Code Tabulation Areas, or ZCTAs, which represent geographical data for the census by zip code rollup. (Zip codes actually have no geographic boundaries, so in order to use them effectively, you have to do some data manipulation.)

- Add the dataset you need to your kernel.

- Create a DataFrame mapping ZCTAs to unique store_ids across all liquor stores.

- Group the data by ZCTA and perform the same visualization.

In order to encourage you to use Kaggle a bit more, I uploaded this population dataset publicly to Kaggle.[6] You can add it to your project and start playing around. In the following AutoML example, we'll start to look at the county level too.

Using the styling features of pandas, which uses matplotlib, you can easily get images like these. Other libraries will take dataframes and produce publication-quality images. Since you've created this plot programmatically, you can easily change it until it looks like what you want. You can change the number of items you want to see, create new filters, or exclude certain items or format the strings. You could even replace the title string with a variable that automatically updates to your parameters, for example, ("Top 20 Liquors Sold in Iowa by Volume and Day, 2017–2018"). You could programmatically produce every static chart you wanted for whatever purpose you needed. If you ever wonder how the *New York Times* is able to produce such interactive and detailed data visualizations so quickly after the news breaks, here it is.

Now consider that you can share this with your stakeholders, including descriptive Markdown to annotate each step. This notebook is a living document that you can continue to use for ongoing analysis without losing your place, from anywhere in the world. Try doing **that** with BigQuery alone.

And because this data is coming straight from your live BigQuery instance, you can create things like monthly analyses that use your streaming business data as soon as it arrives. You can use Dataflows combining every source in your organization and beyond.

Jupyter Magics

I've been holding out on you. Since we haven't worked with notebooks or pandas yet, I wanted to show the full syntax for everything we were doing. But "magics," or magic commands, are shortcuts you can take to avoid even writing the little code we have. More good news: The BigQuery library supports its own magics. Querying a table and loading into a dataframe is actually as simple as writing a SQL query inline and prefixing it with

```
%%bigquery df
```

[6]www.kaggle.com/markmucchetti/2010-census-iowa-population-by-zcta/

This will automatically write the code to load the SQL query into a string, execute it, and load it into a DataFrame object named df, thereby saving you several cells.

A note: If you're trying to do this from within Kaggle, you also need to import the magics library in from the default bigquery library, like so:

```
from google.cloud.bigquery import magics
magics.context.project = 'YOUR-PROJECT-ID'
```

Magics are a feature inherited from IPython, the wrapper around the Python interpreter that allows it to accept interactive statements. You can read about built-in magics at the IPython documentation site.[7] Most of the libraries you'd use within Jupyter environments have their own magics.

AutoML Tables

AutoML Tables, currently in beta, is a Google product from the AutoML Platform. The AutoML Platform aims to make machine learning accessible to non-experts in a variety of areas. Its current areas include ML-aided vision and video processing, natural language, and Tables. The Tables product is designed to operate on structured data from files or BigQuery. Many of the things we discussed in the previous chapter such as feature engineering, data cleanup, and interpretability are handled directly for you by AutoML Tables. If you are finding that BQML doesn't meet your needs or is taking a lot of your effort to extract and train your models, you might try the same exercise using AutoML Tables and see if it gets you closer to your goal with less effort.

A disclaimer before we begin: AutoML is **expensive**. This sort of computational work pushes machines to the limit. AutoML Tables training, at this writing, costs $19.32 per hour, using 92 n1-standard-4 machines in parallel. Batch prediction on AutoML Tables is $1.16 per hour, using 5.5 machines of equivalent class.[8]

AutoML Tables currently offers a free trial of 6 node hours each for training and batch prediction. Those hours expire after a year. The basic example here is probably not worth the activation of your trial unless you have no other plans to use AutoML Tables.

---

[7]https://ipython.readthedocs.io/en/stable/interactive/magics.html
[8]https://cloud.google.com/automl-tables/pricing

AutoML Tables, similarly to BQML, supports two basic kinds of models: regression and classification. Regression models attempt to use existing data to predict the value of a data point based on its other variables. We'll be using that model in the example.

The other type, classification, takes input and attempts to sort it into buckets based on what type it probably is. This is the type of model that automatic object classification uses. Given an image, a classification model would attempt to classify it according to the types you've provided, for example, things that are hot dogs and things that are not hot dogs.

Importing a Dataset

The first thing you have to do is have AutoML Tables import your dataset, after which you can specify the parameters and begin training. Just for fun, we'll use the notebook to facilitate the connection between BigQuery and AutoML Tables. There's no special reason we need the notebook here; you can do this entirely from the AutoML Tables console. However, if you are experimenting and want to test various ML methodologies against each other, for example, BQML, AutoML Tables, and TensorFlow, you could do them all from within the same notebook, sourced initially from the same BigQuery dataset.

Before you start, make sure you go to the AutoML Tables console[9] and enable the API, or the notebook script will tell you that the project doesn't exist. After you execute the script, you will see Auto ML Tables loading in your dataset. The data import process can take up to an hour. When I uploaded the full 5 GB Iowa dataset, it took about ten minutes.

If you want to try the full dataset, the kernel code to do this is the following. Otherwise, keep reading, as we'll generate a more tuned query for our prediction model.

```
PROJECT_ID = 'YOUR-PROJECT-ID'
from google.cloud import automl_v1beta1 as automl
client = automl.TablesClient(project=PROJECT_ID)
datasetURI = 'bq://bigquery-public-data.iowa_liquor_sales.sales'
displayName = 'iowa_liquor_sales'
client.create_dataset(dataset_display_name=displayName)
response = client.import_data(dataset_display_name=displayName, bigquery_
input_uri=datasetURI)
```

---

[9]https://console.cloud.google.com/automl-tables/datasets

The last command initiates the transfer. Since you're transferring directly from BigQuery to AutoML, the data doesn't need to come down into your notebook—you just coordinated the transfer from one part of Google Cloud Platform to another.

Configuring the Training

For a prediction to be useful, we have to know what we're trying to get out of it. For the regression modeling we'll be using, we will use some fields in the table to predict the value of a target column.

Let's try to predict the total volume in liters sold by county in 2019. We already have the answer to this, but the model won't. The easiest way to test a model like this is in three parts—training, testing, and unseen data. AutoML Tables splits the data you give it into training and testing. While training the model, the process will hide the testing data and then use it to see how well training is going.

Once the model has assessed itself, you can try to predict data it has never seen before, but which you know the answer to. If that does well too, then the quality of the prediction model is good.

We'll give it all the data from the beginning of the dataset up to the end of 2018. Knowing what we want to target, let's write another query to clean things up. Date aggregation is good, but let's go down to the week level. We'll obviously need the county number too. We won't need any of the store-level data, though, since we'll aggregate across the county.

Total volume sold should have a pretty strong correlation with the number of sales dollars. It might also be useful to have category as a predictor, since we should get a fairly strong signal if there's a lot of variation by categories, which our earlier analysis suggests there might be. In fact, let's not even worry about individual items or the bottle data. We'll focus solely on volume as a function of time, location, and category. That gets us the following query:

```
INSERT INTO `your-project.dataset.table_name`
SELECT
DATE_TRUNC(date, WEEK) period,
county_number,
category,
ROUND(SUM(sale_dollars),2) sale_dollars,
ROUND(SUM(volume_sold_liters),2) volume_sold_liters,
```

```
FROM `bigquery-public-data.iowa_liquor_sales.sales`
WHERE date <= DATE(2018, 12, 31)
GROUP BY period, county_number, category
```

You can run this query from the kernel or from BigQuery itself. It generates about 1.2 million rows and takes roughly 8 seconds.

If you want to test with this more focused query, you can go back up to the previous code sample and replace the public dataset URI with your own.

After that, you have to set the target column. In this case we want to predict the number of liters that will be sold, a sort of rudimentary supply chain forecast:

```
client.set_target_column(
    dataset=dataset,
    column_spec_display_name='volume_sold_liters'
)
```

Then you can create the model:

```
response = client.create_model(
    MODEL_DISPLAY_NAME,
    dataset_display_name='iowa-liquor-modelss,
    train_budget_milli_node_hours=2000,
    exclude_column_spec_names=[ volume_sold_liters ],
)
```

Caution   Make sure you set the training budget! The property for this is train_budget_milli_node_hours, which specifies the number of millihours[10]/node you want training to last. For an example run, I wouldn't exceed 2000 millihours/node (2 hours) even if it degrades the model results. Your total free trial, measured in millihours/node, is 6000 (6 hours). Note that if AutoML finds the best solution before time runs out, it will stop and you won't be charged for the remainder.

---

[10]A millihour, as you might have guessed, is 1/1000 of an hour, or 3.6 seconds.

In addition to the actual training time, AutoML has to build out the infrastructure cluster before it can begin training. This takes some time on its own, so the actual time before your model is complete will be more than the budget you specified.

This code sample will actually start the model. At this point, since you've seen it running entirely from the notebook, you can also go to the AutoML Tables console and configure it interactively. The UI offers a lot of helpful hints, and you can look at options we haven't configured here. The console also offers some interesting dataset statistics.

Training the Model

Regardless of whether you ran the notebook or clicked "Start Training" in the UI, AutoML will now go and build out your 92 compute nodes and initiate training. This process will take several hours, based primarily on what you specified in your training budget. Once the training has finished, an email will arrive to let you know.

After the training finishes, we're going to jump into the AutoML Tables console to look at the results. If you like, you can spin down any Jupyter kernels you created now; we're done with them for this last part. You could also continue writing cells to pull the analysis back into a DataFrame.

Evaluating the Model

The model is scored on a number of factors to indicate the relative quality of the model. This should give you some idea of the quality of the model's predictions. It's also good to look at this in the console because it has helpful tooltips telling you what each of the scores means.

This is also where you get a sense of how well you prepared the dataset. If the model is not very accurate, you can often improve it by tweaking the granularity, outliers, or columns you provided. When working on your own data, you can use your knowledge of your business domain to help target the right information.

Describing the various measures and contributing statistical analyses is far out of scope here, but the one statistical measure you may remember from school is the R^2 measure, or the coefficient of determination. In basic terms, this takes the real values, fits them against the predicted values from the model, and assesses the fit on a scale between 0 and 1. The higher the R^2, the closer the predictions fit the data. See Figure 20-7 for a visualization.

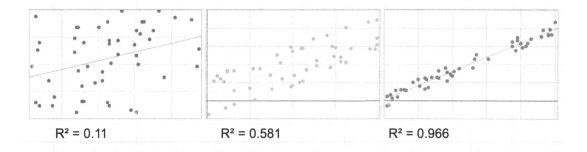

R² = 0.11   R² = 0.581   R² = 0.966

Figure 20-7. *Plots of low R^2 vs. high R^2*

This is a gross oversimplification, and there are reasons why you might expect a lower score and situations where a high score means a false signal. No data analyst would let me get away without repeating the fundamental axiom: **correlation is not causation**. Even if you forgot your linear algebra, you probably remember that. A well-known collector of useless correlations is Tyler Vigen,[11] who among other things notes that the per-capita consumption of cheese in the United States correlates nearly directly with the total revenue generated by golf courses, year over year. Eating cheese does not increase revenue for golf courses. However, you could make a reasonable guess that both of these factors are driven by the size of the US economy, and thus all economic measures are likely to follow a similar pattern.

All of that disclaimer to say that our training model generated an R^2 of 0.954. This looks pretty good, but think about why that might be. The model knows the total sales in dollars—it's a pretty good bet that the ratio of money to volume is going to stay pretty stable over time. It's possible that the only signal we picked up here is that inflation remained in the same range in 2019 as it had in the previous years. This would be known as "target leakage"—the data includes features that the training data couldn't have known about at the time, but which were applied later.

For example, if we had included the volume sold in gallons in our test data, the model would have learned that it can predict the volume sold in liters, because it is always about 0.264 times the gallons column. That doesn't tell us anything except the conversion factor between gallons and liters, which we already knew. On real data, we're not going to know the volume in gallons. If we did, we wouldn't need a machine learning model—only a calculator. So if the model performs perfectly, something is probably wrong.

---

[11]www.tylervigen.com/spurious-correlations

Even if that's the case, it doesn't mean our model is useless. We now have lots of hypotheses to test around the relationship between the economy and liquor consumption in Iowa. This also means we can look for examples that are not well predicted by this and use them to zero in on a better model that could help us forecast anomalies. As we add other likely variables to the model, we might learn that one of them has a significant effect on the model.

Making Predictions

In order to actually use a model you've created, you must first deploy it. AutoML Tables provides 6 free trial hours of batch prediction. The predictions described here run in a few minutes each.

The last panel on the AutoML Tables console sets up the batch prediction. Using batch prediction on the model, we can feed in a BigQuery table with all of the other variables, and it will generate its results. Since we have the 2019 data, we can do a direct comparison between the predicted and actual values.

The query to generate the input batch table is the same as the preceding one, with two changes. First, don't use the target column. Second, change the date range to be between DATE(2019, 1, 1) and DATE(2019, 12, 31).

Select Data from BigQuery for the input dataset and give it your 2019 table. Then set the result to your BigQuery project and project ID, and click "Send Batch Prediction." Within a few minutes, you'll have a results directory, which will be a BigQuery dataset with two tables in it.

If all went well, most of the rows will be in the predictions table, and few will be in the errors row. If you did something wrong, the rows in the errors row will tell you what the problems were. When I got the input dataset form correct, my errors table was empty, so all of the rows should process.

Now, you can go to the dataset and compare the actual 2019 values against the prediction values. You can use all of the other things we did in this chapter to analyze the quality of the model and look for variances. You can plot this data by county or across other variables, or you can rejoin the original dataset to get the metadata like the names of the counties or more granular data about top sellers. Basically I am saying you could get lost in this data for a very long time.

As for me, I was interested only in one thing: the top-level results. So I extracted the actual total volume for 2019, excluded null categories and county data, and compared it with the model's predicted volume:

```
Actual volume sold: 27,397,234 liters
Predicted volume sold: 28,167,027 liters
Error: 769,793 liters (2.8%)
Not bad.
```

Bonus Analysis

It can be pretty difficult to get out of the rabbit hole. I started to wonder which rows had predicted the results exactly, or at least down to a margin of about 2 teaspoons. This is called "data fishing" and it is a bad practice in statistics. XKCD,[12] a well-known web comic, illustrated the practice and its implications for bad science. Nonetheless, I was curious what factors might lead to a successful prediction, and as you might have noticed, this is far from a rigorous scientific analysis. I didn't find anything obvious.

I found 236 rows (out of nearly 200,000, mind you) where the model had predicted the volume within 0.01 liters of accuracy. They crossed date ranges, counties, and categories, which means this is likely complete noise; even a broken clock is right twice a day.

I then checked, based on popularity of category and thus likely amount of training data, how accurate the model had been across categories. There was no substantial correlation between popularity of category and accuracy of prediction, in either direction. While the model didn't bias to popularity, it does mean that some popular categories were way off, and some niche categories did fairly well.

I ended my fishing expedition by looking at the best category/period prediction, for which one county's Tennessee whiskey sales appeared to have been predicted accurately across all of 2019. The reason? The county is tiny and the categorization had changed. There was only one sale in the category that year. Noise!

We could spend days or weeks refining the data inputs, retraining models, and seeking better predictions. And on the surface, this is a public dataset of limited interest to most people. What are you thinking about doing with your own data?

---

[12]https://xkcd.com/882/

The Data ➤ Insight Funnel

You've probably thought of a number of applications for these techniques that would work on your own data. I hope that the time spent peering across the abyss was inspiring. Until now, the focus has been almost exclusively on high-velocity, automated pipelines for passing terabytes around. Suddenly the focus has shifted to a single dataset, poking around and exploring individual results. This indicates that at long last, we've reached the bottom of the funnel. This is the process of moving from data ➤ information ➤ insight, a common thread that has been running since the introduction to BigQuery. See Figure 20-8.

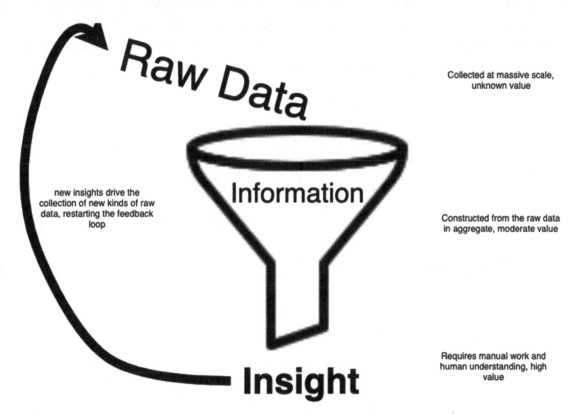

Figure 20-8. *A funnel shape showing how raw data, information, and insight interact*

The term "data mining" really earns the analogy here. Tons of raw ore must be mined to find veins from which a tiny amount of precious metal can be extracted. So it is with data. You now have tools which can take you all the way from one end to the other.

Summary

Jupyter Notebooks are an open source application for doing data analysis, statistics, and machine learning. There are many implementations available in various clouds. Through one of these offerings, you can access a Jupyter notebook environment from which you can access BigQuery. Using Python, you can access all of the latest numerical computing, statistical modeling, and machine learning and apply them to your datasets in BigQuery. By doing this, you can go the final distance in your journey to extract valuable insight from your organization's data. Taking actions on high-quality insight can transform your data program, your organization, and the world around you.

CHAPTER 21

Conclusion

Running an enterprise-grade data program is no easy feat.

BigQuery lowers the barrier to entry. For free, you can create a data warehouse that runs 24/7 without maintenance: no operating system, no patching, no running out of hard drive space. That was the promise we explored in this book. However, this warehouse also starts out completely empty and valueless. Your empty warehouse is the first blank page of a book called *Data Warehousing at Your Company with BigQuery*, and you must write it yourself. Much of it will be literal documentation, code, and configuration. An equal part will be abstract. By forging the right relationships with your business stakeholders and constructing the right process for your organization, you will succeed at establishing your data program. You can then build on that success for the medium- and long-term vision.

There's a relevant analogy in the comparison between software architecture and building architecture. When a building is finished, it's there. When you go to the coordinates, you will be at that building. It may have structural flaws, like the Leaning Tower of Pisa, but it's still the only building at coordinates (43.7229559, 10.394403).

No such guarantee for software! You can construct the most perfect algorithm or write the most brilliant code of all time, and it's possible that no one will ever know. It would be as if you could build the Leaning Tower of Pisa in an extra-dimensional pocket and then "deploy" it to those coordinates. Of course, then you could also dismiss the engineers, patch the building, and redeploy it.[1]

This property of software creates an unresolvable tension between "getting it right" and "getting it done." No value is added by constructing a masterpiece in an extra-dimensional pocket and leaving it there. The first challenge of your data program is to ensure its existence. Success rests at least as much on the people as it does on the technology. Thus, BigQuery projects can still fail. Maybe the complacency that comes

---

[1]PATCH-12331227: fixed skew in matrix translation function, breaking change, recompiling all stories.

© Mark Mucchetti 2020
M. Mucchetti, *BigQuery for Data Warehousing*, https://doi.org/10.1007/978-1-4842-6186-6_21

with a painless setup makes them even more prone to do so—that's definitely not a technology problem. The good news is that you have the necessary tools to surmount this problem for all three edges of the golden triangle.

You can and should read books about databases, books about organizational theory, and books about application management lifecycles. Through the individual examination of each facet, it becomes clear that the triangle's central force is data.

Think about it: a process needs real-world data to understand and improve it. Personal conflicts often result from poor communication and conversely could be prevented with accurate, accessible data. (How many bar fights have been prevented by the Internet?) Then, technology makes it possible to grapple with these giant, global-size problems. You can't sustain a modern data program with thousands of cuneiform tablets eroding in a cave.

In the end, the biggest catalyst is the interaction between humans and technology. As the data program takes off, it will begin to produce insights. Those insights will inspire people to do a thing a little better. That increased motivation and ability will manifest in data streaming into the warehouse. That improved data will produce even greater insight. And so the cycle continues.

With the addition of real-time data analysis, those insights will arrive at a faster and faster rate. Returns multiply. Sifting through all the data in your organization and beyond will spark new connections that no one dreamed of alone. The impossible becomes obvious. The obvious becomes ambient. The process of discovery produces unexpected answers and even more unexpected questions. And you sit at the center of it all.

Cloud Shell and Cloud SDK

While most of the exercises in this book can be completed with the user interfaces available in Google Cloud Platform, they can also be completed via the command line or with the Google Cloud API. Google also offers SDKs in multiple languages for programmatic access. We used the Python SDK in this book, but SDKs are available in many languages including Go, Node.js, PHP, C#, and Java. Regardless of which language(s) you choose to use, being able to work on the command line directly can be a huge timesaver over visiting all of the respective tools in the console.

From the Console

The easiest way to access the Google Cloud Shell is just to use the built-in virtual machine from the web console itself. You can do this by clicking the icon in the upper right with the command prompt and the tooltip "Activate Cloud Shell." A window will pop up from the bottom and indicate that it is provisioning a shell, and after a short while, you'll be dropped to the terminal.

Cloud VM Capabilities

Google Cloud Shell is a fully functional Linux virtual machine running on Google Compute Engine. It has access to the Internet as well, so you can install packages or run external scripts as necessary. Your home directory has 5 GB of space with which to work. The full hard drive space is about 70 GB, and while you can place files outside the home directory, they will be deleted when the ephemeral instance is wiped. You also have full administrative access to this machine (yes, including root user).

© Mark Mucchetti 2020
M. Mucchetti, *BigQuery for Data Warehousing*, https://doi.org/10.1007/978-1-4842-6186-6_22

Specifications

My machine identified itself as a dual-core Intel Xeon running at 2.20 GHz[1]—but the detailed CPU inspections name it only as a "Google" processor running at a 2 GHz clock speed, so who knows. The 2 GB of RAM (actually 1.7 GB) runs with a VirtIO Memory Balloon, which means that it may relinquish memory you're not using back to the host system; you won't notice this in practice. The system identifies itself as Debian GNU/Linux 9 (stretch) running on QEMU, although the root file system and kernel identify themselves as Chrome OS. You get access to 0.5 vCPU through this system.

When you're not using the machine, it will shut down. However, as long as you are regularly accessing the machine (currently, at least once every 120 days), your home directory will remain intact. There are some quotas to be aware of, though: currently the cloud shell may only be used 50 hours per week. This is plenty for most day-to-day work but won't suffice for keeping long-running processes active.

Boost Mode

You can also engage an experimental mode by going to the More menu and selecting "Boost Mode." This will increase the capabilities of your cloud shell VM for the subsequent 24 hours. In practice, it will modify your VM from an e2-small to an e2-medium instance, raising your vCPU count to 1.0.

The only reported hardware change was that the RAM increased from 2 GB to 4 GB. The number of processors continued to report as dual Xeon 2.2 GHz chips. Running a stress test comparison showed that the default (e2-small) mode had equivalent performance as boost mode. This is likely due to the fact that the g1-small can burst to 1.0 vCPU when necessary.[2] This probably means you don't need boost mode unless you intend to use the full 1 vCPU for longer than short bursts. (Google doesn't define how long a short burst is.)

---

[1]Your results may vary.

[2]However, if you like doubling your RAM at the press of a button, I have a program called SoftRAM 95 to sell you.

Console Options

From inside the console, you can take advantage of a few additional features. These features elevate the cloud shell to an IDE, opening up other interesting scenarios like coding on an iPad or Chromebook.

Editor

You can open the editor with the pencil in the upper right. This will load an in-browser editor in which you can browse directories on the machine. The editor supports automatic syntax highlighting based on file extension, configuration of keyboard shortcuts, and multiple themes (yes, dark mode). You can upload and download files with the machine through the browser. You can save and load your workspaces too, so depending on your needs, there may already be enough functionality to support all of your development.

The editor is actually a Google version of the Eclipse Theia[3] open source IDE. Google will likely adopt enhancements from Theia as they arrive.

Web Preview

While you can't open your own ports to the Internet from the cloud shell directly, the console provides a neat way to do this. Click the "Web Preview" icon in the upper right, and either click "Preview on port 8080" or change the port to one of the other available ones. This will open an HTTP connection to your cloud shell instance using the local port you specified. This link is under auth and can only be accessed by you.

Basic HTTP Server

Setting up a local web server couldn't be easier, since cloud shell comes provisioned with Python. Just type

```
nohup python3 -m http.server 8080 > server.log 2>&1 &
```

(Quick breakdown if you're not familiar with Linux: nohup keeps the job running even if you log out of the terminal, although it will still be killed when the machine shuts down. Python3 starts a simple web server on port 8080 and will log its standard output

---

[3]https://github.com/eclipse-theia/theia

to the server.log file. The 2>&1 redirects the standard error into the same output, and the final & sends the process to the background. The important part of the command is just "python3 -m http.server 8080.")

Once you do this, you can open the web preview to that port, and you will see your folder load. The http.server uses index.html as a default page so if your folder has a file by that name, it will display in the browser.

From the Internet

If you do have some need to share your local cloud shell development to unauthenticated users, you can do this with a tool called ngrok. Note that your server will still go offline when the machine is deprovisioned, so this can only be used for testing. Instructions for installing ngrok may change over time, but as of this writing, the following commands will work:

```
wget https://bin.equinox.io/c/4VmDzA7iaHb/ngrok-stable-linux-386.zip
unzip ./ngrok.zip
```

Then, after you have run the preceding local HTTP server command, add this command:

```
./ngrok http 8080
```

Replace 8080 with the same port you used for the HTTP server, if you changed it. When you do this, you'll get a full-screen view which will construct a tunnel between the cloud shell and ngrok.io. You can click either of the forwarding links and see your web server running on the public Internet.

A couple notes: First, ngrok.io has a free tier, but is also a paid service to allow you to construct tunnels on an ongoing basis or with longer lifetimes. It has lots of other features, so check it out,[4] as it may solve other local development pain you have. Second, be aware of potential security issues when doing this. The machine is ephemeral, so "breaking" it or otherwise corrupting it is not a huge deal, unless you somehow ruin your home folder. However, if you're storing private keys and tokens that would not meet your organizational security policies, be very careful before doing this.

---

[4]https://ngrok.com/

From a Local Machine

If you don't want to or can't use the cloud shell for some reason, it is still an option to install gcloud on your local machine. It's also useful to have gcloud installed on your local machine so you can do maintenance on your GCP instances without spinning up the cloud shell.

Installation

Google provides full documentation for installation of the SDK in all supported environments.[5] For Linux and MacOS installations, simply download the installation script and run it:

```
curl https://sdk.cloud.google.com > install.sh
bash install.sh --disable-prompts
```

For Windows, there is an installer program,[6] as well as a simple PowerShell script to accomplish the same thing.[7]

In addition to gcloud, this installation will give you gsutil (for Google Storage) and bq (for BigQuery, which we'll discuss in the following). There are many other Google Cloud utilities for other services, including cbt (Bigtable), kubectl (Kubernetes), and various emulators for Pub/Sub, DataStore, and so on.

Once gcloud is installed, initialize it with

```
gcloud init
```

This will take care of logging you into your GCP project, picking your desired project (if you have one), and choosing a default region. If you already have a configuration, you can make a new one and switch between them.

---

[5]https://cloud.google.com/sdk/docs/quickstarts
[6]https://dl.google.com/dl/cloudsdk/channels/rapid/GoogleCloudSDKInstaller.exe
[7]https://cloud.google.com/sdk/docs/downloads-interactive#windows

Accessing Cloud Shell from Local Machine

Intriguingly, it is possible to access the cloud shell VM even from the local gcloud instance. This is another way of copying files between your local machine and the cloud instance or if you want to use a persistent machine across multiple client machines. To do this, run

```
gcloud alpha cloud-shell ssh
```

The tool will automatically install the necessary public keys for your access and then give you the same terminal you would receive on your web version. (If you don't have the alpha components, it will install those as well.)

You can log into a boost mode version of your cloud shell with the switch --boosted. And just as the -t switch allows you to run a command over the SSH pipe, you can use the --command switch to do the same thing with your cloud shell.

Creating New Projects

Once the gcloud tool is functioning, you can easily make a new project with

```
gcloud projects create YOUR-PROJECT-NAME
```

Assuming the name is not taken, this will create the new project automatically. Then, set it as active with

```
gcloud config set project YOUR-PROJECT-NAME
```

That's it! You can now go back to whatever exercise you were working on with a project ready to go.

Creating New Service Accounts

Another task you will frequently find yourself performing is creating service accounts with permissions to access various services in Google Cloud. Google does this automatically in many cases and will provision an appropriate service account. Also, since we've stayed within the GCP boundaries most of the time, the authentication mechanisms are transparent. For example, when connecting Kaggle to BigQuery in Chapter 20 or using Cloud Functions in Chapter 12, the default service account principals already had access to the necessary scopes. However, we could have created a new one on our own. Understanding service accounts may constitute part of the security portion of your data governance program.

Service accounts are essentially user profiles for machines. Automated systems have long discouraged using a real person's account in any automated fashion, and the GCP-specific terminology for the account you use instead is the service account.

To make a service account from the cloud command lines, you use the iam command:

```
gcloud iam service-accounts create --account-name {YOUR_ACCOUNT_NAME}
--display-name {YOUR_DISPLAY_NAME}
```

This creates an email address for the service account, which you use as the authenticating principal for actions going forward. Typically the format will be something like

```
{YOUR_ACCOUNT_NAME}@{YOUR_PROJECT_ID}.iam.gserviceaccount.com
```

Then, depending on the service you need to authenticate to, you add a policy binding to give the account the appropriate scope. You can do this through the IAM Console UI as well:

```
gcloud projects add-iam-policy-binding {YOUR_PROJECT_ID} \
  --member serviceAccount:{YOUR_SERVICE_ACCOUNT_EMAIL}
  --role {ROLE_NAME}
```

Note the "serviceAccount" prefix, which is required to refer to service accounts in this context. The Google documentation should provide the right role; occasionally I have footnoted it where appropriate.

The bq Command-Line Tool

If you've just created a new project, BigQuery is already active. If you're using an existing project, you can go to the console to enable the BigQuery API.[8] You can test this with the command

```
bq ls
```

---

[8]https://console.cloud.google.com/flows/enableapi?apiid=bigquery

This command will show you all of the datasets you have in your project, which will also confirm that your project is set properly, your connection is working, and you have a successful gcloud installation. If this fails, try on the Google Cloud Shell or check the instructions from the previous section.

Through the bq tool, you have even more access to BigQuery capabilities than what is provided in the console. This book sticks mostly to the UI for ease of use and conceptual explanations, but once you start getting adept with BigQuery concepts, you will begin to use the command line more and more. This may also be familiar to you if you've used similar tools for PostgreSQL or MySQL.

Here are some highlights of the bq tool. If you want the full rundown, just use

```
bq help
```

Querying

Running a query using bq uses the "query" command

```
bq query 'SELECT 42'
```

By default, you'll get a text rendering of the results. Using the --format flag, you can specify the return in another format, including JSON, CSV, and pretty-print. CSV and JSON are designed to be piped to file or to other locations, as in the command

```
bq query --sync --format csv 'SELECT ...' > results.csv
```

The sync parameter makes the command line wait until the query has completed, rather than starting a job in the background. For larger commands, you should omit it and poll the job status instead. (The UI also makes jobs in the background, but since you are waiting for the results, it doesn't normally come into play.)

Loading

It's very common to load data from the command line or API instead of using the UI. The UI can accept file uploads only up to 10 MB, and larger files have to be staged through Google Cloud Storage first. Using the command line, you can load your file directly.

As with the UI, you can use all of the same formats, including CSV, Avro, Parquet, JSON(L), and so on. A basic load command looks like this:

```
bq load dataset.table localfile.csv field1:string,field2:string
```

A Google Cloud Storage URL can be used in place of the file. The command will automatically create the table if it doesn't exist.

All of the capabilities of loading were covered in Chapter 5, and the command-line tool replicates all of them and then some. For more detail, read Chapter 5 or check the bq documentation.[9]

Shell

The bq tool even has its own shell, which you can activate with

```
bq shell
```

This allows you to run many statements in sequence without typing the bq each time. For queries, you don't even need to type "query"—you can simply type the query directly into the shell.

Other commands, such as ls and mk, can be run directly from the shell as well.

Creating

The mk command allows you to create datasets and tables. When making tables, you have the same options as when you use the UI. You can also specify a schema as a command-line parameter, either inline or from a file, using the same format as for loading data. For example, to make a new table with a string column

```
bq mk --table dataset.table field1:string,otherfield:string
```

To use a schema file, replace the final parameter with a path to a JSON. The JSON is in the same format used by the UI.[10]

Copying

The cp command allows you to copy an entire table:

```
bq cp source-table destination-table
```

---

[9]https://cloud.google.com/bigquery/docs/reference/bq-cli-reference#bq_load
[10]https://cloud.google.com/bigquery/docs/schemas

Deleting

Once you've finished playing around with bq, you can wipe your dataset and all its tables with the rm command. For example

```
bq rm -r dataset
```

will remove the dataset by that name.

Undeleting

Undeleting isn't explicitly supported by the command-line tool, but if you need to recover data from a table you accidentally deleted, you can replicate the feature by using the same concept as the SQL construct "FOR SYSTEM TIME AS OF."

You cannot recover a table if you overwrote it with CREATE or REPLACE, and you **cannot** undelete a dataset. The limit for querying past versions of tables is 7 days. If you meet all of these criteria, use this bash script to recover your data. The first parameter is the dataset and table you want to recover, and the second parameter is how far back you want to go in seconds. The max value is 604800 (one week):

```
#!/bin/bash
# Usage: bq dataset-table time-in-seconds
bq cp "$1@$(((`date +%s`-$2)*1000))" $1_recovered
```

APPENDIX B

Sample Project Charter

This book repeatedly references the value of starting with a project charter and using it as a document to inform the initial states of your data warehouse construction. Along with your data glossary and maps of your sources of truth, the original project charter becomes a critical piece of documentation for ensuring you are building something that adds value for your users. It also helps to set and maintain expectations so that there are no unwelcome surprises as construction proceeds.

The charter helps to establish a certain formality around the project, as well as date boundaries to ensure that it gets needed support from the organization. Obviously, your organizational practice will vary on how projects are chartered and added to road maps. The best guide will be your stakeholders themselves—they will make it clear what characteristics of the data warehouse you should emphasize. They will also help you formulate the answer to the most basic question: What problem am I trying to solve?

What follows is a sample charter for your data warehouse project. Feel free to adapt it to your needs or to adjust it to your own organization's particular style. While it contains specific references to BigQuery, it can also be adapted for any other data warehouse project or really any technology project in general.

Additionally, it incorporates the separate charter for reporting covered in Chapter 16. This can be used either separately or as an addendum to the main project charter.

There is also a digital version of this charter available, as well as a Google Form you can use as a template to create your own[1].

---

[1]https://virtu.is/sample-data-warehouse-charter

© Mark Mucchetti 2020
M. Mucchetti, *BigQuery for Data Warehousing*, https://doi.org/10.1007/978-1-4842-6186-6_23

DataCorp, Inc. Project Charter Request

Project Submitter	Mark Mucchetti
Project Name	BigQuery Data Warehouse
Review Date	1/1/20xx

Purpose

This project will establish a data warehouse for the organization. The data warehouse will receive and ingest all relevant organizational data. It will also serve as the central store for reporting and analysis. The data warehouse will store historical data for audit and compliance purposes.

Using a centralized data warehouse solution will allow us to make decisions more quickly and efficiently based on accurate data. The warehouse will generate insights about our organization that will reveal new business opportunities, reveal problem areas, and help us respond immediately to market changes.

Justification

Storing and analyzing data from a NoSQL or operational source, Combining data from multiple sources, Cost savings, Real-time or near–real-time streaming, Handling data at terabyte or petabyte scale, Reducing time spent doing database maintenance

Scope

The first phase of this project will establish the overall data warehouse architecture, as well as specific data marts for several departments.

Success Criteria

Migrate five existing reports to be powered by BigQuery.

Decrease time for weekly data analysis tasks by 50%.

Save $50,000 over existing data warehouse technology within 12 months of project launch.

Budget

Estimated usage is $514.80 per month, or $6,177 this year.

Resourcing is internal and no additional costs are expected.

Timeline

These are the expected dates.

Requirements complete	5/1/20xx
Schemas/data glossary complete	7/1/20xx
External Dataflows complete	10/1/20xx
Reporting complete	11/1/20xx
Phase 1 launch date	1/1/20xx

Clarification: These dates are subject to change and are approximate only. Completion dates will align to sprint boundaries and/or weekdays.

Project Assumptions

The cost and resource requests specified by this charter will be met. Project members will have access to the tools they need to do their jobs, including Google Cloud Platform access, BigQuery, and the external data for ingest. Material and personnel costs will not increase measurably through the duration of the project.

Project Risks

Budget Risks	Budget has not been allocated.
Timeline Risks	Lack of experience in this area could cause poor estimation. Other projects may take priority during this timeline.
Resource Risks	Limited number of subject matter experts who know business domain; they are critical for project success. Resources are busy and shared with other teams. They may be pulled off of this project.
Additional Risks	Data literacy in the organization is low.

Reporting

Summary

This solution will replace our existing reporting solution. Major report users will have to change the location, process, or cadence of reports when the solution launches. The data warehouse project will produce user-readable reports at its conclusion.

Existing Reports to be Ported Over

Sales Report

    Marketing Report 1

    These reports will use the same data source as before. They will use equivalent reporting logic.

Improved Versions of Existing Reports

Daily Sales Report

    Monthly Sales Report

    Year-to-Date Revenue

    These reports will use the same data source as before. They will not use the same reporting logic. Both the original version and the improved version can exist side-by-side for a time.

New Reports

Year-to-Date Cost of Goods Sold

    Sales Detail Report

Out of Scope

Whit's Special Network Report

    Test Report B-19

    These reports will not be migrated.

Additional Constraints

None at this time.

Key Stakeholders

Senior Leadership	Hank Scorpio, CEO
Steering Committee	Charles M. Burns, COO
	Lindsay Naegle, CMO
	Artie Ziff, CTO
Subject Matter Experts	Nick Riviera, Sales Director
	Elizabeth Hoover, People Team
	Otto Mann, Special Projects
Data Analysts	Armin Tamzarian, Senior Data Analyst
	Dr. William MacDougal, Data Engineer
Data Engineers/Architects	Dr. Jonathan Frink, Chief Architect
	Kyle Cartwright, Database Architect
Other Stakeholders	Kearney Zzyzwicz, Accounts Payable Analyst
Special Responsibilities	Stakeholders will attend a monthly meeting to review status of the project. In beta they will assist as user acceptance testers for reporting.

Project Sign-Off

	1/1/20xx
Project Manager	Date
	1/1/20xx
Executive Sponsor	Date
	1/1/20xx
Project Approver	Date

Index

A

Abigail's Flowers (AF), 254–258

Amazon Web Services
(AWS), 4, 92, 265, 471

Analysis of variance (ANOVA), 446

Analytic functions
aggregate functions, 286–288
definition, 273–275
navigation functions, 284–286
numeric functions, 276–278
order of operations, 275
partitions, 275
window frame
syntax, 275, 279, 281–284

Artificial intelligence (AI), 420–422, 468

autodetect flag, 80

Automatic *vs* manual refresh, 302

AutoML Tables
bonus analysis, 494
BQML, 488
configuring training, 489, 490
defining, 487
evaluating model, 491–493
importing dataset, 488, 489
predictions, making, 493
training model, 491

Avro, 50, 79

B

Backward-compatible model, 340

BigQuery, 3, 75, 155, 156
aliasing, 9
API, 59
assignments, 65
bq command line, 59
column-oriented approach, 15
commenting, 9
compute costs, 61
datasets, 7, 38
data storage, 62
data structures, 13
data warehouse, 16
flat-rate pricing, 64
FROM, 10
GCP projects, 38
GROUP BY, 10
hierarchical data structure, 42
LIMIT, 11
normalization/denormalization, 39–41
on-demand pricing, 64
ORDER BY, 11
partitioning, 43
principle, 37
query timing, 12
reservations, 65

© Mark Mucchetti 2020
M. Mucchetti, *BigQuery for Data Warehousing*, https://doi.org/10.1007/978-1-4842-6186-6

Printed in the United States
By Bookmasters